Computer Bible Games with Visual Basic®

A Computer Programming Tutorial

For Visual Studio 2019

16th Edition

By
Philip Conrod & Lou Tylee

BIBLEBYTE BOOKS
PO Box 701
Maple Valley, WA 98038
www.BibleByteBooks.com
www.BibleByteGames.com

Published by:
BibleByte Books (A Publishing Division of Kidware Software, LLC)
PO Box 701
Maple Valley, Washington 98038
1.425.413.1185
www.biblebytebooks.com

Printed in the United States of America

ISBN-13: 978-1-951077-14-3 (Paperback Edition)
ISBN-13: 978-1-951077-15-0 (Electronic Edition)

Illustrations by Kevin Brockschmidt

Copy Editor: Stephanie Rogers

This book was previously published as “Computer Bible Games with Visual Basic - 15th Edition”.

This guide was developed for the course, “Computer Bible Games with Microsoft Visual Basic,” produced by BibleByte Books, Maple Valley, Washington. It is not intended to be a complete reference to the Visual Basic language. Please consult the Microsoft website for detailed reference information.

About The Authors

Philip Conrod has authored, co-authored and edited over two dozen computer programming books over the past thirty years. Philip holds a bachelor's degree in Computer Information Systems and a Master's certificate in the Essentials of Business Development from Regis University. Philip has served in various Information Technology leadership roles in companies like Sundstrand Aerospace, Safeco Insurance, FamilyLife, Kenworth Truck Company, and PACCAR. Philip last served as the Chief Information Officer (CIO) for Darigold for over a decade before returning to teaching and writing full-time. Today, Philip serves as the President & Publisher of Kidware Software LLC which is based in Maple Valley, Washington.

Lou Tylee holds BS and MS degrees in Mechanical Engineering and a PhD in Electrical Engineering. Lou has been programming computers since 1969 when he took his first Fortran course in college. He has written software to control suspensions for high speed ground vehicles, monitor nuclear power plants, lower noise levels in commercial jetliners, compute takeoff speeds for jetliners, locate and identify air and ground traffic and to let kids count bunnies, learn how to spell and do math problems. He has written several on-line texts teaching Visual Basic, Visual C# and Java to thousands of people. He taught computer programming courses for over 15 years at the University of Washington and currently teaches math and engineering courses at the Oregon Institute of Technology. Lou also works as a research engineer at a major Seattle aerospace firm. He is the proud father of five children, has six grandchildren and is married to an amazing woman. Lou and his family live in Seattle, Washington.

Acknowledgements

First and foremost I want to thank my best friend Jesus Christ for granting me the wisdom, courage and resources to publish this edition of the book. My life would be nothing without you. Secondly, I would like to thank my three wonderful daughters - Stephanie, Jessica and Chloe, who helped with various aspects of the book publishing process including software testing, book editing, creative design and many other more tedious tasks like finding typos. I could not have published this book without all your hard work, love and support.

Last but definitely not least, I want to thank my multi-talented co-author, Lou Tylee, for doing all the real hard work necessary to develop, test, debug, and keep current all the 'family-friendly' applications and games for this book. Lou has tirelessly poured his heart and soul into so many previous versions of this tutorial and there are so many beginning programmers who have benefited from his work over the years. Lou is by far one of the best application developers and tutorial writers I have ever worked with. Thank you Lou for collaborating with me on this book publishing project.

Table of Contents

3. Your First Visual Basic Project

4. Project Design, Forms, Buttons

5. Labels, Text Boxes, Variables

6. UpDown Control, Decisions, Random Numbers

7. Icons, Group Boxes, Check Boxes, Radio Buttons

8. Panels, Mouse Events, Colors

9. Picture Boxes, Arrays

10. Timers, Animation, Keyboard Events

11. Noah's Ark Project

12. Elijah and the Ravens Project

13. Daniel and the Lions Project

Bonus Projects.

Classic Computer Games using Visual Basic

Introduction

Computer Bible Games with Visual Basic is an interactive, self-paced tutorial providing a complete introduction to the Visual Basic programming language and environment. The tutorial consists of 13 lessons explaining (in simple, easy-to-follow terms) how to build a Visual Basic application. Numerous examples are used to demonstrate every step in the building process. The tutorial also includes detailed computer projects for you to build and try. **Computer Bible Games with Visual Basic** is presented using a combination of course notes (written in Microsoft Word format) and many Visual Basic examples and projects.

Course Prerequisites

To use **Computer Bible Games with Visual Basic**, you should be comfortable working within the Windows environment, knowing how to find files, move windows, resize windows, etc. No programming experience is needed. You will also need the ability to view and print documents saved in Microsoft Word format. This can be accomplished in one of two ways. The first, and easiest, is that you already have Microsoft Word (or a compatible equivalent) on your computer. The second way is that you can download the Microsoft Word Viewer. This is a free Microsoft product that allows viewing and printing Word documents - it is available for download from Microsoft.

https://www.microsoft.com/en-us/download/details.aspx?id=4

Finally, and most obvious, you need to have Microsoft Visual Basic. This is a separate product that must be obtained. It is available for free download from Microsoft. Follow this link for complete instructions for downloading and installing the free Microsoft Visual Studio Community Edition on your computer:

https://www.visualstudio.com/products/free-developer-offers-vs

System Requirements

You will need the following hardware and software to complete the exercises in this book:

- Microsoft Windows 7, 8, or 10
- Microsoft Visual Studio 2019 Community Edition
- 1.6 Ghz Pentium or compatible processor
- 1 GB (32 Bit) or 2 GB (64 Bit) RAM (Add 512 MB if running in a virtual machine)
- 10 GB of available hard disk space
- 5400 RPM hard drive
- DirectX 9 capable video card running at 1024 x 768 or higher-resolution display
- Video Monitor (1024 x768)
- DVD-ROM Drive
- Microsoft Mouse or compatible pointing device

Installing and Using the Downloadable Solution Files

If you purchased this directly from our website you received an email with a special and individualized internet download link where you could download the compressed Program Solution Files. If you purchased this book through a 3rd Party Book Store like Amazon.com, the solutions files this tutorial are included in a compressed ZIP file that is available for download directly from our website at:

http://www.kidwaresoftware.com/cbgvb2019-solutions.htm

Complete the online web form at this webpage above with your name, shipping address, email address, the exact title of this book, date of purchase, online or physical store name, and your order confirmation number from that store. We also ask you to include the last 4 digits of your credit card so we can match it to the credit card that was used to purchase this tutorial. This process helps prevent students from ordering the solutions without your knowledge. After we receive all this information we will email you a download link for the Source Code Solution Files associated with this book.

Warning: If you purchased this book "used" or "second hand" you are not licensed or entitled to download the Program Solution Files. However, you can purchase the Digital Download Version of this book at a highly discounted price which allows you access to the digital source code solutions files required for completing this tutorial.

Installing The Computer Bible Games with Visual Basic Tutorial:

The course notes and code for **Computer Bible Games with Visual Basic** are included in one or more ZIP files. Use your favorite 'unzipping' application to write all files to your computer. The course is included in the folder entitled **BeginVB**. This folder contains two other folders: **BVB Notes** and **BVB Projects**. The **BVB Projects** folder includes all the Visual Basic projects developed during the course.

How To Take the Course:

Computer Bible Games with Visual Basic is a self-paced course. The suggested approach is to do one class a week for thirteen weeks. Each week's class should require about 3 to 6 hours of your time to grasp the concepts completely. Prior to doing a particular week's work, open the class notes file for that week and print it out. Then, work through the notes at your own pace. Try to do each example as they are encountered in the notes. Work through the projects in Classes 3 through 13 (and the Bonus projects). If you need any help, all completed projects are included in the **BVB Projects** folder.

A Note on Visual Basic Naming Conventions

Controls

The accepted standard for naming controls is to assign a three letter (lower case) prefix (identifying the type of control) followed by a descriptive name you assign. Some of the prefixes are:

Control	**Prefix**	**Example**
Form	frm	frmWatch
Button	btn	btnExit, btnStart
Label	lbl	lblStart, lblEnd
Text Box	txt	txtTime, txtName
Menu	mnu	mnuExit, mnuSave
Check Box	chk	chkChoice

Event Procedures

Once a control is named, the standard for naming an event procedure associated with a control is

Private Sub ControlName_Event (**Arguments**) **Handles** ControlName.Event

.

.

End Sub

So, for a button control name **btnExample**, the event procedure for the **Click** event would be named **btnExample_Click**. And, since the earliest days of Visual Studio, if you double-click on a button control named **btnExample**, the event procedure appearing in the code window was:

```
Private Sub btnExample_Click(sender As Object, e As
EventArgs) Handles btnExample.Click

End Sub
```

This has changed with Visual Studio 2019.

In Visual Studio 2019, if you double-click on a button control named **btnExample**, the event procedure appearing in the code window is:

```
Private Sub BtnExample_Click(sender As Object, e As
EventArgs) Handles btnExample.Click

End Sub
```

Note that the first letter of the control name is automatically capitalized. The folks at Microsoft have decided that the first letter of every procedure in Visual Basic should be upper case (and there doesn't appear to be any way to turn off this "feature"). This creates a mismatch between the assigned control name (**btnExample**) and the name used in the event procedure (**BtnExample**). For our Visual Basic tutorials, we needed to decide what to do about this new convention.

Our Naming Conventions

The mismatch between control name and event procedure name would quickly go away if we simply choose to apply a new control naming convention where the first letter of every control name is an upper case letter. We did not take this route – it would require a massive paradigm shift. And, it would require extensive rewriting of all legacy code written using the standard convention. We decided to continue use of the time-tested control naming convention, a three letter lower case prefix, followed by a describing name with mixed upper and lower case letters. This standard has been around forever and will probably remain so. With this decision, we had to choose what to do about event procedure names.

First, realize that the name of the event procedure associated with a control is completely arbitrary. You can give the procedure any name you want as long as it's properly connected to the correct event procedure using the Visual Studio properties window. So, we could continue to use our old standard of naming event procedures, starting with a lower case letter. For a button control named **btnExample**, the **Click** event procedure would be

```
Private Sub btnExample_Click(sender As Object, e As
EventArgs) Handles btnExample.Click

End Sub
```

Such a convention will work in Visual Studio 2019, but comes with problems.

The first problem in using the 'old standard' is that Visual Studio will flag each so named event procedure with an error message saying: 'Naming rule violation: These words must begin with upper case characters: btnExample_Click'. Again, the code will still work, but there will be all these annoying messages.

The second problem in using the 'old standard' in Visual Studio 2019 is that when building a project, if you double-click on a control to establish an event procedure, the first letter will be automatically capitalized. Then, you have to remember to change the case of that letter for every event procedure established. This would be a headache.

We have decided to live with this new naming convention where the first letter of every event procedure is capitalized, realizing there is a mismatch between the control names and associated event procedures. So, in our tutorials, when we refer to the **Click** event procedure for a control named **btnExample**, that procedure's name in code will be **BtnExample_Click**. We recognize this is a change for programmers, but hopefully is something you can get used to. In our experience, it just took a few examples for the new convention to seem 'normal'.

Foreword

For over 20 years I have known Philip Conrod as a best friend, fellow Christian, and my personal IT guy for a variety of computer issues that have come my way. Philip's technological expertise mixed with his spiritual gifts of knowledge and teaching have given him not only a unique set of skills for working in the Information Technology field for over 30 years but also for serving Jesus in the church. He has saved his home church thousands of dollars in needed upgrades, understanding networks intricacies and teaching staff members needed computer skills.

The "other side" of Philip's gifts lie in his amazing ability to teach. Simply put, he makes the "hard concepts" easy to understand! Whether it's doctrinal, devotional or day to day living from the Bible, student after student have grown tremendously from Philip's teaching at New Community Church. Recently I was leading a group of young adults and asked "Which mentor has influenced you the most?" Not surprisingly, Philip Conrod's name quickly rose to the top! He has, for years been a favorite Sunday school teacher for many students in our church, including my own son. Of course the highlight of each year is when a crowded house of teenagers and college graduates, of "Mr. Phil", play hours of computer games intertwined with Christian fellowship in his home every year for over 15 years. It is this very combination that makes Philip the perfect author for the *Computer Bible Games* series of programming books. Making the Bible fun, intriguing and filled with learning enables all of us to grow in our biblical knowledge. Sit back and be prepared to be challenged, captivated and without knowing it, grow in your knowledge and understanding of the Bible!

Ken B. Michell
Sr. Pastor
New Community Church
Maple Valley, Washington USA

www.newcommunity.us

1

Introducing Visual Basic

A Brief History of Visual Basic

In the mid-1960's, most computing was done on large computers taking up entire floors of buildings (these machines had less computational power than the laptop I'm typing these notes on!). Most programming was done in cryptic languages by engineers and mathematicians. Two professors at Dartmouth College wanted to explain programming to "normal" people and developed the **BASIC** (Beginner's All-Purpose Symbolic Code) language to help in that endeavor. BASIC was meant to be a simple language with just a few keywords to allow a little math and a little printing.

In the later 1960's, timeshare computing, where a user could sit at a terminal and interact with the computer, became popular. The primary language used in these interactive sessions was BASIC. The Dartmouth BASIC was not sufficient for the many applications being developed, so many extensions and improvements were made in the BASIC language. Many of the first computer games were written on timeshare terminals using BASIC – gambling games, world simulations and the classic Star Trek game were very popular.

In the mid-1970's, an issue of Popular Science magazine changed the world of computers forever. On the cover was an Altair computer. About all the computer could do was flash some lights according to a program written by the user. But, it was the first home computer. Two young guys in Seattle, Bill Gates and Paul Allen, saw the potential. They developed a BASIC language for the Altair computer and marketed it through their new company – Microsoft. Yes, the first product sold by Microsoft was the BASIC computer language. It sold for $350 and was distributed on a cassette tape.

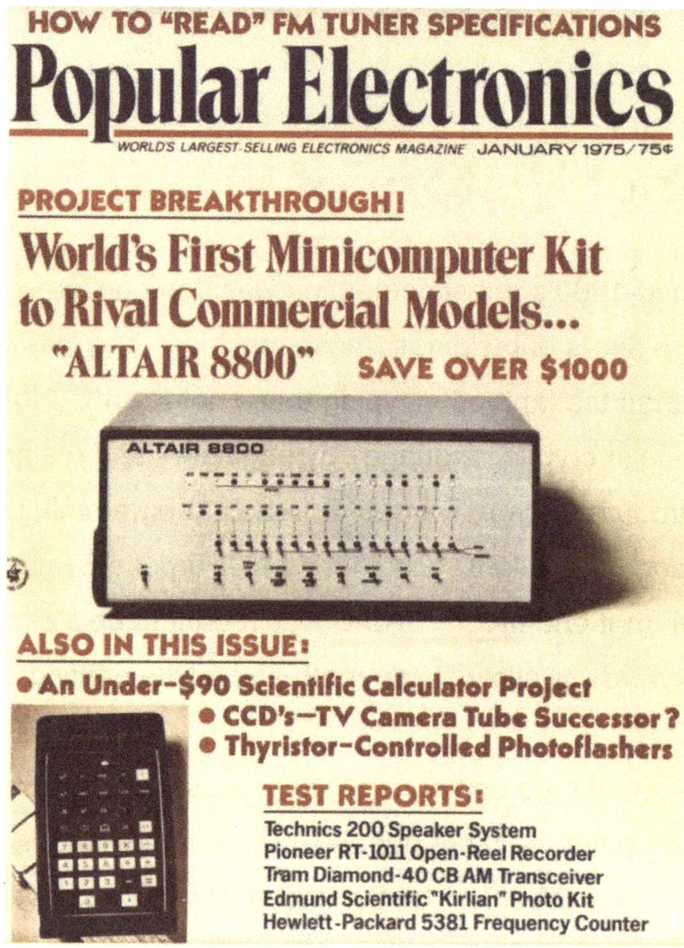

When the big wave of “toy” computers – Radio Shack TRS-80, Commodore 64, Texas Instruments 99/4A, Atari 400, Coleco Adam, Timex Sinclair and the IBM PC-Jr. - flooded the market in the early 1980’s, one thing these machines had in common was that they were all programmed in some version of Microsoft’s BASIC. Microsoft’s name for their BASIC language product has changed over the years, having names like GW-BASIC, QuickBasic, QBasic, Visual Basic, Visual Basic .NET, with one of the newest versions being called **Visual Basic**, the language you are about to learn. Visual Basic is one of the easiest programming languages to learn. Yet, even though it is easy to learn and to use, Visual Basic can also be used to develop very powerful computer programs. Visual Basic provides a sophisticated environment for building and testing Windows-based applications.

You’ve used Windows-based applications before. Microsoft’s programs like Word, Excel, Internet Explorer and the windows that appear within these applications (to open and save files, to print files) are all Windows-based applications. These applications are not written in Visual Basic (they are written in a language called C++), but they do demonstrate the functionality you can put in your Visual Basic applications.

Visual Basic can be used to write computer games, businesses can use Visual Basic to manage their databases, webmasters can use Visual Basic to develop web pages, and people like yourself can use Visual Basic to build Windows applications they want and need in their everyday home and work life. In these notes, you will learn how to use Microsoft’s Visual Basic to write your own Windows-based applications. You may not become a billionaire like Bill and Paul, but hopefully you’ll have some fun learning a very valuable skill.

Let's Get Started

Learning how to use Visual Basic to write a computer program (like learning anything new) involves many steps, many new terms, and many new skills. We will take it slow, describing each step, term, and skill in detail. Before starting, we assume you know how to do a few things:

- You should know how to start your computer and use the mouse.
- You should have a little knowledge on working with your operating system
- You should know how to resize and move windows around on the screen.
- You should know how to run an application on your computer by using the **Start Menu**.
- You should know how to fill in information in Windows that may pop up on the screen.
- You should know about folders and files and how to find them on your computer.
- You should know what file extensions are and how to identify them. For example, in a file named **Example.ext**, the three letters **ext** are called the extension.
- You should know how to click on links to read documents and move from page to page in such documents. You do this all the time when you use the Internet.

You have probably used all of these skills if you've ever used a word processor, spreadsheet, or any other software on your computer. If you think you lack any of these skills, ask someone for help. They should be able to show you how to do them in just a few minutes. Actually, any time you feel stuck while trying to learn this material, never be afraid to ask someone for help. We were all beginners at one time and people really like helping you learn.

Let's get going. And, as we said, we're going to take it slow. In this first class, we will learn how to get Visual Basic started on a computer, how to load a program (or project) into Visual Basic, how to run the program, how to stop the program, and how to exit from Visual Basic. It will be a good introduction to the many new things we will learn in the classes to come.

Starting Visual Basic

We assume you have Visual Basic installed and operational on your computer. If you don't, you need to do this first. Again, this might be a good place to ask for someone's help if you need it. Visual Basic is available for free download from Microsoft.

Visual Basic is included as a part of **Microsoft Visual Studio 2019 Community Edition**. Visual Studio includes not only Visual Basic, but also Visual C++ and Visual C#. All three languages use the same development environment. Follow this link for complete instructions for downloading and installing Visual Basic on your computer:

https://www.visualstudio.com/products/free-developer-offers-vs

Once installed, to start Visual Studio:

- Click on the **Start** button on the Windows task bar.
- Then select **Visual Studio 2019**

Visual Studio should start. Several windows will appear on the screen, with the layout depending on settings within your product.

Upon starting (and clearing the start screen), my screen shows:

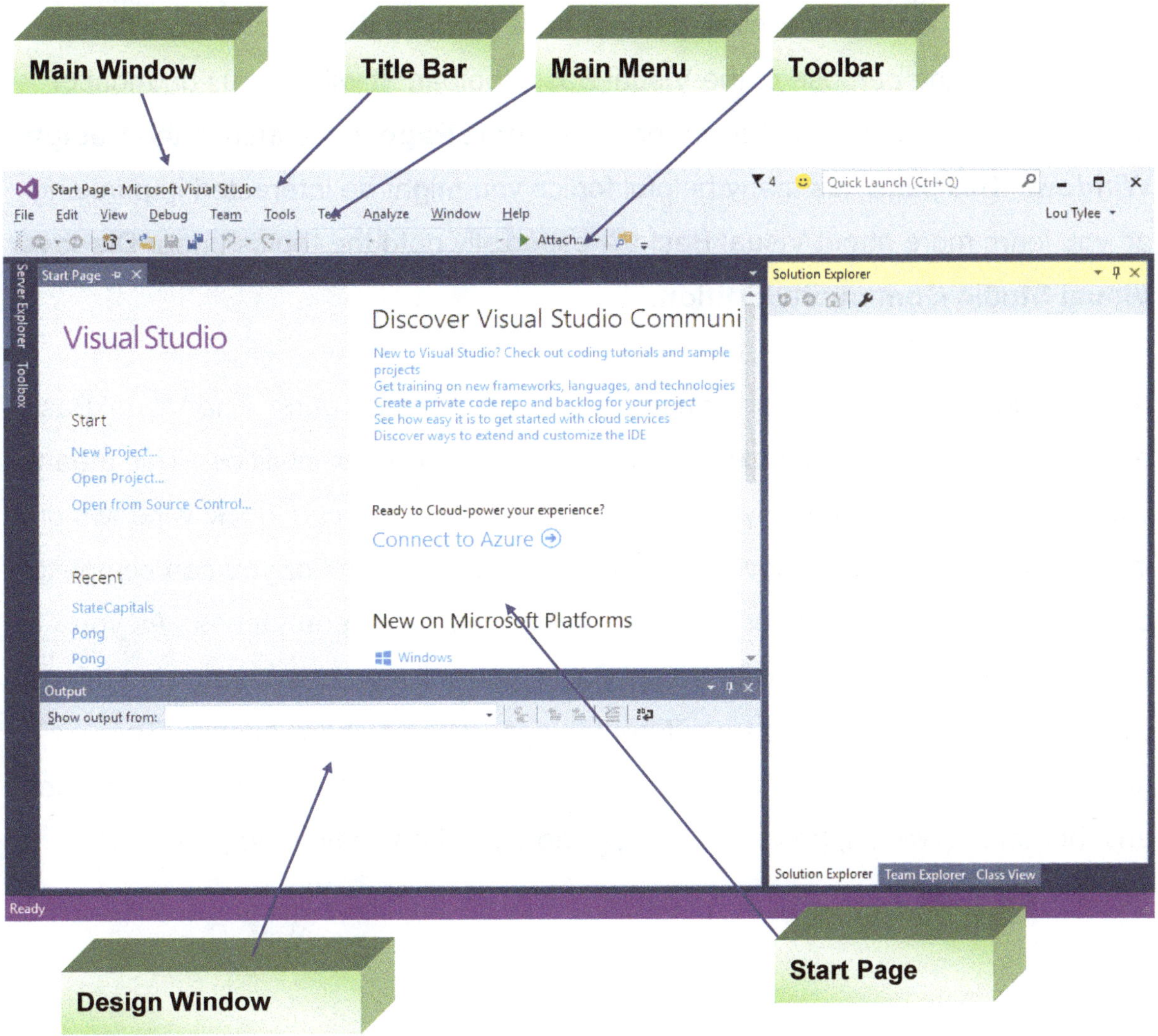

This screen displays the Visual Basic **Integrated Development Environment (IDE)**. This is where we build, run and work with our applications. Let's point out just a few items on the screen. There are many windows on the screen. At the top of the screen is the Visual Basic **Main Window**. At the top of the main window is the **Title Bar**. The title bar gives us information about what program we're using and what Visual Basic program we are working with. Below the title bar is the **Main Menu** from where we can control the Visual Basic program. You should be familiar with how menus work from using other programs like word processors and games. Under the main menu is a **Toolbar**. Here, little buttons with pictures also allow us to control Visual Basic, much like the main menu. If you put the mouse cursor over one of these buttons for a second or so, a little 'tooltip' will pop up and tell you what that particular button does - try it! Almost all Windows applications (spreadsheets, word processors, games) have toolbars that help us do different tasks. This is the purpose of the Visual Basic toolbar. It will help us do most of our tasks. In the middle of the screen is the **Start Page**, contained in the **Design Window**. This page has many helpful topics you might be interested in pursuing as you learn more about Visual Basic. – especially note the topics under **Discover Visual Studio Community Edition**.

At any time, your particular screen may look different than ours. The Visual Basic environment can be customized to an infinite number of possibilities. This means you can make things look anyway you want them to. You can 'dock' windows or 'float' windows. You can move windows wherever you want or you can completely delete windows. And, different windows will appear at different times. As you become more experienced with Visual Basic, you will learn ways you want things to be. We encourage you to try different things. Try moving windows. Try docking and floating. We won't talk a lot about how to customize the development environment. (We will, however, always show you how to find the particular window you need.)

Opening a Visual Basic Project

What we want to do right now is **open a project**. Windows applications written using Visual Basic are referred to as **solutions**. A solution is made up of one or more **projects**. Projects include all the information we need for our computer program. In this course, our applications (solutions) will be made up of a single project. Because of this, we will use the terms application, solution and project interchangeably. Included with these notes are many Visual Basic projects you can open and use. Let's open one now.

We will open a project using the main menu. Follow these steps:

- Select **File** from the main menu, then click **Open,** then **Project/Solution**. An **Open Project** window will appear:

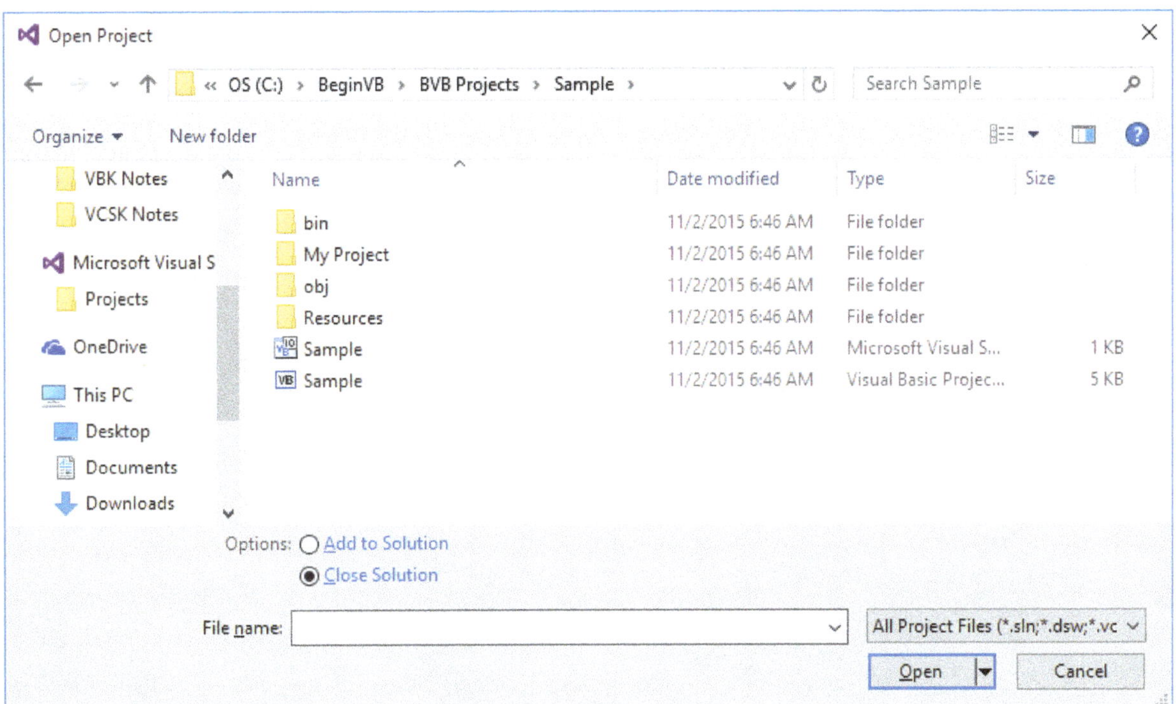

- Find the folder named **CBGVB** (stands for **Computer Bible Games Visual Basic**). This is the folder that holds the notes and projects for this course. Open that folder.

* Find and open the folder named **BVB Projects.** This folder holds all the projects for the course

Remember how you got to this folder. Throughout the course, you will go to this folder to open projects you will need. Open the project folder named **Sample**.

In this project folder, among other things is a **Visual Studio Solution** file named **Sample** and a **Visual Basic Project** file named **Sample**. Open the **Sample** solution file (as shown in the example Open Project window). Since there is only one project in this solution, you could also open the project file and get the same results, but it is better to always open the solution file.

Once the project is opened, many windows are now on the screen:

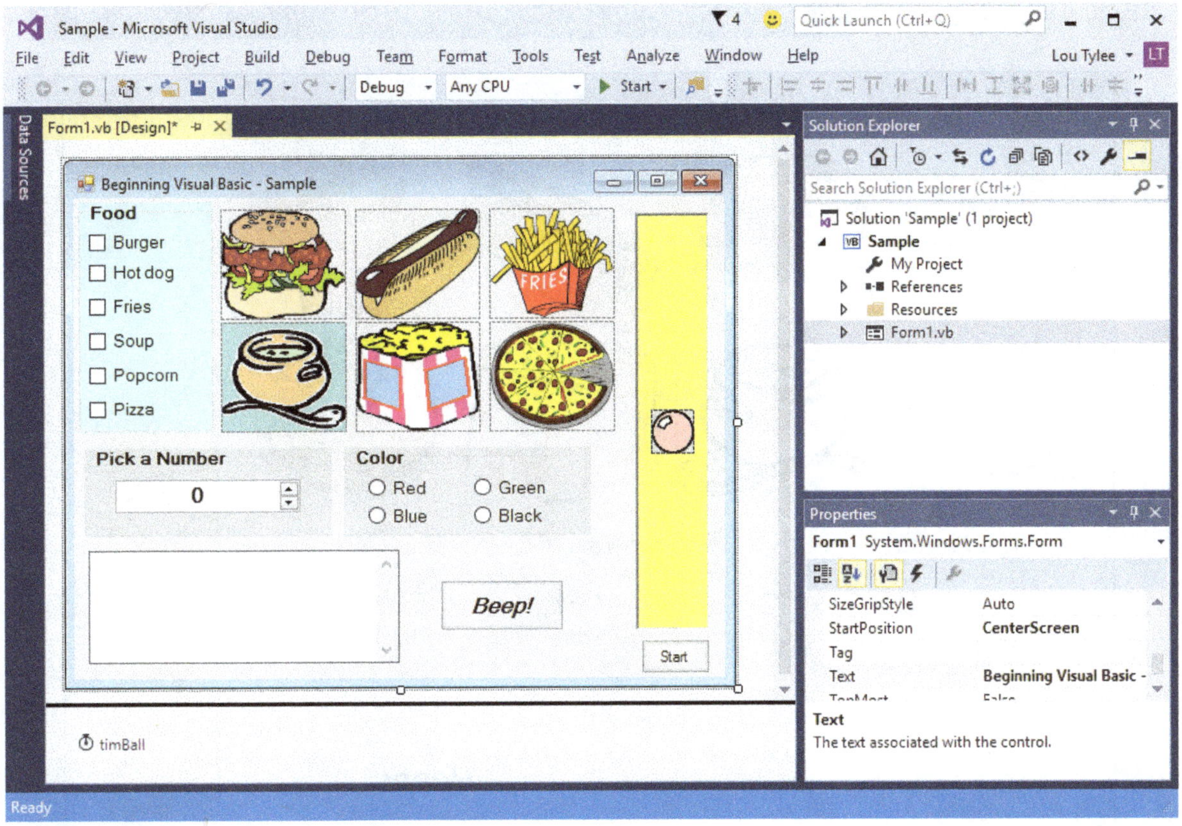

Look for the **Solution Explorer** window (if it is not there, choose **View** in the menu and select **Solution Explorer**). This lists the files in our solution. Right-click the file **Form1.vb** and choose **Open**.

In the **Design** window will appear a window that looks something like this:

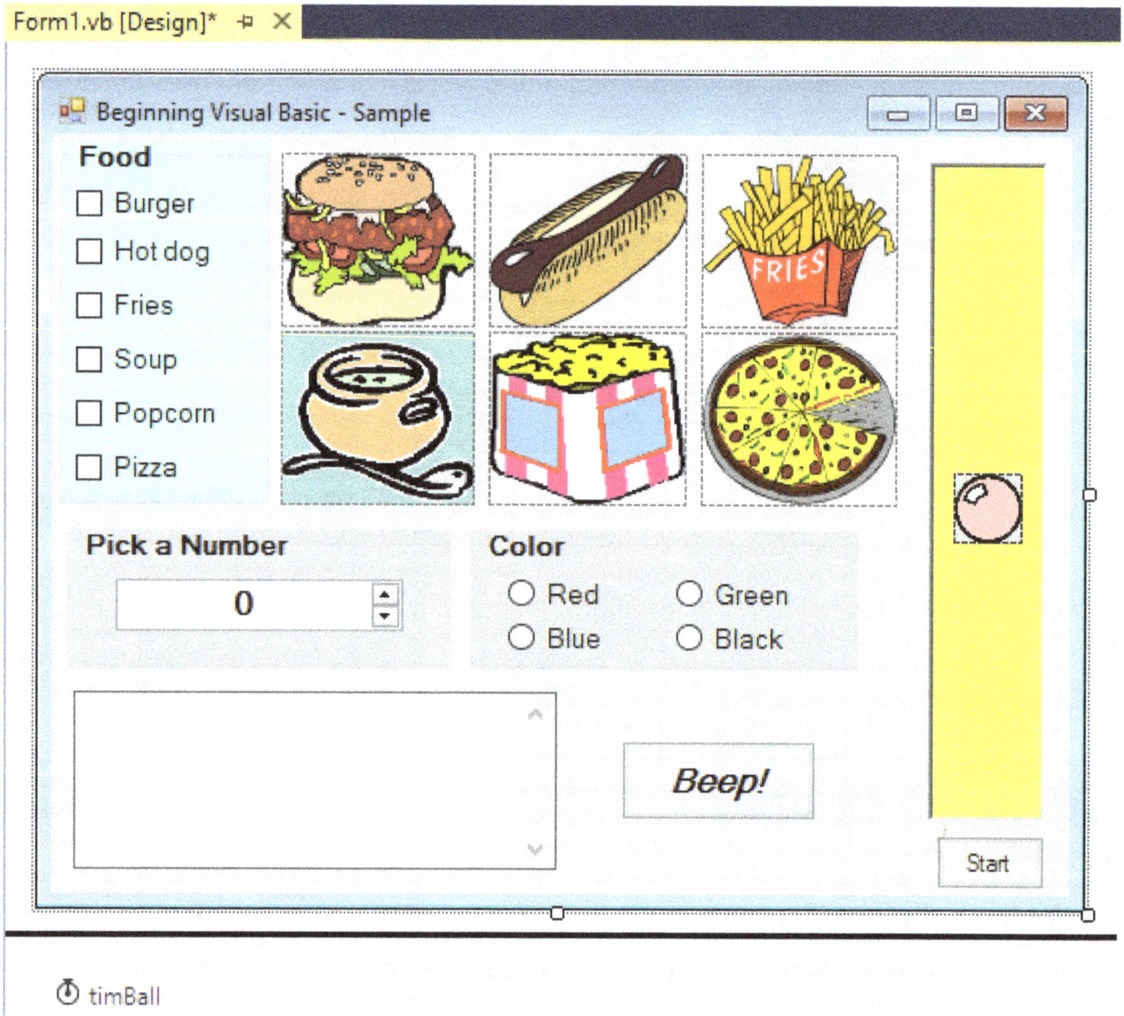

This is our project named **Sample**. We're going to spend a bit of time explaining everything that is displayed here. This will introduce you to some of the words, or vocabulary, we use in Visual Basic. There are lots of terms used in Visual Basic. Don't try to memorize everything - you'll see these new words many times through the course.

We call the displayed project window a **Form**. All Visual Basic projects or programs are built using forms. In fact, you have probably noticed that all Windows applications are built using forms of some type. At the top of the form is the **Title Bar**. It has an **icon** (little picture) related to the form, a description of what the form does (**Beginning Visual Basic - Sample**), and three smaller buttons that control form appearance (we won't worry about these buttons right now). There are lots of other things on the form. These other things are the 'heart' of a Visual Basic computer program.

You see a set of square buttons with food names next to them. You see pictures of food. You see a set of round buttons with color names next to them. There is a little box you can type in with something called a scroll bar on the right side. There's a big button that says **Beep!!** There's a little device for picking the value of a number. And, there's a ball in a big rectangle with a button that says **Start** and, below the form, a little thing that looks like a stopwatch. We call all of these other things on the form **Controls** or **Objects**. Controls provide an **interface**, or line of communication, between you (or the user of your program) and the computer. You use the controls to tell the computer certain things. The computer then uses what it is told to determine some results and displays those results back to you through controls. By the way, the form itself is a control. If you've used any Windows applications, you've seen controls before - you probably just didn't know they were called controls. As examples, buttons on toolbars are controls, scroll bars to move through word processor documents are controls, menu items are controls, and the buttons you click on when opening and saving files are controls.

I think you get the idea that controls are a very important part of Visual Basic, and you're right. They are the most important part of Visual Basic - they are what allow you to build your applications. We will spend much of this course just learning about controls. Right now, though, let's run this program and get some insight into how a Visual Basic project (and its controls) works.

Running a Visual Basic Project

After developing a Visual Basic project, you want to start or run the program. This gets the program going and lets the user interact with the **controls** on the form and have the computer do its assigned tasks. We can run a project also using the toolbar under the Visual Basic menu. Look for a button that looks like the **Play** button on a VCR, CD player, or cassette tape player:

Start Project
Toolbar Button

Click this button to run **Sample** (the project we opened previously).

You can also run a project by: (1) selecting the **Debug** menu heading, then clicking **Start Debugging**, or (2) pressing the **<F5>** function key.

The project form will appear and look something like this.

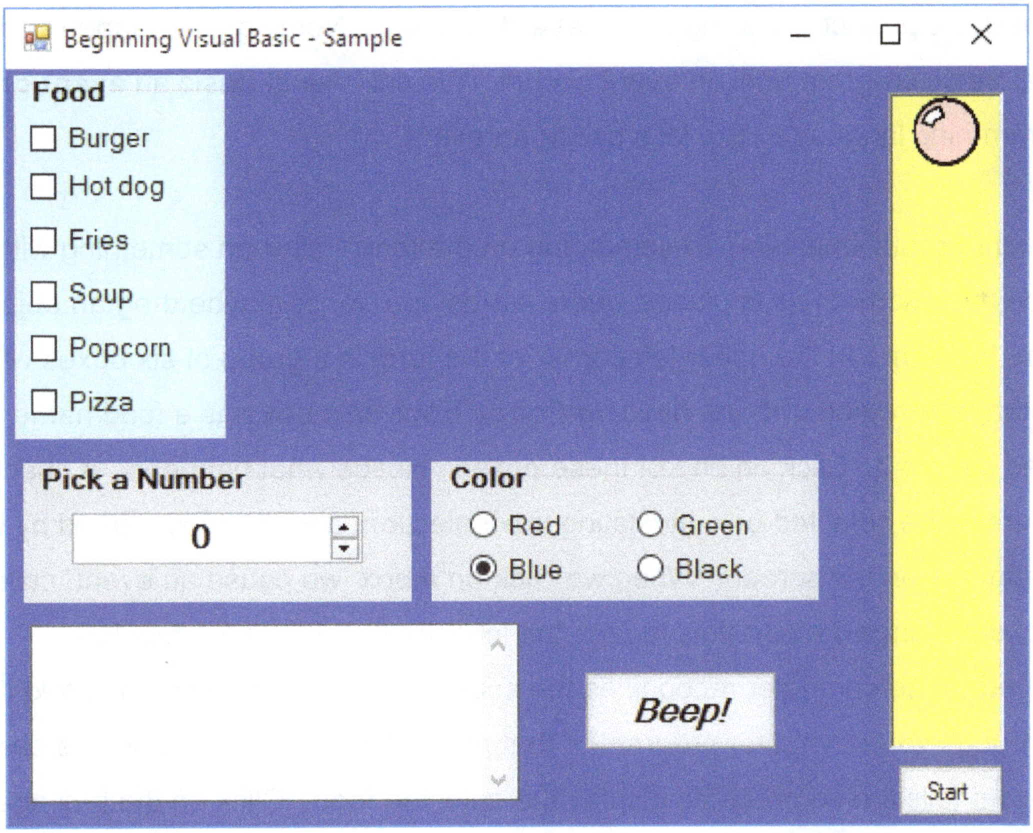

Your form may appear slightly different depending on the particular Windows operating system you are using. We use both Windows Vista (seen here) and Windows XP in these notes:

Notice a few things have changed. All the foods have disappeared. The background color of the form is blue. The circle button next to **Blue** has a black dot in it. The little stopwatch control is not visible. The little ball has moved near the top of the big rectangle. What happened? We'll find out how and why all this happened as we learn more about Visual Basic. Also, notice in the Visual Basic title bar (in the main window) that the word **Running** appears in parentheses next to the project name. It is important to always know if you are running or designing a program – this indication in the title bar will tell you.

The project is now running, but what is it doing? Nothing is happening, or is it? At this point, Visual Basic is waiting for you, the user, to do something. We say your Visual Basic project is waiting for an **event** to occur. Nothing can happen in a Visual Basic program until an event occurs. We call Visual Basic an **event-driven** programming language. So, let's cause an event.

An event occurs when you do something on the form - click on something with the mouse, type something in places where words can go, or maybe drag an object across the form. In the upper left corner of the form is a group of six boxes within a rectangular region with the heading **Food**. Each little box has a food name printed next to it. Click on one of these boxes. Notice what happens. A check appears in the selected box, indicating box selection, and the food named by that box appears on the screen. When we click on a box, we cause an event, called a **CheckedChanged** event (this means the 'checked' status of the box has changed). The computer recognizes the event and does what you have told it to do (through your computer program) if that particular event occurs. In this case, the event tells the computer to display the selected food. Click on the box again. The check mark and the food disappear. You have caused another event and told the computer to make the food disappear. This particular control is called a **check box**. Notice you can check as many boxes as you want, picking which foods (if any) you want displayed on your screen. Check boxes are used when you want to select items from a list. Two other controls are used in this food example. The rectangular region holding the check boxes is called a **group box**. The region each food picture is displayed in is called a **picture box** control. Now, let's look at causing events with the other controls on the form.

Near the middle of the screen is a group of four round buttons in a group box with the heading **Color**. Each button has a color name printed next to it. The **Blue** button has a black dot in it, indicating it is the currently selected color (notice the form is blue). Click on another of these buttons. Notice what happens. The form color changes to the selected color. This **CheckedChanged** (meaning the 'checked' or actually 'dotted' status of the button has changed) event tells the computer to change the form background color. Notice that when you select a new color, the black dot appears in the selected button and disappears in the previously selected button. Unlike the check boxes we saw earlier, you can only select one of these buttons. This makes sense - the form can only be one color! These round buttons are called **radio buttons**. Radio buttons are used when you need to choose exactly one option from a list of many. They are called radio buttons because, on a radio, you can only choose one option (station) at a time.

Under the **Food** group box is another group box with the heading **Pick a Number**. There we see a control called a **numeric up-down** control. There is a **label** area displaying a number and next to the number is another control with one arrow pointing up and one pointing down (a **scroll bar**). You've probably seen scroll bars in other applications you have used. The scroll bar is used to change the displayed number. Click on the arrow on the top of the scroll bar. The displayed value will increase by 1. Continued clicking on that arrow will continue to increase the value. Clicking the lower arrow will decrease the value. In this example, the computer is responding to the numeric up-down control's **ValueChanged** event, which occurs each time an arrow is clicked, changing the displayed value.

Under the **Pick a Number** group box is a region with a scroll bar on the right side. This control is called a **text box**. You can click in it, then type in any text you want. Try it. The text box is like a little word processor in itself. Each time you type something in the text box, several events occur. There is a **KeyPress** event when you press a key and a **Change** event that is called each time the text in the box changes.

Next to the text box is a button that says **Beep!!** Click the button and you should hear a beep on your computer's speaker. This control is called a **button** and is one of the most widely used controls in Visual Basic. The **Click** event told the computer to make the speaker beep.

The last thing on our form is a tall, yellow, rectangular control called a **panel** that contains a **picture box** control displaying a ball. Under the panel is a button that says **Start**. Click on that button, that is, cause a **Click** event. The ball starts moving down. It continues moving down until it hits the bottom of the panel, then starts moving back up. It will continue to do this until you click the button that now says **Stop**. Remember the little stopwatch that was below our form in design mode, but disappeared when we ran the project. It is being used by the bouncing ball example - it is called a **timer** control. The Click event on the button, in addition to changing what the button says to **Stop**, also started this timer control. The timer control generates **Tick** events all by itself at preset time intervals. In this example, a **Tick** event is generated every 1/10th of a second and, in that event, the ball position is changed to give the appearance of movement. Notice that even while the ball is bouncing, you can change the form color, make toys appear and disappear, type text, and make the computer beep. So, Visual Basic even has the capability of handling multiple events.

Obviously, this project doesn't do much more than demonstrate what can be done with Visual Basic, but that is a important concept. It points out what you will be doing in building your own Visual Basic projects. A project is made up of the controls that let the user provide information to the computer. By causing events with these controls, the computer will generate any required results. We haven't worried about how to use the events to determine these results, but we will in all the later classes. By the time you have finished this course, you will be able to build projects that do everything (and more) that the **Sample** project does. Let's look now at how to stop the project.

Stopping a Visual Basic Project

There are many ways to stop a Visual Basic project. We will use the toolbar. Look for a button that looks like the **Stop** button on a VCR, CD player, or cassette tape player (you may have to move the project form down a bit on the screen to see the toolbar):

Stop Project
Toolbar Button

Click on this button (you may have to click it twice). The project will stop and Visual Basic will return to design mode.

Alternate ways to stop a project are:

- Selecting the **Debug** menu heading, then clicking **Stop Debugging**
- Click the **Close** button found on the form. It is the little button that looks like an **X** in the upper right corner of the form.

Stopping Visual Basic

When you are done working with a Visual Basic project, you want to leave the Visual Basic program and the design environment. It is the same procedure used by nearly all Windows applications:

- Select **File** in the main menu.
- Select **Exit** (at the end of the File menu).

Stop Visual Basic now. Visual Basic will close all open windows and you will be returned to the Windows desktop. In stopping Visual Basic with **Sample** active, you may be asked if you want to save certain files. Answer **No**. Like with stopping a project, an alternate way to stop Visual Basic is to click on the close button in the upper right hand corner of the main window. It's the button that looks like an **X**.

Summary

We covered a lot of new material here. As we said earlier, you learned a lot of new words and concepts. Don't worry if you don't remember everything we talked about here. You will see the material many times again. It's important that you just have some concept of what goes into a Visual Basic project and how it works. And you know how to start and stop Visual Basic itself.

In summary, we saw that a Visual Basic project is built upon a **form**. **Controls** (also called **objects**) are placed on the form that allow the user and computer to interact. The user generates **events** with the controls that allow the computer to do its job. In the next class, you will begin to acquire the skills that will allow you to begin building your own Visual Basic projects. You will see how the parts of a project fit together. Using project **Sample** as an example, you will learn how to locate important parts of a project. Then, in Class 3, you will actually build your first project!

2

The Visual Basic Design Environment

Review and Preview

In Class 1, we learned the important parts of a Visual Basic **project**. We saw that a project is built on a **form** using **controls** (also called **objects**). By interacting with the controls using **events**, we get the computer to do assigned tasks via instructions we provide. In this second class, we will learn the beginning steps of building our own Visual Basic projects by looking at the different parts of the project and where they fit in the Visual Basic design environment. Like Class 1, there are also a lot of new terms and skills to learn.

Parts of a Visual Basic Project

In Class 1, we saw that there are four major components in a Visual Basic application: the solution, the project, the form, and the controls. A **solution** can contain multiple projects. In this course, solutions will only contain a single project, so the words solution and project are used interchangeably. **Project** is the word used to encompass everything in a Visual Basic project. Other words used to describe a project are **application** or **program**. The **form** is the window where you create the interface between the user and the computer. **Controls** are graphical features or tools that are placed on forms to allow user interaction (text boxes, labels, scroll bars, command buttons). Recall the form itself is a control. Controls are also referred to as **objects**. Pictorially, a project is:

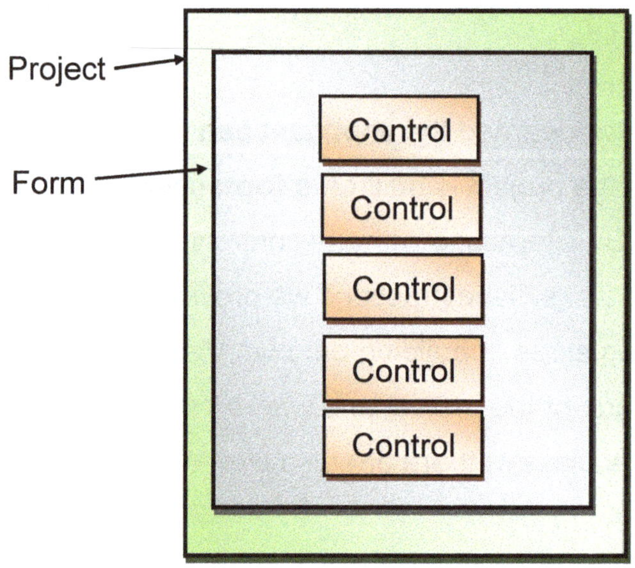

So, in simplest terms, a project consists of a form containing several (and some projects contain hundreds) controls.

Every characteristic of a control (including the form itself) is specified by a **property**. Example control properties include names, any text on the control, width, height, colors, position on the form, and contents. Properties are used to give your project the desired appearance. For each control studied in this class, we will spend a lot of time talking about properties.

In Class 1, we saw that by interacting with the controls in the **Sample** project (clicking buttons, choosing different options, typing text), we could make things happen in our project by generating control **events**. We say that Visual Basic is an **event-driven** language and it is governed by an **event processor**. That means that nothing happens in a Visual Basic project until some event occurs. Once an event is detected, the project finds a series of instructions related to that event, called an **event procedure**. That procedure is executed, then program control is returned to the event processor:

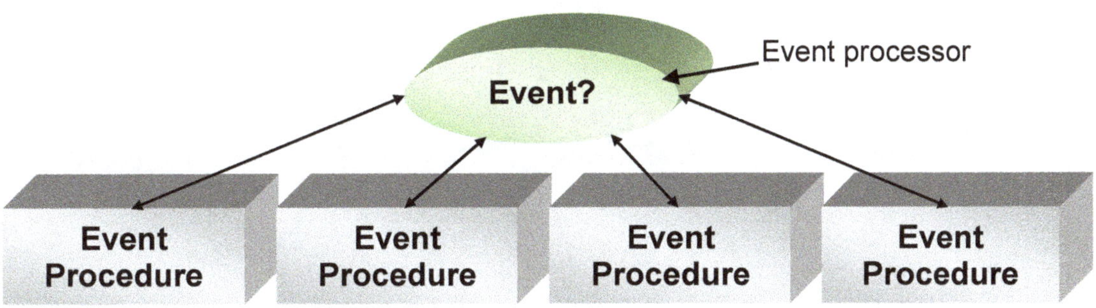

Event procedures associated with various controls are where we do the actual computer programming. These procedures are where we write BASIC language statements. You will learn a lot of programming and BASIC language in this class. The BASIC you will learn is very similar to the original BASIC used by Bill Gates and Paul Allen when starting Microsoft.

In summary, the major parts of a Visual Basic project are:

- **form**
- **controls**
- control **properties**
- control **event procedures**

Now, let's take a look at the Visual Basic programming environment and identify where we can access each of these project components.

Parts of the Visual Basic Environment

Visual Basic is more than just a computer language. It is a project building environment. Within this one environment, we can begin and build our project, run and test our project, eliminate errors (if any) in our project, and save our project for future use. With other computer languages, many times you need a separate text editor to write your program, something called a compiler to create the program, and then a different area to test your program. Visual Basic integrates each step of the project building process into one environment. Let's look at the parts of the Visual Basic environment. To help in this look, we first need to get a new project started. We won't do anything with this project. We just use it to identify parts of the Visual Basic environment.

Starting a New Visual Basic Project

Every time you want to build a project using Visual Basic, a first step is to create a new project. Start Visual Basic using the procedure learned in Class 1. We start a new project also using the toolbar under the Visual Basic menu. Look for this button (the first button on the left):

New Project
Toolbar Button

You can also start a new project by selecting **File** from the menu, then clicking **New**, then **Project**.

Click the **New Project** button and a **New Project** box appears:

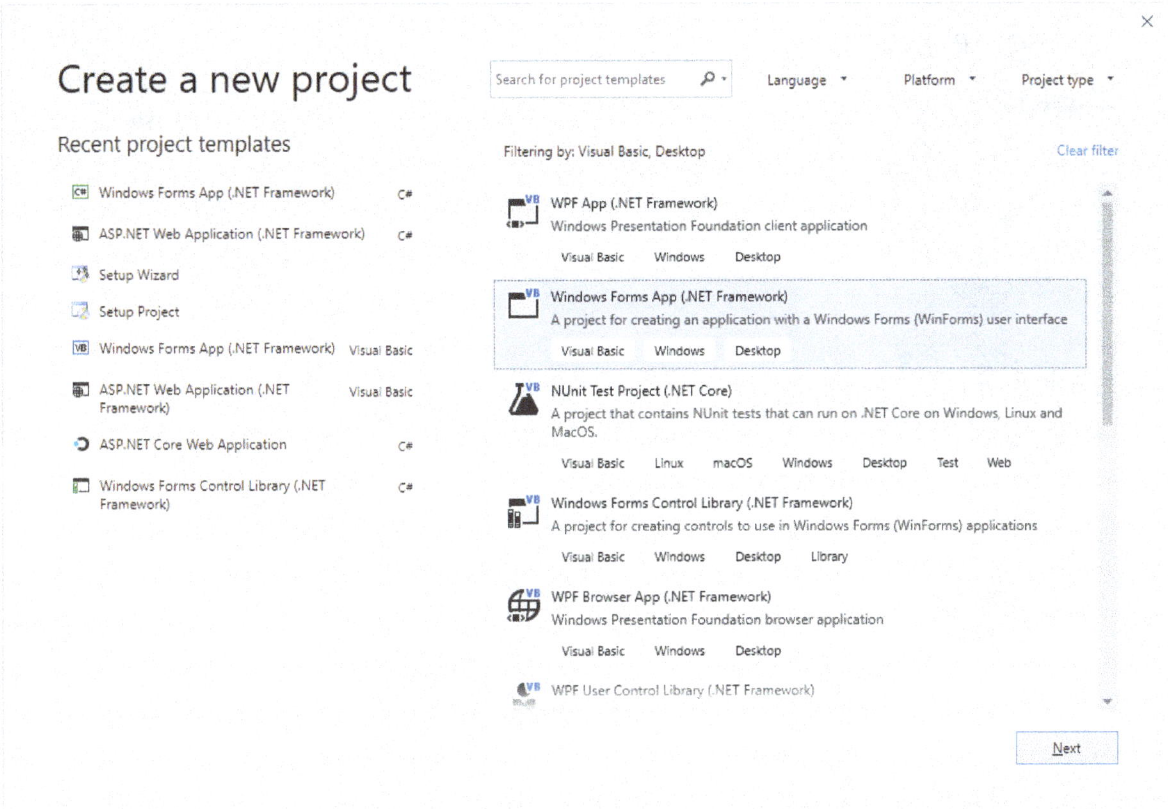

We want to build a Windows Visual BAsic desktop application. In the **Language** drop-down box, choose **Visual Basic**. In the **Platform** drop-down box, choose **Windows**. In the **Project type** drop-down box, choose **Desktop**. Then, select the **Windows Forms App** template. Click **Next**. The selected options will be saved to your IDE environment, so you don't have to reselect them each time you create a new project.

This window appears

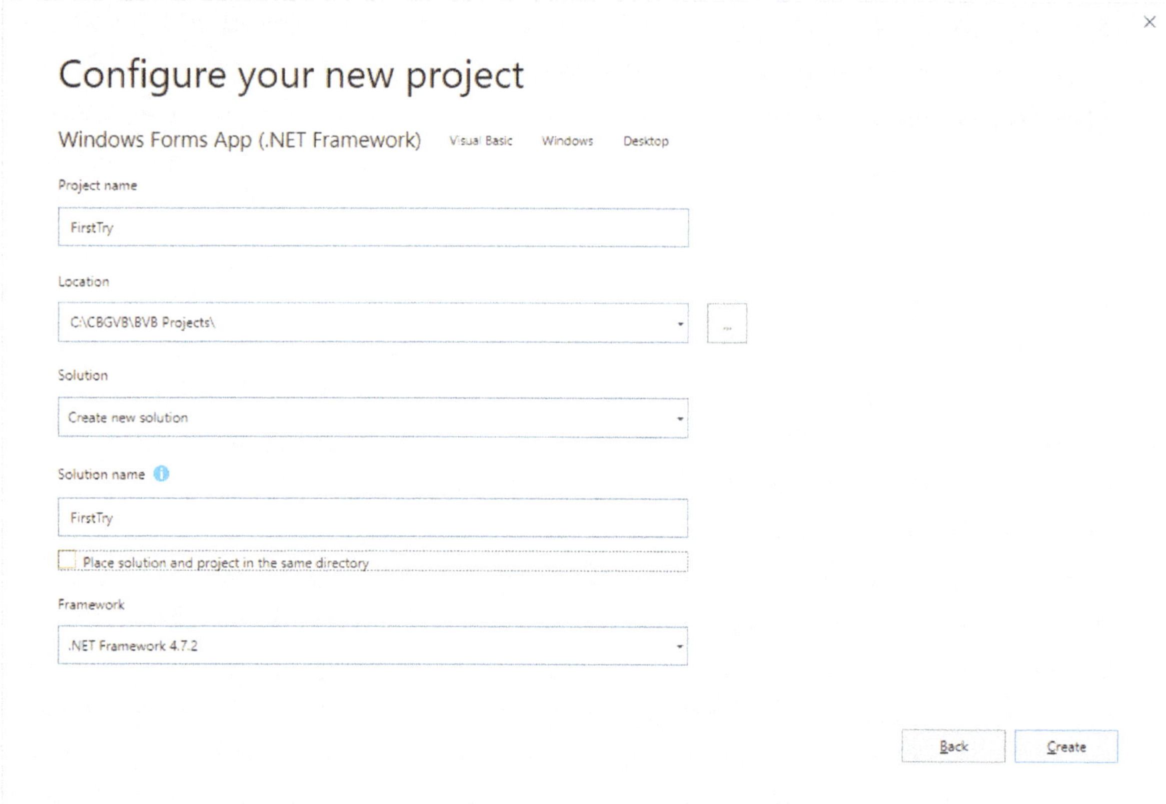

Assign a **Name** to your project (mine is named **FirstTry**). **Location** should show the directory your project folder will be in. You can **Browse** to an existing location or create a new directory by checking the indicated box. For this course, we suggest saving each of your project folders in the same directory. For the course notes, all project folders are saved in the **\CBGVB\BVB Projects** folder, with additional folders for each individual class' projects. We suggest you save your projects in a folder you create.

Once done, click **Create** and the Visual C# development environment will appear. Your project will consist of a single Windows form.

Main Window

The **Main Window** is used to control most aspects of the Visual Basic project building and running process:

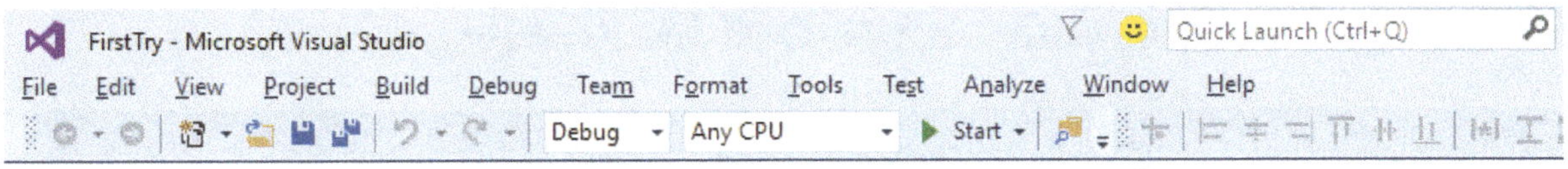

The main window consists of the title bar, menu bar, and toolbars. The title bar indicates the project name (here, **FirstTry**). The menu bar has drop-down menus from which you control the operation of the Visual Basic environment. The toolbars have buttons that provide shortcuts to some of the menu options. You should be able to identify the **New Project** button. Also, look for the buttons we used in Class 1 to start and stop a project.

Solution Explorer Window

The **Solution Explorer Window** shows which files make up your project:

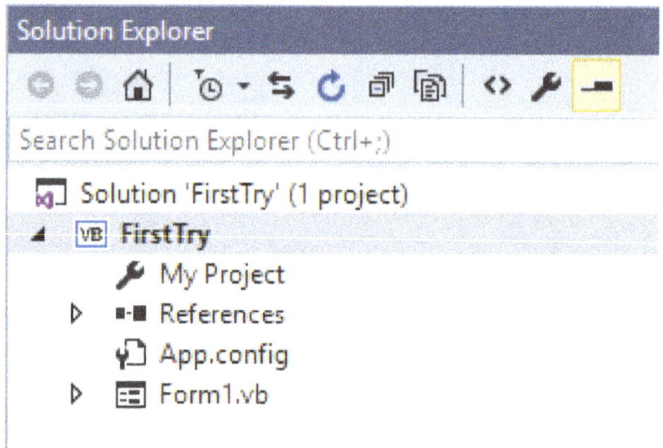

If the Solution Explorer window is not present on the screen, click **View** on the main menu, then **Solution Explorer**. If you select the form file (**Form1.vb**), you can obtain a view of the project form by choosing the **View** menu, then **Designer**. Or, you see the actual BASIC coding within a form by clicking the **View Code** button in the **Solution Explorer** window. We will look at this code window soon.

Design Window

The **Design Window** is central to developing Visual Basic applications. It is where you build your form and write actual code. You should see a blank form in this window:

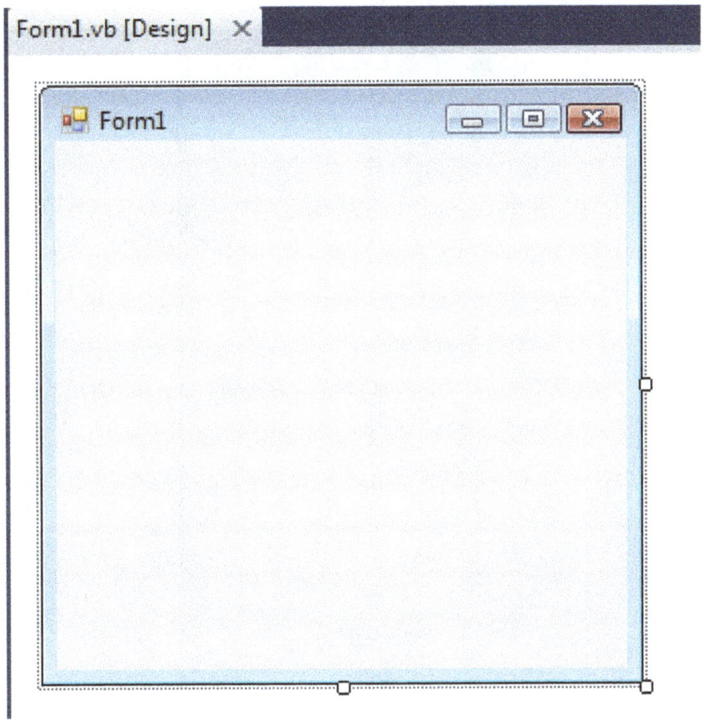

If the form is not present on the screen, select **Form1.vb** in the **Solution Explorer** window. Then, click **View** on the main menu, then **Designer**. Or, press the **<F7>** function key while holding down **<Shift>.**

Toolbox Window

The **Toolbox Window** is the selection menu for controls used in your application. Many times, controls are also referred to as **objects** or **tools**. So, three words are used to describe controls: objects, tools, and, most commonly, controls.

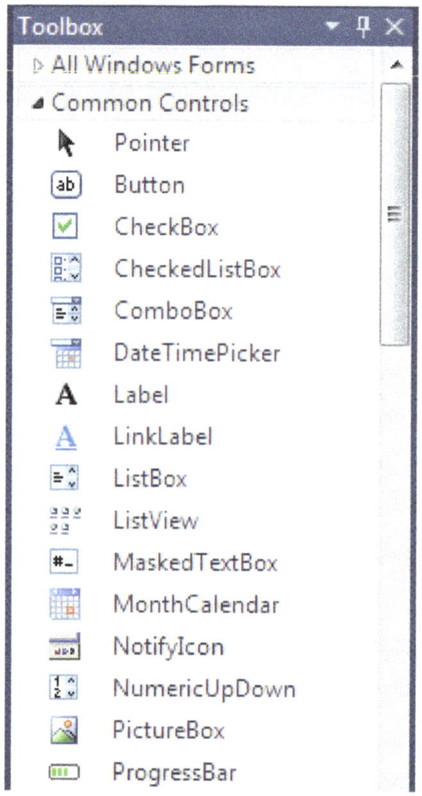

If the toolbox window is not present on the screen, click **View** on the main menu, then **Toolbox**. Make sure you are viewing the **Common Controls**. See if you can identify some of the controls we used in Class 1 with our **Sample** project.

Properties Window

The **Properties Window** is used to establish initial property values for controls. The drop-down box at the top of the window lists all controls on the current form. Under this box are the available properties for the currently selected object (the **Form** in this case). Different views of the properties are selected using the toolbar near the top of the window. Two views are available: **Alphabetic** and **Categorized**. We will always used the Alphabetic view.

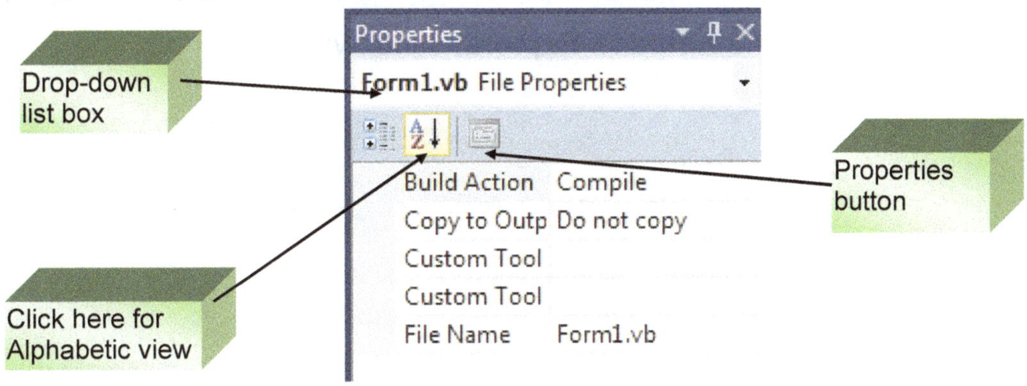

If the properties window is not present on the screen, click **View** on the main menu, then **Properties Window**. Click the **Properties** button (next to the Alphabetic view button) to see the properties. As an alternate, if the window does not show up, press the **F4** function key. Note the properties window will only display when the form and any controls are displayed in the Design window.

You should be familiar with each of the Visual Basic environment windows and know where they are and how to locate them, if they are not displayed. Next, we'll revisit the project we used in Class 1 to illustrate some of the points we've covered here.

Moving Around in Visual Basic

Solution Explorer Window

Open the project named **Sample** that we used in Class 1 (use the **File** menu option, then select **Open Project** reviewing the steps in Class 1 if needed). Once **Sample** is opened (recall it is in the **Sample** folder in the **\CGBVB\BVB Projects** folder), find and examine the **Solution Explorer** window:

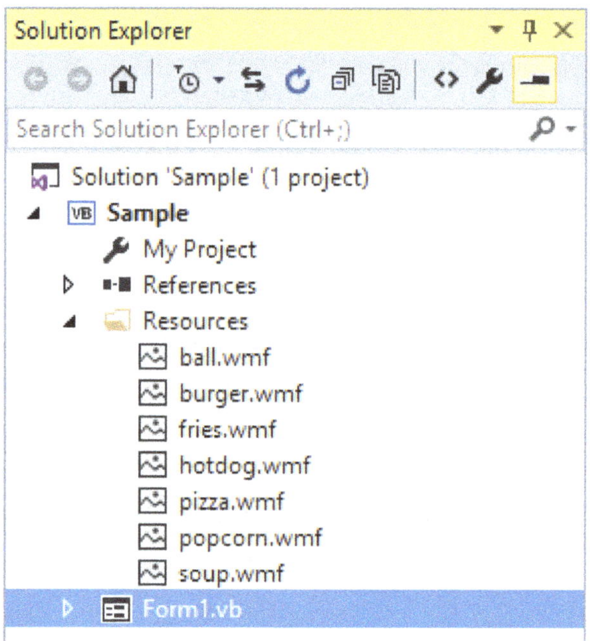

The Solution Explorer window indicates we have a solution with a project file named **Sample.** The project contains a single form saved as **Form1.vb**. The project also includes a file named **My Project** and a folder named **Resources** containing several graphics files (the ones with **wmf** extensions). The only file we're really worried about for now is the form.

Properties Window

Now, find the **Properties** window. Remember it can only be shown when the form is displayed. So, you may have to make sure the form is displayed first. Review the steps that get the desired windows on your screen.

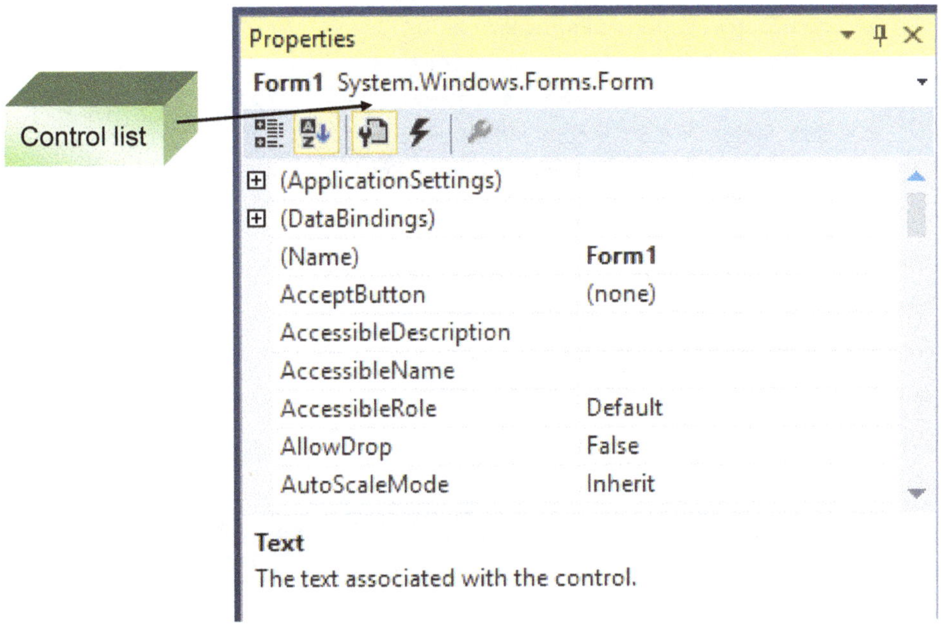

The drop-down box at the top of the properties window is called the **control list**. It displays the name (the **Name** property) of each control used in the project, as well as the type of control it is. Notice, as displayed, the current control is the **Form** and it is named **Form1**. The properties list is directly below this box. In this list, you can scroll (using the scroll bar) through the properties for the selected control. The property name is on the left side of the list and the current property value is on the right side. Scroll through the properties for the form. Do you see how many properties there are? You'll learn about many of these as you continue through the course. Don't worry about them for now, though.

Click on the down arrow in the control list (remember that's the drop-down box at the top of the properties window):

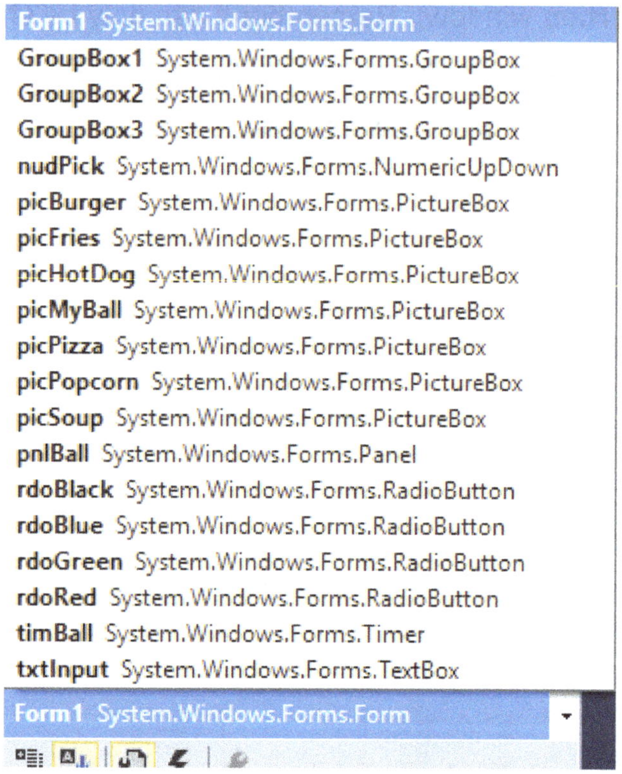

Scroll through the displayed list of all the controls on the form. There are a lot of them. Notice the assigned names and control types. Notice it's pretty easy to identify which control the name refers too. For example, **picBurger** is obviously the **picture box** control holding a picture of a burger. We always want to use proper control naming - making it easy to identify a control just by it's name. We'll spend time talking about control naming in the later classes.

Select a control and scroll through the properties for that control. Look at the properties for several controls. Notice every control has many properties. Most properties are assigned by default, that is the values are given to it by Visual Basic. We will change some properties from their default values to customize them for our use. We will look at how to change properties in Class 3.

Code Window

Let's look at a new window. Recall Visual Basic is event-driven - when an event is detected, the project goes to the correct **event procedure**. Event procedures are used to tell the computer what to do in response to an event. They are where the actual computer programming (using the BASIC language) occurs. We view the event procedures in the **Code Window**. There are many ways to display the code window. One way is to use the **View Code** button found in the Solution Explorer window. Another is to click **View** on the main menu, then **Code**. Or, as an alternate, press the **F7** function key. Find the code window for the **Sample** project. It will appear in the design window under the **Form1.vb** tab:

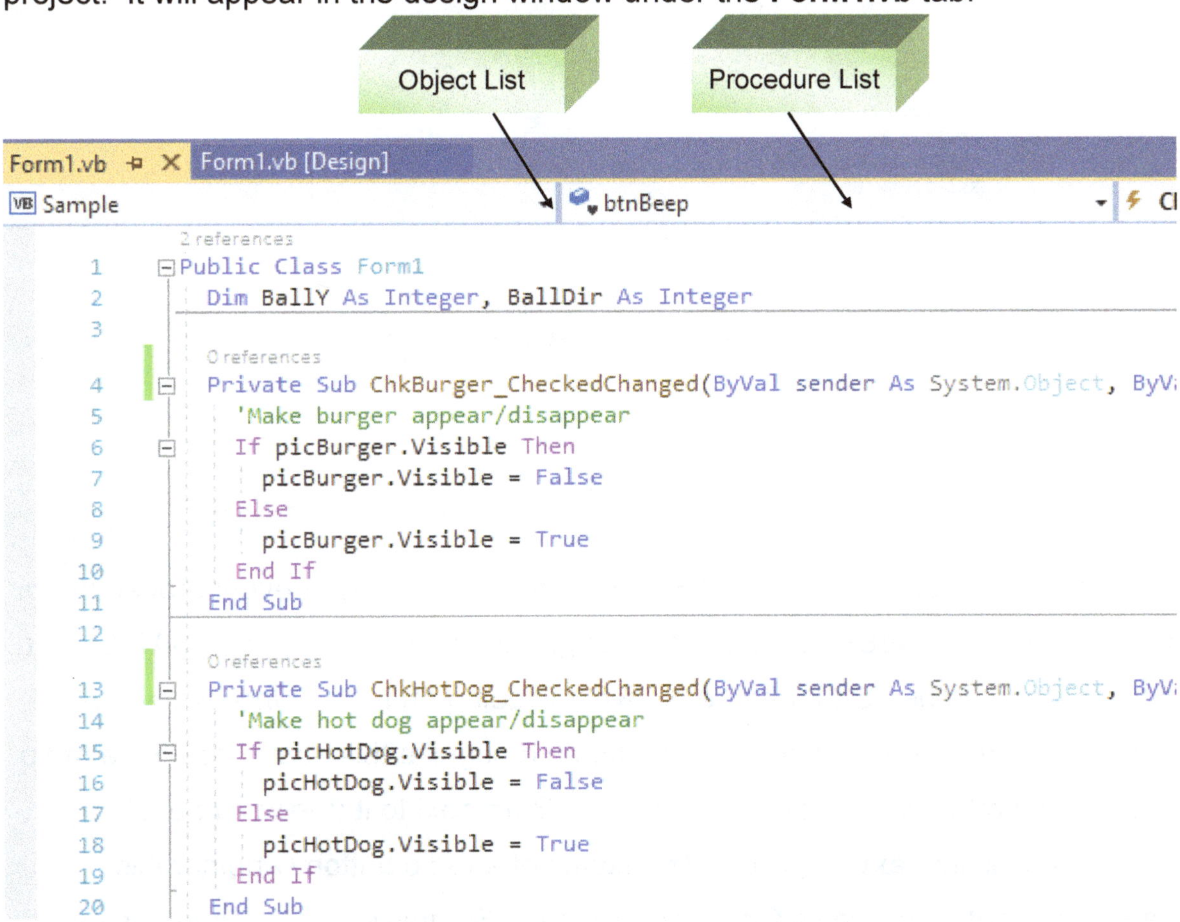

At the top of the code window are two boxes, the **object** (or control) **list** and the **procedure list**. The object list is similar to the control list in the properties window. It lists all objects on the form by name. Once an object, or control, name is selected in that list, the procedure list shows all possible event procedures for that control. Click on the drop-down arrow in the objects list. Select **rdoBlue** as the object. Select **CheckedChanged** as the procedure. You should see this:

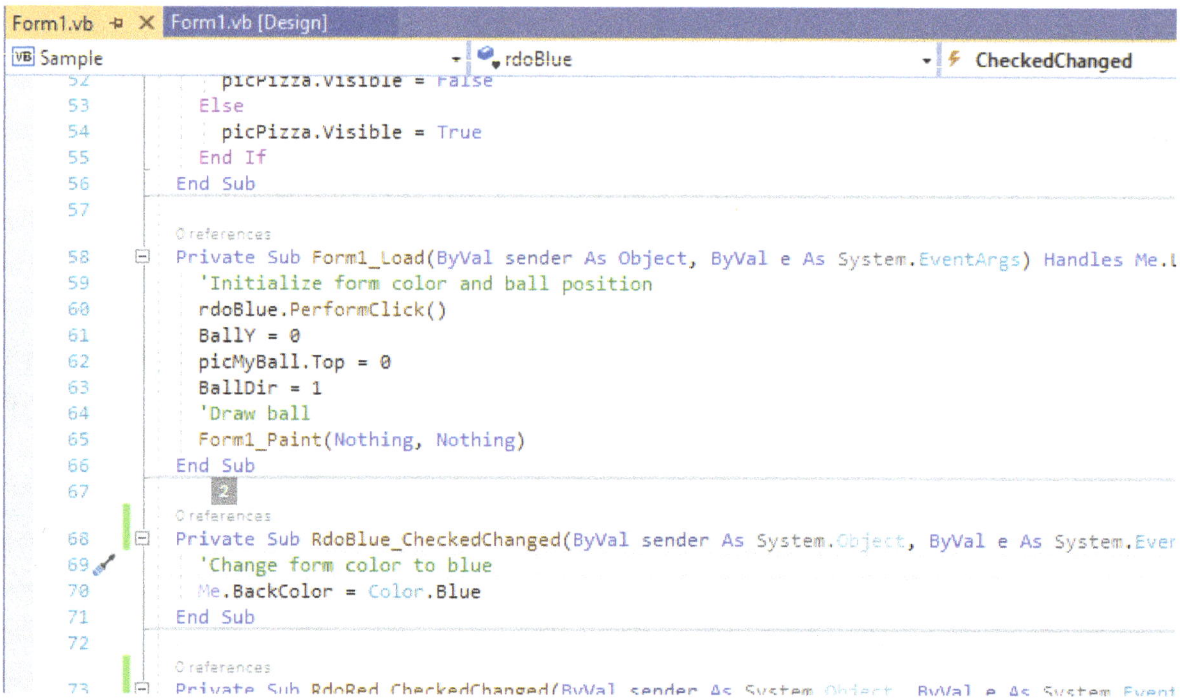

Near the middle of the code window is the **CheckedChanged** event procedure for the control name **rdoBlue**. And even though you may not know any BASIC right now, you should be able for figure out what is going on here. Since we will be careful in how we name controls, you should recognize this control to be the radio button (one with a little circle) with the word **Blue** next to it (the word next to a radio button is its **Text** property). The status of a radio button (whether it is selected or not) is called its **Checked** property. So, this event procedure is called whenever we click on the Blue radio button and change its Checked property.

Notice the procedure has a single line of instruction (ignore the other lines for now):

```
Me.BackColor = Color.Blue
```

What this line of BASIC code says is set the **BackColor** property of the control named **Me** (a word used by Visual Basic to refer to the form) to Blue (represented by the words **Color.Blue**). Pretty easy, huh?

Choose the **rdoBlue** button again in the Object list, then click on the drop-down arrow in the procedures list box. Notice all the other possible event procedures for the rdoBlue control. Fortunately, we don't have to write BASIC code for all of these procedures. We only write code for events we expect will happen when our project is running.

Scroll through the other code in the code window. Much of this code might look like a foreign language right now and don't worry - it should! You'll be surprised though that you probably can figure out what's going on even if you don't know any BASIC. In subsequent classes, you will start to learn BASIC and such code will become easy to read. You'll see that most BASIC code is pretty easy to understand. Writing BASIC code is primarily paying attention to lots of details. For the most part, it's very logical and obvious. And, you're about to start writing your own code!

Summary

In this second class, we've learned the parts of the Visual Basic environment and how to move around in that environment. We've also learned some important new terms like **properties** and **event procedures**. You're now ready to build your first Visual Basic project. In the next class, you'll learn how to place controls on a form, move them around, and make them appear just like you want. And, you will learn the all-important step of how to put BASIC code in the event procedures.

3

Your First Visual Basic Project

Review and Preview

In the first two classes, you learned about **forms**, **controls**, **properties**, and **event procedures**. In this class, you're going to put that knowledge to work in building your first simple Visual Basic project. You'll learn the steps in building a project, how to put controls on a form, how to set properties for those controls, and how to write your own event procedures using a little BASIC.

Steps in Building a Visual Basic Project

There are three primary steps in building a Visual Basic Project:

1. Place (or draw) **controls** on the form.
2. Assign **properties** to the controls.
3. Write **event procedures** for the controls.

Each of these steps is done with Visual Basic in **design** mode.

Start Visual Basic and start a new project (review the steps covered in Class 2, if necessary, naming it whatever you choose). Open the created form in the **Design** window. You should see something like this:

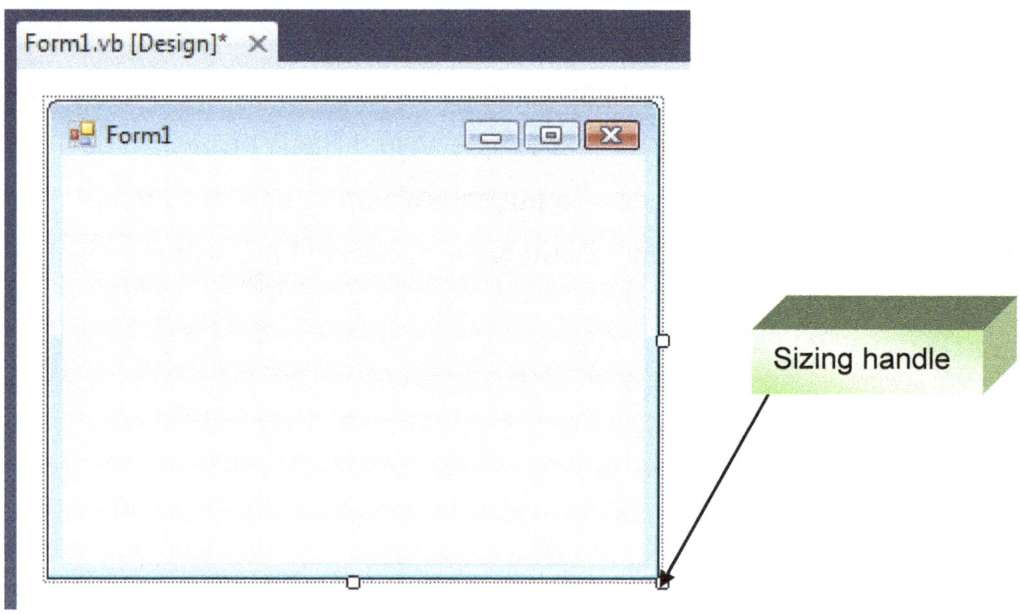

Notice the form has a 'sizing handle' in the lower right corner. You can resize the form if you want. This is one of the 'Windows' techniques you should be familiar with. If you move the cursor over this handle, a little 'double-arrow' will appear. At that point, you can click and drag the corner to its desired position. This allows you to increase the width and height of the form at the same time. If you hold the cursor over the right or lower edge (until the arrow appears), you can resize the width and height, respectively. Practice sizing the form.

Placing Controls on the Form

The first step in building a Visual Basic project is to place controls on the form in their desired positions. So, at this point, you must have decided what controls you will need to build your project. Many times, this is a time-consuming task in itself. And, I guarantee, you will change your mind many times. Right now, we'll just practice putting controls on the form.

Controls are selected from the Visual Basic **Toolbox** window (**Windows Form** controls). Click a tool in the toolbox and hold the mouse button down. Drag the selected tool over to the form. When the cursor pointer is at the desired upper left corner, release the mouse button and the default size control will appear. This is the classic "drag and drop" operation. (There are other ways to put controls on the form, but we'll just use this one). Once the control is on the form, you can still move or resize the control. To **move** a control, left-click the control to select it (crossed-arrows will appear). Drag it to the new location, then release the mouse button. To **resize** a control, left-click the control so that it is selected. If you move the cursor over one its four sizing handles, a little 'double-arrow' will appear. At that point, you can click and drag the corresponding edge or corner to its desired position.

Example

Make sure Visual Basic is still running and there is a form on the screen as well as the **Toolbox** (click **View** on the main menu, then **Toolbox** if it is not there). Go to the toolbox and find the **button** control. It looks like this:

Drag and drop the button onto the form. Your form should look something like this:

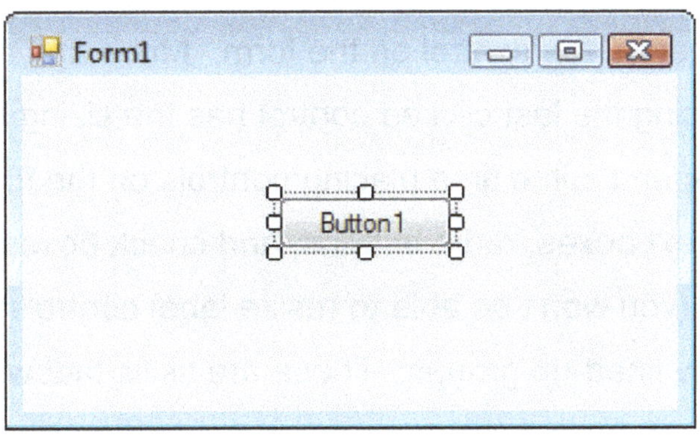

Notice the sizing handles around the button. This indicates this is the **active** control. Click on the form and those handles disappear, indicating the form is now the active control. Click on the button again to make it active.

As mentioned, controls can always be moved and resized. To **move** a control you have drawn, click the object on the form (a cross with arrows will appear). Now, drag the control to the new location. Release the mouse button. To **resize** a control, click the control so that it is selected (active) and sizing handles appear. Use these handles to resize the object.

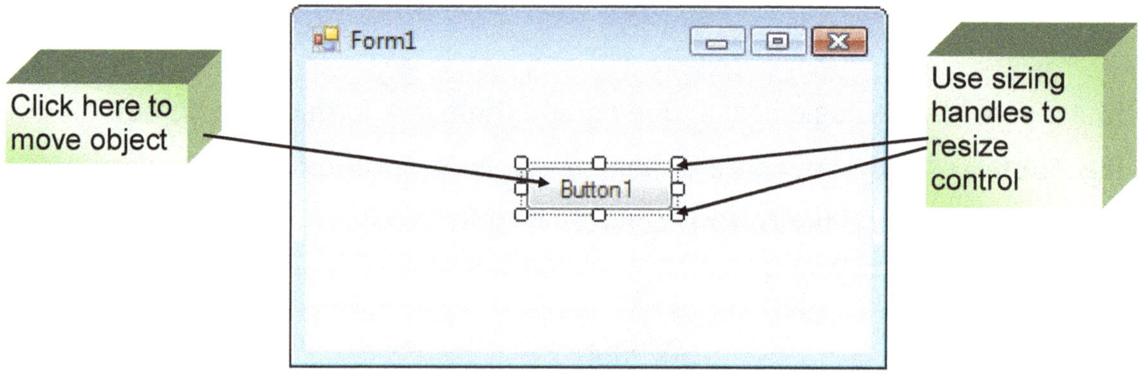

Move the button around and try resizing it. Make a real big button, a real short button, a real wide button, a real tall button. Try moving the button around on the form.

Drag and drop another button control on the form. Move and resize it. Click from button to button noticing the last clicked control has the sizing handles, making it the active control. Spend some time placing controls on the form. Use other controls like labels, text boxes, radio buttons, and check boxes. Move them around, resize them (you won't be able to resize label controls). Try to organize your controls in nicely lined-up groups. These are skills that will be needed in building Visual Basic projects.

You also need to know how to remove controls from a form. It is an easy process. Click on the control you want to remove. It will become the active control. Press the **Del** (delete) key on your keyboard. The control will be removed. Before you delete a control, make sure you really want to delete it.

Setting Control Properties (Design Mode)

Once you have the desired controls on the form, you will want to assign properties to the controls. Recall properties specify how a control appears on the form. They establish such things as control size, color, what a control 'says', and position on the form. When you place a control on the form, it is given a set of default properties by Visual Basic. In particular, its geometric properties (governing size and location) are set when you place and size the control on the form. But, many times, the default properties are not acceptable and you will want to change them. This is done using the **Properties Window**.

If Visual Basic is not running on your computer, start it now. Start another new project. There should be a blank form in the design window. If it's not there, select the **View** menu and choose **Designer**. Find the **Properties Window** (press <**F4**> if it's not there):

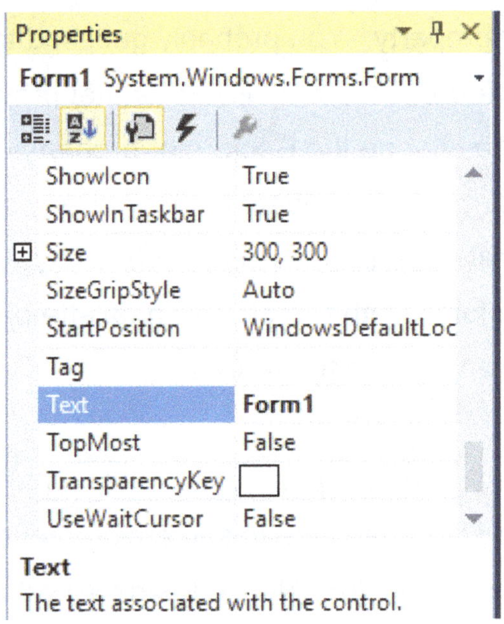

Click the **Alphabetic** view (the button with A-Z on it) if **Categorized** properties are displayed. Also make sure the **Properties** button, next to the Alphabetic view button is depressed (always make sure this button is pressed when working with properties). Recall the box at the top of the properties window is the **control list**, telling us which controls are present on the form. Right now, the list only has one control, that being the form itself. Let's look at some of the form's properties.

First, how big is the form? All controls are rectangular in shape and two properties define the size of that rectangle. Scroll down the list of properties and find the **Size** property. You will see two numbers listed separated by commas. The first number is the **Width** of the form in pixels (a pixel is a single dot on the form). The second number is the **Height** of the form in pixels. Click on the little plus sign (+) in the box next to the Size property. The Width and Height properties will be displayed individually. Resize the form and notice the Height and Width properties change accordingly. You can also change the width and height of the form by typing in values for the desired property in the Properties window. Try it.

Scroll to the **BackColor** property. You probably guessed that this sets the background color of the form. The value listed for that property is probably **Control** (a light gray). To change the BackColor property, click on BackColor, then on the drop-down arrow that appears in the property side of the list. Choose one of the three 'tabs' that appear: **Custom**, **Web**, or **System**, then choose a color. My favorite is Custom. With this choice, a palette of colors will appear, you can choose a new color and notice the results.

Scroll to the **Text** property. This property establishes what is displayed in the form's title bar. Click on Text, then type in something on the right side of the property window and press **<Enter>**. Notice the new Text appears in the form title bar.

That's all there is to setting control properties. First, select the control of interest from the control list. Then, scroll down through properties and find the property you want to change. Click on that property. Properties may be changed by typing in a new value (like the Width and Height values and the Text property) or choosing from a list of predefined options (available as a drop-down list, like color values).

Let's look at some of the **button** properties. Add a button control to your form. Select the button in the control list of the properties window. Like the form, the button is also rectangular. Scroll down to the **Size** property and click on the little plus (+) sign to expand this property. The **Width** property gives its width in pixels and **Height** gives its height in pixels. Two other properties specify the location of the button on the form. Scroll down to the **Location** property and expand it. Values for **X** (the **Left** property) and **Y** (the **Top** property) are displayed. **Left** gives the horizontal position (in pixels) of the left side of the button relative to the left side of the form. Similarly, **Top** is the vertical position (in pixels) of the top side of the button relative to the top of the form (the top of the form being defined as the lower part of the title bar). For a single button, these properties are:

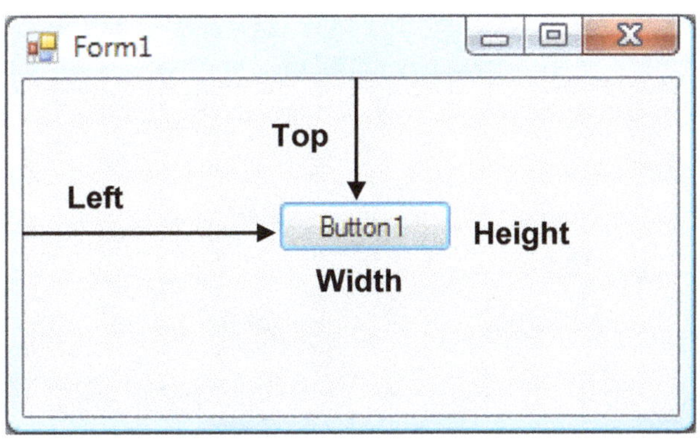

Another important property for a button is the **Text** property. The text appearing on the button is the Text. It should indicate what happens if you click that button. Change the **Text** property of your button. Put a couple more buttons on the form. Move and size them. Change their Text and BackColor properties, if you want.

We have seen that to change from one control to another in the properties window, we can click on the down arrow in the controls list and pick the desired control. A shortcut method for switching the listed properties to a desired control is to simply click on the control on the form, making it the **active** control. Click on one of the buttons. Notice the selected control in the properties window changes to that control. Click on another button - note the change. Click on the form. The selected control becomes the form. You will find this shortcut method of switching from one control to another very useful as you build your own Visual Basic projects.

Naming Controls

The most important property for any control is its **Name**. Because of its importance, we address it separately. When we name a control, we want to specify two pieces of information: the **type** of control and the **purpose** of the control. Such naming will make our programming tasks much easier.

In the Visual Basic programming community, a rule has been developed for naming controls. The first three letters of the control name (called a **prefix**) specify the type of control. Some of these prefixes are (we will see more throughout the class):

Control	Prefix
Button	**btn**
Label	**lbl**
Text Box	**txt**
Check Box	**chk**
Radio Button	**rdo**

After the control name prefix, we choose a name (it usually starts with an upper case letter to show the prefix has ended) that indicates what the control does. The complete control name can have up to 40 characters. The name must start with a letter (this is taken care of by using prefixes) and can only contain letters (lower or upper case), numbers, and the underscore (_) character. Even though you can have 40 character control names, keep the names as short as possible without letting them lose their meaning. This will save you lots of typing.

Let's look at some example control names to give you an idea of how to choose names. These are names used in the **Sample** project looked at in Class 1 and Class 2. Examples:

> **btnBeep** - Button that causes a beep
> **txtType**- Text box where information could be typed
> **rdoBlue** - Radio button that changes background color to Blue
> **chkTop** - Check box that displays or hides the toy top
> **picTop** – Picture box that has the picture of a toy top

This should give you an idea of how to pick control names. We can't emphasize enough the importance of choosing proper names. It will make your work as a programmer much easier.

Note that, unlike most programming languages, the Visual Basic language is <u>not</u> case sensitive. This means the names **picTop** and **PICTOP** are treated the same. Make sure you assign unique names to each control. Even though, Visual Basic is case insensitive, we still suggest mixing upper and lower case letters in your control names for improved readability.

Setting Properties in Run Mode

To illustrate the importance of proper control names, let's look at a common task in Visual Basic. We have seen one of the steps in developing a Visual Basic project is to establish control properties in design mode. You can also establish or change properties while your project is in run mode. For example, in the **Sample** project, when you clicked on a radio button, the **BackColor** property of the form was changed. When you clicked on a food name, that food either appeared or disappeared. To change a property in run mode, we need to use a line of BASIC code (you're about to learn your first line of BASIC!). The format for this code is:

```
ControlName.PropertyName = PropertyValue
```

That is, we type the control's name, a dot (same as a period or decimal point), the name of the property we are changing (found in the properties window), an equal sign (called an assignment operator), and the new value. Such a format is referred to as **dot notation**.

In **Sample**, the code used to display the burger on the form is:

```
picBurger.Visible = True
```

The **Visible** property of a control can be **True** (control is displayed) or **False** (control is not displayed). Notice proper control naming makes this line of code very understandable, even if you don't know any BASIC. It says that the picture box displaying the burger has been made visible.

One exception to the rule we just used is when we set **Form** properties. To set a form property at run-time, you use the Visual Basic keyword **Me** to refer to the form. For example, in Sample, to set the background color of the form to blue, we use:

```
Me.BackColor = Color.Blue
```

How Control Names are Used in Event Procedures

Another place the importance of proper control naming becomes apparent is when we write event procedures (discussed next). When you put a control on a form, all of the possible event procedures that control can have are added to your project. We have seen that these event procedures are viewed in the code window. The structure for these event procedures is:

```
  Private Sub ControlName_EventName(ByVal sender As
System.Object, ByVal e As System.EventArgs) Handles
ControlName.EventName

            [BASIC code goes here]

  End Sub
```

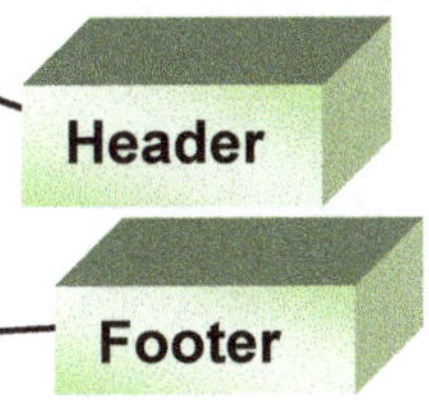

There's a lot to look at. The first, very long line that takes up three lines here, is the **header** line. The last line is the **footer** line. The actual BASIC code goes between these two lines. Let's look at the header, ignoring the information in parentheses for now. Notice the control name is used twice in this header line, as is the event name. The key thing to notice is that, with proper naming, we can easily identify each control's event procedure. One note: Visual Studio 2019 expects all event methods to start with a capital letter. So, in our code, an event method for a control named **controlName** will begin as **ControlName**.

As an example, using **Sample** again, the **CheckedChanged** event procedure for the **rdoBlue** control is:

```
  Private Sub RdoBlue_CheckedChanged(ByVal sender As
System.Object, ByVal e As System.EventArgs) Handles
rdoBlue.CheckedChanged
    'Change form color to blue
    Me.BackColor = Color.Blue
  End Sub
```

We recognize this is the code that is executed when the user changes the **Checked** property (clicks on) of the **rdoBlue** radio button. Proper naming makes identifying and reading event procedures very easy. Again, this will make your job as a programmer much easier. Now, let's write our first event procedure.

Writing Event Procedures

The third step in building a Visual Basic application is to write event procedures for the controls on the form. To write an event procedure, we use the code window. Review ways to display the code window in your project. This step is where we need to actually write BASIC code or do computer programming. You won't learn a lot of BASIC right now, but just learn the process of finding event procedures and typing code.

As just mentioned, when you place a control on a form, the event procedures associated with that control become part of the project and can be accessed using the **code window**. Each control has many event procedures. You don't write BASIC code for each procedure - only the ones you want the computer to respond to. Once you decide an event is to be 'coded,' you decide what you want to happen in that event procedure and translate those desires into actual lines of BASIC code. As seen earlier, the format for each event procedure is:

```
  Private Sub ControlName_EventName(ByVal sender As
System.Object, ByVal e As System.EventArgs) Handles
ControlName.EventName

              [BASIC code goes here]

  End Sub
```

In the header line (remember it's one very long line), the words '**Private Sub'** indicate this is a **Sub**routine (another word for procedure) that is **Private** to the form (only usable by the form - don't worry about what this means right now). The words enclosed in parentheses tell us what information is provided to the event procedure. These values are known as the procedure **arguments** and we won't concern ourselves with them right now. Lastly, the word **Handles** tells us just what event is 'handled' by this procedure. The code goes between this header line and the footer line (**End Sub**).

Writing the BASIC code is the creative portion of developing a Visual Basic application. And, it is also where you need to be very exact. Misspellings, missing punctuation, and missing operators will make your programs inoperable. You will find that writing a computer program requires exactness. So, the process to write event procedures is then:

- Decide which events you want to have some response to
- Decide what you want that response to be
- Translate that response into BASIC code
- Find the event procedure in the code window
- Type in the BASIC code

And, it is a process best illustrated by example. This example project is saved as **FirstCode** in the course projects folder (**\CBGVB\BVB Projects**).

Example

If Visual Basic is not running on your computer, start it and begin a new project. Name it **FirstCode**.

- Put a single button on the form.
- Set the **Text** property of the form to **My First Code**.
- Set the **Name** property of the button to **btnBeep**.
- Set the **Text** property of the button to **Beep!!**

At this point in the design process, your form should look something like this:

We want to write a single event procedure - the procedure that responds to the **Click** event of the button. When we click on that button, we want to computer to make a beep sound.

Display the code window (pressing <**F7**> is one way; choose **View**, then **Code** in the menu is another):

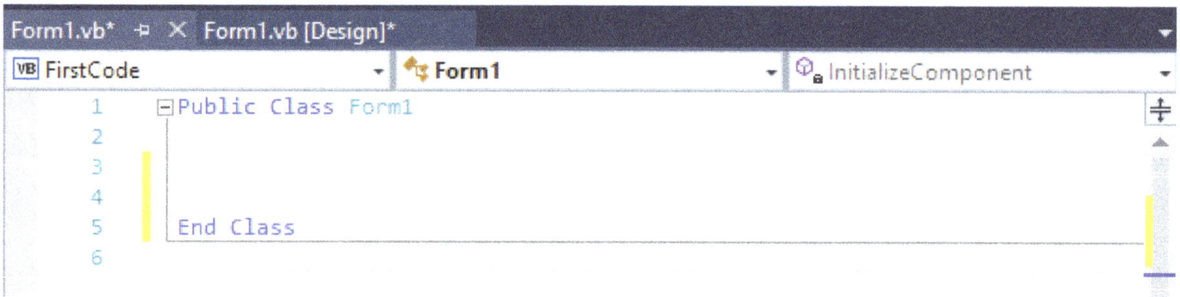

Your code window may not look like this. For example, there are numbers next to each line of code in my code window. You will find it very helpful to have such numbers. To add them, select the **Tools** menu item. Then, choose **Options**. In the left side of the window that appears, choose **Text Editor**, then **Basic**, then **General.** Then, choose the **Line Numbers** option.

The header line (**Public Class Form1**) starts the code and the footer line (**End Class**) ends the code. In Visual Basic, your project is called a **class** – these lines say you're working with the class named **Form1**. These lines must remain. Any code you write needs to go between the two lines displayed in the code window.

Click on the **Object** list's drop-down arrow and select **btnBeep** (the button). Click on the **Procedures** list and choose **Click**. The code window should now look like:

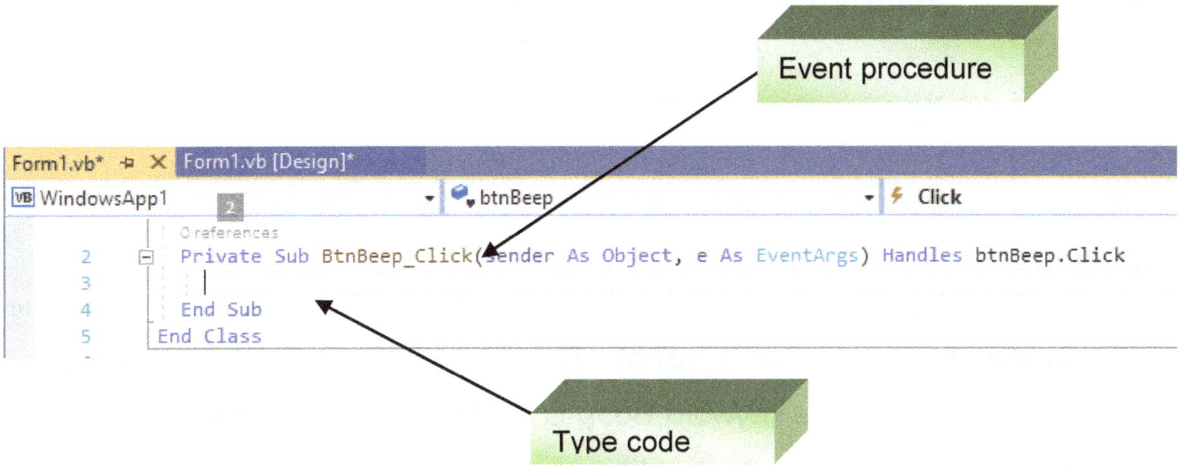

Notice the **Click** procedure for the **btnBeep** button is now displayed This is where we type the code to make the computer beep.

The code window acts like a word processor. You can type text in the window and use many of the normal editing features like cut, paste, copy, find, and replace. As you become a more proficient programmer, you will become comfortable with using the code window. Click on the region between the header and footer lines. Between the header and footer lines, type the single line:

```
Beep
```

The code window should now look like this:

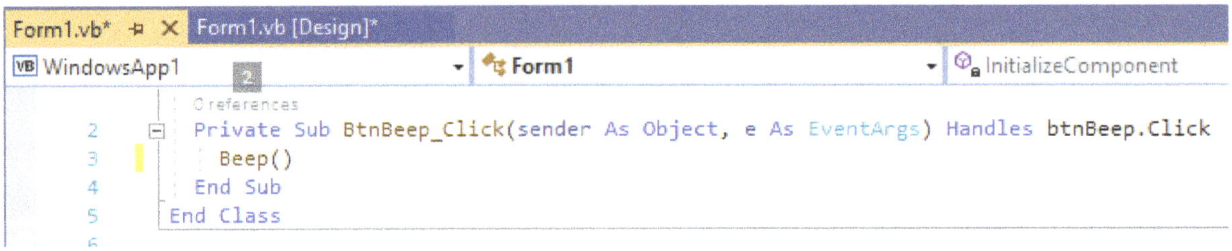

Notice after you typed the line, it was indented and parentheses were added at the end (indicating this is a built-in function). The Visual Basic environment does this additional 'formatting.' The keyword **Beep** is a BASIC instruction that tells the computer to beep. You have now written your first line of BASIC code.

Your project is now ready to run. **Run** the project (click the **Start** button on the toolbar or press <**F5**>). The form will appear:

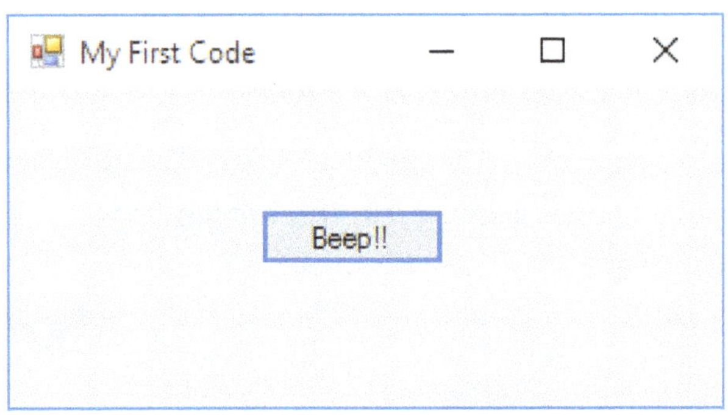

(If it doesn't, go back and make sure you've done all steps properly). Click the button. The computer should beep or some sound like a beep should be heard. You caused a **Click** event on the **btnBeep** control. The computer recognized this and went to the **btnBeep_Click** event procedure. There it interpreted the line of code (Beep) and made the computer beep. Stop your project. Go back to the code window and find the btnBeep_Click event. After the Beep line, add this line:

```
btnBeep.BackColor = Color.Blue
```

Make sure you type it in exactly as shown – code in computer programs must be exact. Run the project again. Click on the button. Explain what happens in relation to the control, the event procedure, and the BASIC code. Stop your project.

You may have noticed when you added this second line of code that as soon as you typed **btnBeep**, then a dot, a little window popped up with lots of choices for completing the line (**BackColor** was one of them). Similarly, once you pressed the equals sign (=), a choice of colors (including **Color.Blue**) popped up. This is the Visual Basic **Intellisense** feature. It helps a lot when it comes to typing code. Intellisense is a very useful part of Visual Basic. You should become acquainted with its use and how to select suggested values. You usually just scroll down the list (you can type the first few letters of a choice for faster scrolling), pick the desired item and continue typing. The choice will be inserted in the proper location. We tell you about the Intellisense feature now so you won't be surprised when little boxes start popping up as you type code.

Summary

You have now finished your first complete Visual Basic project. You followed the three steps of building an application:

1. Place controls on the form
2. Assign control properties
3. Write control event procedures

You follow these same steps, whether building a very simple project like the one here or a very complicated project.

Now, knowing these steps, you're ready to start working your way through the Visual Basic toolbox, learning what each control does. You can now begin learning elements of the BASIC language to help you write programs. And, you can begin learning new features of the Visual Basic environment to aid you in project development. In each subsequent class, you will do just that: learn some new controls, learn some BASIC, and learn more about Visual Basic.

4

Project Design, Forms, Buttons

Review and Preview

You have now learned the parts of a Visual Basic project and the three steps involved in building a project:

1. Place controls on the form.
2. Set control properties.
3. Write desired event procedures.

Do you have some ideas of projects you would like to build using Visual Basic? If so, great. Beginning with this class, you will start to develop your own programming skills. In each class to come, you will learn some new features of the Visual Basic environment, some new controls, and elements of the BASIC language. In this class, you will learn about project design, the form and button controls, and build a complete project.

Project Design

You are about to start developing projects using Visual Basic. We will give you projects to build and maybe you will have ideas for your own projects. Either way, it's fun and exciting to see ideas end up as computer programs. But before starting a project, it's a good idea to spend a little time thinking about what you are trying to do. This idea of proper **project design** will save you lots of time and result in a far better project.

Proper project design is not really difficult. The main idea is to create a project that is easy to use, easy to understand, and free of errors. That makes sense, doesn't it? Spend some time thinking about everything you want your project to do. What information does the program need? What information does the computer determine? Decide what controls you need to use to provide these sets of information. Design a nice user interface (interface concerns placement of controls on the form). Consider appearance and ease of use. Make the interface consistent with other Windows applications, if possible. Familiarity is good in Windows based projects, like those developed using Visual Basic.

Make the BASIC code in your event procedures readable and easy to understand. This will make the job of making later changes (and you will make changes) much easier. Follow accepted programming rules - you will learn these rules as you learn more about BASIC. Make sure there are no errors in your project. This may seem like an obvious statement, but many programs are not error-free. The Windows operating system has many errors floating around!

The importance of these few statements about project design might not make a lot of sense right now, but they will. The simple idea is to make a useful, clearly written, error-free project that is easy to use and easy to change. Planning carefully and planning ahead helps you achieve this goal. For each project built in this course, we will attempt to give you some insight into the project design process. We will always try to explain why we do what we do in building a project. And, we will always try to list all the considerations we make.

Saving a Visual Basic Project

In Class 1, you learned how to open, run, and close a previously-saved Visual Basic project, but we never talked about how a project is saved for future use. Now that you are starting to build your own projects, you need to see how to save them. It's really quite easy. We will use the **Save All** button in the Visual Basic toolbar. Look for a button that looks like several floppy disks. (How much longer do you think people will know what a floppy disk looks like? – most new machines don't even have a floppy disk drive!)

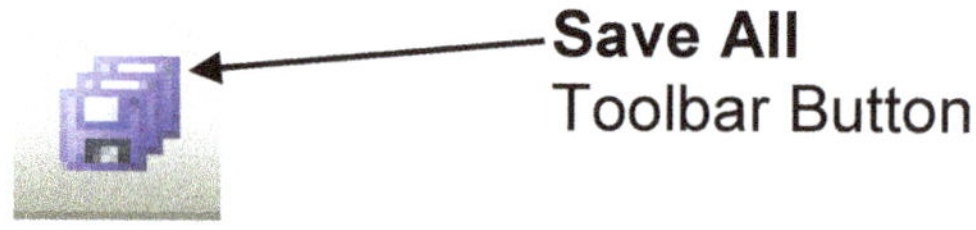

Always make sure to save your project before running it or before leaving Visual Basic.

On-Line Help

Many times, while working in the Visual Basic environment, you will have a question about something. You may wonder what a particular control does, what a particular property is for, what events a control has, or what a particular term in BASIC means. A great way to get help when you're stuck is to ask someone who knows the answer. People are usually happy to help you - they like the idea of helping you learn. You could also try to find the answer in a book and there are lots of Visual Basic books out there! Try searching the Internet. Or, another great way to get help is to use the Visual Basic **On-Line Help** system.

Most Windows applications, including Visual Basic, have help files available for your use. To access the Visual Basic help system, click the **Help** item in the main menu, then **View Help**. At that point, you can search for the topic you need help on or scroll through all the topics. The Visual Basic help system is just like all other Windows help systems. If you've ever used any on-line help system, using the system in Visual Basic should be easy. If you've never used an on-line help system, ask someone for help. They're pretty easy to use. Or, click on **Start** on your Windows task bar, then choose **Help**. You can use that on-line help system to learn about how to use an on-line help system!

A great feature about the Visual Basic on-line help system is that it is 'context sensitive.' What does this mean? Well, let's try it. Start Visual Basic and start a new project. Go to the properties window. Scroll down the window displaying the form properties and click on the word **BackColor**. The word is highlighted. Press the **<F1>** key. A screen of information about the **Form.BackColor** property appears:

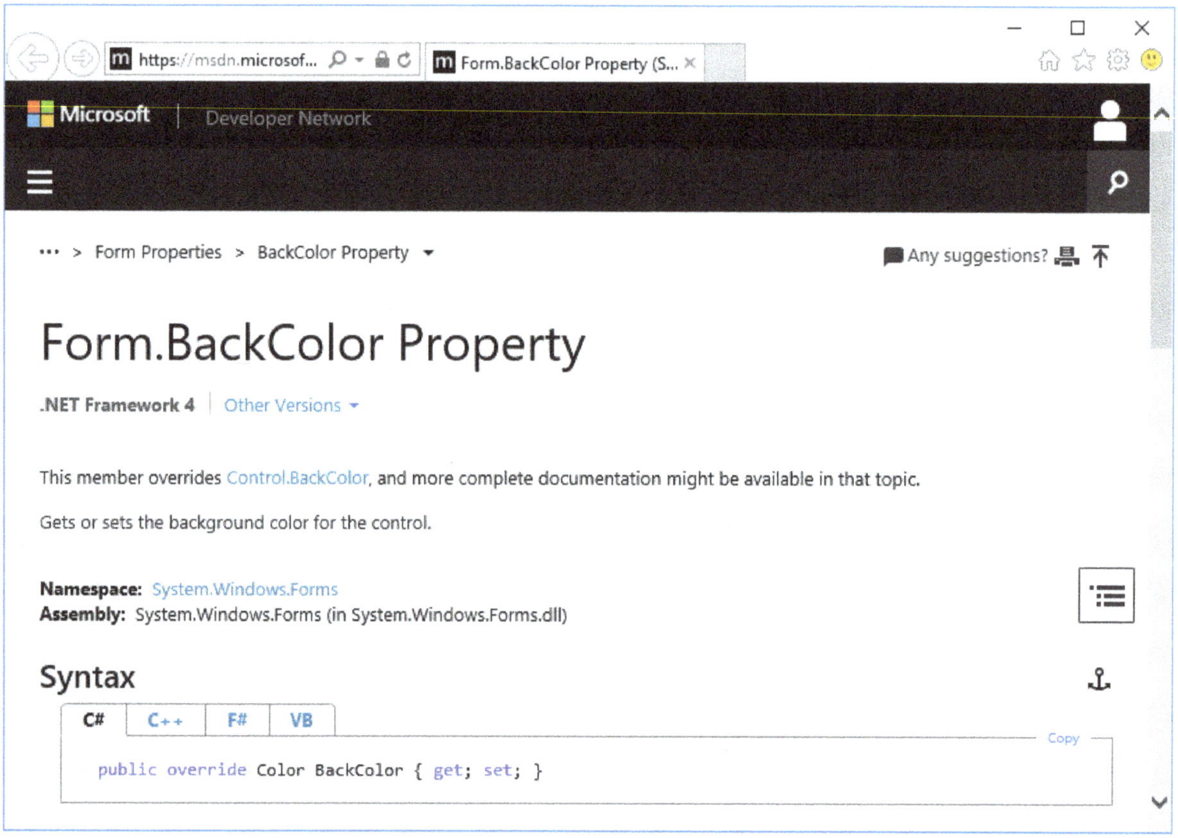

The help system has intelligence. It knows that since you highlighted the word BackColor, then pressed **<F1>** (**<F1>** has always been the key to press when you need help), you are asking for help about BackColor. Anytime you press **<F1>** while working in Visual Basic, the program will look at where you are working and try to determine, based on context, what you are asking for help about. It looks at things like highlighted words in the properties window or position of the cursor in the code window.

As you work with Visual Basic, you will find you will use 'context-sensitive' help a lot. Many times, you can get quick answers to questions you might have. Get used to relying on the Visual Basic on-line help system for assistance. That's enough new material about the Visual Basic environment. Now, let's look, in detail, at two important controls: the form itself and the button. Then we'll start our study of the BASIC language and build a complete project.

The Form Control

We have seen that the **form** is the central control in the development of a Visual Basic project. Without a form, there can be no project! Let's look at some important properties and events for the form control. The form appears when you begin a new project.

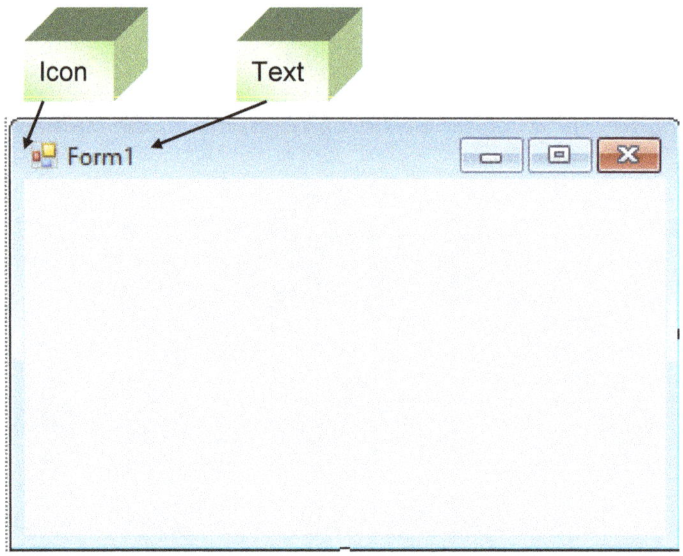

Properties

Like all controls, the form has many (over 40) properties. Fortunately, we only have to know about some of them. The properties we will be concerned with are:

Property	Description
Name	Name used to identify form. In this course, we will always use the default **Form1** for the name.
Text	Text that appears in the title bar of form.
BackColor	Background color of form.
Icon	Reference to icon that appears in title bar of form (we'll look at creating icons in Class 7).
Width	Width of the form in pixels (expand **Size** property)

Height	Height of form in pixels (expand **Size** property)
FormBorderStyle	Form can either be sizable (can resize using the mouse) or fixed size.
StartPosition	Determines location of form on computer screen when application begins (we usually use a value of **CenterScreen**).

The form is primarily a 'container' for other controls. Being a container means many controls (the button control, studied next, is an exception) placed on the form will share the **BackColor** property. To change this behavior, select the desired control (after it is placed on the form) and change the color.

Example

To gain familiarity with these properties, start Visual Basic and start a new project with just a form. Set the Height and Width property values (listed under **Size** in the properties window) and see their effect on form size. Resize the form and notice how those values are changed in the properties window. Set the Text property. Pick a new background color using the selection techniques discussed in Class 3. Try centering the form by changing the StartPosition property (you'll see the effect of this once you run the project). To see the effect of the BorderStyle property, set a value (either **Fixed Single** or **Sizable;** these are the only values we'll use in this course) and run the project. Yes, you can run a project with just a form as a control! Try resizing the form in each case. Note the difference. Stop this example project.

Events

The form does support events. That is, it can respond to some user interactions. We will only be concerned with two form events in this course:

Event	**Description**
Click	Event executed when user clicks on the form with the mouse.
Load	Event executed when the form first loads into the computer's memory. This is a good place to set initial values for various properties and other project values.
FormClosing	Event called when the project is ending. This is a good place to 'clean up' your project.

Locating form event procedures is different than locating procedures for controls - you don't search for procedures by form name. To locate a form event in the code window, click the Object list drop-down arrow and choose **(Form1 Events)**. Once this is selected, you can scroll through the corresponding event procedures in the procedure list.

Typical Use of Form Control

For each control in this, and following chapters, we will provide information for how that control is typically used. The usual design steps for a **Form** control are:

- Set the **Text** property to a meaningful title.
- Set the **StartPosition** property (in this course, this property will almost always be set to **CenterScreen**)
- Set the **FormBorderStyle** to some value. In this course, we will mostly use **FixedSingle** forms.
- Write any needed initialization code in the form's **Load** event. To access this event in the Code window, **Form1 Events** (assumes your form is named Form1), then the **Load** event.
- Write any needed finalization code in the form's **FormClosing** event.

Button Control

The **button** is one of the more widely used Visual Basic controls. Buttons are used to start, pause, or end particular processes. The button is selected from the toolbox. It appears as:

In Toolbox:

On Form (default properties):

Properties

A few useful properties for the button are:

Property	Description
Name	Name used to identify button. Three letter prefix for button names is **btn**.
Text	Text (caption) that appears on the button.
TextAlign	How the caption text is aligned on the button.
Font	Sets style, size, and type of caption text.
BackColor	Background color of button.
ForeColor	Color of text on button.
Left	Distance from left side of form to left side of button (referred to by **X** in properties window, expand **Location** property).
Top	Distance from top side of form to top side of button (referred to by **Y** in properties window, expand **Location** property).

Width	Width of the button in pixels (expand **Size** property).
Height	Height of button in pixels (expand **Size** property).
Enabled	Determines whether button can respond to user events (in run mode).
Visible	Determines whether the button appears on the form (in run mode).

Example

Start Visual Basic and start a new project. Put a button on the form. Move the button around and notice the changes in X and Y properties (listed under **Location** in the properties window). Resize the button and notice how Width and Height change. Set the Text property. Change BackColor and ForeColor properties.

Many controls, in addition to the button, have a Font property, so let's take a little time to look at how to change it. Font establishes what the Text looks like. When you click on Font in the properties window, a button with something called an **ellipsis** will appear on the right side of the window:

Click this button and a **Font Window** will appear:

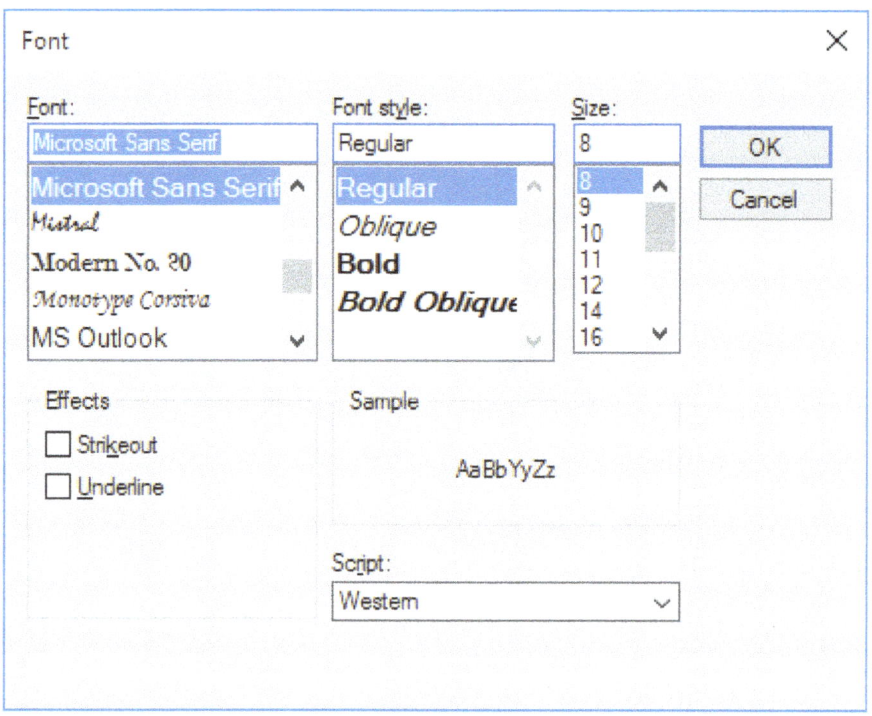

With this window, you can choose three primary pieces of information: **Font**, **Font Style**, and **Size**. You can also have an underlined font. This window lists information about all fonts stored on your computer. To set the Font property, make your choices in this window and click **OK**. Try different fonts, font styles, and font size for the button Text property.

Two other properties listed for the button are Enabled and Visible. Each of these properties can either be **True** (On) or **False** (Off). Most other controls also have these properties. Why do you need these?

If a control's Enabled property is False, the user is unable to access that control. Say you had a stopwatch project with a Start and Stop button:

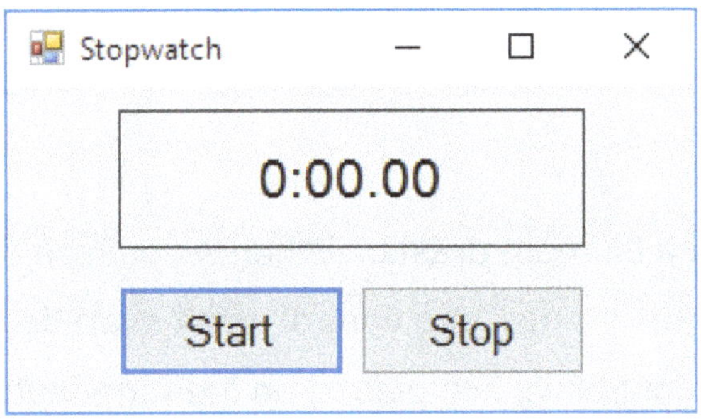

You want the user to click Start, then Stop, to find the elapsed time. You wouldn't want the user to be able to click the Stop button before clicking the Start button. So, initially, you would have the Start button's Enabled property set to True and the Stop button's Enabled property set to False. This way, the user can only click Start. Once the user clicked Start, you would swap property values. That is, make the Start button's Enabled property False and the Stop button's Enabled property True. That way, the user could now only click Stop.

The effects of a False Enabled property are only evident when Visual Basic is in run mode. When a button is not Enabled (Enabled is False), it will appear 'hazy' and the user won't be able to click it. When Stop is not Enabled on the stopwatch, it looks like this:

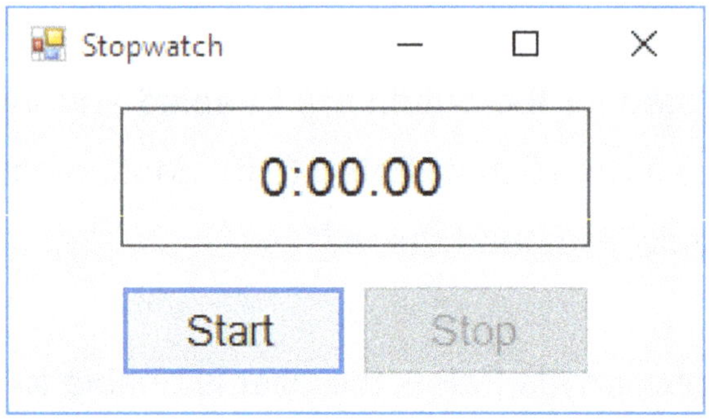

So, use the Enabled property when you want a control on the form to be temporarily disabled. This is a decision made in the project design process we discussed earlier.

The Visible property is a bit more drastic. When a control's Visible property is set to False (its default value is True), the control won't even be on the form! Now, why would we want a control we just placed on the form, set properties for, and wrote event procedures for, to be invisible? The answer is similar to that for the Enabled property. Many times in a project, you will find you want a control to temporarily go away. Remember the **Sample** project in Class 1 where check boxes controlled whether foods were displayed or not. The display of the foods was controlled via the picture box control's Visible property. Or, in the little stopwatch example, instead of setting a button's Enabled property to False to make it 'unclickable,' we could just set the Visible property to False so it doesn't appear on the form at all. Either way, you would obtain the desired result. This is another project design decision. One more thing - like the Enabled property, the effects of Visible being False are only evident in run mode. This makes sense. It would be hard to design a project with invisible controls!

Now, play with the Enabled and Visible properties of the button in the example you have been working with. Once you set either property, run the project to see the results. Note with Enabled set to False, you can't click the button. Note with Visible set to False, the button isn't there. When done, stop the example project.

Events

There is only one button event of interest, but it is a very important one:

Event	Description
Click	Event executed when user clicks on the button with the mouse.

Every button will have an event procedure corresponding to the Click event.

Typical Use of Button Control

The usual design steps for a button control are:

- Set the **Name** and **Text** property.
- Write code in the button's **Click** event.
- You may also want to change the **Font**, **Backcolor** and **Forecolor** properties.

BASIC – The First Lesson

At long last, we are ready to get into the heart of a Visual Basic project - the BASIC language. You have seen that, in a Visual Basic project, event procedures are used to connect control events to actual actions taken by the computer. These event procedures are written using BASIC. So, you need to know BASIC to know Visual Basic. In each subsequent class in this course, you will learn something new about the BASIC language.

Event Procedure Structure

You know, by now, that event procedures are viewed in the Visual Basic code window. Each event procedure has the same general structure. First, there is a **header** line of the form:

```
  Private Sub ControlName_EventName(ByVal sender As
System.Object, ByVal e As System.EventArgs) Handles
ControlName.EventName
```

This tells us we are working with a **Private** (only accessible from our form), **Sub**routine (another name for a event procedure) that is executed when the event **EventName** occurs for the control **ControlName**. Makes sense, doesn't it? Again, for now we will ignore the information contained in the parentheses.

The event procedure code begins following the header line. The event procedure code is simply a set of line-by-line instructions to the computer, telling it what to do. The computer will process the first line, then the second, then all subsequent lines.

Code is processed in a procedure until it reaches the event procedure **footer** line:

```
End Sub
```

The event procedure code is written in the BASIC language. BASIC is a set of keywords and symbols that are used to make the computer do things. There is a lot of content in BASIC and we'll try to look at much of it in this course. Just one warning at this point. We've said it before, but it's worth saying again. Computer programming requires exactness - it does not allow errors! The Visual Basic environment can point out some errors to you, but not all. You must especially be exact when typing in event procedures. Good typing skills are a necessity in the computer age. As you learn Visual Basic programming, you might like also to improve your typing skills using some of the software that's available for that purpose. The better your typing skills, the fewer mistakes you will make in building your Visual Basic applications.

Assignment Statement

The simplest, and most used, statement in BASIC is the **assignment** statement. It has this form:

```
LeftSide = RightSide
```

The symbol **=** is called the **assignment operator**. You may recognize this symbol as the equal sign you use in arithmetic, but it's not called an equal sign in computer programming. Why is that?

In an assignment statement, we say whatever is on the left side of the assignment statement is replaced by whatever is on the right side. The left side of the assignment statement can only be a single term, like a control property. The right side can be just about any legal BASIC expression. It might have some math that needs to be done or something else that needs to be evaluated. If there are such evaluations, they are completed before the assignment. We are talking in very general terms right now and we have to. The idea of an assignment statement will become very obvious as you learn just a little more BASIC.

Property Types

Recall a property describes something about a control: size, color, appearance. Each **property** has a specific **type** depending on the kind of information it represents. When we use the properties window to set a value in design mode, Visual Basic automatically supplies the proper type. If we want to change a property in an event procedure using the BASIC assignment statement, we must know the property type so we can assign a properly typed value to it. Remember we use something called 'dot notation' to change properties in run mode:

```
ControlName.PropertyName = PropertyValue
```

ControlName is the Name property assigned to the control, PropertyName is the property name, and PropertyValue is the new value we are assigning to PropertyName. We will be concerned with four property types.

The first property type is the **integer** type. These are properties that are represented by whole, non-decimal, numbers. Properties like the **Top**, **Left**, **Height**, and **Width** properties are integer type. So, if we assign a value to an integer type property, we will use integer numbers. As an example, to change the width property of a form to 1,100 pixels, we would write in BASIC:

```
Me.Width = 1100
```

Recall the keyword **Me** is used to refer to the form. This says we replace the current Width of the form with the new value of 1100. Notice you write 1,100 as 1100 in BASIC - we can't use commas in large numbers.

A second property type involves **colors**. We need this to set properties like BackColor. Fortunately, Visual Basic has a set of built-in colors to choose from. To set a control color (described by **ColorPropertyName**), we type:

```
ControlName.ColorPropertyName = Color.ColorName
```

As soon as we type the word **Color** and a dot on the right side of the assignment statement, a entire list of color names to choose from magically appears. To change the form background color to blue, use:

```
Me.BackColor = Color.Blue
```

Another property type is the **Boolean** type. It takes its name from a famous mathematician (Boole). It can have two values: **True** or **False**. We saw that the Enabled and Visible properties for the button have Boolean values. So, when working with Boolean type properties, we must insure we only assign a value of True or a value of False. To make a form disappear (not a very good thing to do!), we would use the assignment statement:

```
Me.Visible = False
```

This says the current Visible property of the form is replaced by the Boolean value False. We could make it come back with:

```
Me.Visible = True
```

The last property type we need to look at here is the **string** type. Properties of this type are simply what the definition says - strings of characters. A string can be a name, a string of numbers, a sentence, a paragraph, any characters at all. And, many times, a string will contain no characters at all (an empty string). The Text property is a string type property. We will do lots of work with strings in Visual Basic, so it's something you should become familiar with. When assigning string type properties, the only trick is to make sure the string is enclosed in quotes (""). You may tend to forget this since string type property values are not enclosed in quotes in the properties window. To give our a form a caption in the title bar, we would use:

```
Me.Text = "This is a caption in quotes"
```

This assignment statement says the Text property of the form is replaced by (or changed to) the string value on the right side of the statement. You should now have some idea of how assignment statements work.

Comments

When we talked about project design, it was mentioned that you should follow proper programming rules when writing your BASIC code. One such rule is to properly comment your code. You can place non-executable statements (ignored by the computer) in your code that explain what you are doing. These **comments** can be an aid in understanding your code. They also make future changes to your code much easier.

To place a comment in your code, use the comment symbol, an apostrophe ('). This symbol is to the left of the <Enter> key on most keyboards, not the key next to the 1 key. Anything written after the comment symbol will be ignored by the computer. You can have a comment take up a complete line of BASIC code, like this:

```
 'Change form to blue
Me.BackColor = Color.Blue
```

Or, you can place the comment on the same line as the assignment statement:

```
Me.BackColor = Color.Blue 'Makes form blue
```

You, as the programmer, should decide how much you want to comment your code. We will try in the projects provided in this course to provide adequate comments. Now, on to the first such project.

Project – Form Fun

Project Design

In this project, we will have a little fun with form properties using buttons. We will have a button that makes the form grow, one that makes the form shrink, and two buttons that change the form color. We'll even have a couple of buttons that make the other buttons disappear and reappear. This project is saved as **FormFun** in the course projects folder (**\CBGVB\BVB Projects**).

Place Controls on Form

Start a new project in Visual Basic. Size the form so six buttons will fit on the form. Place six buttons on the form. Resize and move the buttons around until the form looks something like this:

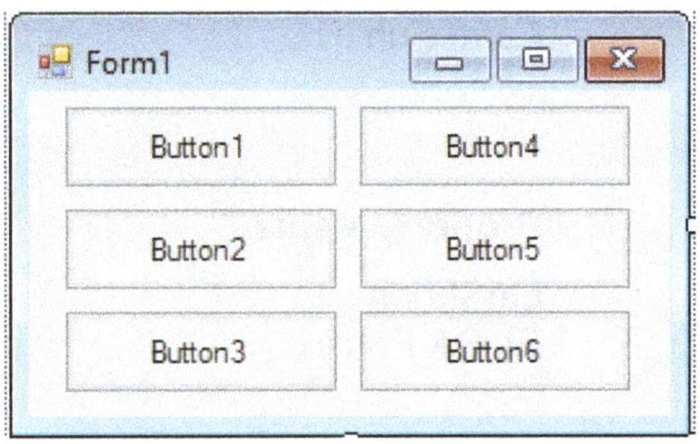

If you've used Windows applications for a while, you have probably used the edit feature known as **Copy** and **Paste**. That is, you can copy something you want to duplicate, move to the place you want your copy and then paste it. This is something done all the time in word processing. You may have discovered, in playing around with Visual Basic, that you can copy and paste controls. Try it here with the button controls and in other projects if you like. It works pretty nicely.

Set Control Properties

Set the control properties using the properties window. Remember that to change the selected control in the properties window, you can either use the controls list at the top of the window or just click on the desired control. For project control properties, we will always list controls by their default names (those assigned by Visual Basic when the control is placed on the form).

Form1 Form:

Property Name	**Property Value**
StartPosition	CenterScreen
Text	Form Fun

Button1 Button:

Property Name	**Property Value**
Name	btnShrink
Text	Shrink Form

Button2 Button:

Property Name	**Property Value**
Name	btnGrow
Text	Grow Form

Button3 Button:

Property Name	Property Value
Name	btnHide
Text	Hide Buttons

Button4 Button:

Property Name	Property Value
Name	btnRed
Text	Red Form

Button5 Button:

Property Name	Property Value
Name	btnBlue
Text	Blue Form

Button6 Button:

Property Name	Property Value
Name	btnShow
Text	Show Buttons
Visible	False

You can change other properties if you want - maybe change the Font property of the buttons. When you're done setting properties, your form should resemble this:

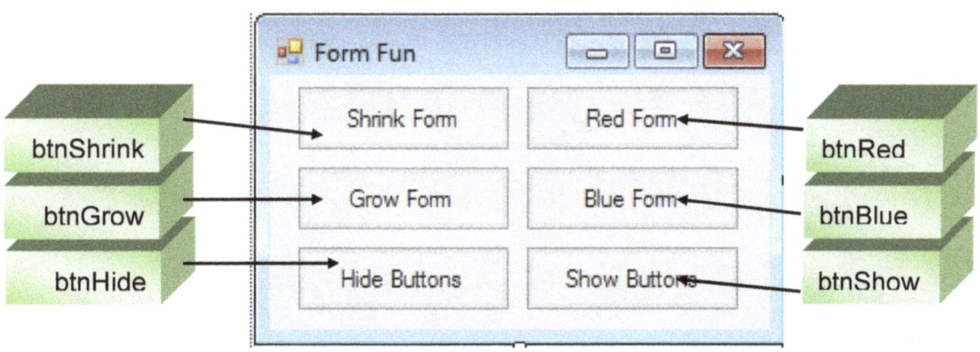

What we have are six buttons, two to change the size of the form, two to change form color, one to make buttons go away, and one to make buttons reappear. Notice the **Show Buttons** button has a Visible property of False. We don't want it on the form at first, since the buttons will already be there. When we make the buttons go away (by changing their Visible property) by clicking the **Hide Buttons** control, we will make the **Show Buttons** button appear. Makes sense, doesn't it? But, why is the **Show Buttons** button there if its Visible property is False? Remember a False Visible property will only be seen in run mode.

Write Event Procedures

We have six buttons on our form. We need to write code for the **Click** event procedure for each of these buttons. We'll also want to write a **Click** event procedure for the form - we'll explain why. We have a button on the form that makes the form shrink. What if we shrink it so much, we can't click on the button to make it grow again? We can avoid that by allowing a click on the form to also grow the form. This 'thinking ahead' is one of the project design concepts we talked about.

For each event procedure, you use the code window. Select the control in the object list and the event in the procedures list. Then click in the region between the header line and footer line and start typing code. It's that easy. But, again, make sure you type in everything just as written in these notes. You must be exact!

First, let's type the **btnShrink Click** event procedure. In this procedure, we decrease the form height by 10 pixels and decrease the form width by 10 pixels:

```
  Private Sub BtnShrink_Click(ByVal sender As System.Object,
ByVal e As System.EventArgs) Handles btnShrink.Click
      'Shrink the form
      'Decrease the form height by 10 pixels
      Me.Height = Me.Height - 10
      'Decrease the form width by 10 pixels
      Me.Width = Me.Width - 10
  End Sub
```

Before looking at the other event procedures, let's look a bit closer at this one since it uses a few ideas we haven't clearly discussed. This is the event procedure executed when you click on the button marked **Shrink Form**. You should easily recognize the comment statements. The non-comment statements change the form height and width. Look at the statement to change the height:

```
Me.Height = Me.Height - 10
```

Recall how the assignment operator (=) works. The right side is evaluated first. So, 10 is subtracted (using the - sign) from the current form height. That value is assigned to the left side of the expression, Me.Height. The result is the form Height property is replaced by the Height property minus 10 pixels. After this line of code, the Height property has decreased by 10 and the form will appear smaller on the screen.

This expression also shows why we call the assignment operator (=) just that and not an equal sign. Anyone can see the left side of this expression cannot possibly be equal to the right side of this expression. No matter what Me.Height is, the right side will always be 10 smaller than the left side. But, even though this is not an equality, you will often hear programmers read this statement as "Me.Height equals Me.Height minus 10," knowing it's not true! Remember how assignment statements work as you begin writing your own programs.

Now, let's look at the other event procedures. The **btnGrow Click** procedure increases form height by 10 pixels and increases form width by 10 pixels:

```
  Private Sub BtnGrow_Click(ByVal sender As System.Object,
ByVal e As System.EventArgs) Handles btnGrow.Click
    'Grow the form
    'Increase the form height by 10 pixels
    Me.Height = Me.Height + 10
    'Increase the form width by 10 pixels
    Me.Width = Me.Width + 10
  End Sub
```

The **btnRed Click** event procedure changes the form background color to red:

```
  Private Sub BtnRed_Click(ByVal sender As System.Object,
ByVal e As System.EventArgs) Handles btnRed.Click
    'Make form red
    Me.BackColor = Color.Red
  End Sub
```

while the **btnBlue Click** event procedure changes the form background color to blue:

```
  Private Sub BtnBlue_Click(ByVal sender As System.Object,
ByVal e As System.EventArgs) Handles btnBlue.Click
    'Make form blue
    Me.BackColor = Color.Blue
  End Sub
```

The **btnHide Click** event procedure is used to hide (set the **Visible** property to **False**) all buttons except **btnShow**, which is made **Visible**:

```
  Private Sub BtnHide_Click(ByVal sender As System.Object,
ByVal e As System.EventArgs) Handles btnHide.Click
    'Hide all buttons but btnShow
    btnGrow.Visible = False
    btnShrink.Visible = False
    btnHide.Visible = False
    btnRed.Visible = False
    btnBlue.Visible = False
    'Show btnShow button
    btnShow.Visible = True
  End Sub
```

and the **btnShow Click** event procedure reverses these effects:

```
  Private Sub BtnShow_Click(ByVal sender As System.Object,
ByVal e As System.EventArgs) Handles btnShow.Click
    'Show all buttons but btnShow
    btnGrow.Visible = True
    btnShrink.Visible = True
    btnHide.Visible = True
    btnRed.Visible = True
    btnBlue.Visible = True
    'Hide btnShow button
    btnShow.Visible = False
  End Sub
```

Lastly, the **Form1_Click** event procedure is also used to 'grow' the form, so it has the same code as **BtnGrow_Click**. Recall to 'find' this procedure, choose **(Form1 Events)** from the Object list box in the code window, then **Click** from the procedures box:

```
  Private Sub Form1_Click(ByVal sender As Object, ByVal e As
System.EventArgs) Handles MyBase.Click
    'Grow the form
    'Increase the form height by 10 pixels
    Me.Height = Me.Height + 10
    'Increase the form width by 10 pixels
    Me.Width = Me.Width + 10
  End Sub
```

Save your project by clicking the **Save All** button (the multiple floppy disks button) in the toolbar.

You should easily be able to see what's going on in each of these procedures. Pay special attention to how the Visible property was used in the **btnHide** and **btnShow** button click events. Notice too that many event procedures are very similar in their coding. For example, the **Form1_Click** event is identical to the **BtnGrow_Click** event. This is often the case in Visual Basic projects. We encourage the use of editor features like Copy and Paste when writing code. To copy something, highlight the desired text using the mouse - the same way you do in a word processor. Then, select **Edit** in the Visual Basic main menu, then **Copy**. Move the cursor to where you want to paste. You can even move to other event procedures. Select **Edit**, then **Paste**. Voila! The copy appears. The pasted text might need a little editing, but you will find that copy and paste will save you lots of time when writing code. And, this is something you'll want to do since you probably have noticed there's quite a bit of typing in programming, even for simple project such as this. Also useful are **Find** and **Replace** editor features. Use them when you can.

The **Intellisense** feature of Visual Basic is another way to reduce your typing load and the number of mistakes you might make. While you are writing BASIC in the code window, at certain points little boxes will pop up that display information that would logically complete the statement you are working on. This way, you can select the desired completion, rather than type it.

Run the Project

Go ahead! Run your project - click the **Start** button on the Visual Basic toolbar. If it doesn't run properly, the only suggestion at this point is to stop the project, recheck your typing, and try again. We'll learn 'debugging' techniques in the next class. Here's a run I made where I grew the form and made it red:

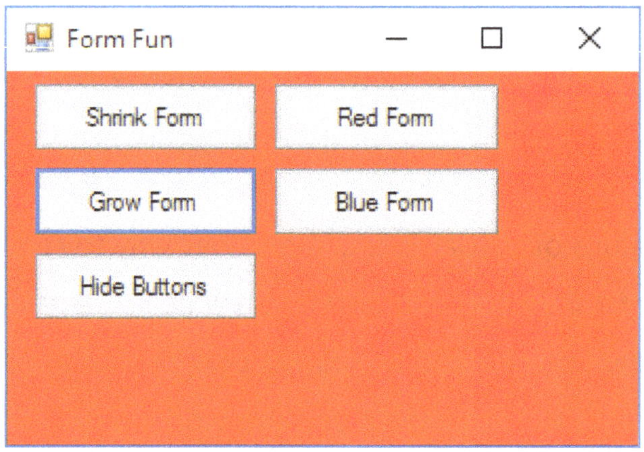

Try all the buttons. Grow the form, shrink the form, change form color, hide the buttons, make the buttons reappear. Make sure you try every button and make sure each works the way you want. Make sure clicking the form yields the desired result. This might seem like an obvious thing to do but, for large projects, sometimes certain events you have coded are never executed and you have no way of knowing if that particular event procedure works properly. This is another step in proper project design - thoroughly testing your project. Make sure every event works as intended. When done trying out this project, stop it (click the Visual Basic toolbar **Stop** button).

Other Things to Try

For each project in this course, we will offer suggestions for changes you can make and try. Modify the **Shrink Form** and **Grow Form** buttons to make them also move the form around the screen (use the Left and Top properties). Change the form color using other color values. Change the **Hide Buttons** button so that it just sets the buttons' Enabled property to False, not the Visible property. Similarly, modify the **Show Buttons** button.

Summary

Congratulations! You have now completed a fairly detailed (at least there's more than one control) Visual Basic project. You learned about project design, saving projects, details of the form and button controls, and how to build a complete project. You should now be comfortable with the three steps of building a project: placing controls, setting properties, and writing event procedures. We will continue to use these steps in future classes to build other projects using new controls and more of the BASIC language.

5

Labels, Text Boxes, Variables

Review and Preview

We continue our look at the Visual Basic environment and learn some new controls and new BASIC statements. As you work through this class, remember the three steps for building a Visual Basic project: (1) place controls on form, (2) assign properties to controls, and (3) write event procedures. In this class, you will examine how to find and eliminate errors in your projects, learn about the label and text box controls, and about BASIC variables. You will build a project that helps you plan your savings.

Debugging a Visual Basic Project

No matter how well you plan your project and no matter how careful you are in implementing your ideas in the controls and event procedures, you will make mistakes. Errors, or what computer programmers call **bugs**, do creep into your project. You, as a programmer, need to have a strategy for finding and eliminating those bugs. The process of eliminating bugs in a project is called **debugging**. Unfortunately, there are not a lot of hard, fast rules for finding bugs in a program. Each programmer has his or her own way of attacking bugs. You will develop your ways. We can come up with some general strategies, though, and that's what we'll give you here.

Project errors, or bugs, can be divided into three types:

- **Syntax** errors
- **Run-time** errors
- **Logic** errors

Syntax errors occur when you make an error setting a property in design mode or when typing a line of BASIC code. Something is misspelled or something is left out that needs to be there. Your project won't run if there are any syntax errors. **Run-time errors** occur when you try to run your project. It will stop abruptly because something has happened beyond its control. **Logic errors** are the toughest to find. Your project will run OK, but the results it gives are not what you expected. Let's examine each error type and address possible debugging methods.

Syntax Errors

Syntax errors are the easiest to identify and eliminate. The Visual Basic program is a big help in finding syntax errors. Syntax errors will most likely occur as you're setting properties for the controls or writing BASIC code for event procedures.

Start a new project in Visual Basic. Go to the project window and try to set the form **Width** property to the word **Junk**. (Click the plus sign next to the **Size** property to see **Width**.) What happened? You should see a little window like this:

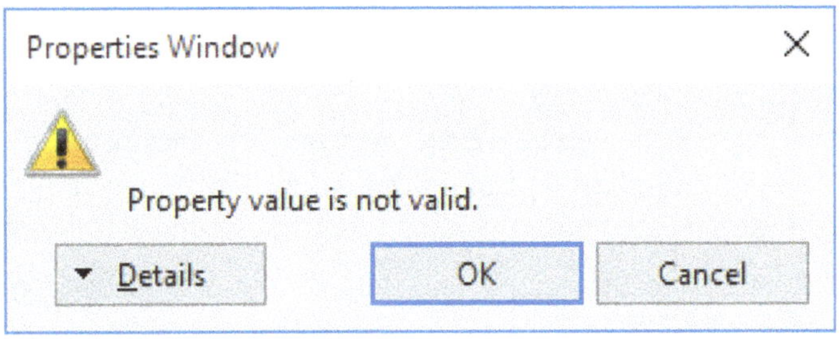

Click **Details** and you will see an explanation of the problem. Remember that property values must be the proper type. Assigning an improper type to a property is a **syntax** error. But, we see Visual Basic won't let us make that mistake. Click **Cancel** to restore the **Width** to what it was before you tried to change it.

What happens if you cause a syntax error while writing code. Let's try it. Open the code window for the **Form1_Load** procedure. Under the header line, type this line, then press <**Enter**>:

```
Me.BackColor 0 Color.Red
```

This would happen if you typed **0** instead of **=** in the assignment statement. What happened? In the code window, the line will appear underlined with a squiggle, similar to what Microsoft Word does when you misspell a word:

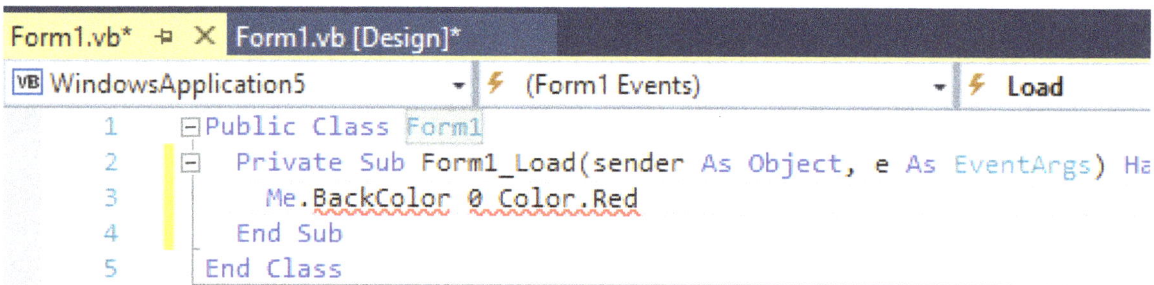

Visual Basic has recognized that something is wrong with this statement. You should be able to see what. Any line with an error will be 'squiggled.' Placing the cursor over a squiggled line will give some indication of your error. In this case, it will tell you that you need to assign a value to Me.BackColor.

So, if you make a syntax error, Visual Basic will usually know you've done something wrong and make you aware of your mistake. The on-line help system is a good resource for debugging your syntax errors. Note that syntax errors usually result because of incorrect typing - another great reason to improve your typing skills, if they need it.

Run-Time Errors

Once you successfully set control properties and write event procedures, eliminating all identified syntax errors, you try to run your project. If the project runs, great! But, many times, your project may stop and tell you it found an error - this is a run-time error. You need to figure out why it stopped and fix the problem. Again, Visual Basic and on-line help will usually give you enough information to eliminate run-time errors. Let's look at examples.

Working with the same example as above, try to run the project with the incorrect line of code. After you click the **Start** button on the toolbar, the following window should appear:

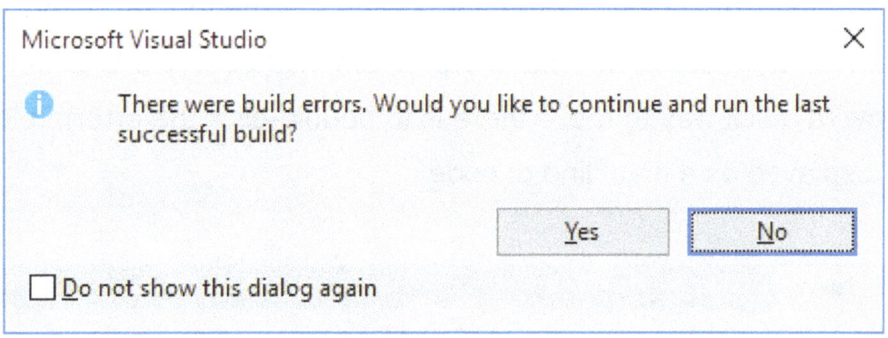

This tell us an error has occurred in trying to 'build' the project. Click **No** – we don't want to continue. We want to find the error. If 'build errors' occur, they are listed in another Visual Basic window – the **Error List**. This list shows you all errors detected in trying to run your program. Go to that window now (if it's not there already, choose **View** in menu, select **Error List**). Error List appears in the Design window. Yours might be floating or docked somewhere.

My Error List window is:

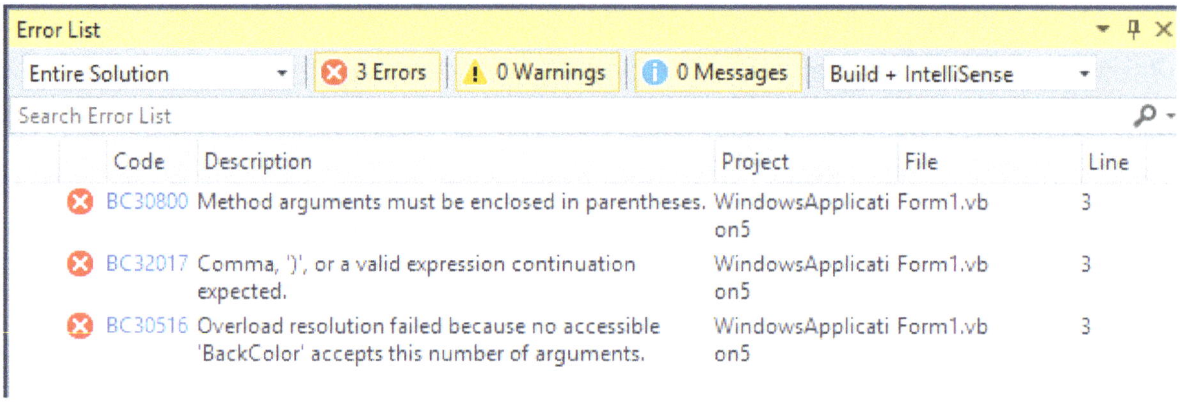

It has three errors that must be cleared before the program will run. Note each task refers to Line 3 on Form1, pointing to the offending line. This is why we number the lines of code in the code window – it makes finding errors much easier. The third error implies we need to assign a value to a property. The other two lines are other 'guesses' at what the problem might be. Go to Line 3 in the code window (a quick way to move there is to double-click the error). Line 3 should be displayed as a 'bad' line of code:

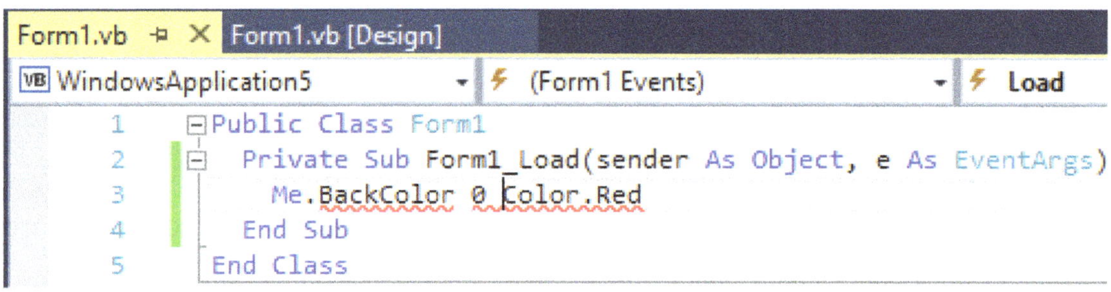

Visual Basic is telling you that there is something wrong with how you used this particular line of code. Using the hints from the task list, you should be able to see that the assignment operator (=) is missing. If you don't see the problem, clicking **<F1>** might give you more help.

Let's say we corrected our error by adding the **=** sign, but we accidentally left out the letter '**k**' in the **BackColor** property name, or we typed:

```
Me.BacColor = Color.Red
```

Try running the project and you'll see another 'build error' window. Choose not to continue and go to the Error List:

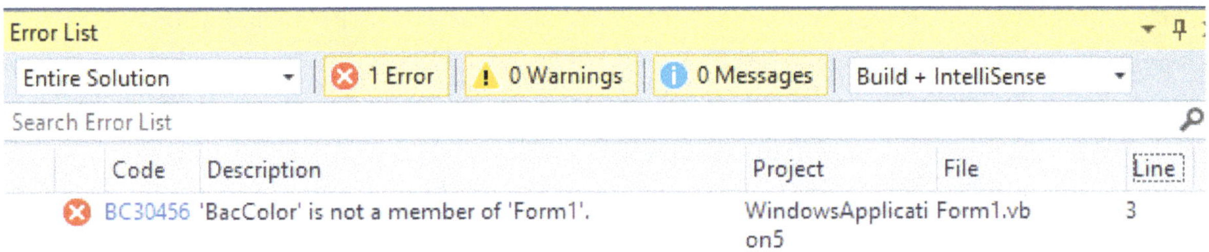

The message again points to Line 3, saying '**BacColor**' is not a **member** (property or event) associated with the form. Again, go to Line 3 (double-click the error message) in the code window and you should see:

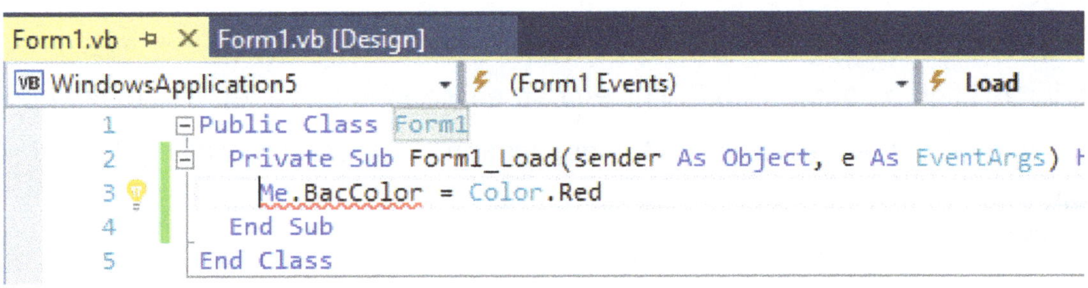

The cursor is next to **Me.BacColor**. Visual Basic is telling you it can't find this property for the particular control (the form). You should note the misspelling and correct it.

Now, let's say you correct the property name, but mess up again and type **Mee** instead of **Me** when referring to the form:

```
Mee.BackColor = Color.Red
```

Run the project. You will get another build error, choose not to continue and view the Task list:

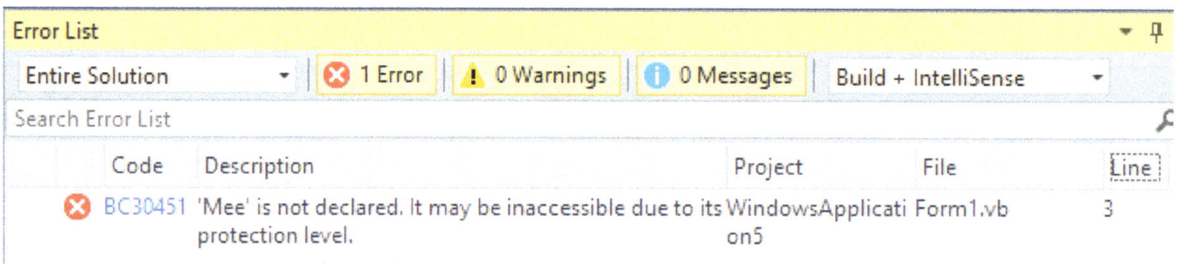

The key message here is 'Name … is not declared.' This usually appears when you have misspelled the assigned name of a control in BASIC code. Visual Basic is trying to assign a property to something using the 'dot notation':

```
ControlName.PropertyName = Value
```

But, it can't find a control with the given name (**Mee** in this case). Go to the code window, correct the error and run the application. You should finally get a red form!!

The errors we've caused here are three of the most common run-time errors: misspelling an assigned Name property, misspelling a property name, or leaving something out of an assignment statement. Notice each run-time error seen was detected prior to running, resulting in a build error. There are other run-time errors that may occur while your application is actually running.

Visual Basic refers to some run-time errors as **exceptions**. If a window appears saying you have some kind of exception, the line with the detected error will be shown with suggestions for fixing the error. Be sure to stop the program before trying to fix the error.

We've seen a few typical run-time errors. There are others and you'll see lots of them as you start building projects. But, you've seen that Visual Basic is pretty helpful in pointing out where errors are and on-line help is always available to explain them. One last thing about run-time errors. Visual Basic will not find all errors at once. It will stop at the first run-time error it encounters. After you fix that error, there may be more. You have to fix run-time errors one at a time.

Logic Errors

Logic errors are the most difficult to find and eliminate. These are errors that don't keep your project from running, but cause incorrect or unexpected results. The only thing you can do at this point, if you suspect logic errors exist, is to dive into your project (primarily, the event procedures) and make sure everything is coded exactly as you want it. Finding logic errors is a time-consuming art, not a science. There are no general rules for finding logic errors. Each programmer has his or her own particular way of searching for logic errors.

With the example we have been using, a logic error would be setting the form background color to blue, when you expected red. You would then go into the code to see why this is happening. You would see the color **Color.Blue** instead of the desired value **Color.Red**. Making the change would eliminate the logic error and the form will be red.

Unfortunately, eliminating logic errors is not as easy as this example. But, there is help. Visual Basic has something called a **debugger** that helps you in the identification of logic errors. Using the debugger, you can print out properties and other values, stop your code wherever and whenever you want, and run your project line-by-line. Use of the debugger is an advanced topic and will not be talked about in this course. If you want to improve your Visual Basic skills, you are encouraged to eventually learn how to use the debugger.

Now, let's improve your skills regarding Visual Basic controls. We'll look at two new controls: the **label** and the **text box**.

Label Control

A **label** is a control that displays information the user cannot edit directly. It is most often used to provide titles for other controls. And, it is used to display the results of some computer operation. The label control is selected from the toolbox. It appears as:

In Toolbox:

On Form (default properties):

Properties

A few useful properties for the label are:

Property	Description
Name	Name used to identify label. Three letter prefix for label names is **lbl**.
Text	Text (string type) that appears in the label.
TextAlign	Specifies how the label text is positioned.
Font	Sets style, size, and type of Text text.
BackColor	Sets label background color.
ForeColor	Sets color of Text text.
Left	Distance from left side of form to left side of label (referred to by X in properties window, expand **Location** property).
Top	Distance from top side of form to top side of label (referred to by Y in properties window, expand **Location** property).
Width	Width of the label in pixels (expand **Size** property).

Height	Height of label in pixels (expand **Size** property).
BorderStyle	Determines type of label border.
Visible	Determines whether the label appears on the form (in run mode).
AutoSize	If **True** (default value), label adjusts to size of text. If **False**, label can be resized.

Note, by default, the label control has no resizing handles. To resize the label, set AutoSize to False.

Example

Make sure Visual Basic is running and start a new project. Put a label on the form. Resize it (you need to set AutoSize to False) and move it, if desired. Set the Text property. Try different Fonts. See the difference among the BorderStyle possibilities; notice the default value (**None**) makes the button match with the form, **Fixed Single** places a box around the label, and **Fixed3D** gives the label a three-dimensional inset look. Change the BackColor and ForeColor properties. You may find certain color combinations that don't do a very good job of displaying the Text when in color. Make sure you are aware of combinations that do and don't work. You want your user to be able to read what is displayed.

The most used label property is Text. It holds the information that is displayed in the label control. There are two things you need to be aware of. First, by default, the label will 'grow' to hold any Text you might provide for it. If the label size is not acceptable, you can try things like changing **Font** or **AutoSize**. If the label is made to be larger than the text it holds (by setting AutoSize to False), you will also want to set the TextAlign property. Try different values of the TextAlign property; there are nine different alignments selected from a 'graphical' menu:

Vertical choices are: top, middle, and bottom justification. Horizontal choices are: left, center, and right justification.

The second thing you need to know is that Text is a string type property. It can only hold string values. When setting the Text property in run mode, the Text information must be in quotes. For example, if you have a label control named **lblExample** and you want to set the **Text** property to **My Label Box**, you would use the BASIC code (note the dot notation):

```
lblExample.Text = "My Label Box"
```

You don't have to worry about the quotes when setting the Text in design mode. Visual Basic knows this is a string value.

Events

There is only one label event of interest:

Event	Description
Click	Event executed when user clicks on the label with the mouse.

With this event, you could allow your user to choose among a set of displayed label boxes. Why would you want to do this? Example applications include multiple choice answers in a test or color choices.

Typical Use of Label Control

The usual design steps for the label control to display unchanging text (for example, to provide titling information) are:

- Set the **Name** (though not really necessary since you rarely write code for a label control) and **Text** property.
- You may also want to change the **Font**, **Backcolor** and **Forecolor** properties.

To use the label control for changing text, for example, to show some computed results, use these steps:

- Set the **Name** property. Initialize **Text** to desired string.
- Set **AutoSize** to **False**, resize control and select desired value for **TextAlign**.
- Assign **Text** property (String type) in code where needed.
- You may also want to change the **Font**, **Backcolor** and **Forecolor** properties.

Text Box Control

The **text box** control is used to display information entered in design mode, by a user in run mode, or assigned within an event procedure. Just think of a text box as a label whose contents your user can (or may not be able to) change. The text box is selected from the Visual Basic toolbox. It appears as:

In Toolbox:

On Form (default properties):

Properties

The text box has a wealth of useful properties:

Property	Description
Name	Name used to identify text box. Three letter prefix for text box names is **txt**.
Text	Text (string value) that appears in text box.
TextAlign	Sets whether Text is left-justified, right-justified, or centered in text box.
Font	Sets style, size, and type of Text.
MultiLine	Specifies whether text box displays one line or multiple lines.
ScrollBars	Specifies type of displayed scroll bar(s).
MaxLength	Maximum length of displayed Text. If **0**, length is unlimited.
BackColor	Sets text box background color.
ForeColor	Sets color of Text.

Left	Distance from left side of form to left side of text box (X in the properties window, expand **Location** property).
Top	Distance from top side of form to top side of text box (Y in the properties window, expand **Location** property).
Width	Width of the text box in pixels (expand **Size** property).
Height	Height of text box in pixels (expand **Size** property).
ReadOnly	If **True**, user can't change contents of text box (run mode only).
TabStop	If **False**, the control cannot be 'tabbed' to.
BorderStyle	Determines type of text box border.
Visible	Determines whether the text box appears on the form (in run mode).

Example

Start a new Visual Basic project. Put a text box on the form. Resize it and move it, if desired. Set the Text property. Try different Fonts. Try different values of the TextAlign property. See the difference among the BorderStyle possibilities. The label box used **None** as default, the text box uses **Fixed3D**. Change the BackColor and ForeColor properties. Set MultiLine to **True** and try different ScrollBars values. I think you can see the text box is very flexible in how it appears on your form.

Like the Text property of the label control, the Text property of a text box is a string value. So, when setting the Text property in run mode, we must enclose the value in quotes (“) to provide a proper assignment. Setting the Text property in design mode does not require (and you shouldn’t use) quotes.

Events

The most important property of the text box is the Text property. As a programmer, you need to know when this property has changed in order to make use of the new value. There are two events you can use to do this:

Event	Description
TextChanged	Event executed whenever **Text** changes.
Leave	Event executed when the user leaves the text box and causes an event on another control.

The **TextChanged** event is executed a lot - every time a user presses a key while typing in the text box, the TextChanged event procedure is called. Looking at the Text property in this event procedure will give you its current value.

The **Leave** event is the more useful event for examining Text. Remember in placing controls on the form in design mode, you can make one control 'active' by clicking on it. There is a similar concept while an application is in run mode. A user can have interaction with only one control at a time. The control the user is interacting with (causing events) is said to have **focus**. While a user is typing in a text box, that box has focus. The Leave event is executed when you leave the text box and another control gets focus. At that point, we know the user is done typing in the text box and is done changing the Text property. That's why this event procedure is a good place to find the value of the Text property.

Typical Use of Text Box Control

There are two primary ways to use a text box – as an input control or as a display control. If the text box is used to accept some input from the user, the usual design steps:

- Set the **Name** property. Initialize **Text** property to desired string.
- If it is possible to input multiple lines, set **MultiLine** property to **True**. Also, set **ScrollBars** property, if desired.
- You may also want to change the **Font**, **Backcolor** and **Forecolor** properties.

If using the control just to display some information (no user modification possible), follow these usual design steps:

- Set the **Name** property. Initialize **Text** property to desired string.
- Set **ReadOnly** property to **True** (once you do this, note the background color will change).
- Set **TabStop** to False.
- If displaying more than one line, set **MultiLine** property to **True**.
- Assign **Text** property in code where needed.
- You may also want to change the **Font**, **Backcolor** and **Forecolor** properties.

BASIC – The Second Lesson

In this class, you will learn some new BASIC concepts. We will discuss variables (name, type, declaring), arithmetic operations, and some functions and techniques for working with strings.

Variables

All computer programs work with information of one kind or another. Numbers, text, colors and pictures are typical types of information they work with. Computer programs need places to store this information while working with it. We have seen one type of storage used by Visual Basic projects - control properties. Control properties store information like control size, control appearance, control position on the form, and control colors.

But, control properties are not sufficient to store all information a project might need. What if we need to know how much ten bananas cost if they are 25 cents each? We would need a place to store the number of bananas, the cost of each banana, and the result of multiplying these two numbers together. To store information other than control properties in Visual Basic projects, we use something called **variables**. They are called variables because the information stored there can change, or vary, during program execution. Variables are the primary method for moving information around in a Visual Basic project. And, certain rules must be followed in the use of variables. These rules are very similar to those we have already established for control properties.

Variable Names

You must **name** every variable you use in your project. Rules for naming variables are:

- No more than 40 characters.
- Can only use letters, numbers, and the underscore (_) character.
- The first character must be a letter. It is customary, though not required, in Visual Basic that this first letter be upper case.
- You cannot use a word reserved by Visual Basic (for example, you can't have a variable named Form or one named Beep).

The most important rule is to use variable names that are meaningful. You should be able to identify the information stored in a variable by looking at its name. As an example, in our banana buying example, good names would be:

Quantity	Variable Name
Cost of each banana	BananaCost
Number of bananas purchased	Bananas
Cost of all bananas	TotalBananaCost

As mentioned in an earlier class, the Visual Basic language is <u>not</u> case sensitive. This means the names **BananaCost** and **bananacost** refer to the <u>same</u> variable. Make sure you assign unique names to each variable. As with control names, we suggest mixing upper and lower case letters for improved readability. You will notice, as you type code, that the Visual Basic editor will adjust the case of control names, variables and reserved BASIC keywords, as necessary.

Variable Types

We need to know the **type** of information stored by each variable. The same types used for properties can be applied to variables: **integer**, **Boolean** and **string**. There are other types too - consult on-line help for types you might want to use.

Here, we look at one more type we will use with variables: the **single** type. Up to now, all the projects we've worked with have used integer (or whole number) values. But, we know most 'real-world' mathematics involves decimal numbers. The single type is just that - a number that has a decimal point. In computer language, we call it a **floating point number**. The 'point' that is floating (moving around) is the decimal. Examples of single type numbers are:

2.00 -1.2 3.14159

Variables can appear in assignment statements:

```
VariableName = NewValue
```

Only a single variable can be on the left side of the assignment operator (=) while any legal BASIC expression, using any number of variables, can be on the right side of the operator. Recall that, in this statement, **NewValue** is evaluated first, then assigned to **VariableName**. The major thing we need to be concerned with is that NewValue is the same **type** as VariableName. That is, we must assign a properly typed value to the variable. This is the same thing we had to do with property values.

Declaring Variables

Once we have named a variable and determined what type we want it to be, we must relay this information to our Visual Basic project. We need to **declare** our variables. (We don't have to declare control properties since Visual Basic already knows about them.) The statement used to declare a variable named **VariableName** as type **Type** is:

```
Dim VariableName As Type
```

We need a declaration statement like this for every variable in our project. This may seem like a lot of work, but it is worth it. Proper variable declaration makes programming easier, minimizes the possibility of program errors, and makes later program modification easier.

So, where do we put these variable declarations. Start a new Visual Basic project and bring up the code window. The code window will look like this:

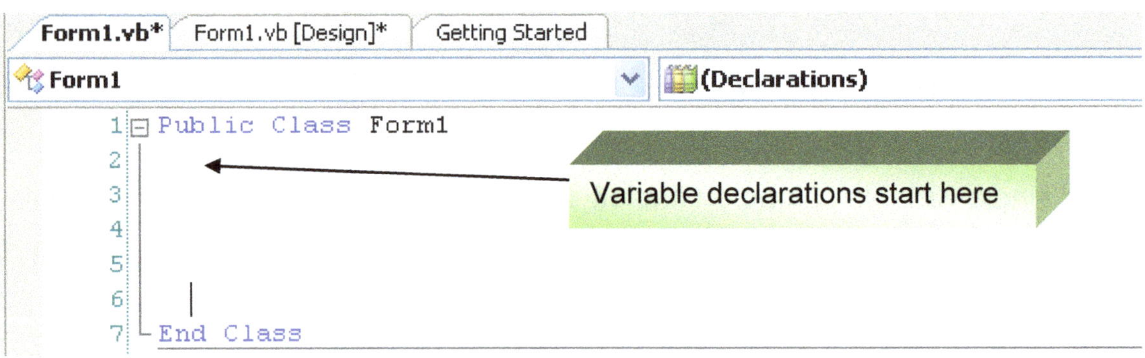

We will put variable declaration statements directly beneath the header line (**Public Class Form1**) and before any event procedures. In this particular window, we would start at Line 2. This location in the code window is known as the general declarations area and any variables declared here can be used (the value can be accessed and/or changed) in any of the project's event procedures.

A little secret: depending on the settings of your installation of Visual Basic, it may not really be necessary to declare every variable you want to use, even though it's a very good idea. Most likely, your installation is set up to require variable declaration, but let's check. Follow these steps:

- Make sure Visual Basic is running.
- Start a new project, if one isn't already loaded.
- Go to the **Solution Explorer** window. Right-click the project name and select **Properties**. Make sure you right-click the project name and not the solution name.

This project properties window should appear. Click **Compile** on the left side of the window:

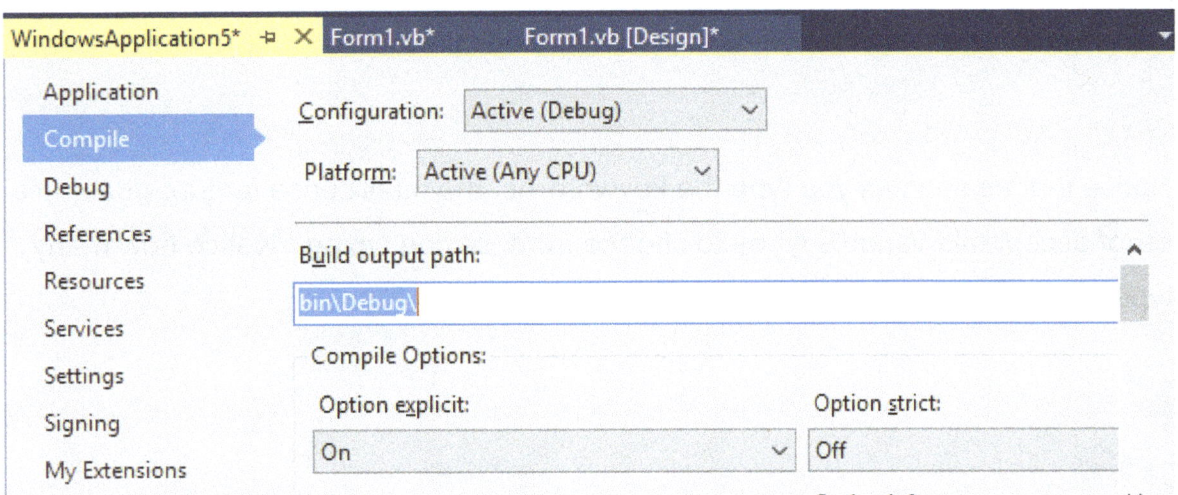

If the word **On** does not appear next to the **Option Explicit** (meaning we need to **explicitly** declare all variables) choice, change it so it does, then close the window (click the **X** in the upper right corner). This change will be in effect for all projects built in Visual Basic. So, for every project you build, all variables must be declared. We will see how this helps in making our programming tasks easier as we build the project in this class.

Try typing some variable declarations in the code window. Here are some examples to try:

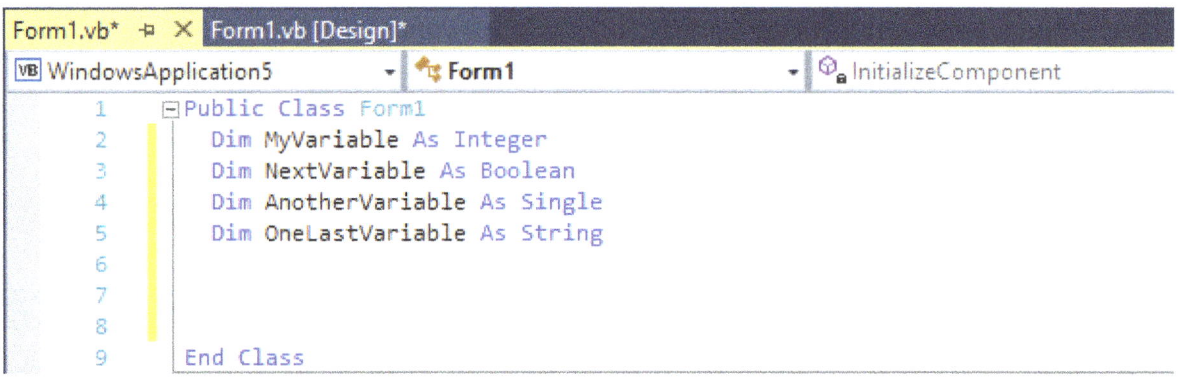

Notice that as soon as you type the keyword As, the Intellisense feature pops up a list of acceptable variable types to choose from, saving typing. Notice how many types there are!

Arithmetic Operators

One thing computer programs are very good at is doing arithmetic. They can add, subtract, multiply, and divide numbers very quickly. We need to know how to make our Visual Basic projects do arithmetic. There are seven **arithmetic operators** in the BASIC language.

Addition is done using the plus (+) sign and **subtraction** is done using the minus (-) sign. Simple examples are:

Operation	**Example**	**Result**
Addition	7 + 2	9
Addition	3 + 8	11
Subtraction	6 - 4	2
Subtraction	11 - 7	4

Multiplication is done using the asterisk (*) and **division** is done using the slash (/). Simple examples are:

Operation	**Example**	**Result**
Multiplication	8 * 4	32
Multiplication	2 * 12	24
Division	12 / 2	6
Division	42 / 6	7

I'm sure you've done addition, subtraction, multiplication, and division before and understand how each operation works. The three other BASIC arithmetic operators may not familiar to you, though.

The next operator is the **exponentiation** operator, represented by a caret symbol (**^**) or sometimes called a 'hat.' The caret is typed when you hold down <**Shift**> while typing a **6**. Exponentiation is used when you want to multiply a number times itself a certain number of times. You've probably 'squared' numbers before, or multiplied a number times itself - this is an example of an exponentiation. If you have an integer variable named A and one named B, A ^ B means you would multiply A times itself B times. Some examples:

Example	**Result**
5 ^ 2	25
2 ^ 4	16
3 ^ 3	27

The other arithmetic operators are concerned with dividing integer numbers. The **integer division** operator is a backslash character (\). This works just like normal division except only integer (whole number) answers are possible - any remainder from the division is ignored. Conversely, the **modulus operator**, represented by the BASIC keyword **Mod**, divides two integer numbers, ignores the main part of the answer, and just gives you the remainder! It may not be obvious now, but the modulus operator is used a lot in computer programming. Examples of both of these operators are:

Operation	**Example**	**Division Result**	**Operation Result**
Integer division	7 \ 2	3 Remainder 1	3
Integer division	23 \ 10	2 Remainder 3	2
Integer division	18 \ 3	6 Remainder 0	6
Modulus	7 Mod 4	1 Remainder 3	3
Modulus	14 Mod 3	4 Remainder 2	2
Modulus	25 Mod 5	5 Remainder 0	0

Study these examples so you understand how integer division works in BASIC.

What happens if an assignment statement contains more than one arithmetic operator? Does it make any difference? Look at this example:

7 + 3 * 4

What's the answer? Well, it depends. If you work left to right and add 7 and 3 first, then multiply by 4, the answer is 40. If you multiply 3 times 4 first, then add 7, the answer is 19. Confusing? Well, yes. But, BASIC takes away the possibility of such confusion by having rules of **precedence**. This means there is a specific order in which arithmetic operations will be performed. That order is:

1. Exponentiation (^)
2. Multiplication (*) and division (/)
3. Integer division (\)
4. Modulus (Mod)
5. Addition (+) and subtraction (-)

So, in an assignment statement, all exponentiations are done first, then multiplications and divisions, then integer divisions, then modulus operations, and lastly, additions and subtractions. In our example (7 + 3 * 4), we see the multiplication will be done before the addition, so the answer provided by BASIC would be 19.

If two operators have the same precedence level, for example, multiplication and division, the operations are done left to right in the assignment statement. For example:

```
24 / 2 * 3
```

The division (24 / 2) is done first yielding a 12, then the multiplication (12 * 3), so the answer is 36. But what if we want to do the multiplication before the division - can that be done? Yes - using the BASIC **grouping operators** - parentheses **()**. By using parentheses in an assignment statement, you force operations within the parentheses to be done first. So, if we rewrite our example as:

```
24 / (2 * 3)
```

the multiplication (2 * 3) will be done first yielding 6, then the division (24 / 6), yielding the desired result of 4. You can use as many parentheses as you want, but make sure they are always in pairs - every left parenthesis needs a right parenthesis. If you type an assignment statement in the Visual Basic code window with unmatched parentheses (a syntax error), the end of the statement will be 'squiggled' indicating an error. If you nest parentheses, that is have one set inside another, evaluation will start with the innermost set of parentheses and move outward. For example, look at:

```
((2 + 4) * 6) + 7
```

The addition of 2 and 4 is done first, yielding a 6, which is multiplied by 6, yielding 36. This result is then added to 7, with the final answer being 43. You might also want to use parentheses even if they don't change precedence. Many times, they are used just to clarify what is going on in an assignment statement.

As you improve your programming skills, make sure you know how each of the arithmetic operators work, what the precedence order is, and how to use parentheses. Always double-check your assignment statements to make sure they are providing the results you want.

Val and Str Functions

A common task in any Visual Basic project is to take numbers input by the user, do some arithmetic operations on those numbers, and output the results of those operations. How do you do this? With the Visual Basic knowledge you have up to this point, you probably see you could use text box controls to allow the user to input numbers. Then you could use the arithmetic operators to do the math and label controls to display the results of the math. And, that's just what you would do. But, there are two problems:

> **Problem One**: Arithmetic operators can only work with numbers (for example, integer variables and integer properties), but the value provided by a text box control (the Text property) is a string. You can't add and multiply string type variables and properties!
>
> **Problem Two**: The result of arithmetic operations is a number. But the Text property of a label control (where we might want to display these results) is a string type. You can't store numerical data in a string quantity!

We need solutions to these two problems. The solutions lie in the **BASIC built-in functions**. We need ways to convert strings to numbers and, conversely, numbers to strings. With this ability, we could take the Text property from a text box, convert it to a number, do some math, and convert that numerical result to a string that could be used as a Text property in a label box. This is a very common task in BASIC and BASIC has a large set of functions that help us do such common tasks. The two functions that will solve our current problems are the **Val** function and the **Str** function. We will look at these in a bit, but first let's define just what a function is.

A BASIC function is a built-in procedure that, given some information by us, computes some desired value. The format for using a function is:

```
FunctionValue = FunctionName(ArgumentList)
```

FunctionName is the name of the function and **ArgumentList** is a list of values (separated by commas) provided to the function so it can do its work. In this assignment statement, FunctionName uses the values in ArgumentList to compute a result and assign that result to the variable we have named **FunctionValue**. We must insure the variable FunctionValue has the same type as the value computed by FunctionName. How do we know what BASIC functions exist, what type of information they provide, and what type of **arguments** they require? Use the Visual Basic on-line help system and search for **Functions**. You'll see that there are lots of them. We'll cover some of them in this class, but you'll have to do a little studying on your own to learn about most of them. Now, let's look at our first two BASIC functions: **Val** and **Str**. Maybe look them up in the on-line help system to do a little 'get-ahead' reading.

The BASIC **Val** function will convert a string type variable (or control property) to a numerical value. The format for using this function is:

```
YourNumber = Val(YourString)
```

The **Val** function takes the **YourString** variable (remember this is called an argument of the function), converts it to a numerical value, and assigns it to the variable **YourNumber**. We could then use YourNumber in any arithmetic statement. Recall strings must be enclosed in quotes. An example using Val:

```
YourNumber = Val("23")
```

Following this assignment statement, the variable YourNumber has a numerical value of 23.

The BASIC **Str** function will convert a numerical variable (or control property) to a string. The format for using this function is:

```
YourString = Str(YourNumber)
```

The **Str** function takes the **YourNumber** argument, converts it to a string type value, and assigns it to the variable named **YourString**. In the example:

```
YourString = Str(23)
```

the variable YourString has a string value of "23".

You should be comfortable with converting numbers to strings and strings to numbers using the Val and Str functions. As mentioned, this is one of the more common tasks you will use when developing Visual Basic projects.

String Concatenation

A confession - in the above discussion, you were told a little lie. The statement was made that you couldn't add and multiply strings. Well, you can't multiply them, but you can do something similar to addition. Many times in Visual Basic projects, you want to take a string variable from one place and 'tack it on the end' of another string. The fancy word for this is **string concatenation**. The concatenation operator is an ampersand (**&**) and it is easy to use. As an example:

```
NewString = "Visual " & "Basic Express"
```

After this statement, the string variable NewString will have the value "Visual Basic". In some books about BASIC and Visual Basic, you may also see the plus sign (**+**) used as a concatenation operator and it will work. We will only use the ampersand here to distinguish string concatenation from the arithmetic operation of addition.

As you've seen, string variables are a big part of Visual Basic. As you develop as a programmer, you need to become comfortable with strings and working with them. You're now ready to attack a new project.

Project – Savings Account

Project Design

In this project, we will build a savings account calculator. We will input how much money we can put into an account each week and the number of weeks we put money in the account. The project will then compute how much we saved. We will use text boxes as both the input controls and for output information. A button will be used to do the computation. This project is saved as **Savings** in the course projects folder (**\CBGVB\BVB Projects**).

Place Controls on Form

Start a new project in Visual Basic. Place three text box controls, three label controls, and two buttons on the form. Your form should resemble this:

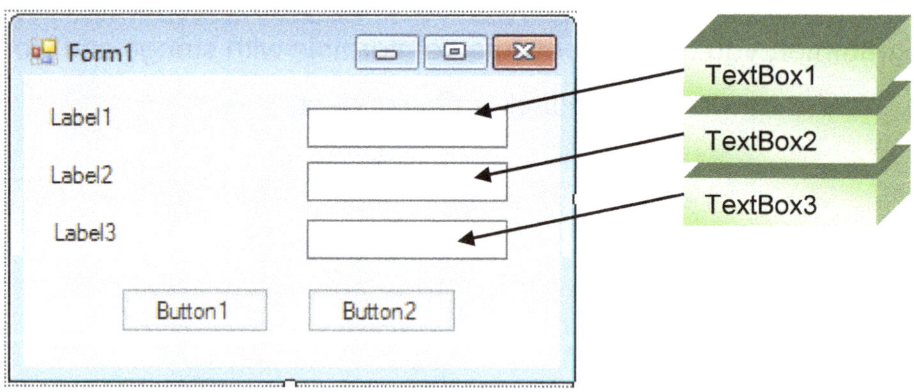

Again, try using copy and paste for the similar controls.

Set Control Properties

Set the control properties using the properties window (remember, controls are listed by their default name):

Form1 Form:

Property Name	Property Value
Text	Savings Account
FormBorderStyle	Fixed Single
StartPosition	CenterScreen

Label1 Label:

Property Name	Property Value
Name	lblDepositHeading
Text	Weekly Deposit
Font	Arial
Font Size	10

Label2 Label:

Property Name	Property Value
Name	lblWeeksHeading
Text	Number of Weeks
Font	Arial
Font Size	10

Label3 Label:

Property Name	Property Value
Name	lblTotalHeading
Text	Total Savings
Font	Arial
Font Size	10

TextBox1 Text Box:

Property Name	**Property Value**
Name	txtDeposit
TextAlign	Right
Font	Arial
Font Size	10

TextBox2 Text Box:

Property Name	**Property Value**
Name	txtWeeks
TextAlign	Right
Font	Arial
Font Size	10

TextBox3 Text Box:

Property Name	**Property Value**
Name	txtTotal
TextAlign	Right
Font	Arial
Font Size	10
ReadOnly	True
BackColor	White
TabStop	False

(Note the background color changes when setting ReadOnly to True. Hence, we set BackColor to White to match the appearance of the other two text boxes.)

Button1 Button:

Property Name	**Property Value**
Name	btnCompute
Text	Compute

Button2 Button:

Property Name	**Property Value**
Name	btnExit
Text	Exit

Note this is the first time you have been asked to change Font properties. Review the procedure for doing this (Class 4 under Button Control), if necessary. Change any other properties, like colors, if you would like. When you are done, your form should resemble this:

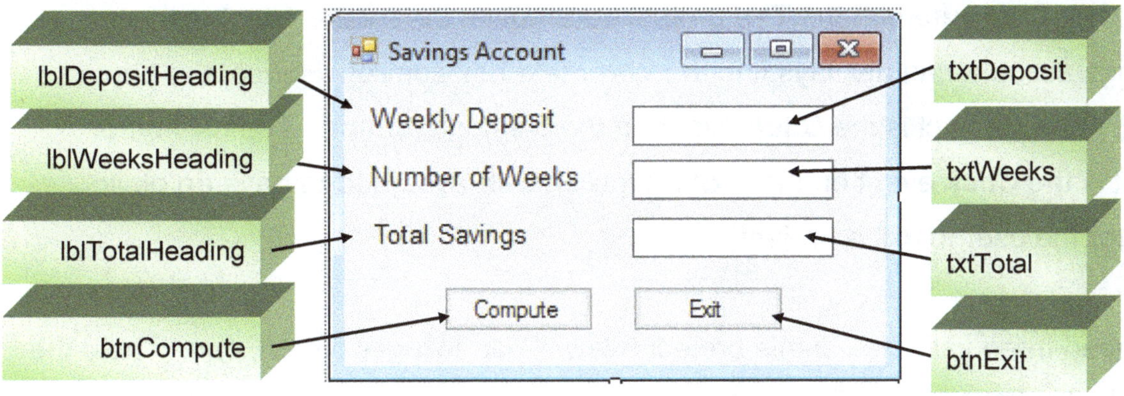

Write Event Procedures

In this project, the user types an amount in the **Weekly Deposit** text box. Then, the user types a value in the **Number of Weeks** text box. Following this, the user clicks the **Compute** button. The project determines the total amount in the savings account and displays it in the lower text box control. Hence, the primary event in this project is the **Click** event on the Compute button. The only other event is the **Click** event on the **Exit** button. It's always good to have an obvious way for the user to exit a project.

We need three variables in this project (we will use **Integer** types), one to hold the weekly deposit amount (**Deposit**), one to store the number of weeks (**Weeks**), and one to store the total savings (**Total**). Open the code window and find the **general declarations**. Declare these three variables:

```
Dim Deposit As Integer
Dim Weeks As Integer
Dim Total As Integer
```

The code window should appear as:

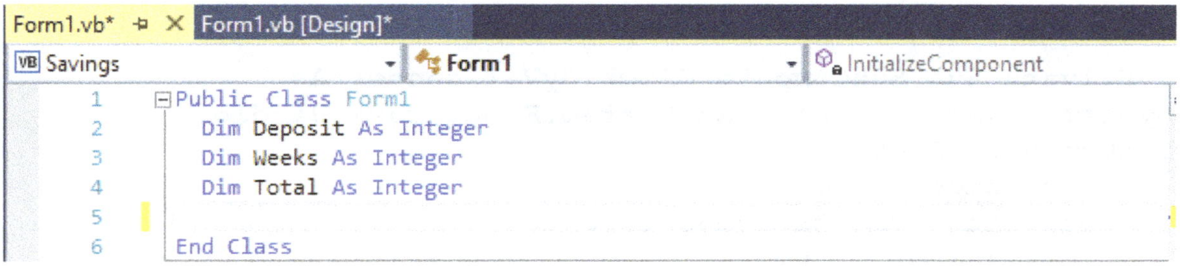

The event procedures will start <u>after</u> Line 4.

The **btnCompute Click** event implements the following steps:

1. Convert input deposit value (**txtDeposit.Text**) to a number and store it in the variable **Deposit**.
2. Convert input number of weeks (**txtWeeks.Text**) to a number and store it in the variable **Weeks**.
3. Multiply Deposit times Weeks and store the result in the variable **Total**.
4. Convert the numerical value **Total** to a string, concatenate it with a dollar sign ($), and store it in **Text** property of **txtTotal**.

Establish the **btnCompute Click** event procedure the code window and type this code (which translates the steps above):

```
  Private Sub BtnCompute_Click(ByVal sender As
System.Object, ByVal e As System.EventArgs) Handles
btnCompute.Click
    'Get deposit amount
    Deposit = Val(txtDeposit.Text)
    'Get number of weeks
    Weeks = Val(txtWeeks.Text)
    'Compute total savings
    Total = Deposit * Weeks
    'Display Total
    txtTotal.Text = "$" & Str(Total)
  End Sub
```

Notice how is easy it is to translate the listed steps to actual BASIC code. It is just paying attention to details. In particular, look at the use of Str and Val for string-number conversion.

The **btnExit Click** procedure is simply one line of code that stops the program by closing the form:

```
  Private Sub BtnExit_Click(ByVal sender As System.Object,
ByVal e As System.EventArgs) Handles btnExit.Click
    Me.Close()
  End Sub
```

Save your project by clicking the **Save All** button.

Run the Project

Run the project. Click in the **Weekly Deposit** text box and type some value. Do the same with **Number of Weeks**. Click the **Compute** button. Your answer should appear in the **Total** text box control. Make sure the answer is correct. Remember, a big step in project design is making sure your project works correctly! If you say you want to save 10 dollars a week for 10 weeks and your computer project says you will have a million dollars by that time, you should know something is wrong somewhere! Click **Exit** to make sure it works. Save your project if you changed anything. Here's a run I made:

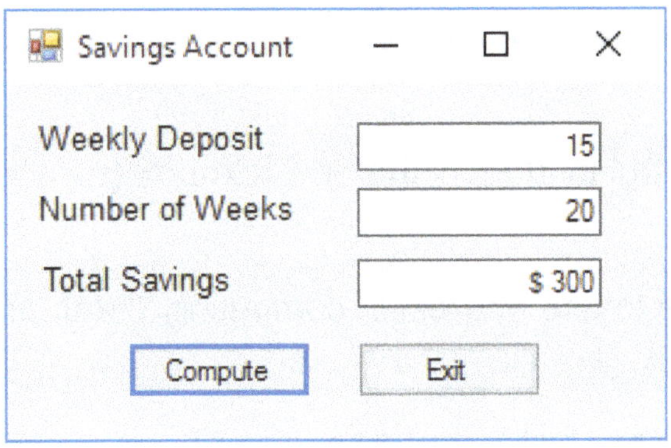

This project may not seem all that complicated. And it isn't. After all, we only multiplied two numbers together. But, the project demonstrates steps that are used in every Visual Basic project. Valuable experience has been gained in recognizing how to read input values, convert them to the proper type, do the math to obtain desired results, and output those results to the user.

Other Things to Try

Most savings accounts yield interest, that is the bank actually pays you for letting them use your money. This savings account project has ignored interest. But, it is fairly easy to make the needed modifications to account for interest - the math is just a little more complicated. We will give you the steps, but not show you how, to change your project. Give it a try if you'd like:

- Define a variable **Interest** to store the yearly savings interest rate. Interest rates are decimal numbers, so use the **Single** type for this variable (it's the first time we've used decimals!).
- Add another text box to allow the user to input this interest rate. Name it **txtInterest**.
- Add a label control to identify the new text box (set the **Text** to **Interest Rate**).
- Modify the code to use Interest in computing **Total**. Interest is found using:

```
Interest = Val(txtInterest.Text)
```

Then, **Total** (get ready - it's messy looking) is computed using:

```
Total = 5200 * (Deposit * ((1 + Interest / 5200) ^
Weeks - 1) / Interest)
```

Make sure you type this all on one line - the word processor has made it look like it is on two. As we said, this is a pretty messy expression, but it's good practice in using parentheses and some other arithmetic operators. The number '5200' is used here to convert the interest from a yearly value to a weekly value.

Now, run the modified project. Type in values for Deposit, Weeks, and Interest. Click Compute button. Make sure you get reasonable answers. (As a check, if you use a Deposit value of 10, a Weeks value of 20, and an Interest value of 6.5, the Total answer should be $202 - note you'd have $200 without interest, so this makes sense). The project automatically converts Total to an integer (since it is declared that type) even though there is probably a decimal (some cents) involved in the answer. Save your project.

Before leaving this project, let's look at one more thing. Remember we said that, even though we don't have to, we will declare every variable we use in our projects? Let's demonstrate a good reason why we do this. Open the Savings Account project, if it's not already opened. This example will work whether or not the interest computation has been programmed. Go to the **btnCompute_Click** event procedure and purposely misspell the variable Deposit. For example, change the line:

```
Deposit = Val(txtDeposit.Text)
```

to:

```
Depsit = Val(txtDeposit.Text)
```

Run the project. You receive a 'build error.' Don't continue and go to the Error List window, where you will see a message saying "Name Depsit is not declared" and be given a line number for the offending line. Go to that line in the code window (double-click the error message) and the misspelled variable **Depsit** should be highlighted in the code window. Visual Basic is telling you there is no declared variable with that name. It is pointing out your misspelling. It has shown you your mistake. Do <u>not</u> correct the error.

What happens in this case if variable declaration is not required? Go to the Project Explorer window, right-click the project name (don't right-click the solution name) and select **Properties**. In the **Savings Project Properties** window that appears, click the **Compile** tab. Turn **Off** the **Option Explicit** choice. You have now removed the requirement that we declare all variables in your project. Close the properties window.

Run the project now (it should run without build errors). Type in some numbers. Click **Compute**. Enter some values. Notice the program seems to run OK, but the answer is wrong. Visual Basic thinks Depsit and Deposit are variables in your project. Since Deposit is never evaluated, it is assumed to be zero. So, no matter what values you input, the computed Total will always be zero. You have a logic error in your code. You know something is wrong, but you would have to look into your code to figure out what. Visual Basic gives you no help in identifying your mistake in this case. With required variable declarations, the variable error was obvious. Hence, by declaring all of our variables, we make the process of writing error-free event procedures a little easier. Stop the project. Restore the **Option Explicit** value to **On** by reversing the earlier steps for project properties. Rerun the project to make sure it is working properly again.

Summary

In this class, you have learned a lot of new material. You learned about the label and text box controls. You learned about variables: naming them, their types and how to declare them properly. And, you learned functions that allow you to change from string variables to numbers and from number to strings. You learned how to do arithmetic in BASIC. Like we said, a lot of new material. In subsequent classes, we will stress new controls and new BASIC statements more than new features about the Visual Basic environment. You should be fairly comfortable in that environment, by now.

6

UpDown Control, Decisions, Random Numbers

Review and Preview

You're halfway through the course! You should now feel comfortable with the project building process and the controls you've studied. In the rest of the classes, we will concentrate more on controls and BASIC and less on the Visual Basic environment. In this class, we look at the numeric updown control, at decisions using BASIC, and at a very fun concept, the random number. You will build a 'Guess the Number' game project.

Numeric UpDown Control

The **Numeric UpDown** control is used to obtain a numeric input. It looks like a text box control with two small arrows. Clicking the arrows changes the displayed value, which ranges from a specified minimum to a specified maximum. The user can even type in a value, if desired. These controls are useful for supplying an integer number, such as a date in a month. The numeric updown control is selected from the Visual Basic toolbox. It appears as:

In Toolbox:

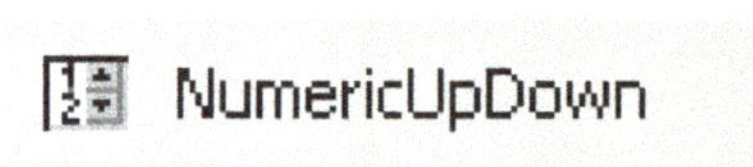

On Form (default properties):

Properties

The numeric updown properties are:

Property	Description
Name	Name used to identify numeric updown control. Three letter prefix for numeric updown name is **nud**.
Value	Value assigned to the updown control.
Increment	Amount to increment (increase) or decrement (decrease) the updown control when the up or down buttons are clicked.
Maximum	Maximum value for the updown control.
Minimum	Minimum value for the updown control.
TextAlign	Sets whether displayed value is left-justified, right-justified or centered.

Font	Sets style, size, and type of displayed value text.
BackColor	Sets updown control background color.
ForeColor	Sets of color of displayed value text.
Left	Distance from left side of form to left side of updown control (X in properties window, expand **Location** property).
Top	Distance from top side of form to top side of updown control (Y in properties window, expand **Location** property).
Width	Width of the updown control in pixels (expand **Size** property).
Height	Height of updown control in pixels (expand **Size** property).
ReadOnly	Determines whether the text may be changed by the use of the up or down buttons only.
Enabled	Determines whether updown control can respond to user events (in run mode).
Visible	Determines whether the updown control appears on the form (in run mode).

Operation of the numeric updown control is actually quite simple. The **Value** property can be changed by clicking either of the arrows (value will be changed by **Increment** with each click) or, optionally by typing a value (if **ReadOnly** is **False**). If using the arrows, the value will always lie between **Minimum** and **Maximum**. If the user can type in a value, you have no control over what value is typed.

Example

Start Visual Basic and start a new project. We will create a numeric updown control that provides numbers from 0 to 20. Put a numeric updown control on the form. (Make sure you choose the **numeric updown** control and not the domain updown control.) Resize it and move it, if desired. Set the following properties:

Property	**Value**
Value	10
Increment	1
Minimum	0
Maximum	20
ReadOnly	False

If you like, try changing colors, font and any other properties too. This numeric updown control has an initial Value of 10. The smallest Value can be is 0 (Minimum), the largest it can be is 20 (Maximum). Value will change by 1 (Increment) when an arrow is clicked. The user can type a value (ReadOnly is False) if desired.

Run the project. The numeric updown control will appear and display a value of 10. Click the end arrows and see the value change. Notice the value will not drop below 0 or above 20, the limits established at design time. Click the display area and type in a value of 100. Note that, even though this is higher than the maximum of 20, you can type the value. Try increasing the value, it will not increase. Hit **<Enter>** or try to decrease the value and it is immediately adjusted within the limits you set. So, Visual Basic makes some attempts to make sure the user doesn't type illegal values. Stop the project.

Events

We will only use a single numeric updown event:

Event	Description
ValueChanged	Occurs when the Value property has been changed in some way.

The **ValueChanged** event is executed whenever Value changes. This is where you can use the current value. If the user is allowed to type a value in the control, you might have to check if it is within acceptable limits.

Typical Use of Numeric UpDown Control

The usual design steps for a numeric updown control are:

- Set the **Name, Minimum** and **Maximum** properties. Initialize **Value** property. Decide on value for **ReadOnly**.
- Monitor **ValueChanged** event for changes in Value.
- You may also want to change the **Font**, **Backcolor** and **Forecolor** properties.

BASIC – The Third Lesson

In the BASIC lesson for this class, we learn about one of the more useful functions of a computer program - decision making. We will discuss expressions and operators used in decisions and how decisions can be made. We will also look at a new BASIC function - the random number. This function is the heart of every computer game.

Logical Expressions

You may think that computers are quite smart. They appear to have the ability to make amazing decisions and choices. Computers can beat masters at chess and help put men and women into space. Well, computers really aren't that smart - the only decision making ability they have is to tell if something is **True** or **False**. But, computers have the ability to make such decisions very quickly and that's why they appear smart (and because, unlike the True or False tests you took in school, computers always get the right answer!). To use BASIC for decision making, we write all possible decisions in the form of **True or False?** statements, called **logical expressions**. We give the computer a logical expression and the computer will tell us if that expression is True or False. Based on that decision, we can take whatever action we want in our computer program. Note the result of a logical expression is a **Boolean** value. We have used Boolean values in setting control properties like Enabled and Visible.

Say, in a computer program we need to know if the value of the variable A is larger than the value of the variable B. We would ask the computer (by writing some BASIC code) to provide an answer to the True or False? statement: "A is larger than B." This is an example of a logical expression. If the computer told us this was True, we could take one set of BASIC steps. If it was False, we could take another. This is how decisions are done in BASIC.

To make decisions, we need to know how to build and use logical expressions. The first step in building such expressions is to learn about comparison operators.

Comparison Operators

In the last class, we looked at one type of BASIC operator - arithmetic operators. In this class, we introduce the idea of a **comparison operator**. Comparison operators do exactly what they say - they compare two values, with the output of the comparison being a Boolean value. That is, the result of the comparison is either **True** or **False**. Comparison operators allow us to construct logical expressions that can be used in decision making.

There are six comparison operators. The first is the "**equal to**" operator represented by the equal (**=**) sign. This operator tells us if two values are equal to each other. Examples are:

Comparison	**Result**
6 = 7	False
4 = 4	True

There is also a "**not equal to**" operator represented by the symbol **<>** (you need to type two characters to form this symbol). Examples of using this operator:

Comparison	**Result**
6 <> 7	True
4 <> 4	False

Notice the "equal to" operator (=) is the same as the assignment operator. This shouldn't be confusing since the "equal to" operator will be in logical expressions and the assignment operator will only appear immediately following a variable in an assignment statement. Some computer languages (like ones called C and

C++) use different operators for assignments and comparisons, to avoid such confusions.

There are other operators that let us compare the size of numbers. The "**greater than**" operator (**>**) tells us if one number (left side of operator) is greater than another (right side of operator). Examples of its usage:

Comparison	**Result**
8 > 3	True
6 > 7	False
4 > 4	False

The "**less than**" operator (**<**) tells us if one number (left side of operator) is less than another (right side of operator). Some examples are:

Comparison	**Result**
8 < 3	False
6 < 7	True
4 < 4	False

The last two operators are modifications to the "greater than" and "less than" operators. The "**greater than or equal to**" operator (**>=**, again two characters need to be typed) compares two numbers. The result is True if the number on the left of the operator is greater than or equal to the number on the right. Otherwise, the result is False. Examples:

Comparison	**Result**
8 >= 3	True
6 >= 7	False
4 >= 4	True

Similarly, the "**less than or equal to**" operator (**<=**) tells us if one number (left side of operator) is less than or equal to another (right side of operator). Examples:

Comparison	**Result**
8 <= 3	False
6 <= 7	True
4 <= 4	True

Comparison operators have equal precedence among themselves, but are lower than the precedence of arithmetic operators. This means comparisons are done after any arithmetic. Comparison operators allow us to make single decisions about the relative size of values and variables. What if we need to make multiple decisions? For example, what if we want to know if a particular variable is smaller than one number, but larger than another? We need ways to combine logical expressions - logical operators can do this.

Logical Operators

Logical operators are used to combine logical expressions built using comparison operators. Using such operators allows you, as the programmer, to make any decision you want. As an example, say you need to know if two variables named A and B are both greater than 0. Using the "greater than" comparison operator (>), we know how to see if A is greater than zero and we know how to check if B is greater than 0, but how do we combine these expressions and obtain one Boolean result (True or False)?

We will look at two logical operators (there are actually several in BASIC, but we will only use these two). The first is the **And** operator. The format for using this operator is (using two logical expressions, **X** and **Y,** each with a Boolean result):

X **And** Y

This expression is asking the question "are X and Y both true?" That's why it is called the And operator. The And operator will return a True value only if both X and Y are True. If either expression is False, the And operator will return a False. The four possibilities for **And** are shown in this **logic table**:

X	**Y**	**X And Y**
True	True	True
True	False	False
False	True	False
False	False	False

Notice the And operator would be used to solve the problem mentioned in the beginning of this section. That is, to see if the variables A and B are both greater than zero, we would use the expression:

A > 0 And B > 0

The other logical operator we will use is the **Or** operator. The format for using this operator is:

X **Or** Y

This expression is asking the question "is X or Y true?" That's why it is called the Or operator. The Or operator will return a True value if either X or Y is True. If both expressions are False, the Or operator will return a False. The four possibilities for **Or** are:

X	Y	X Or Y
True	True	True
True	False	True
False	True	True
False	False	False

The Or operator is second in precedence to the And operator (that is, And is done before Or), and all logical operators come after the comparison operators in precedence. Use of comparison operators and logical operators to form logical expressions is key to making proper decisions in BASIC. Make sure you understand how all the operators (and their precedence) work. Let's look at some examples to help in this understanding.

In these examples, we will have two integer variables A and B, with values:

A = 14, B = 7

What if we want to evaluate the logical expression:

A > 10 And B > 10

Comparisons are done first, left to right since all comparison operators share the same level of precedence. A (14) is greater than 10, so A > 10 is True. B (7) is not greater than 10, so B > 10 is False. Since one expression is not True, the result of the And operation is False. This expression 'A > 10 And B > 10' is False. What is the result of this expression:

A > 10 Or B > 10

Can you see this expression is True (A > 10 is True, B > 10 is False; True Or False is True)?

There is no requirement that a logical expression have just one logical operator. So, let's complicate things a bit. What if the expression is:

A > 10 Or B > 10 And A + B = 20

Precedence tells us the arithmetic is done first (A and B are added), then the comparisons, left to right. We know A > 10 is True, B > 10 is False, A + B = 20 is False. So, this expression, in terms of Boolean comparison values, becomes:

True Or False And False

How do we evaluate this? Precedence says the And is done first, then the Or. The result of 'False And False' is False, so the expression reduces to:

True or False

which has a result of True. Hence, we say the expression 'A > 10 Or B > 10 And A + B = 20' is True.

Parentheses can be used in logical expressions to force precedence in evaluations. What if, in the above example, we wanted to do the Or operation first? This is done by rewriting using parentheses:

(A > 10 Or B > 10) And A + B = 20

You should be able to show this evaluates to False (do the Or first). Before, without parentheses, it was True. The addition of parentheses has changed the value of this logical expression! It's always best to clearly indicate how you want a logical expression to be evaluated. Parentheses are a good way to do this. Use parentheses even if precedence is not affected. If we moved the parentheses in this example and wrote:

A > 10 Or (B > 10 And A + B = 20)

the result (True) is the same as if the parentheses were not there since the And is done first anyway. The parentheses do, however, clearly indicate the And is performed first. Such clarity is good in programming.

Comparison and logical operators are keys to making decisions in BASIC. Make sure you are comfortable with their meaning and use. Always double-check any logical expression you form to make sure it truly represents the decision logic you intend. Use parentheses to add clarity, if needed. And, note that, even though the examples here only used variables, we can also build logical expressions using control properties.

Decisions – The If Statement

We've spent a lot of time covering comparison operators and logical operators and discussed how they are used to form logical expressions. But, just how is all this used in computer decision making? We'll address that now by looking at the BASIC **If** statement. Actually, the If statement is not a single statement, but rather a group of statements that implements some decision logic. It is conceptually simple.

The If statement checks a particular logical expression. It executes different groups of BASIC statements, depending on whether that expression is True or False. The BASIC structure for this logic is:

```
If Expression Then
    [BASIC code to be executed if Expression is True]
Else
    [BASIC code to be executed if Expression is False]
End If
```

Let's see what goes on here. We have some logical **Expression** which is formed from comparison operators and logical operators. **If** Expression is True, **Then** the first group of BASIC statements is executed. **Else** (meaning Expression is not True, or it is False), the second group of BASIC statements is executed. The If statement group is ended with an **End If** statement (all **If** statements require a matching **End If** statement). Whether Expression is True or False, program execution continues with the first line of BASIC code after the End If statement.

The Else keyword and the statements between Else and End If are optional. If there is no BASIC code to be executed if Expression is False, the If structure would simply be:

```
If Expression Then
    [BASIC code to be executed if Expression is True]
End If
```

Let's try some examples.

Pretend your neighbor kid just opened a lemonade stand and you want to let the computer decide how much she should charge for each cup sold. Define a integer type variable **Cost** (cost per cup in cents - our foreign friends can use some other unit here) and another integer variable **Temperature** (outside temperature in degrees F - our foreign friends would, of course, use degrees C). We will write an If/End If structure that implements a decision process that establishes a value for Cost, depending on the value of Temperature. Look at the BASIC code:

```
If Temperature > 90 Then
  Cost = 50
Else
  Cost = 25
End If
```

We see that if Temperature > 90 (a warm day, hence we can charge more), a logical expression, is True, the Cost will be 50, else (meaning Temperature is not greater than 90) the Cost will be 25. Not too difficult. Notice that we have indented the lines of BASIC code following the If and Else statements. This is common practice in writing BASIC code. It clearly indicates what is done in each case and allows us to see where an If structure begins and ends (with the End If statement). The Visual Basic environment will actually handle the indenting for you. And, also, as soon as you type an If statement, it will add an End If for you.

We could rewrite this (and get the same result) without the Else statement. Notice, this code is equivalent to the above code:

```
Cost = 25
If Temperature > 90 Then
  Cost = 50
End If
```

Here, before the If/End If structure, Cost is 25. Only if Temperature is greater than 90 is Cost changed to 50. Otherwise, Cost remains at 25. Even though, in these examples, we only have one line of BASIC code that is executed for each decision possibility, we are not limited to a single line. We may have as many lines of BASIC code as needed in If/End If structures.

What if, in our lemonade stand example, we want to divide our pricing structure into several different Cost values, based on several different Temperature values. The If/End If structure can modified to include an **ElseIf** statement to consider multiple logical expressions. Such a structure is:

```
If Expression1 Then
   [BASIC code to be executed if Expression1 is True]
ElseIf Expression2 Then
   [BASIC code to be executed if Expression2 is True]
ElseIf Expression3 Then
   [BASIC code to be executed if Expression3 is True]
Else
   [BASIC code to be executed if Expression1, Expression 2, and
   Expression3 are all False]
End If
```

Can you see what happens here? It's pretty straightforward - just work down through the code. If Expression1 is True, the first set of BASIC code is executed. If Expression1 is False, the program checks to see if Expression2 (using the

ElseIf) is True. If Expression2 is True, that section of code is executed. If Expression2 is False, Expression3 is evaluated. If Expression3 is True, the corresponding code is executed. If Expression3 is False, and note by this time, Expression1, Expression2, and Expression3 have all been found to be False, the code in the Else section (and this is optional) is executed.

You can have as many ElseIf statements as you want. You must realize, however, that only one section of BASIC code in an If/End If structure will be executed. This means that once BASIC has found a logical expression that is True, it will execute that section of code then leave the structure and execute the first line of code following the End If statement. For example, if in the above example, both Expression1 and Expression3 are True, only the BASIC statements associated with Expression1 being True will be executed. The rule for If/End If structures is: only the statements associated with the first True expression will be executed.

How can we use this in our lemonade example? A more detailed pricing structure is reflected in this code:

```
If Temperature > 90 Then
  Cost = 50
ElseIf Temperature > 80 Then
  Cost = 40
ElseIf Temperature > 70 Then
  Cost = 30
Else
  Cost = 25
End If
```

What would the Cost be if Temperature is 85? Temperature is not greater than 90, but is greater than 80, so Cost is 40. What if this code was rewritten as:

```
If Temperature > 70 Then
  Cost = 30
ElseIf Temperature > 80 Then
  Cost = 40
ElseIf Temperature > 90 Then
  Cost = 50
Else
  Cost = 25
End If
```

This doesn't look that different - we've just reordered some statements. But, notice what happens if we try to find Cost for Temperature = 85 again. The first If expression is True (Temperature is greater than 70), so Cost is 30. This is not the result we wanted and will decrease profits for our lemonade stand! Here's a case where the "first True" rule gave us an incorrect answer - a logic error.

This example points out the necessity to always carefully check any If/End If structures you write. Make sure the decision logic you want to implement is working properly. Make sure you try cases that execute all possible decisions and that you get the correct results. The examples used here are relatively simple. Obviously, the If/End If structure can be more far more complicated. Using multiple variables, multiple control properties, multiple comparisons and multiple operators, you can develop very detailed decision making processes. In the remaining class projects, you will see examples of such processes.

Random Number Generator

Let's leave decisions for now and look at a fun BASIC function - the random number. Have you ever played the Windows solitaire card game or Minesweeper or some similar game? Did you notice that every time you play the game, you get different results? How does this happen? How can you make a computer program unpredictable or introduce the idea of "randomness?" The key is the BASIC random number generator. This generator simply produces a different number every time it is referenced.

Why do you need random numbers? In the Windows solitaire card game, the computer needs to shuffle a deck of cards. It needs to "randomly" sort fifty-two cards. It uses random numbers to do this. If you have a game that rolls a die, you need to randomly generate a number between 1 and 6. Random numbers can be used to do this. If you need to flip a coin, you need to generate Heads or Tails randomly. Yes, random numbers are used to do this too.

Visual Basic has several methods for generating random numbers. We will use just one of them – a random generator of integers (whole numbers). The generator uses what is called the **Random** object. Don't worry too much about what this means –just think of it as another variable type. Follow these few steps to use it. First create a **Random** object (we'll name it **MyRandom**) using the **constructor**:

```
Dim MyRandom As New Random
```

This statement is placed with the variable declaration statements.

Now, whenever you need a random integer value, use the **Next** method of this Random object we created:

```
MyRandom.Next(Limit)
```

This statement generates a random integer value that is greater than or equal to 0 and less than **Limit**. Note it is less than Limit, not equal to. For example, the method:

```
MyRandom.Next(5)
```

will generate random numbers from 0 to 4. The possible values will be 0, 1, 2, 3 and 4.

Let's try it. Start Visual Basic and start a new project. Put a button (default name **Button1**) and label control (default name **Label1**) on the form. We won't worry about properties or names here - we're just playing around, not building a real project. In fact, that's one neat thing about Visual Basic, it is easy to play around with. Add this line to create the random number object:

```
Dim MyRandom As New Random
```

Then, put this code in the **Button1 Click** event procedure:

```
  Private Sub Button1_Click(ByVal sender As System.Object,
ByVal e As System.EventArgs) Handles Button1.Click
    Label1.Text = Str(MyRandom.Next(10))
  End Sub
```

This code simply generates a random integer between 0 and 9 (**Next** uses a limit of 10) and displays its value in the label control (after converting it to a string type). Run the project. Click the button. A number should appear in the label control. Click the button again and again. Notice the displayed number changes with each click and there is no predictability to the number - it is random. The number printed should always be between 0 and 9. Try other limit values if you'd like to understand how the random object works.

So, the random number generator object can be used to introduce randomness in a project. This opens up a lot of possibilities to you as a programmer. Every computer game, video game, and computer simulation, like sports games and flight simulators, use random numbers. A roll of a die can produce a number from 1 to 6. To use our **MyRandom** object to roll a die, we would write:

```
DieNumber = MyRandom.Next(6) + 1
```

For a deck of cards, the random integers would range from 1 to 52 since there are 52 cards in a standard playing deck. Code to do this:

```
CardNumber = MyRandom.Next(52) + 1
```

If we want a number between 0 and 100, we would use:

```
YourNumber = MyRandom.Next(101)
```

Check the examples above to make sure you see how the random number generator produces the desired range of integers. Now, let's move on to a project that will use this generator.

Project – Guess the Number Game

Back in the early 1980's, the first computers intended for home use appeared. Brands like Atari, Coleco, Texas Instruments, and Commodore were sold in stores like Sears and Toys R Us (sorry, I can't type the needed 'backwards' R). These computers didn't have much memory, couldn't do real fancy graphics, and, compared to today's computers, cost a lot of money. But, these computers introduced a lot of people to the world of computer programming. And, guess what language they were programmed in? That's right - BASIC. Many games written in BASIC appeared at that time and the project you will build here is one of those classics.

Project Design

You've all played the game where someone said "I'm thinking of a number between 1 and 10" (or some other limits). Then, you try to guess the number. The person thinking of the number tells you if you're low or high and you guess again. You continue guessing until you finally guess the number they were thinking of. We will develop a computer version of this game here. The computer will pick a number between 0 and 100 (using the random number generator). You will try to guess the number. Based on your guess, the computer will tell you if you are Too Low or Too High.

Several controls will be needed. Buttons will control game play (one to tell the computer to pick a number, one to tell the computer to check your guess, and one to exit the program). We will use a numeric updown control to set and display your guess. A label control will display the computer's messages to you. This project is saved as **GuessNumber** in the course projects folder (**\CBGVB\BVB Projects**).

Place Controls on Form

Start a new project in Visual Basic. Place three buttons, a text box, and a numeric updown control on the form. Move and size controls until your form should look something like this:

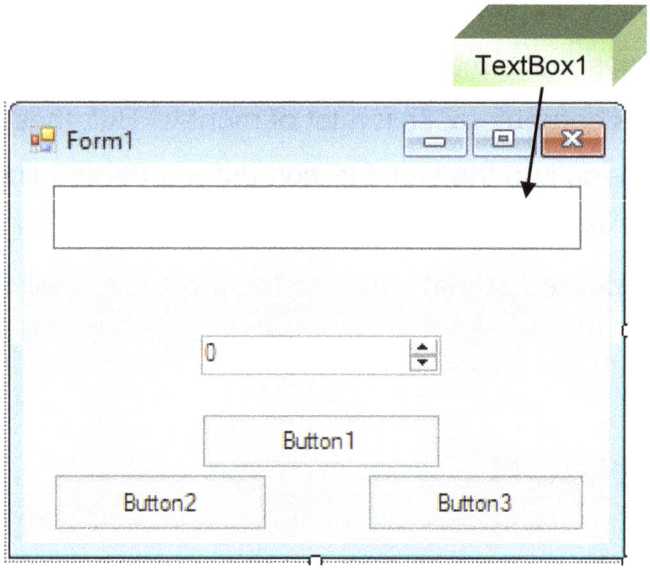

Set Control Properties

Set the control properties using the properties window:

Form1 Form:

Property Name	Property Value
Text	Guess the Number
FormBorderStyle	Fixed Single
StartPosition	CenterScreen

TextBox1 Text Box:

Property Name	Property Value
Name	txtMessage
TextAlign	Center
Font	Arial
Font Size	16
BackColor	White
ForeColor	Blue
ReadOnly	True
TabStop	False

NumericUpDown1 Numeric UpDown:

Property Name	Property Value
Name	nudGuess
Font	Arial
Font Size	16
BackColor	White
ForeColor	Red
TextAlign	Center
Value	50
Minimum	0
Maximum	100
Increment	1
ReadOnly	True
Enabled	False

Button1 Button:

Property Name	**Property Value**
Name	btnCheck
Text	Check Guess
Enabled	False

Button2 Button:

Property Name	**Property Value**
Name	btnPick
Text	Pick Number

Button3 Button:

Property Name	**Property Value**
Name	btnExit
Text	Exit

When done, your form should look something like this (you may have to move and resize a few controls around to get things to fit):

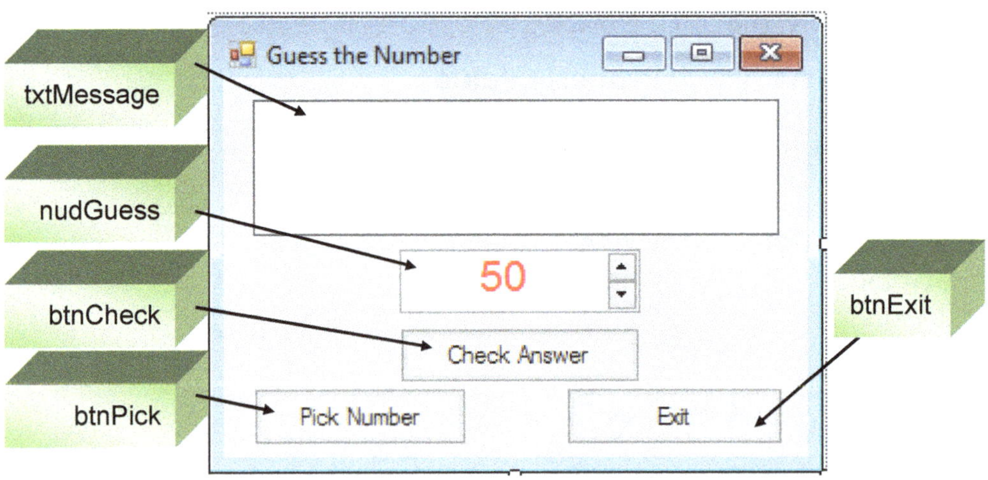

We have set the **Enabled** properties of **btnCheck** and **nudGuess** to **False** initially. We do not want to allow guesses until the **Pick Number** button is clicked.

Write Event Procedures

How does this project work? You click **Pick Number** to have the computer pick a number to guess. This click event will 'enable' the numeric updown control and **Check Guess** button (remember we set their Enabled properties initially at False). Input your guess using the numeric updown control, then click Check Guess. The computer will tell you if your guess is too low, too high, or correct by using the message box (**txtMessage**). So, we need a **Click** event procedure for each button.

Two variables are needed in this project, both **Integer** types. One variable will store the number selected by the computer (the number you are trying to guess). We call this variable **TheNumber**. Your current guess will be saved in the variable **MyGuess**. You will also need a Random object named **MyRandom**. Open the code window and declare these variables in the **general declarations** area:

```
Dim TheNumber As Integer
Dim MyGuess As Integer
Dim MyRandom As New Random
```

After typing these lines, the code window should appear as:

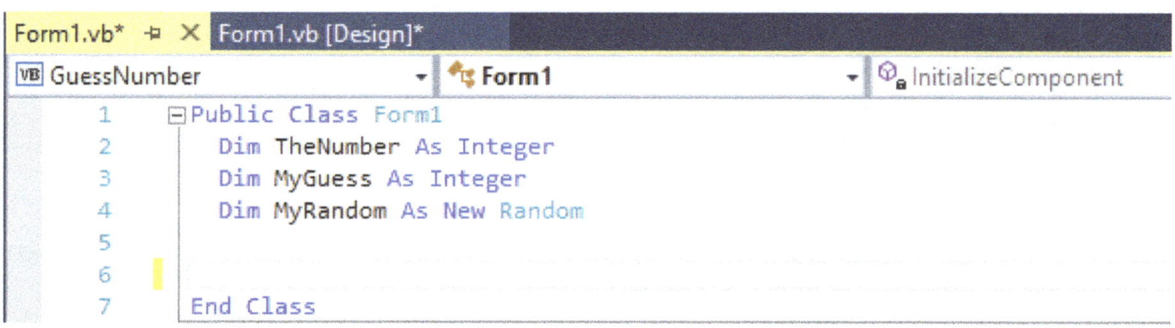

When you click **Pick Number**, the computer needs to perform the following steps:

- Pick a random integer number between 0 and 100.
- Display a message to the user.
- Enable the numeric updown control to allow guesses.
- Enable the Check Guess button to allow guesses.

And, we will add one more step. Many times in Visual Basic, you might want to change the function of a particular control while the program is running. In this game, once we click Pick Number, that button has no further use until the number has been guessed. But, we need a button to tell us the answer if we choose to give up before guessing it. We will use **btnPick** to do this. We will change the Text property and add decision logic to see which 'state' the button is in. If the button says "Pick Number" when it is clicked (the initial state), the above steps will be followed. If the button says "Show Answer" when it is clicked (the 'playing' state), the answer will be shown and the form controls returned to their initial state. This is a common thing to do in Visual Basic.

Here's the **btnPick Click** code that does everything:

```
  Private Sub BtnPick_Click(ByVal sender As System.Object,
ByVal e As System.EventArgs) Handles btnPick.Click
    If btnPick.Text = "Pick Number" Then
      'Get new number and set controls
      TheNumber = MyRandom.Next(101)
      txtMessage.Text = "I'm thinking of a number between 0
and 100"
      nudGuess.Value = 50
      nudGuess.Enabled = True
      btnCheck.Enabled = True
      btnPick.Text = "Show Answer"
    Else
      'Just show the answer and re-set controls
      txtMessage.Text = "The answer is" + Str(TheNumber)
      nudGuess.Value = TheNumber
      nudGuess.Enabled = False
      btnCheck.Enabled = False
      btnPick.Text = "Pick Number"
    End If
  End Sub
```

Study this so you see what is going on. Notice the use of indentation in the If/End If structure. Notice in the line where we first set the txtMessage.Text, it looks like two lines of BASIC code. Type this all on one line - the word processor is making it look like two. In fact, keep an eye out for such things in these notes. It's obvious where a so-called "word wrap" occurs.

When you click **Check Answer**, the computer should see if your current guess (MyGuess) is correct. If so, a message telling you so will appear and the form controls return to their initial state, ready for another game. If not, the computer will display a message telling you if you are too low or too high. You can then make another guess. The **btnCheck Click** event that implements this logic is:

```
  Private Sub BtnCheck_Click(ByVal sender As System.Object,
ByVal e As System.EventArgs) Handles btnCheck.Click
    'Guess is the updown control value
    MyGuess = nudGuess.Value
    If MyGuess = TheNumber Then
      'Correct guess
      txtMessage.Text = "That's it!!"
      nudGuess.Enabled = False
      btnCheck.Enabled = False
      btnPick.Text = "Pick Number"
    ElseIf MyGuess < TheNumber Then
      'Guess is too low
      txtMessage.Text = "Too low!"
    Else
      'Guess is too high
      txtMessage.Text = "Too high!"
    End If
  End Sub
```

The last button click event is **btnExit Click**:

```
  Private Sub BtnExit_Click(ByVal sender As System.Object,
ByVal e As System.EventArgs) Handles btnExit.Click
    Me.Close()
  End Sub
```

Save the project by clicking the **Save All** button in the toolbar.

Run the Project

Run the project. Click **Pick Number** to have the computer to pick a number to guess. Use the arrows on the numeric updown control to input your guess. Click **Check Guess**. Continue adjusting your guess (using the computer clues) until you get the correct answer. Make sure the proper messages display at the proper times. Do you see how the text displayed on btnPick changes as the game 'state' changes? Make sure the **Show Answer** button works properly. Again, always thoroughly test your project to make sure all options work. Save your project if you needed to make any changes.

Here's what the form should look like in the middle of a game:

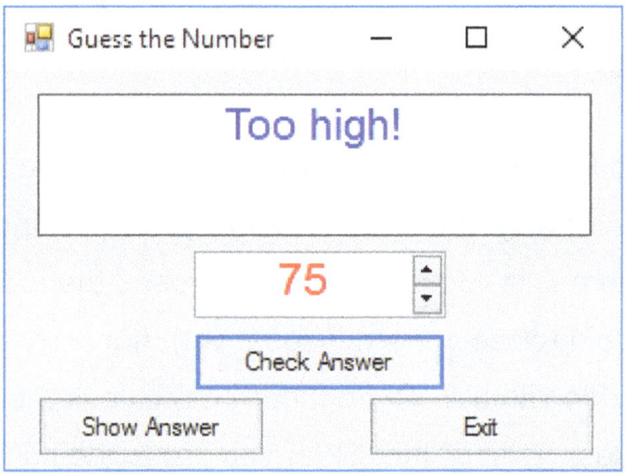

Other Things to Try

You can add other features to this game. One suggestion is to add a text box where the user can input the upper range of numbers that can be guessed. That way, the game could be played by a wide variety of players. Use a maximum value of 10 for little kids, 1000 for older kids.

Another good modification would be to offer more informative messages following a guess. Have you ever played the game where you try to find something and the person who hid the item tells you, as you move around the room, that you are freezing (far away), cold (closer), warm (closer yet), hot (very close), or burning up (right on top of the hidden item)? Try to modify the Guess the Number game to give these kind of clues. That is, the closer you are to the correct number, the warmer you get. To make this change, you will probably need the BASIC **absolute value** function, **Math.Abs**. This function returns the value of a number while ignoring its sign (positive or negative). The format for using Math.Abs is:

```
YourValue = Math.Abs(InputValue)
```

If InputValue is a positive number (greater than zero), YourValue is assigned InputValue. If InputValue is a negative number (less than zero), YourValue is assigned the numerical value of InputValue, without the minus sign. A few examples:

Value	**Math.Abs(Value)**
6	6
-6	6
0	0
-1.1	1.1

In our number guessing game, we can use Math.Abs to see how close a guess is to the actual number. One possible decision logic is:

```
If MyGuess = TheNumber Then
    [BASIC code for correct answer]
ElseIf Math.Abs(MyGuess - TheNumber) <= 2 Then
    [BASIC code when burning up - within 2 of correct answer]
ElseIf Math.Abs(MyGuess - TheNumber) <= 5 Then
    [BASIC code when hot - within 5 of correct answer]
ElseIf Math.Abs(MyGuess - TheNumber) <= 15 Then
    [BASIC code when warm - within 15 of correct answer]
ElseIf Math.Abs(MyGuess - TheNumber) <= 25 Then
    [BASIC code when cold - within 25 of correct answer]
Else
    [BASIC code when freezing - more than 25 away]
End If
```

A last possible change would be the make the project into a math game, and tell the guesser “how far away” the guess is. I’m sure you can think of other ways to change this game. Have fun doing it.

Summary

In this class, you learned about a useful input control for numbers, the numeric updown control. You'll learn about other input controls in the next class. And, you learned about a key part of BASIC programming - decision making. You learned about logical expressions, comparison operators, logical operators, and If/End If structures. And, you will see that the random number object is a fun part of many games. You are well on your way to being a Visual Basic programmer.

7

Icons, Group Boxes, Check Boxes, Radio Buttons

Review and Preview

You should feel very comfortable working within the Visual Basic environment by now and know the three steps of building a project. In this class, we learn about three more controls relating to making choices in Visual Basic: group boxes, check boxes, and radio buttons. We will look at another way to make decisions using the Select Case statement. We'll have some fun making icons for our projects. And, you will build a sandwich making project.

Icons

Have you noticed that whenever you design or run a Visual Basic project, a little picture appears in the upper left hand corner of the form. This picture is called an **icon**. Icons are used throughout the Windows environment. There are probably lots of icons on your Windows desktop - each of these represents some kind of application. Look at files using Windows Explorer. Notice every file has an icon associated with it. Here is a blank Visual Basic form:

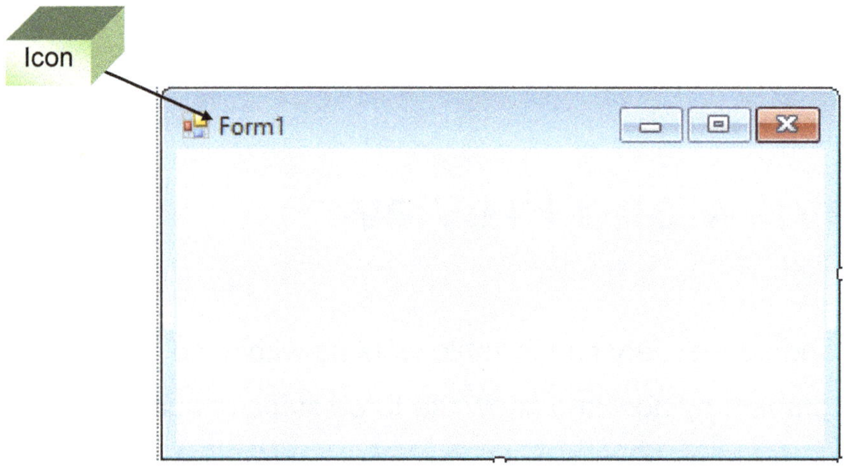

The icon seen is the default Visual Basic icon for forms. It's really kind of boring. Using the **Icon** property of the form, you can change this displayed icon to something a little flashier. Before seeing how to do this, though, let's see how you can design your own icon.

Custom Icons

An icon is a special type of graphics file with an **ico** extension. It is a picture with a specific size of 32 by 32 pixels. The internet has a wealth of free icons you can download to your computer and use. Do a search on 'free 32 x 32 ico files'. You will see a multitude of choices. One site we suggest is:

http://www.softicons.com/toolbar-icons/32x32-free-design-icons-by-aha-soft/

At such a site, you simply download the ico file to your computer and save it.

It is possible to create your own icon using Visual Studio. To create an icon for a particular project, in **Solution Explorer**, right-click the project name, choose **Add**, then **New Item**. This window will appear:

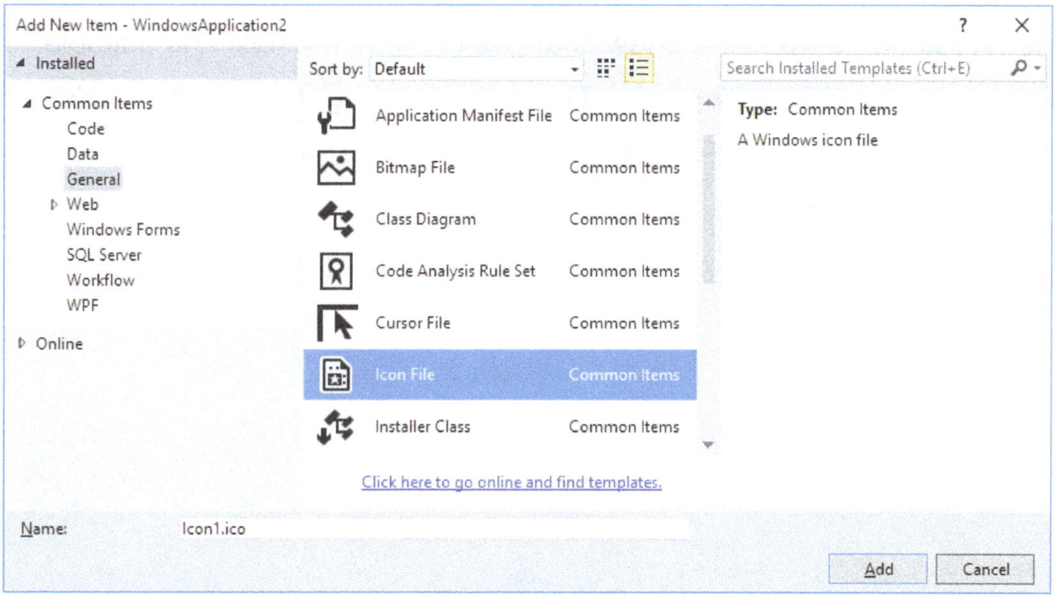

As shown, expand **Common Items** and choose **General**. Then, pick **Icon File**. Name your icon and click **Add**.

A generic icon will open:

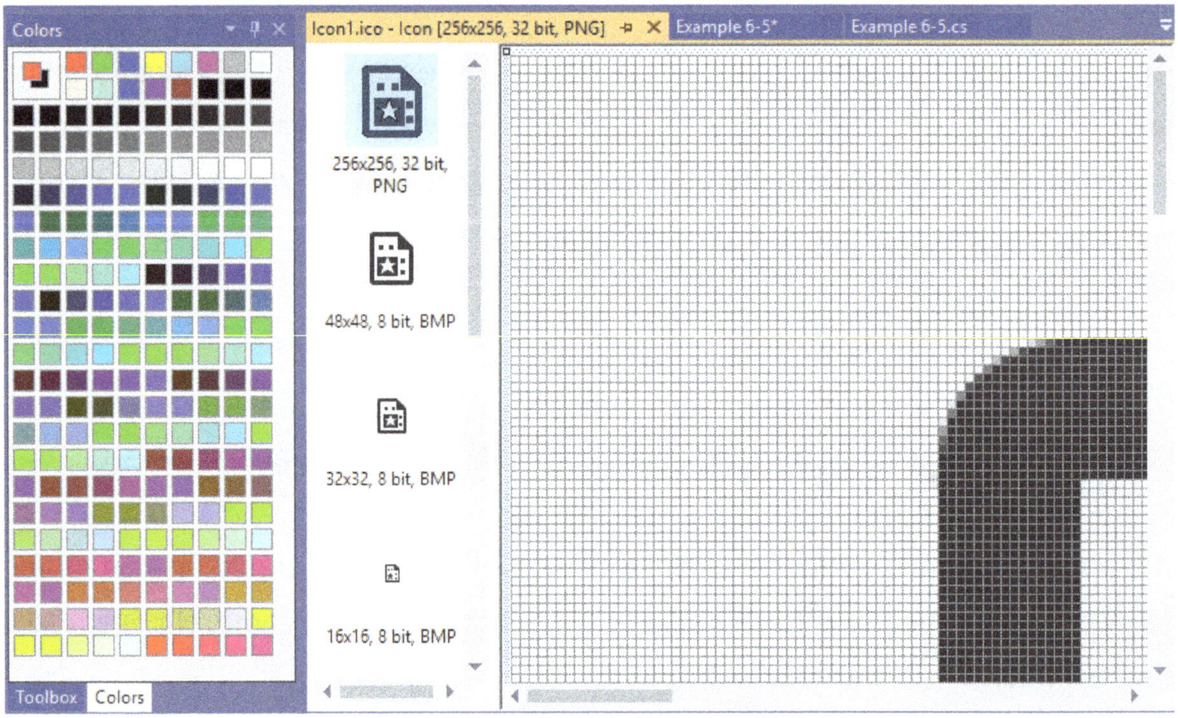

The icon is very large. Let's make a few changes to make it visible and editable. First, resize the image to 32 x 32 pixels. Then, use the magnifying tool to make the image as large as possible. Finally, add a grid to the graphic.

When done, I see:

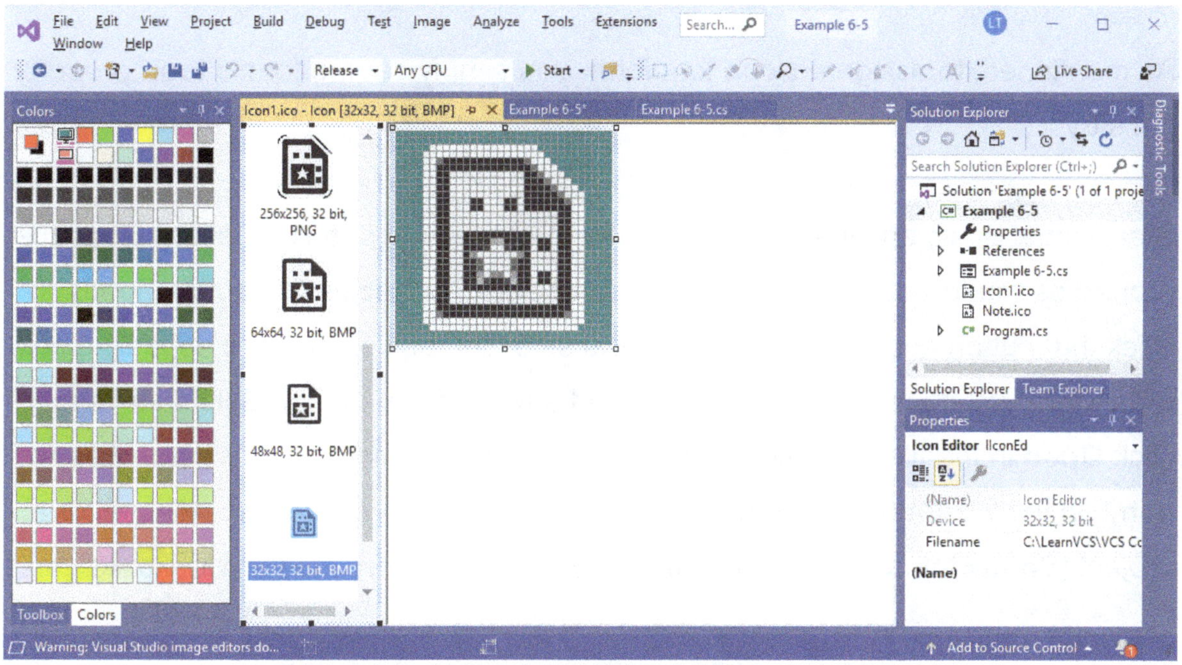

At this point, we can add any detail we need by setting pixels to particular colors. Consult on-line help for the exact steps needed. Once done, the icon will be saved in your project file and can be used by your project. The icon file (**Icon1.ico** in this case) is also listed in **Solution Explorer**:

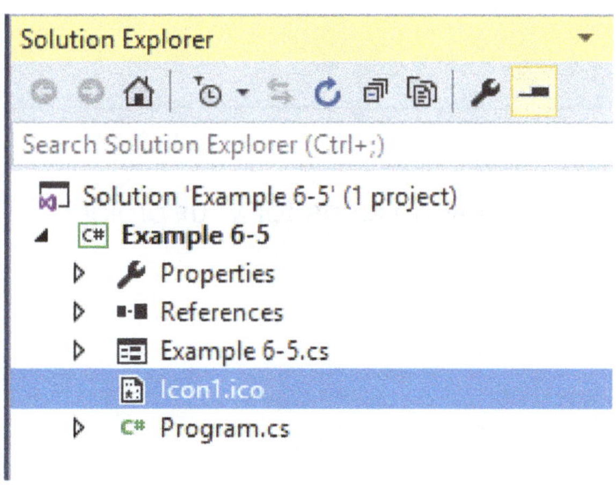

Assigning Icons to Forms

As mentioned, to assign an icon to a form, you simply set the form's **Icon** property. Let's try it.

Start Visual Basic and start a new project. A blank form should appear. Go to the properties window and click on the Icon property. An ellipsis (**...**) button appears. Click that button and a window that allows selection of icon files will appear. Look for an icon you downloaded or created and saved (if you did it). Select an icon, click **Open** in the file window and that icon is now 'attached' to your form. Easy, huh? In the **\CBGVB\BVB Projects\Sandwich** folder is an icon we will use for a project (**Sandwich.ico**). When I attach my sandwich icon, the form looks like this:

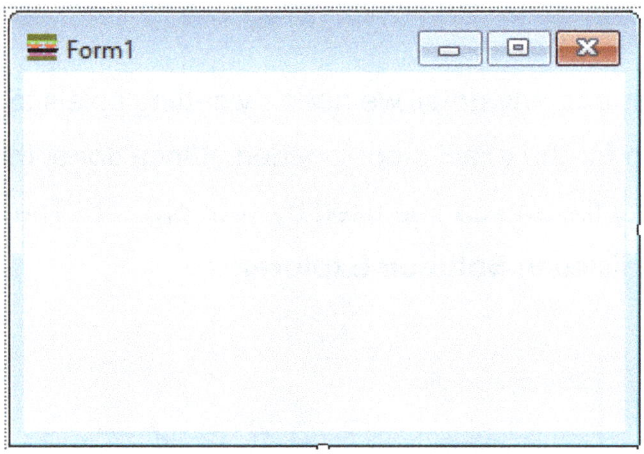

You'll have a lot of fun using unique icons for your projects. It's nice to see a personal touch on your projects.

Group Box Control

A **group box** is simply a control that can hold other controls. Group boxes provide a way to separate and group controls and have an overall enable/disable feature. This means if you disable the group box, all controls in the group box are also disabled. The group box has no events, just properties. The only events of interest are events associated with the controls in the group box. Writing event procedures for these controls is the same as if they were not in a group box. The group box is selected from the toolbox. It appears as:

In Toolbox:

On Form (default properties):

Properties

The group box properties are:

Property	Description
Name	Name used to identify group box. Three letter prefix for group box names is **grp**.
Text	Title information at top of group box.
Font	Sets style, size, and type of title text.
BackColor	Sets group box background color.
ForeColor	Sets color of title text.

Left	Distance from left side of form to left side of group box (X in property window, expand **Location** property).
Top	Distance from top side of form to top side of group box (Y in property window, expand **Location** property).
Width	Width of the group box in pixels (expand **Size** property).
Height	Height of group box in pixels (expand **Size** property).
Enabled	Determines whether all controls within group box can respond to user events (in run mode).
Visible	Determines whether the group box (and attached controls) appears on the form (in run mode).

Like the Form object, the group box is a **container** control, since it 'holds' other controls. Hence, controls placed in a group box will share **BackColor**, **ForeColor** and **Font** properties. To change this, select the desired control (after it is placed on the group box) and change the desired properties.

Moving the group box control on the form uses a different process than other controls. To move the group box, first select the control. Note a 'built-in' handle (looks like two sets of arrows) for moving the control appears at the upper left corner:

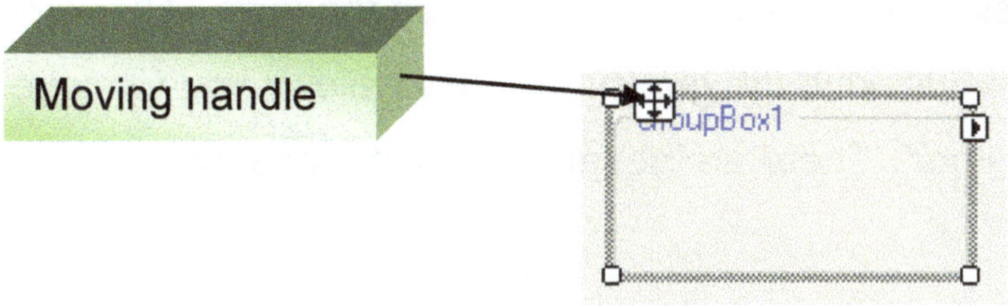

Click on this handle and you can move the control.

Placing Controls in a Group Box

As mentioned, a group box's single task is to hold other controls. To put controls in a group box, you first position and size the group box on the form. Then, the associated controls must be placed in the group box. This allows you to move the group box and controls together. There are several ways to place controls in a group box:

- Place controls directly in the group box using any of the usual methods.
- Draw controls outside the group box and drag them in.
- Copy and paste controls into the group box (prior to the paste operation, make sure the group box is selected).

To insure controls are properly place in a group box, try moving it (use the move handle) and make sure the associated controls move with it. To remove a control from a group box, simply drag it out of the control.

Example

Start Visual Basic and start a new project. Put a group box on the form and resize it so it is fairly large. Select the button control in the Visual Basic toolbox. Drag the control until it is over the group box. Drop the control in the group box. Move the group box and the button should move with it. If it doesn't, it is not properly placed in the group box. If you need to delete the control, select it then press the **Del** key on the keyboard. Try moving the button out of the group box onto the form. Move the button back in the group box.

Put a second button in the group box. Put a numeric updown control in the group box. Notice how the controls are associated with the group box. A warning: if you delete the group box, the associated controls will also be deleted! Run the project. Notice you can click on the buttons and use the numeric updown control. Stop the project. Set the group box Enabled property to False. Run the project again. Notice the group box title (set by the Text property) is grayed and all of the controls on the group box are now disabled - you can't click the buttons or updown control. Hence, by simply setting one Enabled property (that of the group box), we can enable or disable a number of individual controls. Stop the project. Reset the group box Enabled property to True. Set the Visible property to False (will remain visible in design mode). Run the project. The group box and all its controls will not appear. You can use the Visible property of the group box control to hide (or make appear) some set of controls (if your project requires such a step). Stop the project.

Change the Visible property back to True. Place a label control in the group box. Change the BackColor property of the group box. Notice the background color of the label control takes on the same value, while the button controls are unaffected. Recall this is because the group box is a 'container' control. Sometimes, this sharing of properties is a nice benefit, especially with label controls. Other times, it is an annoyance. If you don't want controls to share properties (BackColor, ForeColor, Font) with the group box, you must change the properties you don't like individually. Group boxes will come in very handy with the next two controls we look at: the check box and the radio button. You will see this sharing of color properties is a nice effect with these two controls. It saves us the work of changing lots of colors!

Typical Use of Group Box Control

The usual design steps for a group box control are:

- Set **Name** and **Text** property (perhaps changing **Font**, **BackColor** and **ForeColor** properties).
- Place desired controls in group box. Monitor events of controls in group box using usual techniques.

Check Box Control

A **check box** provides a way to make choices from a group of things. When a check box is selected, a check appears in the box. Each check box acts independently. Some, all, or none of the choices in the group may be selected. An example of where check boxes could be used is choosing from a list of ice cream toppings. You might want it plain, you might want a couple of toppings, you might want it with the works - you decide. Check boxes are also used individually to indicate whether a particular project option is active. For example, it might indicate if a control's text is bold (checked) or not bold (unchecked).

Check boxes are usually grouped in a group box control. The check box control is selected from the toolbox. It appears as:

In Toolbox:

On Form (default properties):

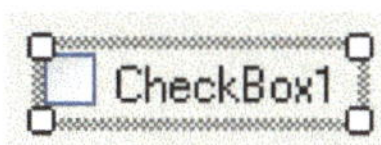

Properties

The check box properties are:

Property	Description
Name	Name used to identify check box. Three letter prefix for check box names is **chk**.
Text	Identifying text next to check box.
TextAlign	Specifies how the displayed text is positioned.
Font	Sets style, size, and type of displayed text.
Checked	Indicates if box is checked (**True**) or unchecked (**False**).

BackColor	Sets check box background color.
ForeColor	Sets color of displayed text.
Left	If on form, distance from left side of form to left side of check box. If in group box, distance from left side of group box to left side of check box (X in properties window, expand **Location** property).
Top	If on form, distance from top side of form to top side of check box. If in group box, distance from top side of group box to top side of check box (Y in properties window, expand **Location** property).
Width	Width of the check box in pixels (expand **Size** property).
Height	Height of check box in pixels (expand **Size** property).
Enabled	Determines whether check box can respond to user events (in run mode).
Visible	Determines whether the check box appears on the form (in run mode).

Pay particular attention to the Left and Top properties. Notice if a check box is in a group box, those two properties give position in the group box, not on the form.

Example

Start Visual Basic and start a new project. Draw a group box - we will always use group boxes to group check boxes. Place three or four check boxes in the group box using techniques discussed earlier. Move the group box to make sure the check boxes are in the group box. Run the project. Click the check boxes and see how the check marks appear and disappear. Notice you can choose as many, or as few, boxes as you like. In code, we would examine each check box's Checked property to determine which boxes are selected. Stop the project. Change the BackColor of the group box. Notice the check box controls' background color changes to match. This is a nice result of using the group box as a container.

Did you notice we didn't have to write any BASIC code to make the check marks appear or go away? That is handled by the check box control. There are check box events, however. Let's look at one.

Events

The only check box event of interest is the CheckedChanged event:

Event	Description
CheckedChanged	Event executed when Checked property of a check box changes.

The event occurs each time a user clicks on a check box, either placing a check mark in the box or removing one.

Typical Use of a Check Box Control

Usual design steps for a check box control are:

- Set the **Name** and **Text** property. Initialize the **Checked** property.
- Monitor **CheckChanged** event to determine when control is clicked. At any time, read **Checked** property to determine check box state.
- You may also want to change the **Font**, **Backcolor** and **Forecolor** properties.

Radio Button Control

A **radio button** provides a way to make a "mutually-exclusive" choice from a group of things. This is a fancy way of saying only <u>one</u> item in the group can be selected. When a radio button is selected, a filled circle appears in the button. No other button in the group can be selected, or have a filled circle. There are many places you can use radio buttons - they can be used whenever you want to make only one choice from a group. Say you have a game for one to four players - use radio buttons to select the number of players. Radio buttons can be used to select background colors. Radio buttons can be used to select difficulty levels in arcade type games. As you write more Visual Basic programs, you will come to rely on the radio button as a device for choice.

Radio buttons always work in groups and each group must be in a separate group box control. Radio buttons in one group box act independently of radio buttons in another group box. So, by using group boxes, you can have as many groups of radio buttons as you want. The radio button control is selected from the toolbox. It appears as:

In Toolbox:

On Form (default properties):

Properties

The radio button properties are:

Property	Description
Name	Name used to identify radio button. Three letter prefix for radio button names is **rdo**.
Text	Identifying text next to radio button.
TextAlign	Specifies how the displayed text is positioned.
Font	Sets style, size, and type of displayed text.
Checked	Indicates if button is selected (**True**) or not selected (**False**). Only one button in a group can have a True value.
BackColor	Sets radio button background color.
ForeColor	Sets color of displayed text.
Left	If on form, distance from left side of form to left side of radio button. If in group box, distance from left side of group box to left side of radio button (X in properties window, expand **Location** property).
Top	If on form, distance from top side of form to top side of radio button. If in group box, distance from top side of group box to top side of radio button (Y in properties window, expand **Location** property).

Width	Width of the radio button in pixels (expand **Size** property).
Height	Height of radio button in pixels (expand **Size** property).
Enabled	Determines whether all controls within radio button can respond to user events (in run mode).
Visible	Determines whether the radio button appears on the form (in run mode).

One button in each group of radio buttons should always have a Checked property set to True in design mode. And, again, if a radio button is in a group box, the Left and Top properties give position in the group box, not on the form.

Example

Start Visual Basic and start a new project. Draw a group box. Remember, each individual group of radio buttons (we need one group for each decision we make) has to be in a separate group box. Place three or four radio buttons in the group box using techniques discussed earlier. Set one of the buttons Checked property to True. Run the project. Notice one button has a filled circle (the one you initialized the Checked property for). Click another radio button. That button will be filled while the previously filled button will no longer be filled. Keep clicking buttons to get the idea of how they work. In event procedures, we would examine each radio button's Checked property to determine which one is selected. Stop the project. Did you notice that, like for check boxes, we didn't have to write any BASIC code to make the filled circles appear or go away? That is handled by the control itself. Change the group box BackColor property and notice all the 'contained' radio buttons also change background color.

Draw another group box on the form. Put two or three radio buttons in that group box and set one button's Checked property to True. As always, make sure the buttons are properly placed in the group box. Run the project. Change the selected button in this second group. Notice changing this group of radio buttons has no effect on the earlier group. Remember that radio buttons in one group box do not affect radio buttons in another. Group boxes are used to implement separate choices. Try more group boxes and radio buttons if you want. Stop the project.

Events

The only radio button event of interest is the CheckedChanged event:

Event	Description
CheckedChanged	Event executed when the Checked property changes.

When one radio button acting in a group attains a Checked property of True, the Checked property of all other buttons in its group is set to False. We don't have to write BASIC code to do this - it is automatic.

Typical Use of a Radio Button Control

Usual design steps for a radio button control are:

- Establish a group of radio buttons by placing them in the same group box control
- For each button in the group, set the **Name** (give each button a similar name to identify them with the group) and **Text** property. You might also change the **Font**, **BackColor** and **Forecolor** properties.
- Initialize the **Checked** property of one button to **True**.
- Monitor the **CheckChanged** event of each radio button in the group to determine when a button is clicked. The 'last clicked' button in the group will always have a **Checked** property of **True**.

BASIC – The Fourth Lesson

By now, you've learned a lot about the BASIC language. In this class, we look at just one new idea - another way to make decisions.

Decisions - Select Case

In the previous class, we studied the If/End If structure as a way of letting Visual Basic make decisions using comparison operators and logical operators. We saw that the If/End If structure is very flexible and allows us to implement a variety of decision logic's. Many times in making decisions, we simply want to examine the value of just one variable or expression. Based on whatever values that expression might have, we want to take particular actions in our BASIC code. We could implement such a logic using If, ElseIf, and End If statements. As an example, say we want to do different things if the variable A is 0, 1, 2, 3, 4, or 5. The BASIC code, using an If/End If structure, to do this is:

```
If A = 0 Then
    [BASIC code for A = 0]
ElseIf A = 1 Then
    [BASIC code for A = 1]
ElseIf A = 2 Then
    [BASIC code for A = 2]
ElseIf A = 3 Then
    [BASIC code for A = 3]
ElseIf A = 4 Then
    [BASIC code for A = 4]
ElseIf A = 5 Then
    [BASIC code for A = 5]
End If
```

This code will work but there is a lot of repetition. It is also difficult to make simple changes to values A might have. BASIC offers another way to make decisions such as this.

The **Select Case** statement is used to make decisions based on the value of a single variable or expression. A typical structure for the Select Case statement is:

```
Select Case TestExpression
Case Comparison1
    [BASIC code to execute if Comparison1 matches TestExpression]
Case Comparison2
    [BASIC code to execute if Comparison2 matches TestExpression]
Case Comparison3
    [BASIC code to execute if Comparison3 matches TestExpression]
Case Comparison4
    [BASIC code to execute if Comparison4 matches TestExpression]
Case Else
    [BASIC code to execute if no comparison matches TestExpression]
End Select
```

The **TestExpression** is any BASIC expression. **Select** Case goes through the list of **Case** statements, top to bottom, until it finds a Case where TestExpression matches the listed Case comparison. The BASIC statements associated with that particular Case are then executed and program execution moves to the first line after the **End Select** statement. If no match is found, the statements associated with **Case Else** are executed. If there is no Case Else and no match is found, none of the statements in the Select Case/End Select structure are executed. There is no limit to the number of Case statements allowed. What do the comparisons in the Case statements look like?

The simplest comparison is just a single value against which TestExpression is tested for equality. For example,

```
Case 6
```

would check to see if the TestExpression is equal to 6. You can use the **To** keyword to check against a range of values. For example,

```
Case 6 To 14
```

checks to see if TestExpression is between 6 and 14 (inclusive). The **Is** keyword can be used with a comparison operator to make a logical comparison. For example,

```
Case Is > 8
```

would check to see if TestExpression is greater than 8. Multiple comparison expressions can be used in one Case statement using commas as separators. The commas act like the **Or** logical operator. To see if TestExpression is between 2 and 4, between 8 and 12, or less than 2, we would use the Case statement:

```
Case 2 To 4, 8 To 12, Is < 2
```

Whenever you are making multiple checks on a value of an expression, consider the **Select Case** statement instead of the **If** statement.

As mentioned, you can have as many Case statements as you want. But, like the If/End If structure, only one section of BASIC code in a Select Case structure will be executed. This means that once BASIC has found a Case comparison that matches the Select Case expression, it will execute that section of code then leave the structure and execute the first line of code following the End Select statement. The rule for Select Case structures is: only the statements associated with the first matching Case will be executed.

A good example where Select Case is more appropriate than If was provided at the end of last class. Remember the 'Guess the Number' game? We suggested a variation where, rather than tell the user if they are high or low, we would tell the user how "warm" they were. An If/End If structure that implements such a logic was given as (recall TheNumber is the correct answer and MyGuess is the user's guess):

```
If MyGuess = TheNumber Then
    [BASIC code for correct answer]
ElseIf Math.Abs(MyGuess - TheNumber) <= 2 Then
    [BASIC code when burning up - within 2 of correct answer]
ElseIf Math.Abs(MyGuess - TheNumber) <= 5 Then
    [BASIC code when hot - within 5 of correct answer]
ElseIf Math.Abs(MyGuess - TheNumber) <= 15 Then
    [BASIC code when warm - within 15 of correct answer]
ElseIf Math.Abs(MyGuess - TheNumber) <= 25 Then
    [BASIC code when cold - within 25 of correct answer]
Else
    [BASIC code when freezing - more than 25 away]
End If
```

Can you see how this more concise Select Case/End Select structure might be a little easier to understand and modify, if necessary?

```
Select Case Math.Abs(MyGuess - TheNumber)
Case 0
    [BASIC code for correct answer]
Case Is <= 2
    [BASIC code when burning up - within 2 of correct answer]
Case Is <= 5
    [BASIC code when hot - within 5 of correct answer]
Case Is <= 15
    [BASIC code when warm - within 15 of correct answer]
Case Is <= 25
    [BASIC code when cold - within 25 of correct answer]
Case Else
    [BASIC code when freezing - more than 25 away]
End Select
```

Project – Sandwich Maker

The local sandwich shop has heard about your fantastic Visual Basic programming skills and has hired you to make a computer version of their ordering system. What a great place to try out your skills with group boxes, check boxes, and radio buttons!

Project Design

In a project like this, making a computer version of an existing process (ordering a sandwich), the design steps are usually pretty straightforward. We asked the sandwich shop how they do things and this is what they told us:

- Three bread choices (can only pick one): white, wheat, rye
- Five meat choices (pick as many as you want): roast beef, ham, turkey, pastrami, salami
- Three cheese choices (can only pick one): none, American, Swiss
- Six condiment choices (pick as many as you want): mustard, mayonnaise, lettuce, tomato, onion, pickles

It should be obvious what controls are needed.

We will need a group of three radio buttons for bread, a group of five check boxes for meat, a group of three radio buttons for cheese, and six check boxes for condiments. We'll add a button for clearing the menu board, a button to 'build' the sandwich, and a text box, with a label for titling information, where we will print out the sandwich order. This project is saved as **Sandwich** in the course projects folder (**\CBGVB\BVB Projects**).

Place Controls on Form

Start a new project in Visual Basic. Place and resize four group boxes on the form. Place three radio buttons (for bread choices) in the first group box (remember how to properly place controls in a group box). Place five check boxes (for meat choices) in the second group box. Place three radio buttons (for cheese choices) in the third group box. Place six check boxes (for condiment choices) in the fourth group box. Add two buttons, a label and a text box. My form looks like this:

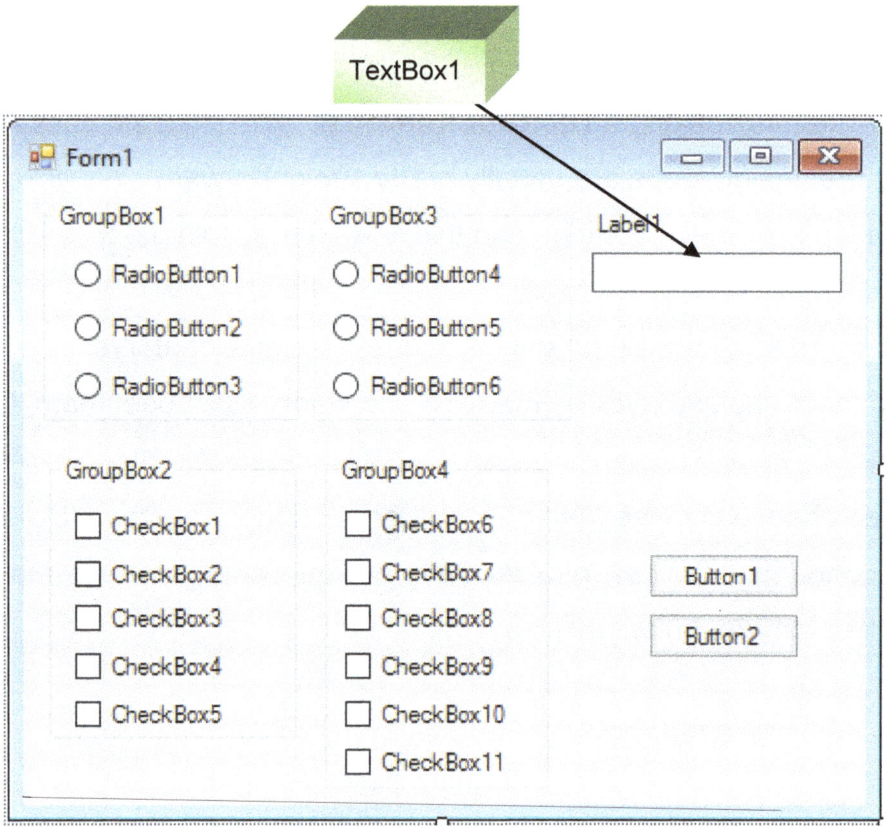

Yes, there are lots of controls involved when working with check boxes and radio buttons, and even more properties. Get ready!

Set Control Properties

Set the control properties using the properties window:

Form1 Form:

Property Name	Property Value
Text	Sandwich Maker
FormBorderStyle	Fixed Single
StartPosition	CenterScreen
Icon	[Pick one you make with IconEdit or you can use my little sandwich icon]

GroupBox1 Group Box:

Property Name	Property Value
Name	grpBread
Text	Bread
Font Size	10
Font Style	Bold

RadioButton1 Radio Button:

Property Name	Property Value
Name	rdoWhite
Text	White
Font Size	8
Font Style	Regular
Checked	True

RadioButton2 Radio Button:

Property Name	Property Value
Name	rdoWheat
Text	Wheat
Font Size	8
Font Style	Regular

RadioButton3 Radio Button:

Property Name	Property Value
Name	rdoRye
Text	Rye
Font Size	8
Font Style	Regular

GroupBox2 Group Box:

Property Name	Property Value
Name	grpMeats
Text	Meats
Font Size	10
Font Style	Bold

CheckBox1 Check Box:

Property Name	Property Value
Name	chkRoastBeef
Text	Roast Beef
Font Size	8
Font Style	Regular

CheckBox2 Check Box:

Property Name	Property Value
Name	chkHam
Text	Ham
Font Size	8
Font Style	Regular

CheckBox3 Check Box:

Property Name	Property Value
Name	chkTurkey
Text	Turkey
Font Size	8
Font Style	Regular

CheckBox4 Check Box:

Property Name	Property Value
Name	chkPastrami
Text	Pastrami
Font Size	8
Font Style	Regular

CheckBox5 Check Box:

Property Name	Property Value
Name	chkSalami
Text	Salami
Font Size	8
Font Style	Regular

GroupBox3 Group Box:

Property Name	Property Value
Name	grpCheese
Text	Cheese
Font Size	10
Font Style	Bold

RadioButton4 Radio Button:

Property Name	Property Value
Name	rdoNone
Text	None
Font Size	8
Font Style	Regular
Checked	True

RadioButton5 Radio Button:

Property Name	Property Value
Name	rdoAmerican
Text	American
Font Size	8
Font Style	Regular

RadioButton6 Radio Button:

Property Name	Property Value
Name	rdoSwiss
Text	Swiss
Font Size	8
Font Style	Regular

GroupBox4 Group Box:

Property Name	Property Value
Name	grpCondiments
Text	Condiments
Font Size	10
Font Style	Bold

CheckBox6 Check Box:

Property Name	Property Value
Name	chkMustard
Text	Mustard
Font Size	8
Font Style	Regular

CheckBox7 Check Box:

Property Name	Property Value
Name	chkMayo
Text	Mayonnaise
Font Size	8
Font Style	Regular

CheckBox8 Check Box:

Property Name	Property Value
Name	chkLettuce
Text	Lettuce
Font Size	8
Font Style	Regular

CheckBox9 Check Box:

Property Name	Property Value
Name	chkTomato
Text	Tomato
Font Size	8
Font Style	Regular

CheckBox10 Check Box:

Property Name	Property Value
Name	chkOnions
Text	Onions
Font Size	8
Font Style	Regular

CheckBox11 Check Box:

Property Name	Property Value
Name	chkPickles
Text	Pickles
Font Size	8
Font Style	Regular

Label1 Label:

Property Name	Property Value
Name	lblOrder
Text	Order:
Font Size	10
Font Style	Bold

TextBox1 Text Box:

Property Name	Property Value
Name	txtOrder
MultiLine	True
ScrollBars	Vertical

Button1 Button:

Property Name	**Property Value**
Name	btnOrder
Text	Order

Button2 Button:

Property Name	**Property Value**
Name	btnClear
Text	Clear

When done, my form looks like this:

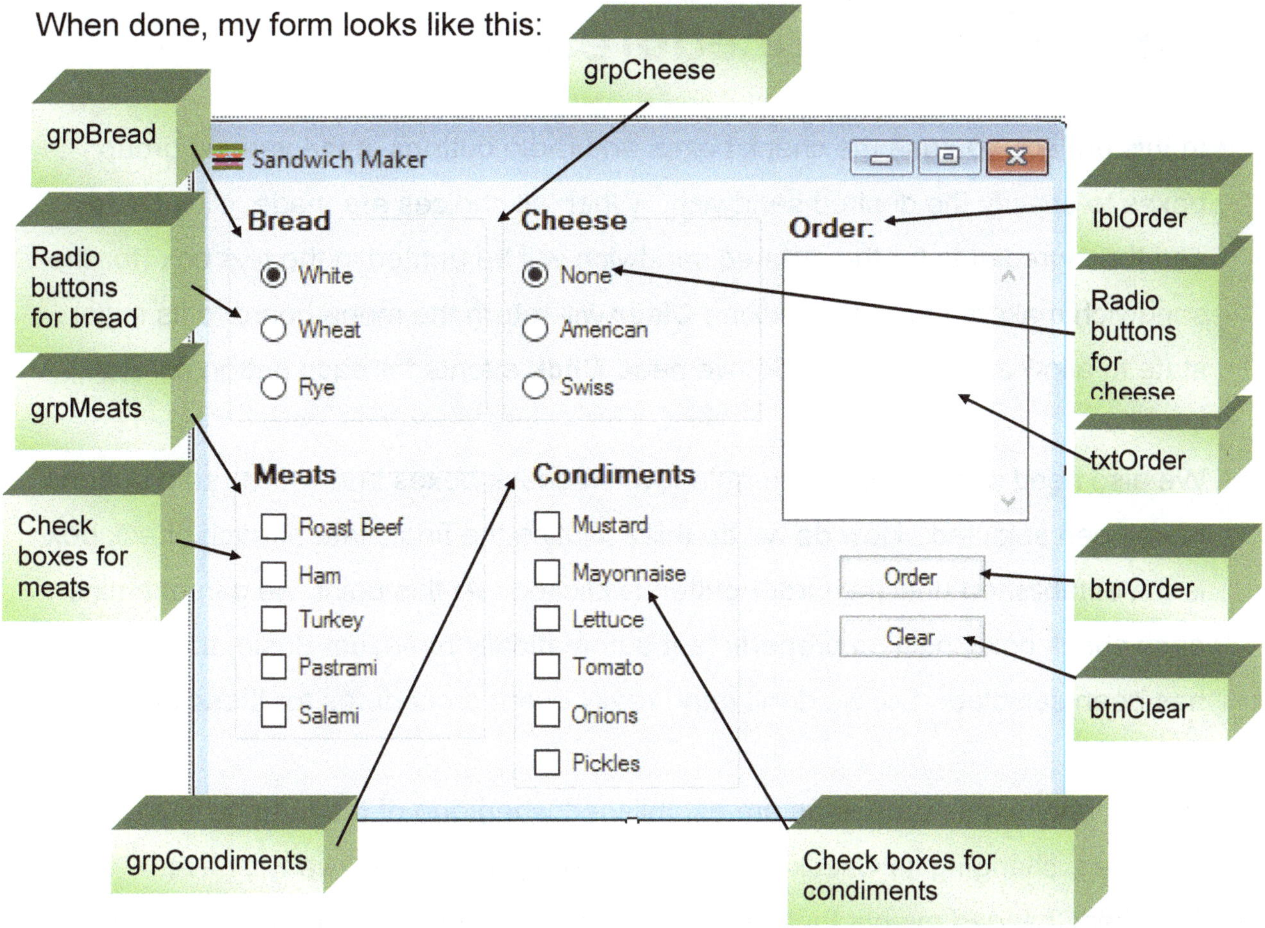

As we said, there is a lot of work involved when working with check boxes and radio buttons - many controls to place in group boxes and many properties to set. This is a part of developing computer applications. Many times, the work is tedious and uninteresting. But, you have the satisfaction of knowing, once complete, your project will have a professional looking interface with controls every user knows how to use. Now, let's write the event procedures - they're pretty easy.

Write Event Procedures

In this project, you use the check boxes and radio buttons in the various group boxes to specify the desired sandwich. When all choices are made, click **Order** and the ingredients for the ordered sandwich will be printed in the text box (for the sandwich makers to read). Clicking **Clear** will return the menu board to its initial state to allow another order. So, we need **Click** events for each button control.

We also need some way to determine which check boxes and which radio buttons have been selected. How do we do this? Notice the final state of each check box is not established until the Order button is clicked. At this point, we can examine each check box Checked property (set automatically by Visual Basic) to see if it has been selected. So, we don't need really event procedures for these boxes.

Radio button value properties are established when one of the buttons in a group is clicked, changing its Checked property. For radio buttons, we will have CheckedChanged events that keep track of which button in a group is currently selected. Two integer variables are needed, one to keep track of which bread (**BreadChoice**) is selected and one to keep track of which cheese (**CheeseChoice**) is selected. We will use these values to indicate choices:

BreadChoice:

Value	Selected Bread
1	White
2	Wheat
3	Rye

CheeseChoice:

Value	Selected Cheese
0	None
1	American
2	Swiss

Using variables to indicate radio button choices is common.

We will add two more variables (**NumberMeats** and **NumberCondiments**) to count how many meats and condiments are selected. Open the code window and declare these variables in the **general declarations** area:

```
Dim BreadChoice As Integer
Dim CheeseChoice As Integer
Dim NumberMeats as Integer
Dim NumberCondiments As Integer
```

The code window should look like this:

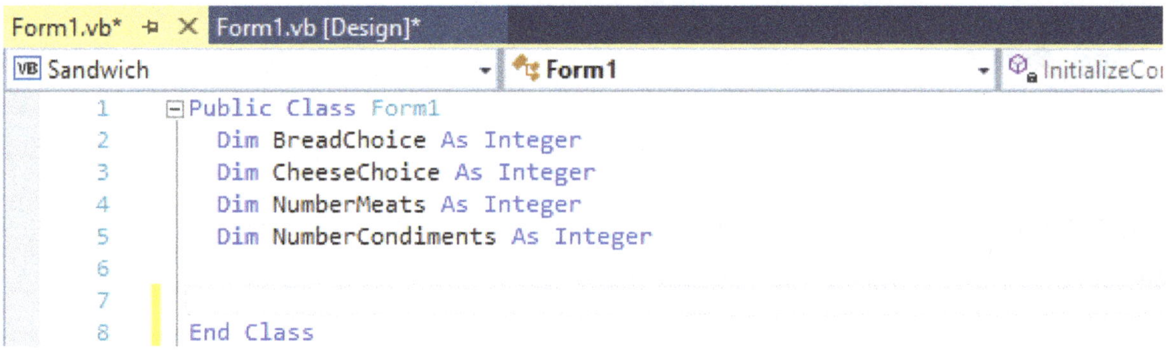

BreadChoice and CheeseChoice must be initialized to match the initially selected radio buttons: **rdoWhite** (white bread) has an initial True value (for Checked property) in the bread group, so BreadChoice is initially 1; **rdoNone** (no cheese) has an initial True value (for Checked property) in the cheese group, so CheeseChoice is initially 0. Set these initial values in the **Form1 Load** procedure (recall this is always a good place to set values the first time you use them):

```
  Private Sub Form1_Load(ByVal sender As Object, ByVal e As
System.EventArgs) Handles MyBase.Load
    'Initialize bread and cheese choices
    BreadChoice = 1
    CheeseChoice = 0
  End Sub
```

After all choices have been input on the sandwich menu board, you click **Order**. At this point, the computer needs to do the following:

- Decide which bread was selected
- Decide which meats (if any) were selected
- Decide which cheese (if any) was selected
- Decide which condiments (if any) were selected
- Place 'order' in text box

Let's look at how each decision is made.

The bread and cheese decisions are similar - they both use radio buttons. The selected bread is given by the variable BreadChoice. BreadChoice is established in the CheckedChanged events for each of the three bread radio buttons. It is easy code. First, **rdoWhite CheckedChanged:**

```
  Private Sub RdoWhite_CheckedChanged(ByVal sender As
System.Object, ByVal e As System.EventArgs) Handles
rdoWhite.CheckedChanged
    'White bread selected
    BreadChoice = 1
  End Sub
```

rdoWheat CheckedChanged:

```
  Private Sub RdoWheat_CheckedChanged(ByVal sender As
System.Object, ByVal e As System.EventArgs) Handles
rdoWheat.CheckedChanged
    'Wheat bread selected
    BreadChoice = 2
  End Sub
```

rdoRye CheckedChanged:

```
  Private Sub RdoRye_CheckedChanged(ByVal sender As
System.Object, ByVal e As System.EventArgs) Handles
rdoRye.CheckedChanged
    'Rye bread selected
    BreadChoice = 3
  End Sub
```

Similar code is used to determine CheeseChoice. The **rdoNone CheckedChanged** event procedure:

```
  Private Sub RdoNone_CheckedChanged(ByVal sender As
System.Object, ByVal e As System.EventArgs) Handles
rdoNone.CheckedChanged
    'No cheese selected
    CheeseChoice = 0
  End Sub
```

rdoAmerican CheckedChanged:

```
  Private Sub RdoAmerican_CheckedChanged(ByVal sender As
System.Object, ByVal e As System.EventArgs) Handles
rdoAmerican.CheckedChanged
    'American cheese selected
    CheeseChoice = 1
  End Sub
```

rdoSwiss CheckedChanged:

```
  Private Sub RdoSwiss_CheckedChanged(ByVal sender As
System.Object, ByVal e As System.EventArgs) Handles
rdoSwiss.CheckedChanged
    'Swiss cheese selected
    CheeseChoice = 2
  End Sub
```

With the above code, we see that by the time Order is clicked, the bread and cheese choices will be known. We do not know the meat and condiment choices, however. The only way to determine these choices is to examine each individual check box Checked property to see if it is checked or not. This is done in the **btnOrder Click** event procedure. We also place the complete order in the text box control in this procedure. Let's see how.

The displayed information in the text box is stored in its **Text** property. We build this multi-line Text property in stages. The stages are:

- Establish bread type in Text property (use Select Case).
- Replace Text property with previous value plus any added meat(s) (use an If/End If for each meat).
- Replace Text property with previous value plus any added cheese (use Select Case).
- Replace Text property with previous value plus any added condiments(s) (use an If/End If for each condiment).
- Text property is complete.

As items are added to the Text property (we'll be using lots of concatenations), we would also like to put each item on a separate line. We use a Visual Basic **control character constant** to do that – **ControlChars.CrLf**. This is a value that tells the Text property to begin a new line. The letters at the end stand for carriage return (Cr) and line feed (Lf), a throwback to typewriter days! Here's the **btnOrder Click** event procedure that implements the steps of determining meat and condiments and building the Text property of txtOrder:

```
  Private Sub BtnOrder_Click(ByVal sender As System.Object,
ByVal e As System.EventArgs) Handles btnOrder.Click
    'Start Text with bread type
    txtOrder.Text = "Sandwich Order:" & ControlChars.CrLf
    Select Case BreadChoice
      Case 1
        txtOrder.Text = txtOrder.Text & "White Bread" &
ControlChars.CrLf
      Case 2
        txtOrder.Text = txtOrder.Text & "Wheat Bread" &
ControlChars.CrLf
      Case 3
        txtOrder.Text = txtOrder.Text & "Rye Bread" &
ControlChars.CrLf
    End Select
    'Add and count meats
```

```
    NumberMeats = 0
    If chkRoastBeef.Checked Then
      NumberMeats = NumberMeats + 1
      txtOrder.Text = txtOrder.Text & "Roast Beef" &
ControlChars.CrLf
    End If
    If chkHam.Checked Then
      NumberMeats = NumberMeats + 1
      txtOrder.Text = txtOrder.Text & "Ham" &
ControlChars.CrLf
    End If
    If chkTurkey.Checked Then
      NumberMeats = NumberMeats + 1
      txtOrder.Text = txtOrder.Text & "Turkey" &
ControlChars.CrLf
    End If
    If chkPastrami.Checked Then
      NumberMeats = NumberMeats + 1
      txtOrder.Text = txtOrder.Text & "Pastrami" &
ControlChars.CrLf
    End If
    If chkSalami.Checked Then
      NumberMeats = NumberMeats + 1
      txtOrder.Text = txtOrder.Text & "Salami" &
ControlChars.CrLf
    End If
    'If no meats picked, say so
    If NumberMeats = 0 Then
      txtOrder.Text = txtOrder.Text & "No Meat" &
ControlChars.CrLf
    End If
    'Add cheese type
    Select Case CheeseChoice
      Case 0
        txtOrder.Text = txtOrder.Text & "No Cheese" &
ControlChars.CrLf
      Case 1
        txtOrder.Text = txtOrder.Text & "American Cheese" &
ControlChars.CrLf
      Case 2
        txtOrder.Text = txtOrder.Text & "Swiss Cheese" &
ControlChars.CrLf
    End Select
    'Finally, add  and count condiments
    NumberCondiments = 0
    If chkMustard.Checked Then
      NumberCondiments = NumberCondiments + 1
```

```
      txtOrder.Text = txtOrder.Text & "Mustard" &
ControlChars.CrLf
    End If
    If chkMayo.Checked Then
      NumberCondiments = NumberCondiments + 1
      txtOrder.Text = txtOrder.Text & "Mayonnaise" &
ControlChars.CrLf
    End If
    If chkLettuce.Checked Then
      NumberCondiments = NumberCondiments + 1
      txtOrder.Text = txtOrder.Text & "Lettuce" &
ControlChars.CrLf
    End If
    If chkTomato.Checked Then
      NumberCondiments = NumberCondiments + 1
      txtOrder.Text = txtOrder.Text & "Tomato" &
ControlChars.CrLf
    End If
    If chkOnions.Checked Then
      NumberCondiments = NumberCondiments + 1
      txtOrder.Text = txtOrder.Text & "Onions" &
ControlChars.CrLf
    End If
    If chkPickles.Checked Then
      NumberCondiments = NumberCondiments + 1
      txtOrder.Text = txtOrder.Text & "Pickles" &
ControlChars.CrLf
    End If
    'If no condiments picked, say so
    If NumberCondiments = 0 Then
      txtOrder.Text = txtOrder.Text & "No Condiments" &
ControlChars.CrLf
    End If
  End Sub
```

Wow! That's one long event procedure. And, after we're done, all we really have is just one very long txtOrder.Text property. But, with your BASIC knowledge, you should be able to see it's really not that complicated, just long. Each step in the procedure is very logical.

A few comments. First, as you type in the procedure from these notes, be aware of places the word processor 'word wraps' a line because it has gone past the right margin. It appears there is a new line, but don't start a new line in your BASIC code. Type each line of code on just one line in the Visual Basic code window. Second, this is a great place to practice your copying and pasting skills. Notice how a lot of the code is very similar. Use copy and paste (highlight text, select **Edit** menu, then **Copy** - move to paste location, select **Edit** menu, then **Paste**). Once you paste text, make sure you make needed changes to the pasted text! Third, for long procedures like this, I suggest typing in one section of code (for example, the cheese choice), saving the project, and then running the project to make sure this section works. Then, add another section and test it. Then, add another section and test it. Visual Basic makes such incremental additions very easy. This also lessens the amount of program "debugging" you need to do.

We need one last event procedure - the **btnClear Click** event. Clicking Clear will reset the bread and cheese choices, clear all the check boxes, and clear the text box. This event is:

```
  Private Sub BtnClear_Click(ByVal sender As System.Object,
ByVal e As System.EventArgs) Handles btnClear.Click
    'Set bread to white
    BreadChoice = 1
    rdoWhite.Checked = True
    'Clear all meat choices
    chkRoastBeef.Checked = False
    chkHam.Checked = False
    chkTurkey.Checked = False
    chkPastrami.Checked = False
    chkSalami.Checked = False
    'Set cheese to none
    CheeseChoice = 0
    rdoNone.Checked = True
    'Clear all condiment choices
    chkMustard.Checked = False
    chkMayo.Checked = False
    chkLettuce.Checked = False
    chkTomato.Checked = False
    chkOnions.Checked = False
    chkPickles.Checked = False
    'Clear text box
    txtOrder.Text = ""
  End Sub
```

You're done! Save your project by clicking the **Save All** button in the toolbar.

Run the Project

Run the project. Make choices on the menu board, then click **Order**. Pretty cool, huh? Here's my favorite sandwich:

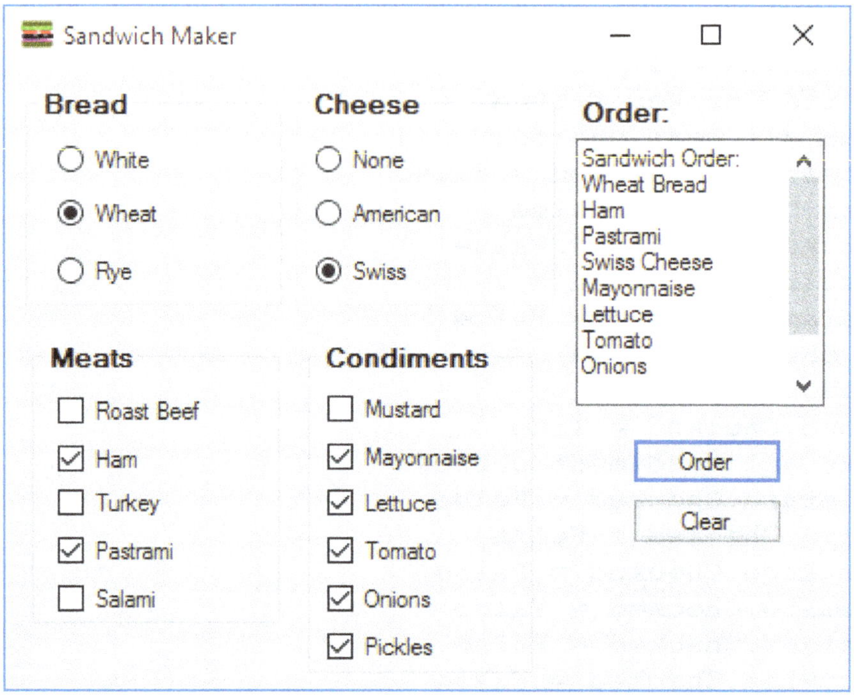

As always, make sure all check boxes and radio buttons work and provide the proper information in the text box. Make sure the **Clear** button works. Notice the text box scroll bar is active only when there is a long sandwich order. If something doesn't work as it should, recheck your control properties and event procedures. Save your project if you needed to make any changes.

Other Things to Try

Notice the only ways to stop this project are to click on the Visual Basic toolbar's Stop button or to click the box that looks like an **X** in the upper right corner of the Sandwich Maker form. We probably should have put an Exit button on the form. Try adding one and its code. Remember the BASIC **Me.Close()** statement stops a project.

The sandwich shop owner liked your program so much, she wants to hook it up to her cash register. She wants you to modify the program so it also prints out (at the bottom) how much the sandwich cost. We'll give the steps - you do the work. The owner says a sandwich costs $3.95. There is an additional $0.75 charge for each extra meat selection (one meat is included in the $3.95 price) and there is an 8% sales tax. Now, the steps: (1) define a single type variable **Cost** to compute the sandwich cost and (2) after setting the text box Text property, compute Cost using this code segment (place this at the end, right before the **End Sub** line in the **btnOrder Click** event procedure):

```
'Start with basic cost
Cost = 3.95
'Check for extra meats
If NumberMeats > 1 Then
  Cost = Cost + (NumberMeats - 1) * 0.75
End If
'Add 8 percent sales tax
Cost = Cost + 0.08 * Cost
'Add cost to text property
txtOrder.Text = txtOrder.Text & Str(Cost)
```

Can you see how this works? Particularly, look at the If/End If to see if we need to charge for extra meat. Now, run the project and see the cost magically appear. The Cost value may have more or less than the two decimals we like to see when working with money. Using the Str function to convert decimal numbers to strings, we have no control on how many (if any) decimals are displayed. There is another

BASIC function that does allow us to do that - the BASIC **Format** function. We'll show you how to use Format to display dollar amounts. To find out more about Format (and it is a very useful function - we just don't use it in this course), consult the Visual Basic on-line help system. To display two decimals for cost, replace the last line of code with:

```
txtOrder.Text = txtOrder.Text & Format(Cost, "$0.00")
```

One last modification to this project might be to add some way to enter how much money the customer gave you for the sandwich and have the computer tell you how much change the customer gets. Can you think of a way to do this? Try it. You would want to use the Format function here. It's difficult to give $1.2345 in change!

Summary

In this class, we learned about three very useful controls for making choices: the group box, check boxes, and radio buttons. And, we looked at another way to make decisions: Select Case. Using these new tools, you built your biggest project yet - the Sandwich Maker. This project had a lot of controls, a lot of properties to set, and a lot of BASIC code to write. But, that's how most projects are. But, I think you see that with careful planning and a methodical approach (following the three project steps), building such a complicated project is not really that hard. In the next class, we start looking at a really fun part of Visual Basic - graphics!

8

Panels, Mouse Events, Colors

Review and Preview

You've seen and learned how to use lots of controls in the Visual Basic toolbox. In this class, we begin looking at a very fun part of Visual Basic - adding graphics capabilities to our projects. A key control for such capabilities is the panel. We will look at this control in detail. We will also look at ways for Visual Basic to recognize mouse events and have some fun with colors. You will build an electronic blackboard project.

Panel Control

The **Panel** control is another Visual Basic 'container' control. It is nearly identical to the **GroupBox** control (seen in Class 7) in behavior. Controls are placed in a Panel control in the same manner they are placed in the GroupBox. Radio buttons in a panel work as an independent group. Yet, panel controls can also be used to display graphics (lines, rectangles, ellipses, polygons, text). In this class, we will look at these graphic capabilities of the panel control. The panel is selected from the toolbox. It appears as:

In Toolbox:

On Form (default properties):

Properties

The panel properties are:

Property	Description
Name	Name used to identify panel. Three letter prefix for panel names is **pnl**.
BackColor	Sets panel background color.
Left	Distance from left side of form to left side of panel (X in properties window, expand **Location** property).
Top	Distance from top side of form to top side of panel (Y in properties window, expand **Location** property).
Width	Width of the panel in pixels (expand **Size** property).
Height	Height of panel in pixels (expand **Size** property).
Enabled	Determines whether all controls within panel can respond to user events (in run mode).
Visible	Determines whether the panel (and attached controls) appears on the form (in run mode).

Like the form and group box objects, the panel is a **container** control, since it 'holds' other controls. Hence, many controls placed in a panel will share the **BackColor** property (notice the panel does not have a Text property). To change this, select the desired control (after it is placed on the group box) and change the background color. Also, note the panel is moved using the displayed 'handle' identical to the process for the group box in the previous class.

Typical Use of the Panel Control

The usual design steps for using a panel control are:

- Set **Name** property.
- Place desired controls in panel control.
- Monitor events of controls in panel using usual techniques.

Graphics Using the Panel Control

As mentioned, the panel control looks much like a group box and its use is similar. Panels can be used in place of group box controls, if desired. A powerful feature of the panel control (a feature the group box does not have), however, is its support of graphics. We can use the control as a blank canvas for self-created works of art! There are many new concepts to learn to help us become computer artists. Let's look at those concepts now.

Graphics Methods

To do graphics (drawing) in Visual Basic, we use the built-in **graphics methods**. A **method** is a procedure or function that imparts some action to an object or control. Most controls have methods, not just the panel. With the panel, a graphics method can be used to draw something on it. Methods can only be used in run mode. The BASIC code to use a method is:

```
ObjectName.MethodName(Arguments)
```

where ObjectName is the object of interest, MethodName is the method being used, and there may be some arguments (information needed by the method to do its task). Notice this is another form of the dot notation we use to set control properties in code. In this class, we will look at graphics methods that can draw colored lines. As you progress in your programming skills, you are encouraged to study the many other graphics methods that can draw rectangles, ellipses, polygons and virtually any shape, in any color. To use the panel for drawing lines, we need to introduce another concept, that of a **graphics object**.

Graphics Objects

You need to tell Visual Basic that you will be using graphics methods with the panel control. To do this, you convert the panel control to something called a **graphics object**. Graphics objects provide the "surface" for graphics methods. Creating a graphics object requires two simple steps. We first declare the object using the standard **Dim** statement. If we name our graphics object **MyGraphics**, the form is:

```
Dim MyGraphics As Graphics
```

This declaration is placed in the **general declarations** area of the code window, along with our usual variable declarations. Once declared, the object is created using the **CreateGraphics** method:

```
MyGraphics = ControlName.CreateGraphics()
```

where **ControlName** is the name of the control hosting the graphics object (in our work, the **Name** property of the panel control). We will create this object in the form **Load** event of our projects.

Once a graphics object is created, all graphics methods are applied to this newly formed object. Hence, to apply a graphics method named **GraphicsMethod** to the **MyGraphics** object, use:

```
MyGraphics.GraphicsMethod(Arguments)
```

where **Arguments** are any needed arguments, or information needed by the graphics method.

There are two important graphics methods we introduce now. First, after all of your hard work drawing in a graphics object, there are times you will want to erase or clear the object. This is done with the **Clear** method:

```
MyGraphics.Clear(Color)
```

This statement will clear a graphics object (MyGraphics) and fill it with the specified **Color**. We will look further at colors next. The usual color argument for clearing a graphics object is the background color of the host control (ControlName), or:

```
MyGraphics.Clear(ControlName.BackColor)
```

Once you are done drawing to an object and need it no longer, it should be properly disposed to clear up system resources. To do this with our example graphics object, use the **Dispose** method:

```
MyGraphics.Dispose()
```

This statement is usually placed in the form **FormClosing** event procedure.

Our drawing will require colors and objects called pens, so let's take a look at those concepts. Doesn't it make sense we need pens to do some drawing?

Colors

Colors play a big part in Visual Basic applications. We have seen colors in designing some of our previous applications. At design time, we have selected background colors (**BackColor** property) and foreground colors (**ForeColor** property) for different controls. Such choices are made by selecting the desired property in the properties window. Once selected, a palette of customizable colors appears for you to choose from.

Most graphics methods and graphics objects use color. For example, the pen object we study next has a **Color** argument that specifies just what color it draws with. Unlike control color properties, these colors cannot be selected at design time. They must be defined in code. How do we do this? There are two approaches we will take: (1) use built-in colors and (2) create a color.

The colors built into Visual Basic are specified by the **Color** structure. We have seen a few colors in some our examples and projects. A color is specified using:

```
Color.ColorName
```

where **ColorName** is a reserved color name. There are many, many color names (I counted 141). There are colors like **BlanchedAlmond**, **Linen**, **NavajoWhite,** **PeachPuff** and **SpringGreen**. You don't have to remember these names. Whenever you type the word **Color**, followed by a dot (.), in the code window, the Intellisense feature of Visual Basic will pop up a list of color selections. Just choose from the list to complete the color specification. You will have to remember the difference between BlanchedAlmond and Linen though!

If for some reason, the selection provided by the **Color** structure does not fit your needs, there is a method that allows you to create over 16 million different colors. The method (**FromArgb**) works with the **Color** structure. The syntax to specify a color is:

```
Color.FromArgb(Red, Green, Blue)
```

where **Red**, **Green**, and **Blue** are integer measures of intensity of the corresponding primary colors. These measures can range from 0 (least intensity) to 255 (greatest intensity). For example, `Color.FromArgb(255, 255, 0)` will produce yellow. Sorry, but I can't tell you what values to use to create **PeachPuff**.

It is easy to specify colors for graphics methods using the **Color** structure. Any time you need a color, just use one of the built-in colors or the **FromArgb** method. These techniques to represent color are not limited to just providing colors for graphics methods. They can be used anywhere Visual Basic requires a color; for example, **Backcolor** and **Forecolor** properties can also be set (at run-time) using these techniques. For example, to change your form background color to **PeachPuff**, use:

```
Me.BackColor = Color.PeachPuff
```

You can also define variables that take on color values. It is a two step process. Say we want to define a variable named **MyRed** to represent the color red. First, in the general declarations area, declare your variable to be of type **Color**:

```
Dim MyRed As Color
```

Then, define your color in code using:

```
MyRed = Color.Red
```

From this point on, you can use **MyRed** anywhere the red color is desired.

Example

Go the course project folder (**\CBGVB\BVB Projects**) and open a project named **RGBColors**. Run this project. Three numeric updown controls are there: one to control the **Red** (R =) content, one to control the **Green** (G =) content, and one to control the **Blue** (B =) content. Set values for each and see the corresponding color assigned using the **FromArgb** function. Play with this project and look at all the colors available with this function. How long does it take to look at all 16 million combinations? A long time! The running project looks like this:

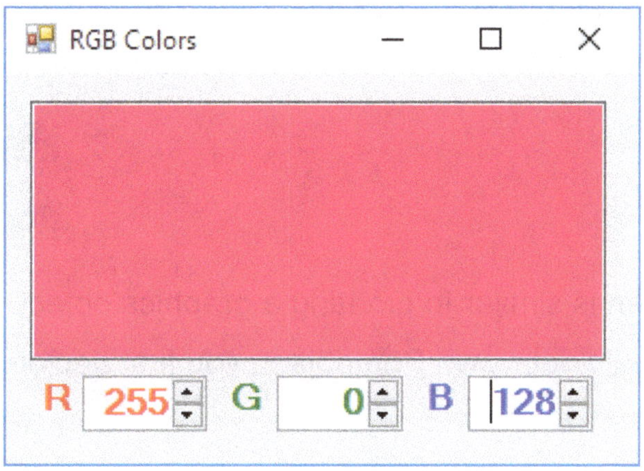

Stop the project when you're done playing with the colors. See if you can figure out how this little project works.

Pen Objects

As mentioned, many of the graphics methods (including the method to draw lines) require a **Pen** object. This virtual pen is just like the pen you use to write and draw. You can choose color and width. You can use pens built into Visual Basic or create your own pen.

In many cases, the pen objects built into Visual Basic are sufficient. These pens will draw a line **1** pixel wide in a color you choose (Intellisense will present the list to choose from). If the selected color is **ColorName** (one of the 141 built-in color names), the syntax to refer to such a pen is:

```
Pens.ColorName
```

Creating your own pen is similar to creating a graphics object, but here we create a **Pen** object. To create your own Pen object, you first declare the pen using:

```
Dim MyPen As Pen
```

This line goes in the **general declarations** area. The pen is then created using the **Pen constructor** function:

```
MyPen = New Pen(Color, Width)
```

where **Color** is the color your new pen will draw in and **Width** is the integer width of the line (in pixels) drawn. The pen is usually created in the form **Load** procedure. This pen will draw a solid line. The **Color** argument can be one of the built-in colors or one generated with the **FromArgb** function.
Once created, you can change the color and width at any time using the **Color** and **Width** properties of the pen object. The syntax is:

```
MyPen.Color = NewColor
MyPen.Width = NewWidth
```

Here, **NewColor** is a newly specified color and **NewWidth** is a new integer pen width.

Like the graphics object, when done using a pen object, it should be disposed using the **Dispose** method:

```
MyPen.Dispose()
```

This disposal usually occurs in the form **FormClosing** procedure.

We're almost ready to draw lines – be patient! Just one more concept and we're on our way.

Graphics Coordinates

We will use Visual Basic to draw lines using a method called the **DrawLine** method. Before looking at this method, let's look at how we specify the points used to draw and connect lines. All graphics methods use a default **coordinate system**. This means we have a specific way to refer to individual points in the control (a panel in our work) hosting the graphics object. The coordinate system used is:

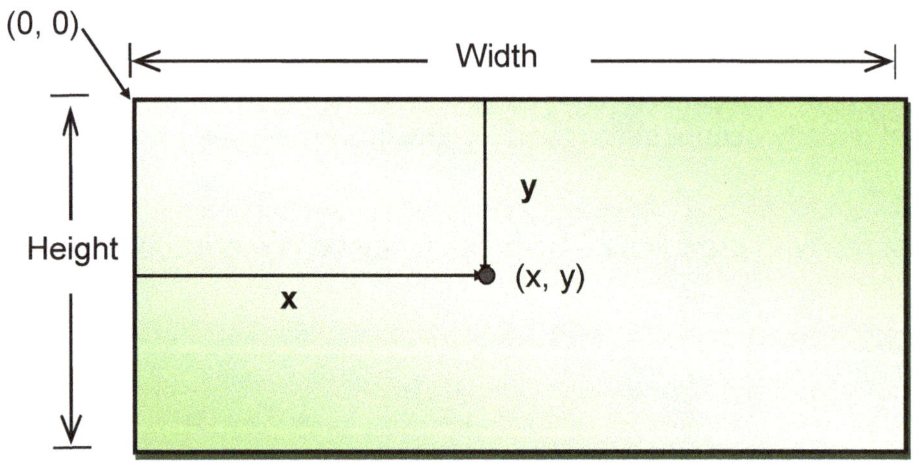

We use two values (coordinates) to identify a single point in the panel. The **x** (horizontal) coordinate increases from left to right, starting at **0**. The **y** (vertical) coordinate increases from top to bottom, also starting at **0**. Points in the panel are referred to by the two coordinates enclosed in parentheses, or **(x, y)**. Notice how x and y, respectively, are similar to the Left and Top control properties. All values shown are in units of **pixels**.

At long last, we're ready to draw some lines.

DrawLine Method

The Visual Basic **DrawLine** method is used to connect two points with a straight-line segment. It operates on a previously created graphics object. If that object is **MyGraphics** and we wish to connect the point (**x1**, **y1**) with (**x2**, **y2**) using a pen object **MyPen**, the statement is:

```
MyGraphics.DrawLine(MyPen, x1, y1, x2, y2)
```

The pen object can be either one of the built-in pens or one you create using the pen constructor just discussed. Each coordinate value is an integer type. Using a built-in black pen (**Pens.Black**), the **DrawLine** method with these points is:

```
MyGraphics.DrawLine(Pens.Black, x1, y1, x2, y2)
```

This produces on a panel (**MyGraphics** object):

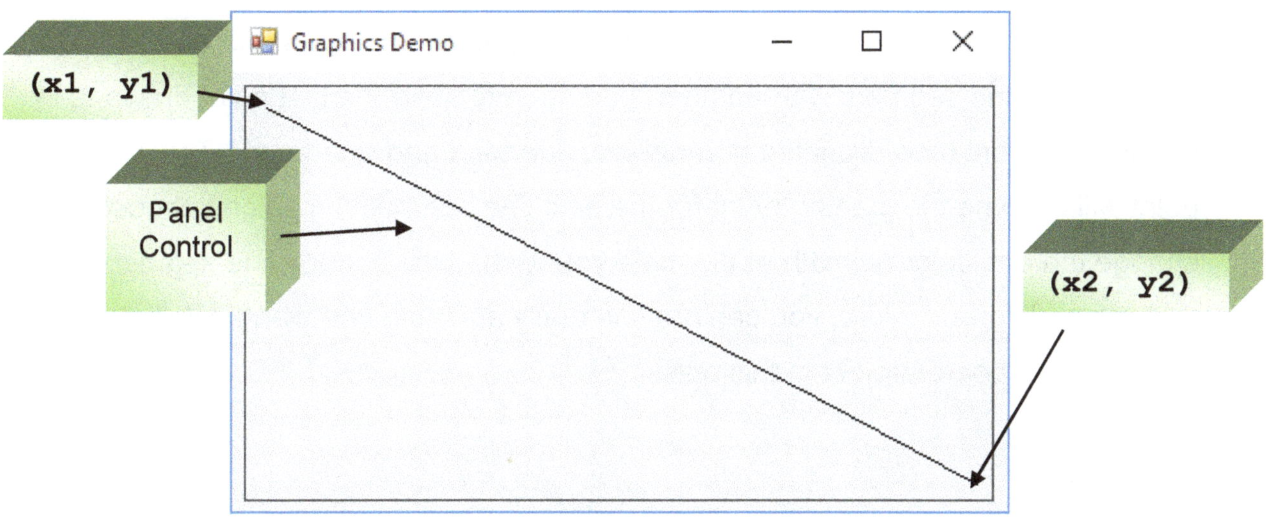

To connect the last point (**x2, y2**) to another point (**x3, y3**), use:

```
MyGraphics.DrawLine(Pens.Black, x2, y2, x3, y3)
```

This produces on a panel (**MyGraphics** object):

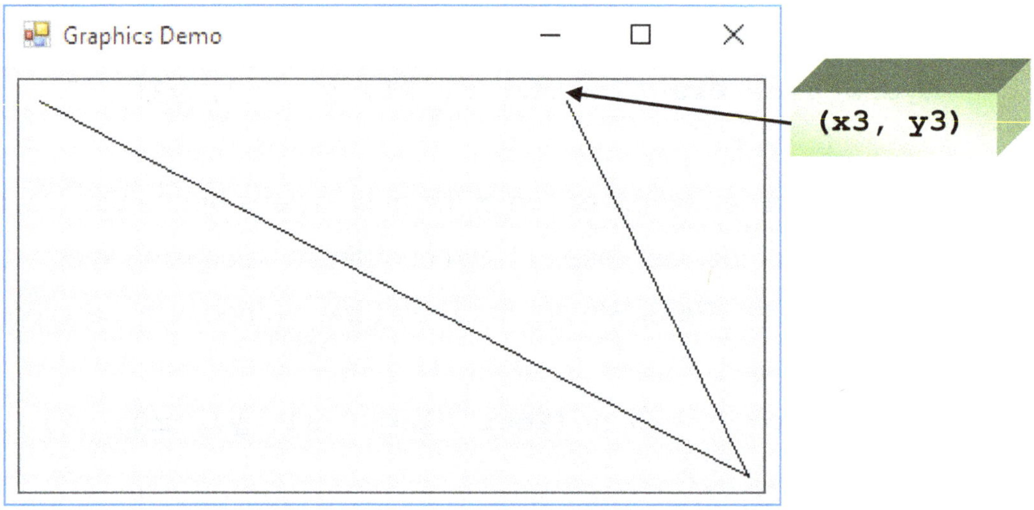

For every line segment you draw, you need a separate **DrawLine** statement. To connect one line segment with another, you need to save the last point drawn to in the first segment (use two integer variables, one for x and one for y). This saved point will become the starting point for the next line segment. You can choose to change the pen color or width at any time you wish. Using many line segments, with many different colors, you can draw virtually anything you want! We'll do that with the blackboard project in this class.

Graphics Review

We've covered lots of new material here, so it's probably good to review the steps necessary to use the **DrawLine** method to draw line segments:

- **Declare** a **graphics object** in the general declarations area.
- **Create** a **graphics object** in the form Load event procedure.
- **Select** a **pen object** using the built-in Pens object or **create** your own **pen object**.
- **Draw** to **graphics object** using DrawLine method and specified coordinates.
- **Dispose** of **graphics object** and **pen object** (if created) in the form FormClosing event procedure.

The process is like drawing on paper. You get your paper (graphics object) and your pens. You do all your drawing and coloring and then put your supplies away!

Example

Start a new project in Visual Basic. Place a panel control on the form. Make it fairly large. Set its **BackColor** property to white. Place a button control on the form. My form looks like this:

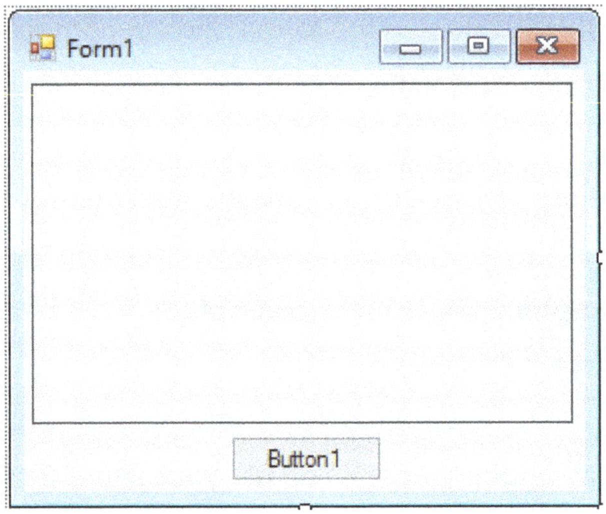

Write down the **Width** and **Height** properties of your panel control (look at the **Size** property; my values are Width = 270 and Height = 170).

In the general declarations area of the code window, declare your graphics object using:

```
Dim MyGraphics As Graphics
```

In the **Form1_Load** event, add this line of code to create the graphics object:

```
MyGraphics = Panel1.CreateGraphics()
```

In the **Button1 Click** event, write a line of code that draws a line starting at the point (10, 10) and goes to a point (Width – 10, Height – 10), where Width and Height are the dimensions of your panel control. Using a black pen, this line of code for my panel is:

```
MyGraphics.DrawLine(Pens.Black, 10, 10, 260, 160)
```

And, in the **Form1 FormClosing** event, dispose of your graphics object using:

```
MyGraphics.Dispose()
```

Make sure your code window looks like this:

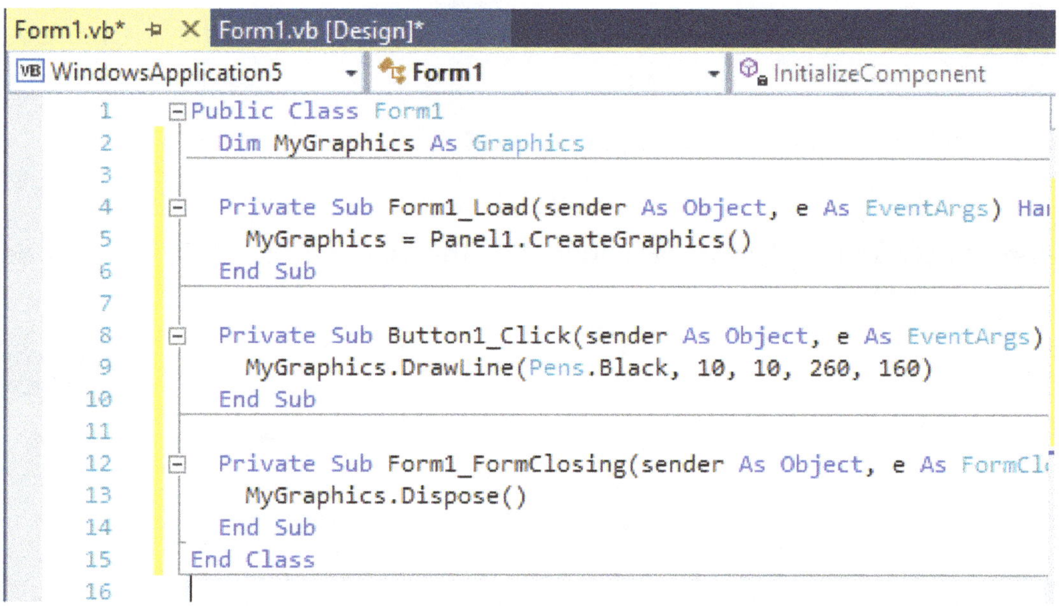

Especially note the placement of the **Dim** statement declaring the graphics object.

Run the project. Click the button. The code draws a black line from (10, 10), near the upper left corner, to (260, 160), near the lower right corner:

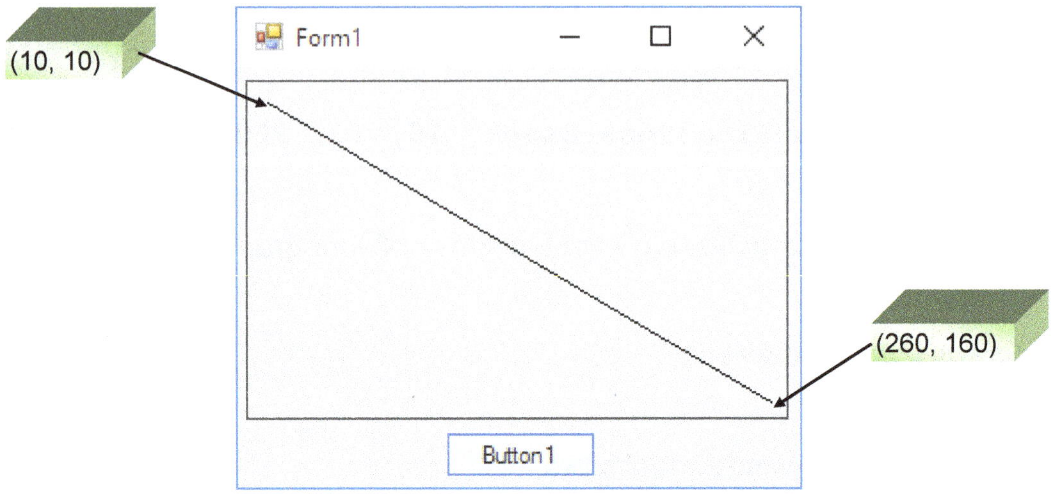

Stop the project and add this line after the current line in the Button1_Click event:

```
MyGraphics.DrawLine(Pens.Red, 260, 160, 260, 10)
```

Run the project again. A red line, connecting the last point to (260, 10) is added:

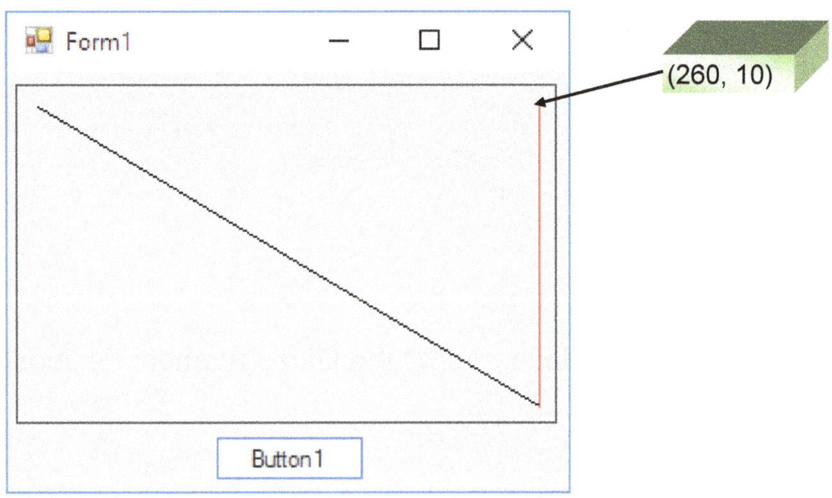

Stop the project. Let's create a wide pen. Add this line in the general declarations area to declare **MyPen**:

```
Dim MyPen As Pen
```

Add this line of code in the **Form1_Load** event to create MyPen as a blue pen with a drawing width of 10:

```
MyPen = New Pen(Color.Blue, 10)
```

Add this line of code in the **Form1_FormClosing** event to dispose of MyPen:

```
MyPen.Dispose()
```

Now add this line after the lines already in the **Button1_Click** event to draw a 'wide' blue line that completes a little triangle:

```
MyGraphics.DrawLine(MyPen, 260, 10, 10, 10)
```

Run the project and you should see:

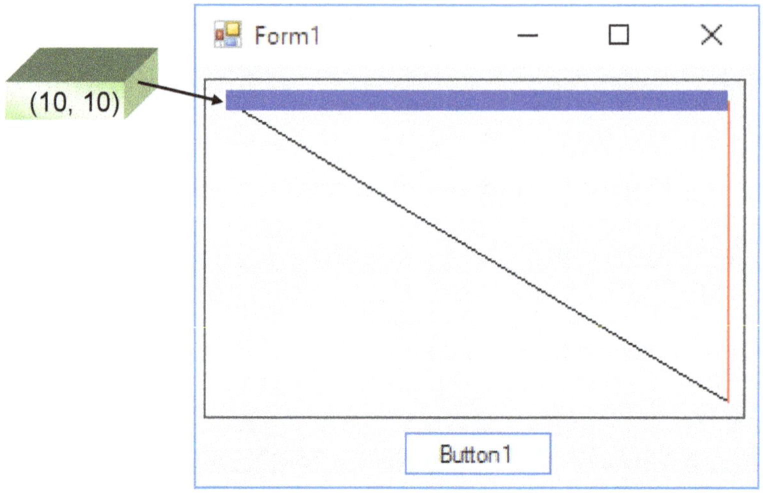

Add more line segments, using other points and colors if you like. Try creating other pens with different colors and drawing widths. Save this project – we'll continue working with it. I think you get the idea of drawing. Just pick some points, pick some colors, and draw some lines. But, it's pretty boring to just specify points and see lines being drawn. It would be nice to have some user interaction, where points could be drawn using the mouse. And, that's just what we are going to do. We will use our newly gained knowledge about graphics methods to build a Visual Basic drawing program. To do this, though, we need to know how to use the mouse in a project. We do that now.

BASIC – The Fifth Lesson

In the BASIC lesson for this class, we examine how to recognize mouse events (clicking and releasing buttons, moving the mouse) to help us build a drawing program with a panel control.

Mouse Events

Related to graphics methods are **mouse events**. The mouse is a primary interface for doing graphics in Visual Basic. We've already used the mouse to **Click** on controls. Here, we see how to recognize other mouse events in controls. Many controls recognize mouse events - we are learning about them to allow drawing in panel controls.

MouseDown Event

The **MouseDown** event procedure is triggered whenever a mouse button is pressed while the mouse cursor is over a control. The form of this procedure is:

```
  Private Sub ControlName_MouseDown(ByVal sender As Object,
ByVal e As System.Windows.Forms.MouseEventArgs) Handles
ControlName.MouseDown

       [BASIC code for MouseDown event]

  End Sub
```

This is the first time we will use the arguments (information in parentheses) in an event procedure. This is information BASIC is supplying, for our use, when this event procedure is executed. Note this procedure has two arguments: **sender** and **e**. **Sender** is the control that was clicked to cause this event (MouseDown) to occur. In our case, it will be the panel control. The argument **e** is an event handler revealing which button was clicked and the coordinate of the mouse cursor when a button was pressed. We are interested in three properties of the event handler **e**:

Value	Description
e.Button	Mouse button pressed. Possible values are: **MouseButtons.Left**, **MouseButtons.Center**, **MouseButtons.Right**
e.X	X coordinate of mouse cursor in control when mouse was clicked
e.Y	Y coordinate of mouse cursor in control when mouse was clicked

Only one button press can be detected by the MouseDown event - you can't tell if someone pressed the left and right mouse buttons simultaneously. In drawing applications, the **MouseDown** event is used to initialize a drawing process. The point clicked is used to start drawing a line and the button clicked is often used to select line color.

Example

Let's try the MouseDown event with the example we just used with graphics methods. Recall we just have a panel control and a button on a form. Delete the button control from the form and the Button1_Click event procedure from the code window. Add two label boxes (one with default Name **Label1** and one with default name **Label2**) near the bottom of the form- we will use these to tell us which button was clicked and display the mouse click coordinate. My form looks like this:

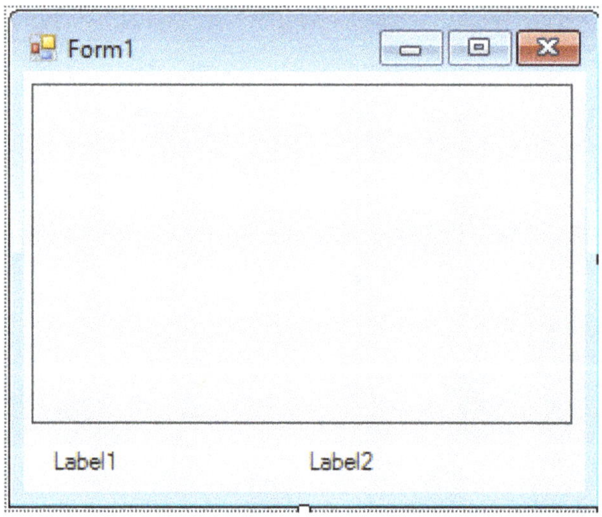

Put these lines of code in the **Panel1 MouseDown** event (make sure you select the correct event in the code window):

```
  Private Sub Panel1_MouseDown(ByVal sender As Object, ByVal
e As System.Windows.Forms.MouseEventArgs) Handles
Panel1.MouseDown
    Select Case e.Button
      Case MouseButtons.Left
        Label1.Text = "Left"
      Case MouseButtons.Middle
        Label1.Text = "Middle"
      Case MouseButtons.Right
        Label1.Text = "Right"
    End Select
    Label2.Text = Str(e.X) & "," & Str(e.Y)
  End Sub
```

Here, we use a Select Case to specify which button was clicked (displayed in Label1 Text property) and we display e.X and e.Y (separated by a comma) in the Label2 Text property. Run the project. Click the panel and notice the displayed button and coordinate. Here's an example of a point I clicked:

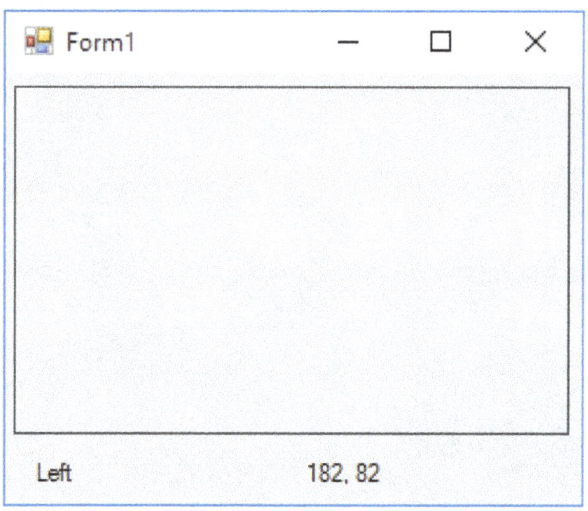

Try different mouse buttons. Click various spots in the panel and see how the coordinates change. Click near the upper left corner. Is (X, Y) close to (0, 0)? It should be. Play with this example until you are comfortable with how the MouseDown event works and what the coordinates mean. Stop and save the project.

MouseUp Event

The **MouseUp** event is the opposite of the MouseDown event. It is triggered whenever a previously pressed mouse button is released. The procedure format is:

```
  Private Sub ControlName_MouseUp(ByVal sender As Object,
ByVal e As System.Windows.Forms.MouseEventArgs) Handles
ControlName.MouseDown
```

[BASIC code for MouseUp event]

```
  End Sub
```

Notice the arguments for MouseUp are identical to those for MouseDown. The only difference here is **e.Button** tells us which mouse button was released. In a drawing program, the **MouseUp** event signifies the halting of the current drawing process.

Example

Cut the code from the **Panel1 MouseDown** procedure in our example (highlight the code, click the **Edit** menu, then **Cut**) and paste it in the **Panel1 MouseUp** procedure (click **Edit**, then **Paste**). Make sure you have the correct procedure before pasting. Run the project. Click the panel, move the mouse, then release the mouse. Note the displayed button and coordinates. Become comfortable with how the MouseUp event works and how it differs from the MouseDown event. Stop and save the project.

MouseMove Event

The **MouseMove** event is continuously triggered whenever the mouse is being moved. The event procedure format is:

```
Private Sub ControlName_MouseMove(ByVal sender As Object, ByVal e As System.Windows.Forms.MouseEventArgs) Handles ControlName.MouseDown

    [BASIC code for MouseMove event]

End Sub
```

And, yes, the arguments are the same. **e.Button** tells us which button is being pressed (if any) as the mouse is moving over the control and (e.X, e.Y) tell us the mouse position. In drawing processes, the **MouseMove** event is used to detect the continuation of a previously started line. If drawing is continuing, the current point is connected to the previous point using the current pen.

Example

Cut the code from the **Panel1 MouseUp** procedure in our example and paste it in the **Panel1 MouseMove** procedure. Run the project. Move the mouse over the panel. Notice the coordinates (X, Y) appear and continuously change as the mouse is moving. Click the panel and move the mouse. Notice the label boxes tell you which button was pressed and the current coordinates of the mouse in the panel. Stop the project.

You should now know how the three mouse events work and how they differ. Now let's use the panel control, DrawLine method, mouse events, pens and colors we've studied to build a fun drawing project

Project – Blackboard Fun

Have you ever drawn on a blackboard with colored chalk? You'll be doing that with the "electronic" blackboard you build in this project. This project is saved as **Blackboard** in the course projects folder (**\CBGVB\BVB Projects**).

Project Design

This is a simple project in concept. Using the mouse, you draw colored lines on a computer blackboard. A panel control will represent the blackboard. Radio buttons will be used to choose "chalk" color. Mouse events will control the drawing process. Two command buttons will be used: one to erase the blackboard and one to exit the program.

Place Controls on Form

Start a new project in Visual Basic. Place a panel control (make it fairly large), a group box, and two command buttons on the form. Place eight small radio buttons (used for color choice) in the group box. When done, my form looks like this:

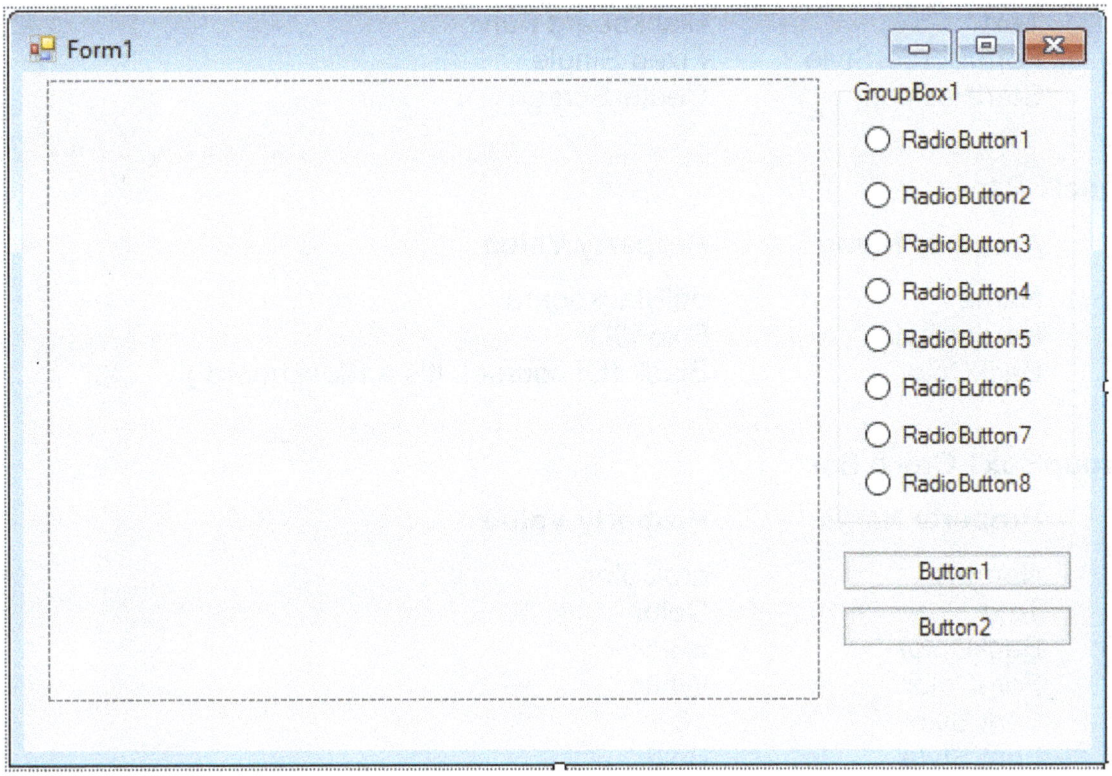

Set Control Properties

Set the control properties using the properties window:

Form1 Form:

Property Name	Property Value
Text	Blackboard Fun
FormBorderStyle	Fixed Single
StartPosition	CenterScreen

Panel1 Panel:

Property Name	Property Value
Name	pnlBlackboard
BorderStyle	Fixed3D
BackColor	Black (Of course! It's a Blackboard!)

GroupBox1 Group Box:

Property Name	Property Value
Name	grpColor
Text	Color
BackColor	Black
ForeColor	White
Font Size	10
Font Style	Bold

RadioButton1 Radio Button:

Property Name	Property Value
Name	rdoGray
Text	10 to 15 spaces (need some blank space to display color)

RadioButton2 Radio Button:

Property Name	Property Value
Name	rdoBlue
Text	10 to 15 spaces

RadioButton3 Radio Button:

Property Name	Property Value
Name	rdoGreen
Text	10 to 15 spaces

RadioButton4 Radio Button:

Property Name	Property Value
Name	rdoCyan
Text	10 to 15 spaces

RadioButton5 Radio Button:

Property Name	Property Value
Name	rdoRed
Text	10 to 15 spaces

RadioButton6 Radio Button:

Property Name	Property Value
Name	rdoMagenta
Text	10 to 15 spaces

RadioButton7 Radio Button:

Property Name	Property Value
Name	rdoYellow
Text	10 to 15 spaces

RadioButton8 Radio Button:

Property Name	**Property Value**
Name	rdoWhite
Text	10 to 15 spaces

Button1 Button:

Property Name	**Property Value**
Name	btnErase
Text	Erase

Button2 Button:

Property Name	**Property Value**
Name	btnExit
Text	Exit

My form looked like this when I was done:

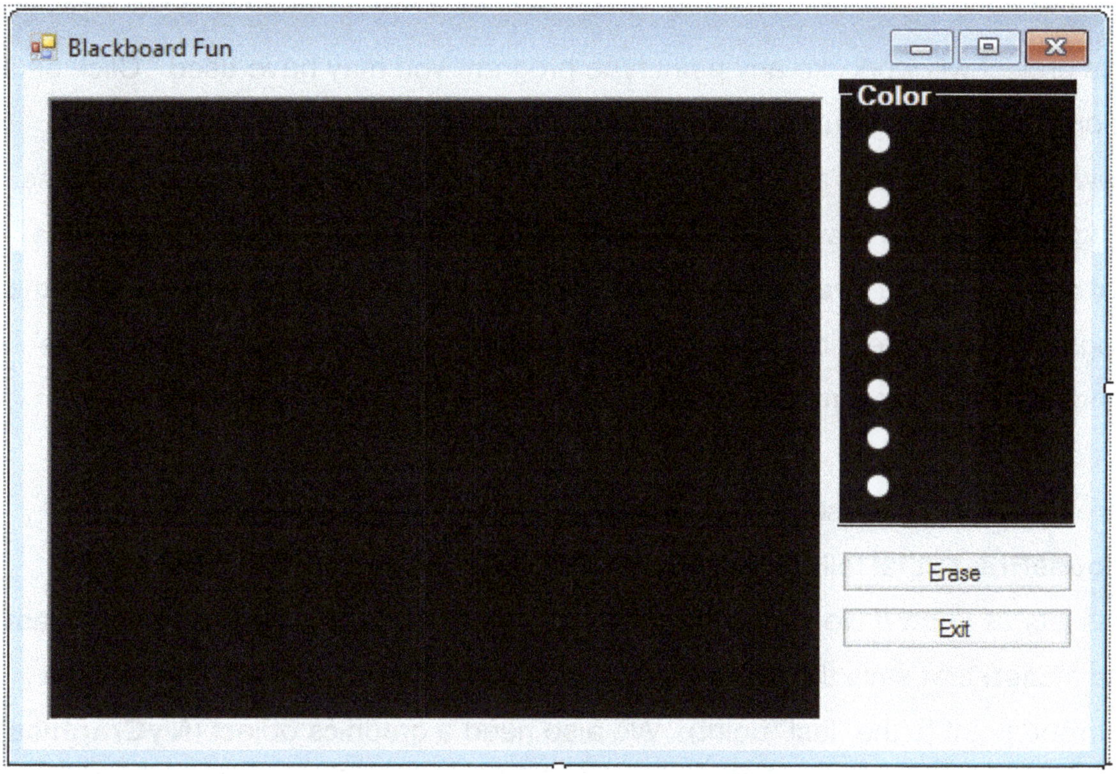

You may be asking – are you crazy? All the radio button Texts are empty spaces - how can these be used for picking colors? Wait a minute and you'll see.

Write Event Procedures

This project will work like any paint type program you may have used. Click on a color in the **Color** group box (we'll see colors there soon) to choose a color to draw with. Then, move to the blackboard, left-click to start the drawing process. Drag the mouse to draw lines. Release the mouse button to stop drawing. It's that easy. Clicking **Erase** will clear the blackboard and clicking **Exit** will stop the program. Every step, but initializing a few things and stopping the program, is handled by the panel mouse events.

Three variables are used in this project. We need a Boolean variable (**MousePress**) that tells us whether the left mouse button is being held down. This lets us know if we should be drawing or not. We need two variables (**XLast** and **YLast**) that save the last point drawn in a line (we will always connect the "current" point to the "last" point). We also need a graphics object (**MyGraphics**) and a pen object (**MyPen**). Open the code window and declare these variables in the **general declarations** area:

```
Dim MousePress As Boolean
Dim XLast As Integer, YLast As Integer
Dim MyGraphics As Graphics
Dim MyPen As Pen
```

We need to establish some initial values. First, we create the graphics object (**MyGraphics**) we will draw on and our pen object (**MyPen**). We will set the pen to an initial drawing color of gray. How will we pick colors? Each radio button has a **BackColor** property. We set each BackColor property to its corresponding color using BASIC code. The user then sees each actual color and not some word describing it. The eight colors we will use are values from the Color structure. These colors were selected to look good on a black background. As seen, the initial color will be Gray, so we set the **rdoGray** radio button **Checked** property to

True. We also initialize **MousePress** to **False** (we aren't drawing yet). All this is done in the **Form1 Load** procedure:

```
  Private Sub Form1_Load(ByVal sender As Object, ByVal e As
System.EventArgs) Handles Me.Load
    'Create graphics and pen objects
    MyGraphics = pnlBlackboard.CreateGraphics
    MyPen = New Pen(Color.Gray, 1)
    'Initialize the eight radio button colors
    rdoGray.BackColor = Color.Gray
    rdoBlue.BackColor = Color.Blue
    rdoGreen.BackColor = Color.LightGreen
    rdoCyan.BackColor = Color.Cyan
    rdoRed.BackColor = Color.Red
    rdoMagenta.BackColor = Color.Magenta
    rdoYellow.BackColor = Color.Yellow
    rdoWhite.BackColor = Color.White
    'Set initial color
    rdoGray.Checked = True
    MousePress = False
  End Sub
```

You'll see that this is pretty cool in how it works. This is a very common thing to do in Visual Basic - initialize lots of properties in the form **Load** procedure instead of using the properties window at design time. It makes project modification much easier.

Each radio button needs a **CheckedChanged** event procedure to set the corresponding **MyPen.Color** values. These eight one-line click events are:

```
  Private Sub RdoGray_CheckedChanged(ByVal sender As
System.Object, ByVal e As System.EventArgs) Handles
rdoGray.CheckedChanged
    'Gray
    MyPen.Color = rdoGray.BackColor
  End Sub
```

```
  Private Sub RdoBlue_CheckedChanged(ByVal sender As
System.Object, ByVal e As System.EventArgs) Handles
rdoBlue.CheckedChanged
    'Blue
    MyPen.Color = rdoBlue.BackColor
  End Sub

  Private Sub RdoGreen_CheckedChanged(ByVal sender As
System.Object, ByVal e As System.EventArgs) Handles
rdoGreen.CheckedChanged
    'Green
    MyPen.Color = rdoGreen.BackColor
  End Sub

  Private Sub RdoCyan_CheckedChanged(ByVal sender As
System.Object, ByVal e As System.EventArgs) Handles
rdoCyan.CheckedChanged
    'Cyan
    MyPen.Color = rdoCyan.BackColor
  End Sub

  Private Sub RdoRed_CheckedChanged(ByVal sender As
System.Object, ByVal e As System.EventArgs) Handles
rdoRed.CheckedChanged
    'Red
    MyPen.Color = rdoRed.BackColor
  End Sub

  Private Sub RdoMagenta_CheckedChanged(ByVal sender As
System.Object, ByVal e As System.EventArgs) Handles
rdoMagenta.CheckedChanged
    'Magenta
    MyPen.Color = rdoMagenta.BackColor
  End Sub

  Private Sub RdoYellow_CheckedChanged(ByVal sender As
System.Object, ByVal e As System.EventArgs) Handles
rdoYellow.CheckedChanged
    'Yellow
    MyPen.Color = rdoYellow.BackColor
  End Sub
```

```
  Private Sub RdoWhite_CheckedChanged(ByVal sender As
System.Object, ByVal e As System.EventArgs) Handles
rdoWhite.CheckedChanged
    'White
    MyPen.Color = rdoWhite.BackColor
  End Sub
```

We'll code the two buttons before tackling the drawing process. The **btnErase** button simply clears the panel. The **btnErase Click** procedure is:

```
  Private Sub BtnErase_Click(ByVal sender As System.Object,
ByVal e As System.EventArgs) Handles btnErase.Click
    'Clear the blackboard
    MyGraphics.Clear(pnlBlackboard.BackColor)
  End Sub
```

And, the **btnExit Click** procedure is, as always:

```
  Private Sub BtnExit_Click(ByVal sender As System.Object,
ByVal e As System.EventArgs) Handles btnExit.Click
    Me.Close()
  End Sub
```

Now, let's code the drawing process. There are three events we look for:

- Left mouse button click - starts drawing
- Mouse moving with left mouse button pressed - continues drawing
- Left mouse button release - stops drawing

Each of these is a separate mouse event.

The **pnlBlackboard MouseDown** event is executed when the left mouse button is clicked. When that happens, we set **MousePress** to **True** (we are drawing) and initialize the "last point" variables, **XLast** and **YLast**. That event procedure is:

```
  Private Sub PnlBlackboard_MouseDown(ByVal sender As
Object, ByVal e As System.Windows.Forms.MouseEventArgs)
Handles pnlBlackboard.MouseDown
    'Start drawing if left click
    If e.Button = MouseButtons.Left Then
      MousePress = True
      XLast = e.X
      YLast = e.Y
    End If
  End Sub
```

The **pnlBlackboard MouseMove** event is executed when the left mouse button is being pressed (**MousePress** is **True**) and the mouse is moving over the panel. In this event, we connect the last point (**XLast, YLast**) to the current point (**e.X, e.Y**) using the **DrawLine** method with **MyPen**. Once done drawing, the "last point" becomes the "current point." This code is:

```
  Private Sub PnlBlackboard_MouseMove(ByVal sender As
Object, ByVal e As System.Windows.Forms.MouseEventArgs)
Handles pnlBlackboard.MouseMove
    'Draw a line if drawing
    If MousePress Then
      MyGraphics.DrawLine(MyPen, XLast, YLast, e.X, e.Y)
      XLast = e.X
      YLast = e.Y
    End If
  End Sub
```

The **pnlBlackboard MouseUp** event is executed when the left mouse button is released. When that happens, we draw the last line segment and set **MousePress** to **False** (we are done drawing). That event procedure is:

```
  Private Sub PnlBlackboard_MouseUp(ByVal sender As Object,
ByVal e As System.Windows.Forms.MouseEventArgs) Handles
pnlBlackboard.MouseUp
    'Finish line
    If e.Button = MouseButtons.Left Then
      MyGraphics.DrawLine(MyPen, XLast, YLast, e.X, e.Y)
      MousePress = False
    End If
  End Sub
```

We're almost done. A last step is to dispose of our graphics and pen objects in the **Form1 FormClosing** event:

```
  Private Sub Form1_FormClosing(ByVal sender As Object,
ByVal e As System.ComponentModel.CancelEventArgs) Handles
Me.FormClosing
    MyGraphics.Dispose()
    MyPen.Dispose()
  End Sub
```

Save the project by clicking the **Save All** button in the toolbar.

Run the Project

Run the project. See how the radio button BackColor property is used to display colors? Choose a color. Draw a line in the panel control. Try other colors. Draw something. Here's my attempt at art:

I've had students draw perfect pictures of Fred Flintstone and Homer Simpson using this program. Make sure each color works. Make sure **Erase** works. Make sure **Exit** works. As always, thoroughly test your project. Save it if you had to make any changes while running it.

Do you see how simple the drawing part of this program is? Most of the code is used just to set and select colors. The actual drawing portion of the code (MouseDown, MouseMove, MouseUp events) is only a few lines of BASIC! This shows two things: (1) those drawing programs you use are really not that hard to build and (2) there is a lot of power in the Visual Basic graphics methods.

Other Things to Try

The Blackboard Fun project offers lots of opportunity for improvement with added options. Have an option to set the pen **Width** property. This way you can draw with very skinny lines or very fat lines. Use a numeric updown control to set the value.

Add the ability to change the background color of the blackboard. Determine and build logic that allows drawing different colored lines depending on whether you press the left or right mouse button. For this, I'd suggest creating a left pen and a right pen. You will also need some way for the user to choose colors for each pen. Then, apply the appropriate pen in the various mouse events depending on what button is pressed.

See if you can figure out ways to get special effects. Here's one possibility to try. Delete (or 'comment out') these lines in the **pnlBlackboard MouseMove** event:

```
XLast = e.X
YLast = e.Y
```

By doing this, the first point clicked (in the MouseDown event) is always the last point and all line drawing originates from this original point. Now, run the project again. Notice the "fanning" effect. Pretty, huh? Play around and see what other effects (change colors randomly, change pen width randomly). Have fun!

There is one effect of the Blackboard Fun project that is annoying. You may have discovered it. You may not have. In the upper right corner of the form is a small button with an "underscore" called the **minimize button**:

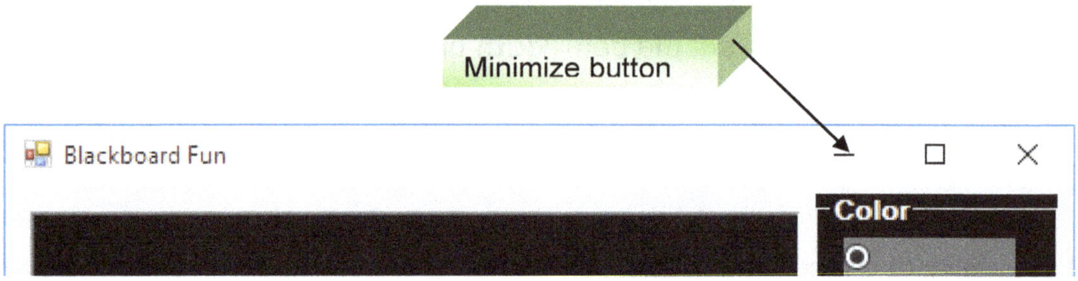

When you click this button, your application window disappears (is minimized) and is moved to the Windows task bar at the bottom of the screen. When you click your application name in the task bar, it will return to the screen. Go ahead and try it. Run the project and draw a few lines. Don't draw anything too elaborate – you'll soon find out why. Minimize your application, then restore your application by clicking the appropriate button in the Windows task bar. Where did your lines go?

Why did the lines disappear when the project went away for a bit? Visual Basic graphics objects have no memory. They only display what has been last drawn on them. If you reduce your form to the task bar and restore it (as we just did), the graphics object cannot remember what was displayed previously – it will be cleared. Similarly, if you switch from an active Visual Basic application to some other application, your Visual Basic form may become partially or fully obscured. When you return to your Visual Basic application, the obscured part of any graphics object will be erased. Again, there is no memory. Notice in both these cases, however, all controls are automatically restored to the form. Your application remembers these, fortunately! The controls are persistent. We also want **persistent graphics**.

The topic of persistent graphics is beyond the scope of this course. To eliminate this annoyance in the blackboard project, however, we will show you coding changes needed to add persistence. Only a few lines need to be changed. Make the changes if you like. In each case, the modified and/or new code is shown as shaded in gray. The idea is that we create a type of graphics object with memory (maintained in the **BackgroundImage** property of the panel control). The new **Form1 Load** procedure to do this is:

```
  Private Sub Form1_Load(ByVal sender As Object, ByVal e As
System.EventArgs) Handles MyBase.Load
    'Create graphics and pen objects
    pnlBlackboard.BackgroundImage = New
Bitmap(pnlBlackboard.Width, pnlBlackboard.Height,
Imaging.PixelFormat.Format24bppRgb)
    MyGraphics =
Graphics.FromImage(pnlBlackboard.BackgroundImage)
    MyPen = New Pen(Color.Gray, 1)
    'Initialize the eight radio button colors
    rdoGray.BackColor = Color.Gray
    rdoBlue.BackColor = Color.Blue
    rdoGreen.BackColor = Color.LightGreen
    rdoCyan.BackColor = Color.Cyan
    rdoRed.BackColor = Color.Red
    rdoMagenta.BackColor = Color.Magenta
    rdoYellow.BackColor = Color.Yellow
    rdoWhite.BackColor = Color.White
    'Set initial color
    rdoGray.Checked = True
    MousePress = False
  End Sub
```

We also need to add a single line (shaded) to the **pnlBlackboard MouseMove** event, **pnlBlackboard_MouseDown** event and **btnErase Click** event. This line refreshes the added memory after each graphics method. The modified event procedures are:

```
  Private Sub PnlBlackboard_MouseMove(ByVal sender As
Object, ByVal e As System.Windows.Forms.MouseEventArgs)
Handles pnlBlackboard.MouseMove
    'Draw a line if drawing
    If MousePress Then
      MyGraphics.DrawLine(MyPen, XLast, YLast, e.X, e.Y)
      pnlBlackboard.Refresh()
      XLast = e.X
      YLast = e.Y
    End If
  End Sub

  Private Sub PnlBlackboard_MouseUp(ByVal sender As Object,
ByVal e As System.Windows.Forms.MouseEventArgs) Handles
pnlBlackboard.MouseUp
    'Finish line
    If e.Button = MouseButtons.Left Then
      MyGraphics.DrawLine(MyPen, XLast, YLast, e.X, e.Y)
      pnlBlackboard.Refresh()
      MousePress = False
    End If
  End Sub

  Private Sub BtnErase_Click(ByVal sender As System.Object,
ByVal e As System.EventArgs) Handles btnErase.Click
    'Clear the blackboard
    MyGraphics.Clear(pnlBlackboard.BackColor)
    pnlBlackboard.Refresh()
  End Sub
```

Try running the project again. You should now be able to minimize the project window without fear of losing your lovely work of art!

Summary

You've now had your first experience with graphics programming in Visual Basic using the DrawLine method. You learned about the versatility of the panel control. You learned about three important control events to help in drawing: MouseDown, MouseMove, and MouseUp. And, you learned a lot about colors. In the next class, we'll continue looking at using graphics in projects. And, we'll look at some ways to design computer games.

9

Picture Boxes, Arrays

Review and Preview

In the last class, we introduced the panel control and ways to draw colored lines in a Visual Basic project. We continue looking at graphics in this class. The picture box control is studied. In particular, we use that control to display graphics files – photos, drawing, pictures. In our BASIC lesson, we look at a new way to declare variables and ways to count and loop. And, as a project, we build a version of the card game War.

Picture Box Control

Many times in projects, you want to display pictures or drawings saved as a graphics file on your computer. Maybe you have a little kid's program where if you type an A, an apple appears, B, a ball, and so on. Maybe you want to show a map of the United States (or some other country) for a geography lesson. Maybe you want to see some of the photos you took using a digital camera. The **picture box** is the control for that use. The picture box is selected from the toolbox. It appears as:

In Toolbox:

On Form (default properties):

Properties

The picture box control properties are:

Property	Description
Name	Name used to identify picture box control. Three letter prefix for picture box names is **pic**.
Image	Establishes the graphics file to display in the picture box.
SizeMode	Indicates how the image is displayed.
BorderStyle	Determines type of picture box border.

Left	Distance from left side of form to left side of picture box (X in properties window, expand **Position** property).
Top	Distance from top side of form to top side of picture box (Y in properties window, expand **Position** property).
Width	Width of the picture box in pixels (expand **Size** property).
Height	Height of picture box in pixels (expand **Size** property).
Enabled	Determines whether picture box can respond to user events (in run mode).
Visible	Determines whether the picture box appears on the form (in run mode).

The **Image** property is used to select the graphic file to display in the picture box and the **SizeMode** property affects how the file is displayed. Let's look at both properties.

Image Property

The picture box **Image** property specifies the graphics file to display. To set the Image property at design time, simply display the **Properties** window for the picture box control and select the **Image** property. An ellipsis (...) will appear. Click the ellipsis and a **Select Resource** window will appear. Select **Import** and an **Open File** dialog box will appear. Use that box to locate the graphics file to display. The picture box can display pictures stored in several different **graphics formats**. The formats we study are:

Bitmap A bitmap is an image represented by pixels (screen dots) and stored as a collection of bits in which each bit corresponds to one pixel. It usually has a **bmp** extension. You can also display icon files (**ico** extension) since they are essentially bitmap files.

GIF A GIF (Graphic Interchange Format, pronounce 'jif' like the peanut butter) file is a compressed bitmap format originally developed by the Internet provider CompuServe. Most graphics you see on the Internet are GIF files. A GIF file has a **gif** extension.

JPEG A JPEG (Joint Photographic Experts Group, pronounced 'jay-peg') file is a compressed bitmap format that is popular on the Internet and is the format usually used to store digital photographs. A JPEG file has a **jpg** extension.

These are standard graphics file types and there are other types that can be displayed. There are many programs (Paint Shop Pro by JASC, Eden Prairie, Minnesota is a good one) available that will convert a file from one type to another that you may find useful.

A good place to find sample Bitmap and GIF files is on the Internet. To save a displayed Internet graphic as a file, right-click the graphic and choose the **Save Picture As** option (make sure it has a **bmp** or **gif** extension). If you have a digital camera, you probably have hundreds of JPEG files.

In the **\CBGVB\BVB Projects\Graphics** folder, we have included one file of each type for use with our examples:

ball.bmp	Bitmap picture of a ball
kidware.gif	GIF file with the logo our company uses on its website
mexico.jpg	Digital picture from a Mexican vacation

Example

Start Visual Basic and start a new project. Place a picture box control on the form. Make it fairly large. Click the Image property and the ellipsis (...) button that appears. A **Select Resource** window will appear. Make sure the **Project resource file** radio button is selected and click the button marked **Import** and a file open window will appear. Move (as shown) to the **\CBGVB\BVB Projects\Graphics** folder and you will see our sample files listed:

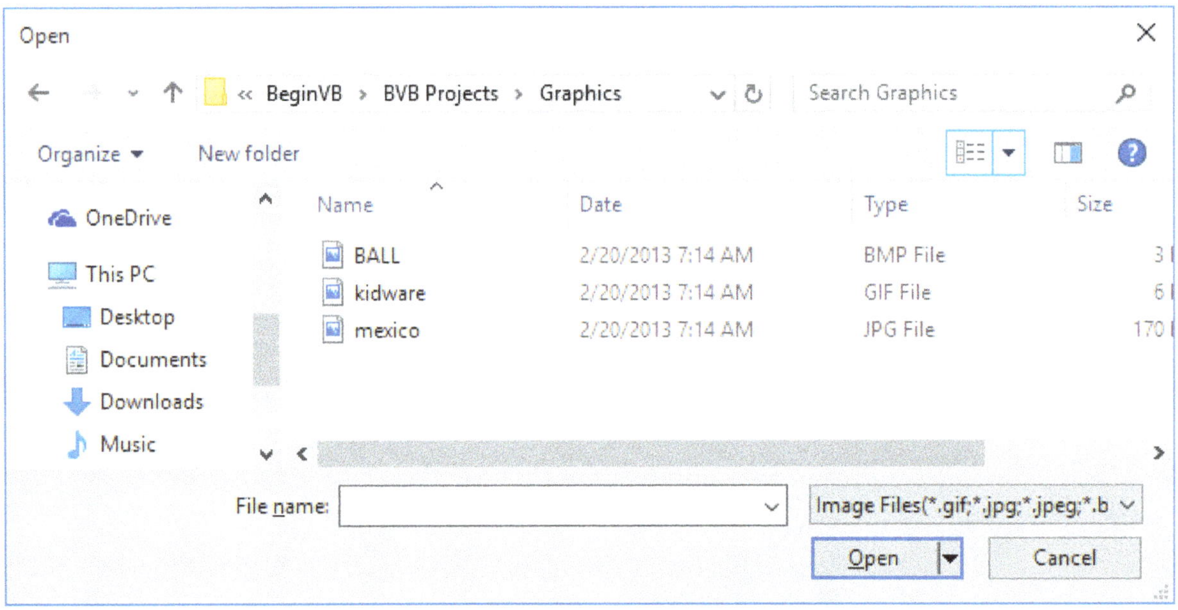

Note six file types are displayed including bitmaps, gifs, and jpegs. Other file types include metafiles (**wmf** extensions) and portable network graphics (**png** extension) – you might like to learn about these other file types on your own. One type not displayed is icon files (**ico** extension). To see these files, which will display just fine, you need to click **Files of type** and choose **All Files**.

Choose the **ball** bitmap file and click **Open**. You will be returned to the Select Resource window and it should look like this:

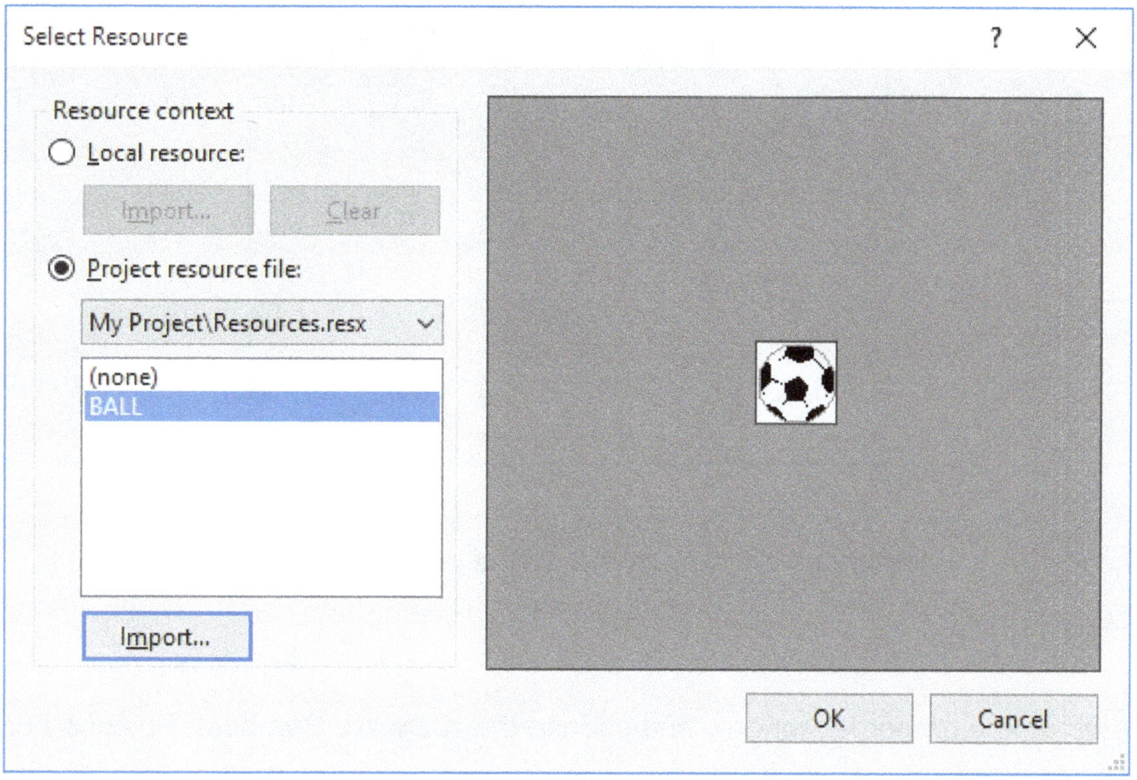

Click the **OK** button.

On your form, you should see something like this (depending on the size of your picture box):

The image is in the upper left hand corner of the picture box. It appears in full-size.

Return to the properties window and choose the **KIDware** Computer Science For Kids logo gif file for the picture box Image property (following the same procedure using the Select Resource window):

In this example, the picture box is shorter than the graphic, so the picture is vertically "cropped." It is located in the upper left hand corner and appears in full-size. If the picture is cropped in your example too, you can resize the picture box control to see the entire graphic.

Lastly, load and view the **mexico** JPEG file:

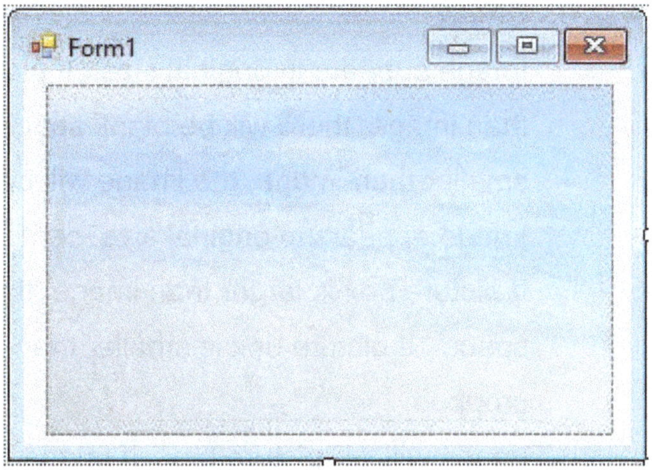

There's not much to see here. The picture box is smaller than the photo, so only the sky is seen. The picture appears in full-size and is seriously cropped.

We see that the bitmap file seems to display satisfactorily. The GIF and JPEG files had cropping problems though. The **SizeMode** property of the picture box control gives us some control on how we want a graphic to display. This will help us solve some of the problems we've seen. We look at that property next, but first a quick look at how to remove a graphic from a picture box.

There are times you may want to delete the graphic displayed in a picture box. To do this, click Image in the properties window. In the right side of the window will be the current file (with a very tiny copy of the graphic). Select this information (double-click to highlight it) and press the keyboard **Del** key. The displayed picture will vanish and the property will read **(None)**.

SizeMode Property

The **SizeMode** property dictates how a particular image will be displayed in a picture box. There are five possible values for this property: **Normal**, **CenterImage, StretchImage**, **AutoSize, Zoom**. The effect of each value is:

SizeMode	Effect
Normal	Image appears in original size. If picture box is larger than image, there will be blank space. If picture box is smaller than image, the image will be cropped.
CenterImage	Image appears in original size, centered in picture box. If picture box is larger than image, there will be blank space. If picture box is smaller than image, image is cropped.
StretchImage	Image will 'fill' picture box. If image is smaller than picture box, it will expand. If image is larger than picture box, it will scale down. Bitmap files do not scale nicely. JPEG and GIF files do scale nicely.
AutoSize	Reverse of StretchImage - picture box will change its dimensions to match the original size of the image. Be forewarned – some files are very large!
Zoom	Similar to StretchImage. The image will adjust to fit within the picture box, however its actual height to width ratio is maintained.

In the previous example, the **SizeMode** property had its default value of **Normal**, so all the images appeared in their original size. In the case of the bitmap file, there was lots of blank space. With the GIF and JPEG files, there was cropping. Similar results would have been seen with the **SizeMode** property changed to **CenterImage**. The most useful (in my opinion) of the **SizeMode** property choices is **StretchImage**. With this property, the image always fills the space you give it.

Example

Continue the previous project. Change the **SizeMode** property of the picture box control to **CenterImage**. Reload each of the three sample graphics files. Note when you click the ellipsis next to Image in the picture box properties window, the Select Resources window will appear as:

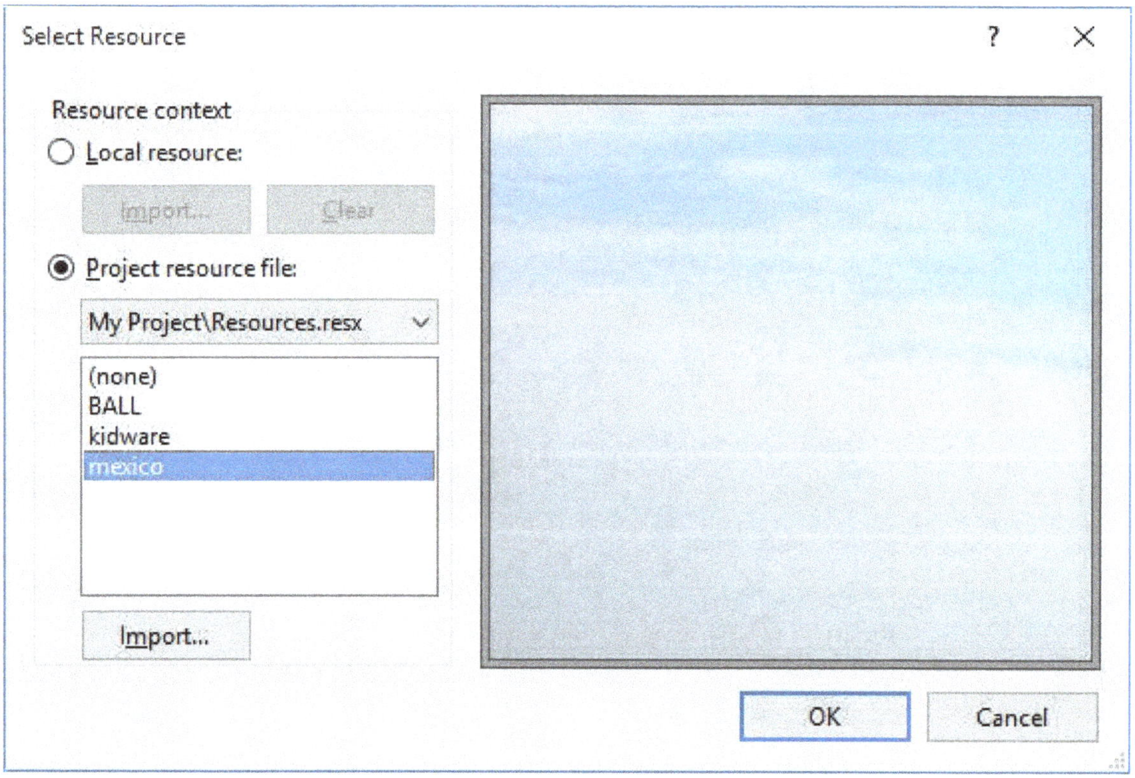

Since each graphic already appears in the Select Resource window (these graphics have become part of the project), there is no need to reload the actual graphics files. You can choose the **Image** property directly from this window. The process is – select the desired graphic (resource) and click **OK**.

With the **CenterImage SizeMode** property, note the difference in how the files are displayed. In particular, the GIF and JPEG files are still cropped, but now they're centered in the control. For example, here is **KIDware Computer Science for Kids** logo graphic with the image centered:

Change the **SizeMode** to **StretchImage**. Reload each of the sample graphics files. Notice how the graphic takes up the entire picture box. Here's the **mexico** graphic:

Try resizing the picture box control. How do the different graphics types resize? After resizing the picture box control, does the picture still look recognizable? You should find that bitmaps (in most cases) scale poorly, while GIF and JPEG graphics scale very nicely. Change the **SizeMode** to **Zoom**. Notice the graphic displays are very similar to those seen with StretchImage. The mexico graphic appears clearer, since the height to width ratio are correct:

Lastly, change the **SizeMode** to **AutoSize**. Load each graphic example and see the results. Watch out! The Mexico photo is very large. **AutoSize** should only be used when you know the size of your images and you allow for that size on your project form. If you like, try finding other graphic files on your computer and view them in the picture box with different SizeMode properties.

Events

The picture box control supports a few events. The important ones are:

Event	Description
Click	Event executed when user clicks on picture box.
MouseDown	Event executed when user presses mouse button while cursor is over picture box.
MouseMove	Event executed when user moves cursor over picture box.
MouseUp	Event executed when user releases mouse button while cursor is over picture box.

You would use the Click event when you are choosing from a group of picture box controls in a multiple choice environment. You would use the mouse events when you need to know which mouse button was pressed or released and/or where the cursor was when a mouse click, move, or release occurred.

Typical Use of Picture Box Control

The usual design steps to use a picture box control for displaying a graphic file are:

- Set the **Name** and **SizeMode** property (most often, **StretchImage**).
- Set **Image** property, either in design mode or at run-time.

BASIC – The Sixth Lesson

In this BASIC lesson, we look at ways to store large numbers of variables, a technique for counting, and some code for shuffling a deck of cards (or randomly sorting a list of numbers).

Variable Arrays

The local school principal has recognized your great Visual Basic programming skills and has come for your help. Everyone (300 students) in the school has just taken a basic skills test. The principal wants you to write a program that stores each student's name and score. The program should rank (put in order) the scores and compute the average score. The code to do this is not that hard. The problem we want to discuss here is how do we declare all the variables we need? To write this test score program, you need 300 string variables to store student names and 300 integer variables to store student scores. We are required to declare every variable we use in the code window general declarations area. Do you want to type 600 lines of code something like this?:

```
Dim Student1 As String
Dim Student2 As String
Dim Student3 As String
    .
    .
Dim Student300 As String
Dim Score1 As Integer
Dim Score2 As Integer
Dim Score3 As Integer
    .
    .
Dim Score300 As Integer
```

I don't think so.

BASIC provides a way to store a large number of variables under the same name - **variable arrays**. Each variable in an array, called an **element**, must have the same data type, and they are distinguished from each other by an array index. A variable array is declared in a way similar to other variables. The **Dim** (actually the origin of the Dim statement is related to arrays - Dim stands for dimension) statement is used. For 300 student names and 300 student scores, we write:

```
Dim Student(300) As String
Dim Score(300) As Integer
```

The number in parentheses is called the array **dimension**. These two lines have the same effect as the 600 declaration lines we might have had to write! And, notice how easy it would be to add 200 more variables if we needed them.

We now have 300 **Student** variables and 300 **Score** variables available for our use. Well, we actually have 301 of each variable! How is this? BASIC array indices begin with 0 and end at the dimension value, in this case 300. That yields 301 array elements. In this class, we will ignore the 0th element. As you progress as a Visual Basic programmer, you will not be able to ignore this 0th element. So, remember it exists.

Each variable in an array is referred to by its declared name and index. For example, to assign the 150th student's information, we could write two lines of code like this:

```
Student(150) = "Billy Gates"
Score(150) = 100
```

Array variables can be used anywhere regular variables are used. They can be used on the left side of assignment statements or in expressions. To add up the first three test scores, you would write:

```
Sum = Score(1) + Score(2) + Score(3)
```

We still need to provide values for each element in each array, but there are also some shortcuts we can take to avoid lots of assignment statements. You will find variable arrays are very useful when working with large numbers (and sometimes, not so large numbers) of similar variables.

For/Next Loops

A common computer programming task is counting. We might like to execute some BASIC code segment a particular number of times - we would need to count how many times we executed the code. In the school score example from above, we need to go through all 300 scores to compute an average. BASIC offers a convenient way to do counting: the **For/Next** loop.

A **For/Next** loop has this structure:

```
For LoopCounter = StartValue To EndValue Step Increment
    [BASIC code to execute goes here]
Next LoopCounter
```

The **For** statement creates a loop (place where code is repeated) in which the variable **LoopCounter** (called the **loop index**) is initialized at **StartValue** and is then incremented (changed) by **Increment** each time the program executes the loop. The words "Step Increment" are optional. If they are omitted, an increment (Step) of one is assumed. The end of the loop is marked by the **Next** statement. The loop is repeated until LoopCounter reaches or exceeds **EndValue**. When the loop is completed, program execution continues after the Next statement. Each **For** statement in your BASIC program must have a matching **Next** statement (the Intellisense feature of Visual Basic will automatically add a Next statement as soon as you type a For statement). The code between the For and Next should be indented (automatically done by the Visual Basic environment). For/Next loops can be nested (one loop in another), but that's beyond this class.

Let's look at a few For/Next examples to see how they work. This loop will repeat 10 times:

```
For LoopCounter = 1 to 10
    [BASIC code to execute goes here]
Next LoopCounter
```

LoopCounter has a value of 1 the first time through loop, 2 the second time through, and repeats until LoopCounter has a value of 10 the final time through. How about a rocket launch countdown? This loop will do the job:

```
For LoopCounter = 10 to 1 Step -1
    [BASIC code to execute goes here]
Next LoopCounter
```

Here LoopCounter starts at 10 and goes <u>down</u> by 1 (Step -1) each time the loop is repeated. Yes, you can have negative Step values. And, you can have increments that are not 1. This loop counts from 0 to 200 by 5's:

```
For LoopCounter = 0 to 200 Step 5
    [BASIC code to execute goes here]
Next LoopCounter
```

How about averaging the scores from our student example. This code will do the job:

```
ScoreSum = 0
For StudentNumber = 1 to 300
  ScoreSum = ScoreSum + Score(StudentNumber)
Next StudentNumber
Average = ScoreSum / 300
```

To find an average of a group of numbers, you add up all the numbers then divide by the number of numbers you have. In this code, ScoreSum represents the sum of all the numbers. We set this to zero to start. Then, each time through the loop, we add the next score to that "running" sum. The loop adds up all 300 scores making use of the Score array. The first time through it adds in Score(1), then Score(2), then Score(3), and so on, until it finishes by adding in Score(300). Once done, the Average is computed by dividing ScoreSum by 300. Do you see how the For/Next loop greatly simplifies the task of adding up 300 numbers? This is one of the shortcut methods we can use when working with arrays. Study each of these examples so you have an idea of how the For/Next loop works. Use them when you need to count.

Procedure Level Variables

Before continuing, let's address an important issue. Notice, at a minimum, the For/Next loop requires the declaration of one variable, the loop index, usually an integer variable. This variable is only used in this loop - it's value is of no use outside of the event procedure it is used in. When we declare a variable in the general declarations area of the code window, its value is available to all event procedures. Such declarations are not necessary with For/Next loop indexes and it becomes a headache if you have lots of For/Next loops. Loop indexes and other variables not needed outside of a particular procedure can be declared within the procedure. We give these variables **procedure level scope** - their value is only known within that procedure. Variables declared in the general declarations area are said to have **form level scope**. Variables are given procedure level scope using the same Dim statement. Just declare any procedure level variables right after the event procedure header line.

As an example of declaring procedure level variables, assume we have a button control (named **btnAverage**) on a form that computes the student average score in our example. The **btnAverage Click** event procedure would look like this:

```
  Private Sub BtnAverage_Click(ByVal sender As
System.Object, ByVal e As System.EventArgs) Handles
btnAverage.Click
    Dim ScoreSum As Integer
    Dim StudentNumber As Integer
    ScoreSum = 0
    For StudentNumber =1 to 300
      ScoreSum = ScoreSum + Score(StudentNumber)
    Next StudentNumber
    Average = ScoreSum / 300
  End Sub
```

In this example, **ScoreSum** and **StudentNumber** are only used and needed in this procedure, hence are declared as procedure level variables. The variable **Average** should be declared in the general declarations area so it has form level scope and is available everywhere in your project. As you write BASIC code, decide whether you want your variables to have procedure level or form level scope and declare them in the proper area in the code window.

Shuffle Routine

A common task in any computer program is to randomly sort a list of consecutive integer values. Why would you want to do this? Say you have four answers in a multiple choice quiz. Randomly sort the integers 1, 2, 3, and 4, so the answers are presented in random order. Or, you have a quiz with 30 questions. Randomly sort the questions for printing out as a worksheet. Or, the classic application is shuffling a deck of standard playing cards (there are 52 cards in such a deck). In that case, you randomly sort the integers from 1 to 52 to "simulate" the shuffling process. Let's build a shuffle routine using the variable array and For/Next knowledge we now have. We call it a shuffle routine, recognizing it can do more than shuffle a card deck. Our routine will sort any number of consecutive integers.

Usually when we need a computer version of something we can do without a computer, it is fairly easy to write down the steps taken and duplicate them in BASIC code. Remember we did that with the Sandwich Maker project in Class 7. When we shuffle a deck of cards, we separate the deck in two parts, then interleaf the cards as we fan each part, making that familiar shuffling noise. I don't know how you could write BASIC code to do this. Other times, the computer version of a process is easy to do on a computer, but hard or tedious to do off the computer. Our shuffle routine is an example of such a process.

We will perform what could be called a "one card shuffle." In a one card shuffle, you pull a single card (at random) out of the deck and lay it aside on a pile. Repeat this 52 times and the cards are shuffled. Try it! I think you see this idea is simple, but doing a one card shuffle with a real deck of cards would be awfully time-consuming. We'll use the idea of a one card shuffle here, with a slight twist. Rather than lay the selected card on a pile, we will swap it with the bottom card in the stack of cards remaining to be shuffled. This takes the selected card out of the deck and replaces it with the remaining bottom card. The result is the same as if we lay it aside.

Here's how the shuffle works with N numbers:

- Start with a list of N consecutive integers.
- Randomly pick one item from the list. Swap that item with the last item. You now have one fewer items in the list to be sorted (called the remaining list), or N is now N - 1.
- Randomly pick one item from the remaining list. Swap it with the item on the bottom of the remaining list. Again, your remaining list now has one fewer items.
- Repeatedly remove one item from the remaining list and swap it with the item on the bottom of the remaining list until you have run out of items. When done, the list will have been replaced with the original list in random order.

Confusing? Let's show a simple example with N = 5 (a very small deck of cards).

The starting list is (with 5 remaining items):

<u>**1 2 3 4 5**</u>
Remaining List

We want to pick one item, at random, from this list. Using the BASIC random number generator, we would choose a random number from 1 to 5. Say it was 3. We take the third item in the list (the 3) and swap it with the last item in the list (the 5). We now have:

<u>**1 2 5 4**</u> **3**
Remaining List

There are now 4 items in the remaining list. Pick a random number from 1 to 4 - say it's 4. The fourth item in the remaining list is 4. Swap it with the last item in the remaining list. Wait a minute! The last item in the remaining list is the 4. In this case, we swap it with itself, or it stays put. If the random number was something other than 4, there really would have been a swap here. We now have:

<u>**1 2 5**</u> **4 3**
Remaining List

There are 3 items in the remaining list. Pick a random number from 1 to 3 - say it's 1. The first item in the list is 1. Swap the 1 with the last item in the remaining list (the 5), giving us:

<u>5 2</u> 1 4 3

Remaining List

There are 2 items in the remaining list. Pick a random number from 1 to 2 - say it's 1. The first item in the list is 5. Swap the 5 with the last item in the remaining list (the 2), giving us the final result, the numbers 1 to 5 randomly sorted:

2 5 1 4 3

Pretty neat how this works, huh?

We want to describe the one card shuffle with BASIC code. Most of the code is straightforward. The only question is how to do the swap involved in each step. This swap is easy on paper. How do we do a swap in BASIC? Actually, this is a common BASIC task and is relatively simple. At first thought, to swap variable A with variable B, you might write:

```
A = B
B = A
```

The problem with this code is that when you replace A with B in the first statement, you have destroyed the original value of A. The second statement just puts the newly assigned A value (B) back in B. Both A and B now have the original B value! Actually, swapping two variables is a three step process. First, put A in a temporary storage variable (make it the same type as A and B and give it procedure level scope). Then, replace A by B. Then, replace B by the temporary variable (which holds the original A value). If T is the temporary variable, a swap of A and B is done using:

```
T = A
A = B
B = T
```

You use swaps like this in all kinds of Visual Basic applications.

Now, we'll see the BASIC code that uses a one card shuffle to randomly sort N consecutive integer values. When done the random list of integers is in the array **NumberList**, which should be declared in the general declarations area of your project with the proper dimension. Also declare the variable, **NumberOfItems**, which is the length of the list. For a deck of cards, these declarations would be:

```
Dim NumberList(52) As Integer
Dim NumberOfItems As Integer
```

You need to make sure to assign a value (52) to **NumberOfItems** somewhere, most likely in the form **Load** procedure. All other variables can be given procedure level scope. These variables are:

TempValue - temporary integer variable used for swapping
LoopCounter - integer loop counter variable
ItemPicked - integer variable giving item picked in remaining list
Remaining - integer loop variable giving number of items in remaining list

We also need a random number object (**MyRandom**) with procedure level scope to do all the random number generation.

The code is:

```
'Variable declarations (put at top of procedure)

Dim TempValue As Integer
Dim LoopCounter As Integer
Dim ItemPicked As Integer
Dim Remaining As Integer
Dim MyRandom As New Random

'One card shuffle code
'Initialize NumberList
For LoopCounter = 1 to NumberOfItems
  NumberList(LoopCounter) = LoopCounter
Next LoopCounter
'Work through Remaining values
'Start at NumberOfItems and swap one value
'at each For/Next loop step
'After each step, Remaining is decreased by 1
For Remaining = NumberOfItems to 2 Step -1
  'Pick item at random
  ItemPicked = MyRandom.Next(Remaining) + 1
  'Swap picked item with bottom item
  TempValue = NumberList(Remaining)
  NumberList(Remaining) = NumberList(ItemPicked)
  NumberList(ItemPicked) = TempValue
Next Remaining
```

Study this code and see how it implements the procedure followed in the simple five number example. It's not that hard to see. Understanding how such code works is a first step to becoming a good BASIC programmer. Notice this bit of code uses everything we talked about in this class' BASIC lesson: arrays, For/Next Loops, and procedure level variables.

Project - Card Wars

In this project, we create a simplified version of the kid's card game - War. You play against the computer. You each get half a deck of cards (26 cards). Each player turns over one card at a time. The one with the higher card wins the other player's card. The one with the most cards at the end wins. Obviously, the shuffle routine will come in handy here. We call this project Card Wars! This project is saved as **CardWars** in the projects folder **(\CBGVB\BVB Projects**).

Project Design

We will use a panel control to represent the outline of each player's card. A label control will show the card's value and a picture box control will display the card's suit (hearts, diamonds, clubs, spades). A button will control starting a new game or drawing a new card, depending on game state. Another button will control stopping the game, if playing, or stopping the program, if not playing. The current score (number of cards each player has) will be displayed in a labeled text box control.

Place Controls on Form

Start a new project in Visual Basic. Place two panel controls on the form. Size them to represent the two displayed cards. Place a label and picture box control in each panel. Add two buttons to the form. Add two labels and two text boxes that will be used for the scoring system. Add a large text box to tell us when the game is over. And, add four more picture boxes that will be used to hold the images for each card suit. When done, my form looks like this:

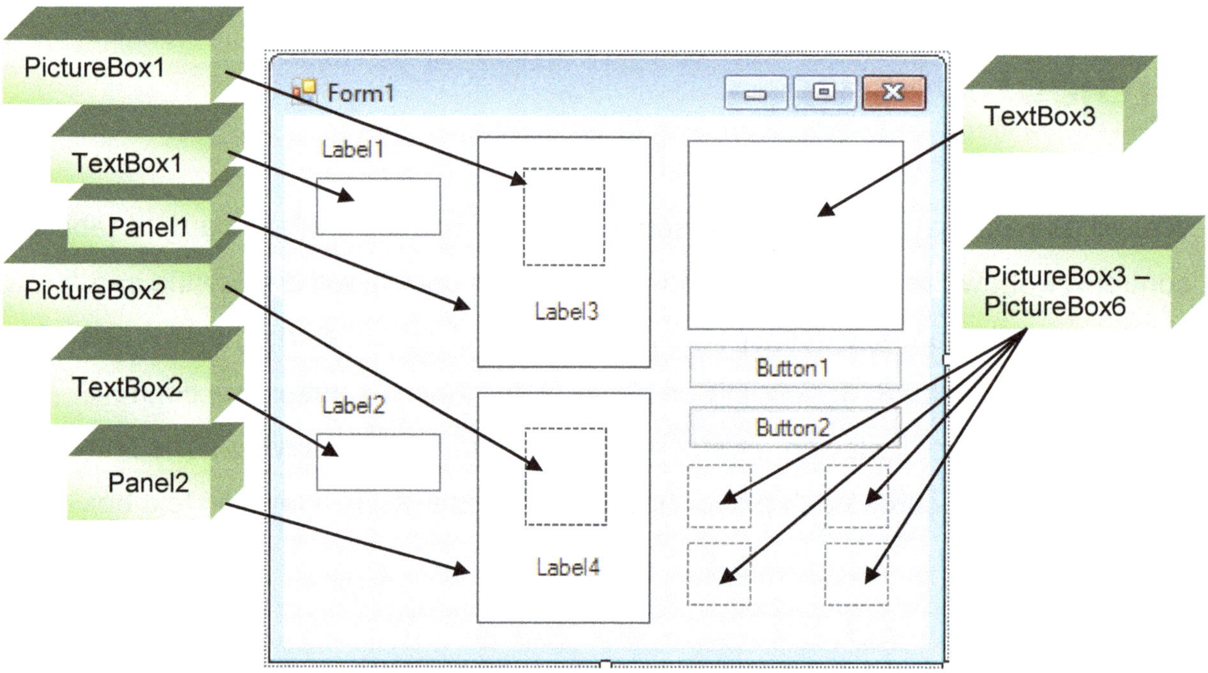

Set Control Properties

Set the control properties using the properties window:

Form1 Form:

Property Name	**Property Value**
Text	Card Wars
FormBorderStyle	Fixed Single
StartPosition	CenterScreen

Panel1 Panel:

Property Name	**Property Value**
Name	pnlPlayer
BackColor	White
BorderStyle	FixedSingle

Panel2 Panel:

Property Name	**Property Value**
Name	pnlComputer
BackColor	White
BorderStyle	FixedSingle

Picture Box1 Picture Box:

Property Name	**Property Value**
Name	picPlayer
SizeMode	StretchImage

Picture Box2 Picture Box:

Property Name	**Property Value**
Name	picComputer
SizeMode	StretchImage

PictureBox3 Picture Box:

Property Name	**Property Value**
Name	picHeart
Image	Heart.ico (in **\CBGVB\BVB Projects\CardWars** folder)
SizeMode	AutoSize
Visible	False

PictureBox4 Picture Box:

Property Name	**Property Value**
Name	picDiamond
Image	Diamond.ico (in **\CBGVB\BVB Projects\CardWars** folder)
SizeMode	AutoSize
Visible	False

PictureBox5 Picture Box:

Property Name	**Property Value**
Name	picClub
Image	Club.ico (in in **\CBGVB\BVB Projects\CardWars** folder)
SizeMode	AutoSize
Visible	False

PictureBox6 Picture Box:

Property Name	**Property Value**
Name	picSpade
Image	Spade.ico (in in **\CBGVB\BVB Projects\CardWars** folder)
SizeMode	AutoSize
Visible	False

The Visible properties for these four picture box controls (picHeart, picDiamond, picClub, picSpade) are purposely False. We don't want them to show up on the form in run mode - we just want to use their stored picture for our card displays. This is done a lot in Visual Basic. When setting the Image property, in the Open File Dialog, you will need to make sure you view **All Files** and not just the **Image Files**. Icon files will not appear unless you make this change.

Label1 Label:

Property Name	**Property Value**
Name	lblYou
Text	You
Font Size	10
TextAlign	LeftCenter

TextBox1 Text Box:

Property Name	**Property Value**
Name	txtYouScore
Text	0
Font Size	12
Font Style	Bold
ReadOnly	True
TextAlign	Center
BackColor	White

Label2 Label:

Property Name	**Property Value**
Name	lblComp
Text	Computer
Font Size	10
TextAlign	LeftCenter

TextBox2 Text Box:

Property Name	Property Value
Name	txtCompScore
Text	0
Font Size	12
Font Style	Bold
ReadOnly	True
TextAlign	Center
BackColor	White

Label3 Label:

Property Name	Property Value
Name	lblPlayer
Text	[Blank]
Font Size	18
Font Style	Bold
TextAlign	MiddleCenter

Label4 Label:

Property Name	Property Value
Name	lblComputer
Text	[Blank]
Font Size	18
Font Style	Bold
TextAlign	MiddleCenter

TextBox3 Text Box:

Property Name	Property Value
Name	txtOver
Text	Game Over
Font Size	14
Font Style	Bold
ReadOnly	True
TextAlign	Center
BackColor	White
ForeColor	Red

Button1 Button:

Property Name	**Property Value**
Name	btnNew
Text	New Game

Button2 Button:

Property Name	**Property Value**
Name	btnExit
Text	Exit

When done, my form looks like this:

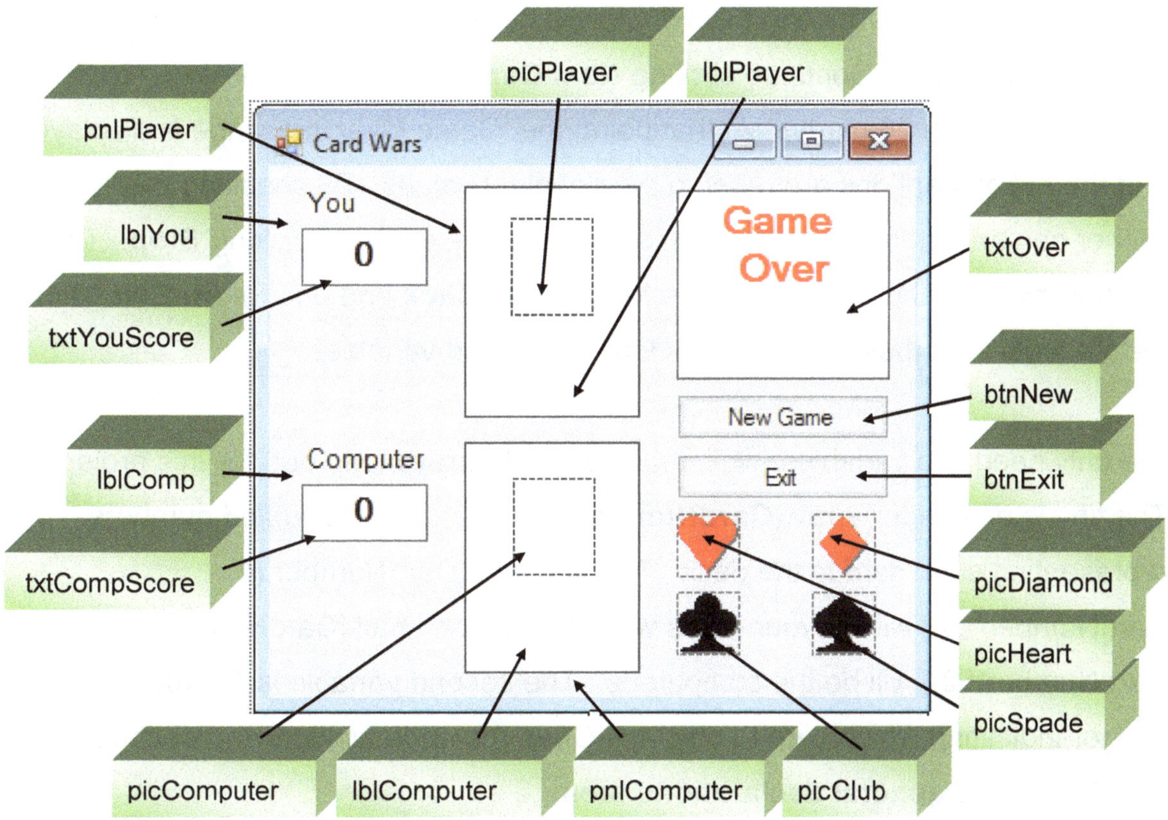

Write Event Procedures

The idea of this game is quite simple. You click the **New Game** button to start. This shuffles the cards, resets the scores to zero and changes the button's Text to **Next Card**. It also changes the **Exit** button Text to **Stop** (for stopping the current game). A card for you (upper card) and a card for the computer (lower card) are displayed. The computer decides which card is higher. The player with the higher card gets two points. If it's a tie, each player gets one point. Scores are displayed under **You** (txtYouScore has your score) and **Computer** (txtCompScore has computer's score). Click **Next Card**. A new card is displayed for each player and the scores updated. Continue clicking **Next Card** until the game is over (each player has shown 26 cards). At that point, the 'Game Over' message is displayed and the button captions are reset to their original values. By checking the score, a winner can be determined. You can stop the game early by clicking **Stop**. There are only two event procedures - one for **btnNew Click** and one for **btnExit Click**. Before looking at these events, let's look at needed variables.

We only need two variables (well, really 53, but, arrays help out) for this project. The first is an integer array (**CardNumber**) that has the 52 shuffled numbers representing each card in the deck. The first half [CardNumber (1) - CardNumber(26)] will be your cards while the second half [CardNumber(27) - CardNumber(52)] will be the computer's. The second variable is **CardIndex**, an integer indicating which card to display. Open the code window and declare these variables in the **general declarations** area:

```
Dim CardNumber(52) As Integer
Dim CardIndex As Integer
```

Now, let's outline the steps involved in the **btnNew Click** event. First, we are letting this command button have two purposes. It either starts a new game (**Text** is **New Game**) and or gets a new card (**Text** is **Next Card**). So, the Click event has two segments. If Text is New Game, the steps are:

- Hide 'Game Over' notice
- Set btnNew Text to "Next Card"
- Set btnExit Text to "Stop"
- Set scores to zero
- Shuffle cards
- Initialize CardIndex to one
- Display first card for each player
- Compare cards - update score

If Text is Next Card, the steps are:

- Display two new cards
- Compare displayed cards - update scores
- Increment CardIndex
- If there are no cards left, stop game - display 'Game Over' message, change button captions. Otherwise, wait for click on Next Card button.

Most of these steps are easily done now that we know how to shuffle a deck of cards. The only tough part is deciding how to display and compare cards. Let's look at that in some detail.

Displaying a card consists of answering two questions: what is the card suit and what is the card value? The four suits are hearts, diamonds, clubs, and spades. The thirteen card values, from lowest to highest, are: 2, 3, 4, 5, 6, 7, 8, 9, 10, Jack (J), Queen (Q), King (K), Ace (A). We've seen in our shuffle routine that a card number will range from 1 to 52. How do we translate that card number to a card suit and value? (Notice the distinction between card **number** and card **value -** card number ranges from 1 to 52, card value can only range from 2 to Ace.) We need to develop some type of translation rule. This is done all the time in BASIC. If the number you compute with or work with does not directly translate to information you need, you need to make up rules to do the translation. For example, the numbers 1 to 12 are used to represent the months of the year. But, these numbers tell us nothing about the names of the month. We need a rule to translate each number to a month name.

We know we need 13 of each card suit. Hence, an easy rule to decide suit is: cards numbered 1 - 13 are hearts, cards numbered 14 - 26 are diamonds, cards numbered 27 - 39 are clubs, and cards numbered 40 - 52 are spades. Suit is represented on the displayed card by the two picture boxes: picPlayer (your card) and picComputer (computer's card). For card values, lower numbers should represent lower cards. A rule that does this for each number in each card suit is:

		Card Numbers		
Hearts	**Diamonds**	**Clubs**	**Spades**	**Card Value**
1	14	27	40	2
2	15	28	41	3
3	16	29	42	4
4	17	30	43	5
5	18	31	44	6
6	19	32	45	7
7	20	33	46	8
8	21	34	47	9
9	22	35	48	10
10	23	36	49	J
11	24	37	50	Q
12	25	38	51	K
13	26	39	52	A

As examples, notice card 23 is a Jack of Diamonds. Card 31 is a 6 of Clubs. The card values are displayed in the lblPlayer and lblComputer label controls. We now can display cards. How do we compare them?

Card comparisons must be based on a numerical value, not displayed card value - it's difficult to check if K is greater than 7, though it can be done. So, one last rule is needed to relate card value to numerical value. It's a simple one - start with a 2 having a numerical value of 1 (lowest) and go up, with an Ace (A) having a numerical value of 13 (highest). This makes numerical card comparisons easy. Notice hearts card numbers already go from 1 to 13. If we subtract 13 from diamonds numbers, 26 from clubs numbers, and 39 from spades numbers, each of those card numbers will also range from 1 to 13. This gives a common basis for comparing cards. This all may seem complicated, but look at the BASIC code and you'll see it really isn't.

The BASIC code that implements the **btnNew Click** event procedure is:

```
  Private Sub BtnNew_Click(ByVal sender As System.Object,
ByVal e As System.EventArgs) Handles btnNew.Click
    'Procedure level variables
    Dim TempValue As Integer
    Dim LoopCounter As Integer
    Dim ItemPicked As Integer
    Dim Remaining As Integer
    Dim MyRandom As New Random
    Dim YourNumber As Integer ' Your card number
    Dim ComputerNumber As Integer ' Computer card number
    If btnNew.Text = "New Game" Then
      'New game clicked
      txtOver.Visible = False
      btnNew.Text = "Next Card"
      btnExit.Text = "Stop"
      'Zero out scores
      txtYouScore.Text = "0"
      txtCompScore.Text = "0"
      'Shuffle cards using one card shuffle code
      'Initialize CardNumbers
      For LoopCounter = 1 To 52
        CardNumber(LoopCounter) = LoopCounter
      Next LoopCounter
      'Work through Remaining values
      'Start at 52 and swap one value
      'at each For/Next loop step
      'After each step, Remaining is decreased by 1
      For Remaining = 52 To 2 Step -1
        'Pick item at random
        ItemPicked = MyRandom.Next(Remaining) + 1
        'Swap picked item with bottom item
        TempValue = CardNumber(Remaining)
        CardNumber(Remaining) = CardNumber(ItemPicked)
        CardNumber(ItemPicked) = TempValue
      Next Remaining
      'Set CardIndex to one
      CardIndex = 1
    End If
    'Display cards
    'Display your card's suit
    'Determine your card's number for comparisons
      Select Case CardNumber(CardIndex)
        Case 1 To 13
          picPlayer.Image = picHeart.Image
```

```
      YourNumber = CardNumber(CardIndex)
    Case 14 To 26
      picPlayer.Image = picDiamond.Image
      YourNumber = CardNumber(CardIndex) - 13
    Case 27 To 39
      picPlayer.Image = picClub.Image
      YourNumber = CardNumber(CardIndex) - 26
    Case 40 To 52
      picPlayer.Image = picSpade.Image
      YourNumber = CardNumber(CardIndex) - 39
  End Select
  'Display your card's value
  Select Case YourNumber
    Case 1 To 9
      lblPlayer.Text = Str(YourNumber + 1) + " "
    Case 10
      lblPlayer.Text = "J"
    Case 11
      lblPlayer.Text = "Q"
    Case 12
      lblPlayer.Text = "K"
    Case 13
      lblPlayer.Text = "A"
  End Select
  'Display computer's card suit
  'Determine computer's number for comparisons
  Select Case CardNumber(CardIndex + 26)
    Case 1 To 13
      picComputer.Image = picHeart.Image
      ComputerNumber = CardNumber(CardIndex + 26)
    Case 14 To 26
      picComputer.Image = picDiamond.Image
      ComputerNumber = CardNumber(CardIndex + 26) - 13
    Case 27 To 39
      picComputer.Image = picClub.Image
      ComputerNumber = CardNumber(CardIndex + 26) - 26
    Case 40 To 52
      picComputer.Image = picSpade.Image
      ComputerNumber = CardNumber(CardIndex + 26) - 39
  End Select
  'Display computer card's value
  Select Case ComputerNumber
    Case 1 To 9
      lblComputer.Text = Str(ComputerNumber + 1) + " "
    Case 10
      lblComputer.Text = "J"
    Case 11
```

```
          lblComputer.Text = "Q"
        Case 12
          lblComputer.Text = "K"
        Case 13
          lblComputer.Text = "A"
      End Select
      'Compare displayed cards
      If YourNumber > ComputerNumber Then
        'You win
        txtYouScore.Text = Str(Val(txtYouScore.Text) + 2)
      ElseIf ComputerNumber > YourNumber Then
        'Computer win
        txtCompScore.Text = Str(Val(txtCompScore.Text) + 2)
      Else
        'A Tie!
        txtYouScore.Text = Str(Val(txtYouScore.Text) + 1)
        txtCompScore.Text = Str(Val(txtCompScore.Text) + 1)
      End If
    CardIndex = CardIndex + 1
    'Check to see if all cards have been used
    If CardIndex > 26 Then
      'Game over
      txtOver.Visible = True
      btnNew.Text = "New Game"
      btnExit.Text = "Exit"
    End If
  End Sub
```

You should be able to see each outlined step in this code. Notice particularly the shuffle routine and how CardIndex is used with the CardNumber array to display your card and the computer card. Remember the computer card is 26 elements ahead of your card in the CardNumber array. Look at how the card numbers are found and how comparisons are made. Check out the tricky way scores are updated without using any variables! Notice, too, how as your programming knowledge expands, there's a lot more happening in the code we write. Remember to use cut and paste where you can - it will make your work easier.

We now need to code the **btnExit Click** event. Like **btnNew**, It also has two purposes. If the button **Text** property is **Exit**, the program stops. If the **Text** is **Stop**, the current game stops. That code is pretty simple:

```
  Private Sub BtnExit_Click(ByVal sender As System.Object,
ByVal e As System.EventArgs) Handles btnExit.Click
    If btnExit.Text = "Exit" Then
      'Stop program
      Me.Close()
    Else
      'Stop game
      txtOver.Visible = True
      btnExit.Text = "Exit"
      btnNew.Text = "New Game"
    End If
  End Sub
```

Save the project by clicking the **Save All** button in the toolbar.

Run the Project

Run the project. Click **New Game** to get started. Click **Next Card** to display each pair of cards. Notice how the different controls are used to make up the cards. Make sure the program works correctly. Here's what my screen looks like in the middle of a game:

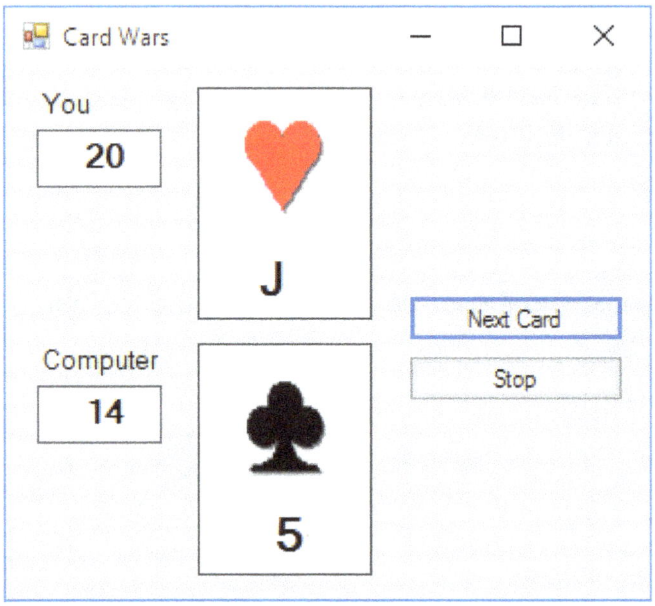

Play through one game and check each comparison to make sure you get the correct result and score with each new card. Make sure the **Stop** and **Exit** buttons work properly. Go through the usual process of making sure the program works as it should. Once you're convinced everything is OK, have fun playing the game. Share your creation with friends. If you made any changes during the running process, make sure you save the project.

Other Things to Try

Possible changes to the Card Wars project are obvious, but not easy. One change would be to have more than two players. Set up three and four player versions. You could also add a message after each comparison to way which player won (or whether it was a tie). You could use the txtOver control that's already there.

In Card Wars, we stop the game after going through the deck one time. In the real card game of War, after the first round, the players pick up the cards they won, shuffle them, and play another round. Every time a player uses all the cards in their "hand," they again pick up their winnings pile, reshuffle and continue playing. This continues until one player has lost all of their cards. Another change to Card Wars would be to write code that plays the game with these rules. As we said, it's not easy. You would need to add code to keep track of which cards each player won, when they ran out of cards to play, how to reshuffle their remaining cards, and new logic to see when a game was over. Such code would use more arrays, more For/Next loops, and more variables. If you want a programming challenge, go for it!

And, while you're tackling challenges, here's another. In the usual War game, when two cards have the same value - War is declared! This means each player takes three cards from their "hand" and lays them face down. Then another card is placed face up. The higher card at that time wins all 10 cards! If it's still a tie, there's another War. Try adding this logic to the game. You might need to change the display to allow more cards. You'll need to figure out how to lay cards "face down" in BASIC. You'll need to check if a player has enough cards to wage War. Another difficult task, but give it a try if you feel adventurous.

Summary

This class presented one of the more challenging projects yet. The code involved in shuffling cards and displaying cards, though straightforward, was quite involved. The use of panel and picture box controls helped in the display. The use of arrays and For/Next loops made the coding a bit easier. If you completely understood the Card Wars project, you are well on your way to being a good Visual Basic programmer. Now, on to the last class.

10

Timers, Animation, Keyboard Events

Review and Preview

It's the last class. By now, you should have some confidence in your abilities as a Visual Basic programmer. In this class, we'll look at one more control that's a lot of fun - the timer control. It's a key control for adding animation (motion) to graphics in projects. We study some animation techniques and we'll examine how to recognize user inputs from the keyboard via keyboard events. Then, you'll build one last project (at least, the last project in this class) - your first video game!

Timer Control

The Visual Basic **timer** control has an interesting feature. It is the one control that can generate events without any input from the user. Timer controls work in your project's background, generating events at time intervals you specify. This event generation feature comes in handy for graphics animation where screen displays need to be updated at regular intervals. The timer control is selected from the toolbox. It appears as:

In Toolbox:

Below Form (default properties):

There is no user interface (nothing to click or nothing to look at) for the timer control, so it will not appear on the form. Such controls are placed in the "tray area" below the form in the design window.

Properties

The timer control properties are:

Property	Description
Name	Name used to identify timer control. Three letter prefix for timer names is **tim**.
Interval	Number of milliseconds between timer events. There are 1000 milliseconds in one second.
Enabled	Used to turn timer control on and off. When True, timer continues to generate events until set to False.

Events

The timer control has a single event:

Event	Description
Tick	Event procedure executed every Interval milliseconds when timer control Enabled property is True.

Examples

A few examples should clarify how the timer control works. It's very simple and very powerful. Here's what happens. If a timer control's **Enabled** property is **True** (the timer is on), every **Interval** milliseconds, Visual Basic will generate an event and execute the corresponding **Tick** event procedure. No user interaction is needed. If your timer is named **timExample**, the Timer event procedure has the form:

```
  Private Sub TimExample_Tick(ByVal sender As System.Object,
ByVal e As System.EventArgs) Handles timExample.Tick

      [BASIC code to be executed every Interval milliseconds]

  End Sub
```

Whatever BASIC code you want to execute is put in this procedure.

The Interval property is the most important timer control property. This property is set to the number of milliseconds between timer events. A millisecond is 1/1000th of a second, or there are 1,000 milliseconds in a second. If you want to generate N events per second, set Interval to 1000 / N. For example, if you want a timer event to occur 4 times per second, set Interval to 250. About the lowest practical value for Interval is 50 and values that differ by 5, 10, or even 20 are likely to produce similar results. It all depends on your particular computer.

The only other property to worry about is the Enabled property. It is used to turn the timer on (True) or off (False). In design mode, the timer control Enabled property is given a default value of False. We will always leave this at False. It is good programming practice to control timers programmatically. This simply means turn your timers on and off in BASIC code. It's a matter of changing the Enabled property. And, always make sure if you turn a timer on that you turn it off when you need to. Now, the first example.

Start Visual Basic and start a new project. Add a timer control (it will appear below the form) and button to the form. In this example, we will use the timer control to make your computer beep every second. The button will turn the timer on and off. Set the timer control (**Timer1** default name) Interval property to 1000 (1000 milliseconds equals one second). Put this code in the **Timer1 Tick** event procedure (it will be one of the few events listed for the timer control in the code window):

```
  Private Sub Timer1_Tick(ByVal sender As System.Object,
ByVal e As System.EventArgs) Handles Timer1.Tick
    Beep()
  End Sub
```

Beep is the BASIC function that makes the computer beep, or is that obvious?

Put this code in the button (default name **Button1**) **Button1 Click** event procedure:

```
  Private Sub Button1_Click(ByVal sender As System.Object,
ByVal e As System.EventArgs) Handles Button1.Click
    If Timer1.Enabled Then
      Timer1.Enabled = False
    Else
      Timer1.Enabled = True
    End If
  End Sub
```

What does this code do? If the timer is on (Timer1.Enabled = True), it turns it off (Timer1.Enabled = False), and vice versa. We say this code "toggles" the timer. Run the project. Click the button. Your computer will beep every second (the Tick event is executed every 1000 milliseconds, the Interval value) until you click the button again. Notice it does this no matter what else is going on. It requires no input (once the timer is on) from you, the user. Click the button. The beeping will stop. Remember to always let your BASIC code turn timer controls on and off. Stop the project when you get tired of the beeping.

Add the two shaded lines of code to the **Timer1 Tick** event, so it now reads:

```
  Private Sub Timer1_Tick(ByVal sender As System.Object,
ByVal e As System.EventArgs) Handles Timer1.Tick
    Beep()
    Dim MyRandom As New Random
    Me.BackColor = Color.FromArgb(MyRandom.Next(256),
MyRandom.Next(256), MyRandom.Next(256))
  End Sub
```

This extra code randomly changes the form (name **Me**) background color using the **FromArgb** method (using random red, green and blue values). Run the project. Click the button. Now, every second, the computer beeps and the form changes color. Stop the timer. Stop the project.

What if we want the computer to beep every second, but want the form color to change four times every second? If events require different intervals, each event needs its own timer. Add another timer control to the form (default name **Timer2**). We'll use this timer to control the form color. Set Timer2's Interval to 250 (Tick event executed every 0.25 seconds, or 4 color changes per second). Copy and paste the line of code in **Timer1 Tick** that sets color into the **Timer2 Tick** event. The two timer Tick events are now:

```
  Private Sub Timer1_Tick(ByVal sender As System.Object,
ByVal e As System.EventArgs) Handles Timer1.Tick
    Beep()
  End Sub

  Private Sub Timer2_Tick(ByVal sender As System.Object,
ByVal e As System.EventArgs) Handles Timer2.Tick
    Dim MyRandom As New Random
    Me.BackColor = Color.FromArgb(MyRandom.Next(256),
MyRandom.Next(256), MyRandom.Next(256))
  End Sub
```

We also need to add code to the **Button1 Click** event to toggle (turn it on and off) this new timer. We could copy and paste the five lines of code there for Timer1 and change all the Timer1 words to Timer2. And, this would work. But, let me show you a quick way to toggle Boolean variables, like the Enabled property. We'll be able to replace five lines of code with one!

Way back in Class 6, we studied logical operators - operators that work with Boolean variables. Remember **And**? Remember **Or**? Well, there's another logical operator that comes in handy - the **Not** operator. This operator works on a single Boolean variable. If we have a Boolean variable named X, it can have two values, True or False. **Not** X has the opposite value of X as shown in this simple logic table:

X	Not X
True	False
False	True

Notice the Not operator toggles the Boolean variable X. If X is on (True), the Not operator turns X off (False). If X is off (False), the Not operator turns X on (True). So, we can use the Not operator to turn timer controls on and off. Use this code in the **Button1 Click** event procedure in our example:

```
  Private Sub Button1_Click(ByVal sender As System.Object,
ByVal e As System.EventArgs) Handles Button1.Click
    Timer1.Enabled = Not (Timer1.Enabled)
    Timer2.Enabled = Not (Timer2.Enabled)
  End Sub
```

Notice how the Not operator simplifies using timer controls. Do you see that one line of BASIC code using Not has exactly the same effect as the five lines of code we used earlier to toggle the timer? Run the project. Click the button. Do you see how the two timer events are interacting? You should hear a beep every four times the screen changes color. Stop the project when you're done playing with it.

Let's use the timer to do some flashier stuff. Start a new project. Add a panel control (default name **Panel1**). Make the panel fairly big – make it wider than it is tall. Add a button (default name **Button1**), and a timer control (default name **Timer1**). Set the timer control Interval property to 50. Declare an Integer variable **Delta** in the general declarations area:

```
  Dim Delta As Integer
```

Toggle the timer in the **Button1 Click** event:

```
  Private Sub Button1_Click(ByVal sender As System.Object,
ByVal e As System.EventArgs) Handles Button1.Click
    Timer1.Enabled = Not (Timer1.Enabled)
  End Sub
```

Put this code in the **Timer1 Tick** event:

```
  Private Sub Timer1_Tick(ByVal sender As System.Object,
ByVal e As System.EventArgs) Handles Timer1.Tick
    Dim MyGraphics As Graphics
    Dim MyPen As Pen
    Dim MyRandom As New Random
    MyGraphics = Panel1.CreateGraphics
    MyPen = New Pen(Color.FromArgb(MyRandom.Next(256),
MyRandom.Next(256), MyRandom.Next(256)), 2)
    MyGraphics.DrawEllipse(MyPen, Delta, Delta, Panel1.Width
- 2 * Delta, Panel1.Height - 2 * Delta)
    Delta = Delta + MyPen.Width
    If Delta > Panel1.Height / 2 Then
      Delta = 0
      MyGraphics.Clear(Panel1.BackColor)
    End If
    MyPen.Dispose()
    MyGraphics.Dispose()
  End Sub
```

You should recognize most of what's here. We've created a graphics object and pen object (with a random color) to do some drawing. Notice, though, we use a graphics method (**DrawEllipse**) we haven't seen before. You should be able to understand it and you'll see it gives a really neat effect in this example. The **DrawEllipse** method has the form:

```
MyGraphics.DrawEllipse(MyPen, X, Y, Width, Height)
```

Here, **MyGraphics** is the graphics object. This command draws an ellipse, with a width **Width** and height **Height**, in the graphics object starting at the point (**X**, **Y**). A picture shows the result:

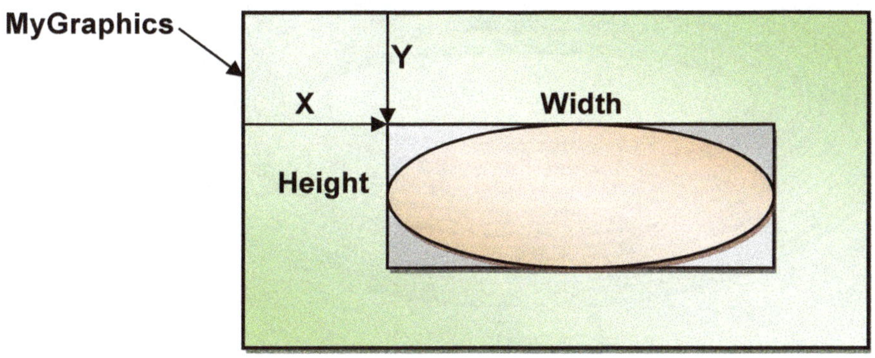

In your work with Visual Basic, you will often see code you don't recognize. Learn to use the on-line help facilities (try it with **DrawEllipse**) in these cases.

Back to the code, you should see the **DrawEllipse** method draws the first ellipse around the border of the panel control (**X = 0** initially). The surrounding rectangle moves "in" an amount **Delta** (in each direction) with each Tick event, resulting in a smaller rectangle (the width and height are decreased by both **2*Delta**). Once Delta (incremented by the pen width in each step) exceeds half of the panel height, it is reset to 0, the panel is cleared and the process starts all over. Run the project. Click the button. Are you hypnotized? Here's a sample of a run I made:

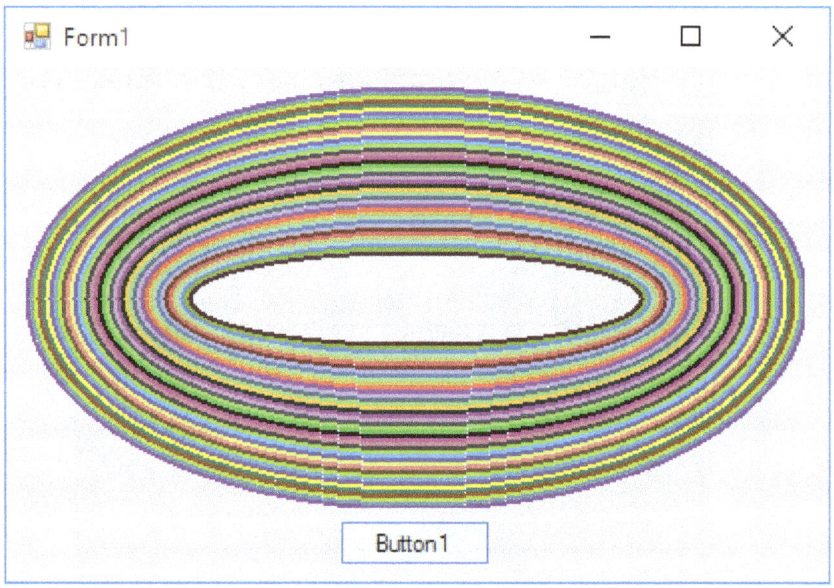

Can you think of other things you could draw using other graphics methods? Look at **DrawRectangle** for example. Try your ideas.

In this last example, the periodic (every 0.050 seconds) changing of the display in the graphics object, imparted by the timer control, gives the appearance of motion – the ellipses seem to be moving inward. This is the basic concept behind a very powerful graphics technique - **animation**. In animation, we have a sequence of pictures, each a little different from the previous one. With the ellipse example, in each picture, we add a new ellipse. By displaying this sequence over time, we can trick the viewer into thinking things are moving. It all has to do with how fast the human eye and brain can process information. That's how cartoons work - 24 different pictures are displayed every second - it makes things look like they are moving, or animated. Obviously, the timer control is a key element to animation, as well as for other Visual Basic timing tasks. In the BASIC lesson for this class, we will look at how to do simple animations and some other things.

Typical Use of Timer Control

The usual design steps to use a timer control are:

- Set the **Name** property and **Interval** property.
- Write code in **Tick** event.
- At some point in your application, set **Enabled** to **True** to start timer. Also, have capability to reset **Enabled** to **False**, when desired.

BASIC – The Final Lesson

In this last BASIC lesson, we study some simple animation techniques, look at math needed with animations, and learn how to detect keyboard events.

Animation - DrawImage Graphics Method

In the last example, we saw that by using a timer to periodically change the display in a panel control, a sense of motion, or animation, is obtained. We will use that idea here to do a specific kind of animation - moving objects around. This is the basis for nearly every video game ever made. The objects we move will be images contained in Visual Basic picture box controls.

Moving images in a panel is easy to do. First, establish an image (set the **Image** property) in the picture box. This image is then placed in the panel control using the **DrawImage** graphics method. Like the other graphics methods we've seen (DrawLine and DrawEllipse), before using DrawImage, you need to establish a graphics object to draw to. The graphics object is declared in the usual manner (usually in the **general declarations** area):

```
Dim MyGraphics As Graphics
```

We then create the graphics object (assume **MyControl** is the host control; we'll use a panel):

```
MyGraphics = MyControl.CreateGraphics()
```

This creation usually occurs in the form **Load** procedure. You dispose of the object in the form **FormClosing** procedure.

Now, assume we have an image in a picture box control named **picExample**. At this point, we can draw **picExample.Image** in **MyGraphics**, using **DrawImage**. The **DrawImage** method that does this is:

```
MyGraphics.DrawImage(picExample.Image, X, Y, W, H)
```

where **X** is the horizontal position of the image within **MyGraphics** and **Y** is the vertical position. The image will have a width value **W** and a height **H**. The width and height can be the original image size or scaled up or down. It's your choice.

A picture illustrates what's going on with **DrawImage**:

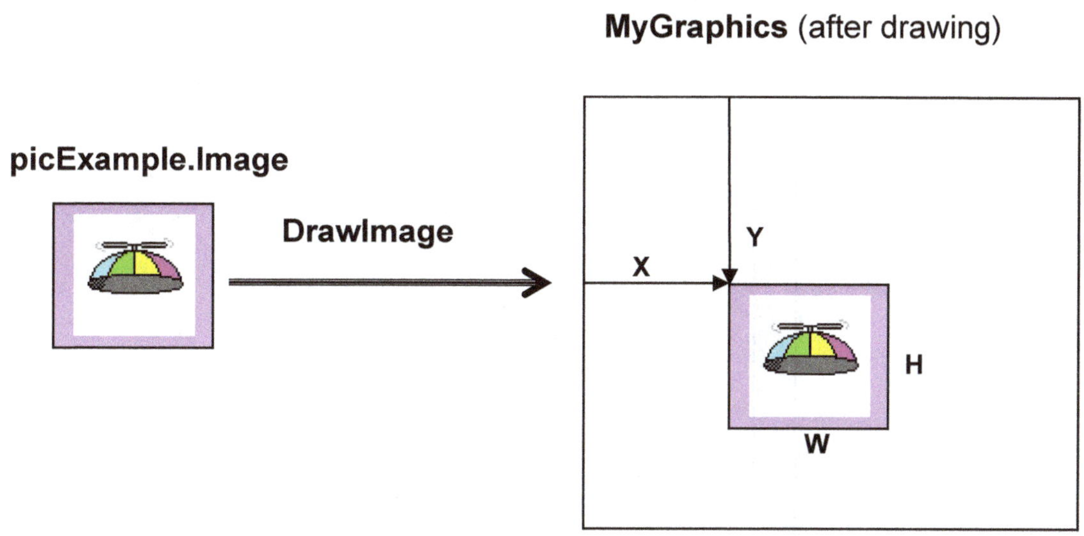

Note how the transfer of the rectangular image occurs. Successive transfers (always erasing the previous position of the image) gives the impression of motion, or animation. Where do we put the DrawImage statement?

Each picture box image to be moved must have an associated timer control. If desired, several images can use the same timer. The DrawImage statement is placed in the corresponding timer control Tick event. Whenever a Tick event is triggered, the image is erased at its old position (by putting a “blank” image in that position), a new image position is computed and the DrawImage method executed. This periodic movement is **animation**. Let’s look at an example to see how simple it really is.

Start Visual Basic and start a new project. Put a panel (default name **Panel1**) on the form - make it fairly tall with a white background color. Put a small picture box on the form. Set its **Image** property (I used the soccer ball bitmap graphic in the **\CBGVB\BVB Projects\Graphics** folder). Place a timer control (default name **Timer1**) on the form. Use an Interval property of 100. Place a button (default name **Button1**) on the form for starting and stopping the timer. We will use this example a lot. Try to make it look something like this:

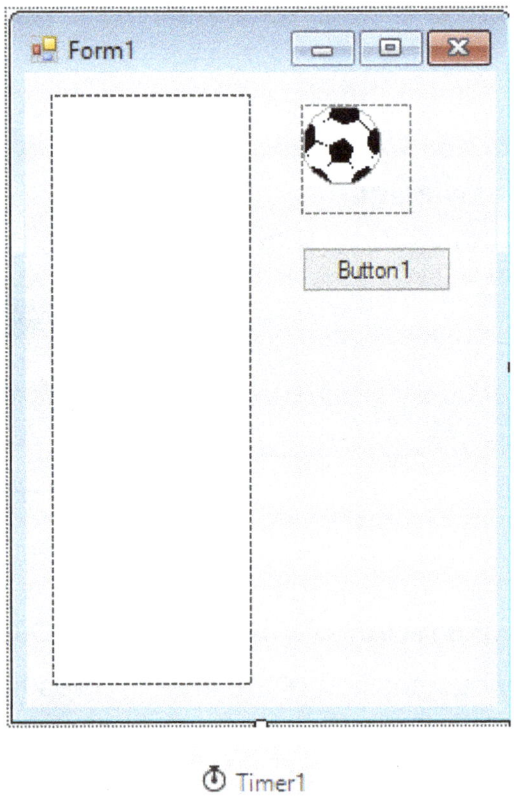

Define the needed graphics object in the **general declarations** area. Also include a variable (**ImageY**) to keep track of the vertical position of the image:

```
  Dim MyGraphics As Graphics
  Dim ImageY As Integer
```

And create the object in the **Form1 Load** event procedure:

```
  Private Sub Form1_Load(ByVal sender As System.Object,
ByVal e As System.EventArgs) Handles MyBase.Load
    MyGraphics = Panel1.CreateGraphics
  End Sub
```

Dispose of the graphics object in the **Form1 FormClosing** event procedure:

```
  Private Sub Form1_FormClosing(ByVal sender As Object,
ByVal e As System.ComponentModel.CancelEventArgs) Handles
MyBase.FormClosing
    MyGraphics.Dispose()
  End Sub
```

Use **Button1 Click** to toggle the timer and initialize the position of **PictureBox1.Image** at the top of the panel control:

```
  Private Sub Button1_Click(ByVal sender As System.Object,
ByVal e As System.EventArgs) Handles Button1.Click
    Timer1.Enabled = Not (Timer1.Enabled)
    ImageY = 0
  End Sub
```

Now, move the image in the **Timer1 Tick** event:

```
  Private Sub Timer1_Tick(ByVal sender As System.Object,
ByVal e As System.EventArgs) Handles Timer1.Tick
    Dim ImageX As Integer
    Dim ImageW As Integer
    Dim ImageH As Integer
    ImageX = 10
    ImageW = 30
    ImageH = 25
    MyGraphics.Clear(Panel1.BackColor)
    ImageY = ImageY + Panel1.Height / 40
    MyGraphics.DrawImage(PictureBox1.Image, ImageX, ImageY,
ImageW, ImageH)
  End Sub
```

In this event, the image width (**ImageW**) and height (**ImageH**) are given values, as is the horizontal location (**ImageX**). Then, the graphics object is cleared to erase the previous image. The vertical position of the image (**ImageY**) is increased by 1/40th of the panel height each time the event is executed (every 0.1 seconds). The picture box image is moving down. It should take 40 executions of this routine, or about 4 seconds, for the image to reach the bottom. Let's try it.

Run the example project. Click the button to start the timer. Watch the image drop. Notice the image is scaled to fit the area defined by the DrawImage method. Pretty easy, wasn't it? How long does it take the image to reach the bottom? What happens when it reaches the bottom? It just keeps on going down through the panel, through the form and out through the bottom of your computer monitor to who knows where! We need to be able to detect this disappearance and do something about it. We'll look at two ways to handle this. First, we'll make the image reappear at the top of the panel, or scroll. Then, we'll make it bounce. Stop the project. Save it too. We'll be using it again.

Image Disappearance

When images are moving in a panel, we need to know when they move out of the panel across a border. Such information is often needed in video type games. We just saw this need with the falling ball example. When an **image disappearance** happens, we can either ignore that image or perhaps make it "scroll" around to other side of the panel control. How do we decide if an image has disappeared? It's basically a case of comparing various positions and dimensions.

We need to detect whether a image has completely moved across one of four panel borders (top, bottom, left, right). Each of these detections can be developed using this diagram of a picture box image (**MyImage**) within a panel (**MyPanel**):

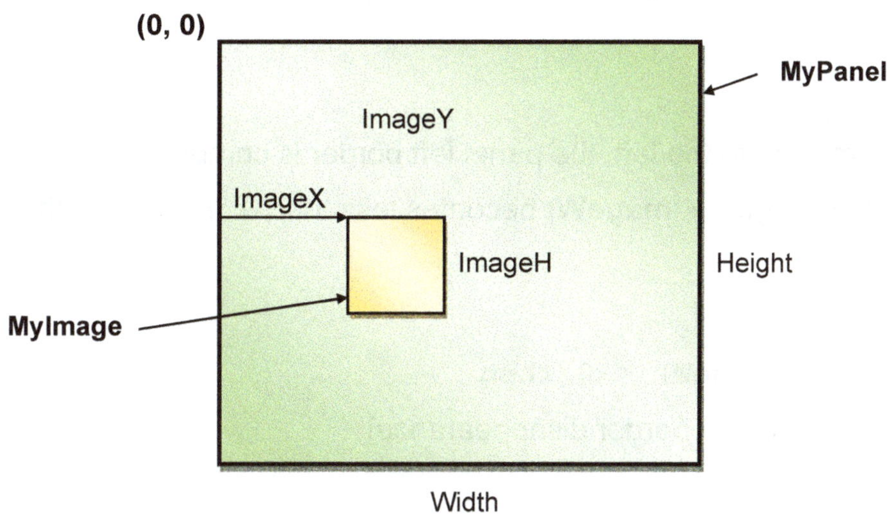

Notice the image is located at (**ImageX**, **ImageY**), is **ImageW** pixels wide and **ImageH** pixels high.

If the image is moving down, it completely crosses the panel bottom border when its top (**ImageY**) is lower than the bottom border. The bottom of the panel is **MyPanel.Height**. BASIC code for a bottom border disappearance is:

```
If ImageY > MyPanel.Height Then
    [BASIC code for bottom border disappearance]
End If
```

If the image is moving up, the panel top border is completely crossed when the bottom of the image (**ImageY + ImageH**) becomes less than 0. In BASIC, this is detected with:

```
If (ImageY + ImageH) < 0 Then
    [BASIC code for top border disappearance]
End If
```

If the control is moving to the left, the panel left border is completely crossed when image right side (**ImageX + ImageW)** becomes less than 0. In BASIC, this is detected with:

```
If (ImageX + ImageW) < 0 Then
    [BASIC code for left border disappearance]
End If
```

If the image is moving to the right, it completely crosses the panel right border when its left side (**ImageX**) passes the border. The right side of the panel is **MyPanel.Width**. BASIC code for a right border disappearance is:

```
If ImageX > MyPanel.Width Then
   [BASIC code for right border disappearance]
End If
```

Let's add disappearance detection to our "falling soccer ball" example. Return to that project. Say, instead of having the image disappear when it reaches the bottom, we have it magically reappear at the top of the panel. We say the image is scrolling. Modify the **Timer1 Tick** event to this (new lines are shaded):

```
  Private Sub Timer1_Tick(ByVal sender As System.Object,
ByVal e As System.EventArgs) Handles Timer1.Tick
    Dim ImageX As Integer
    Dim ImageW As Integer
    Dim ImageH As Integer
    ImageX = 10
    ImageW = 30
    ImageH = 25
    MyGraphics.Clear(Panel1.BackColor)
    ImageY = ImageY + Panel1.Height / 40
    MyGraphics.DrawImage(PictureBox1.Image, ImageX, ImageY,
ImageW, ImageH)
    If ImageY > Panel1.Height Then
      ImageY = -ImageH
    End If
  End Sub
```

We added the bottom border disappearance logic. Notice when the image disappears, we reset its ImageY value so it is repositioned just off the top of the panel. Run the project. Watch the image scroll. Pretty easy, wasn't it? Stop and save the project.

Border Crossing

What if, in the falling image example, instead of scrolling, we want the image to bounce back up when it reaches the bottom border? This is another common animation task - detecting the initiation of **border crossings**. Such crossings are used to change the direction of moving images, that is, make them bounce. How do we detect border crossings?

The same diagram used for image disappearances can be used here. Checking to see if an image has crossed a panel border is like checking for image disappearance, except the image has not moved quite as far. For top and bottom checks, the image movement is less by an amount equal to its Height value (ImageH). For left and right checks, the control movement is less by an amount equal to its width value (ImageW). Look back at that diagram and you should see these code segments accomplish the respective border crossing directions:

```
If ImageY < 0 Then
    [BASIC code for top border crossing]
End If

If (ImageY + ImageH) > MyPanel.Height Then
    [BASIC code for bottom border crossing]
End If

If ImageX < 0 Then
    [BASIC code for left border crossing]
End If
```

```
If (ImageX + ImageW) > MyPanel.Width Then
    [BASIC code for right border crossing]
End If
```

Let's modify the falling image example to have it bounce when it reaches the bottom of the panel. Declare an integer variable **ImageDir** in the **general declarations** area:

```
Dim ImageDir As Integer
```

ImageDir is used to indicate which way the image is moving. When ImageDir is 1, the image is moving down (ImageY is increasing). When ImageDir is -1, the image is moving up (ImageY is decreasing). Change the **Button1 Click** event to (new line is shaded):

```
Private Sub Button1_Click(ByVal sender As System.Object,
ByVal e As System.EventArgs) Handles Button1.Click
    Timer1.Enabled = Not (Timer1.Enabled)
    ImageY = 0
    ImageDir = 1
End Sub
```

We added a single line to initialize ImageDir to 1 (moving down).

Change the **Timer1 Tick** event to this (again, change and/or new lines are shaded):

```
  Private Sub Timer1_Tick(ByVal sender As System.Object,
ByVal e As System.EventArgs) Handles Timer1.Tick
    Dim ImageX As Integer
    Dim ImageW As Integer
    Dim ImageH As Integer
    ImageX = 10
    ImageW = 30
    ImageH = 25
    MyGraphics.Clear(Panel1.BackColor)
    ImageY = ImageY + ImageDir * Panel1.Height / 40
    MyGraphics.DrawImage(PictureBox1.Image, ImageX, ImageY,
ImageW, ImageH)
    If ImageY + ImageH > Panel1.Height Then
      ImageY = Panel1.Height - ImageH
      ImageDir = -1
    End If
      End Sub
```

We modified the calculation of ImageY to account for the ImageDir variable. Notice how it is used to impart the proper direction to the image motion (down when ImageDir is 1, up when ImageDir is –1). We have also replaced the code in the existing If/End If structure for a bottom border crossing. Notice when a crossing is detected, the image is repositioned (by resetting ImageY) at the bottom of the panel (**Panel1.Height - ImageH**) and ImageDir is set to -1 (direction is changed so the image will start moving up). Run the project. Now when the image reaches the bottom of the panel, it reverses direction and heads back up. We've made the image bounce! But, once it reaches the top, it's gone again!

Add top border crossing detection, so the **Timer1 Tick** event is now (changes are shaded):

```
  Private Sub Timer1_Tick(ByVal sender As System.Object,
ByVal e As System.EventArgs) Handles Timer1.Tick
    Dim ImageX As Integer
    Dim ImageW As Integer
    Dim ImageH As Integer
    ImageX = 10
    ImageW = 30
    ImageH = 25
    MyGraphics.Clear(Panel1.BackColor)
    ImageY = ImageY + ImageDir * Panel1.Height / 40
    MyGraphics.DrawImage(PictureBox1.Image, ImageX, ImageY,
ImageW, ImageH)
    If ImageY + ImageH > Panel1.Height Then
      ImageY = Panel1.Height - ImageH
      ImageDir = -1
      Beep()
    ElseIf ImageY < 0 Then
      ImageY = 0
      ImageDir = 1
      Beep()
    End If
  End Sub
```

In the top crossing code (the ElseIf portion), we reset ImageY to 0 (the top of the panel) and change ImageDir to 1. We've also added a couple of Beep statements so there is some audible feedback when either bounce occurs. Run the project again. Your image will now bounce up and down, beeping with each bounce, until you stop it. Stop and save the project.

The code we've developed here for checking and resetting image positions is a common task in Visual Basic. As you develop your programming skills, you should make sure you are comfortable with what all these properties and dimensions mean and how they interact. As an example, do you see how we could compute ImageX so the image is centered in the panel? Try this in the **Timer1 Tick** procedure:

```
ImageX = 0.5 * (Panel1.Width - ImageW)
```

Make sure you put this line after the line setting ImageW. You might want to change the panel **BackColor** to see that this line of code truly does center the image. Save the project one more time.

You've now seen how to do lots of things with animations. You can make images move, make them disappear and reappear, and make them bounce. Do you have some ideas of simple video games you would like to build? You still need two more skills – image erasure and collision detection - which are discussed next.

Image Erasure

In the little example we just did, we had to clear the panel control (using the **Clear** graphics method) prior to each DrawImage method. This was done to erase the image at its previous location before drawing a new image. This “erase, then redraw” process is the secret behind animation. But, what if we are animating many images? The Clear method would clear all images from the panel and require repositioning every image, even ones that haven’t moved. This would be a slow, tedious and unnecessary process.

We will take a more precise approach to erasure. Instead of erasing the entire panel before moving an image, we will only erase the rectangular region previously occupied by the image. To do this, we will use the **FillRectangle** graphics method, a new concept. This method is straightforward and, with your Visual Basic knowledge, you should easily understand how it is used. If applied to a graphics object named **MyGraphics**, the form is:

```
MyGraphics.FillRectangle(MyBrush, X, Y, Width, Height)
```

This line of code will “paint” a rectangular region located at (**X, Y**), **Width** wide, and **Height** high with a brush object (**MyBrush**).

And, yes, there’s another new concept – a **brush** object. A brush is like a “wide” pen. It is used to fill areas with a color. A brush object is declared (assume an object named **MyBrush**) using:

```
Dim MyBrush As Brush
```

Then, a solid brush (one that paints with a single color) is created using:

```
MyBrush = New Drawing.SolidBrush(Color)
```

where you select the **Color** of the brush. Once done with the brush, dispose of the object using the **Dispose** method.

So, how does this work with the problem at hand? We will create a "blank" brush (we'll even name it **BlankBrush**) with the same color as the BackColor property of the panel (**MyPanel**) control. The code to do this (after declaring the brush object) is:

```
BlankBrush = New SolidBrush(MyPanel.BackColor)
```

Then, to erase an image located in **MyGraphics** at (ImageX, ImageY), ImageW pixels wide and ImageH pixels high, we use:

```
MyGraphics.FillRectangle(BlankBrush, ImageX, ImageY,
ImageW, ImageH)
```

This will just paint the specified rectangular region with the panel background color, effectively erasing the image that was there.

Open up the "bouncing soccer ball" example one more time. Add this line of code in the **general declarations** area:

```
Dim BlankBrush As Brush
```

Add this line in the **Form1 Load** procedure:

```
BlankBrush = New SolidBrush(Panel1.BackColor)
```

And, add this line in the **Form1 FormClosing** procedure:

```
BlankBrush.Dispose()
```

These three lines declare, create and dispose of the brush object at the proper times. Finally, in the **Timer1 Tick** procedure, replace the line using the Clear method with this new line of code (selective erasing):

```
  MyGraphics.FillRectangle(BlankBrush, ImageX, ImageY,
ImageW, ImageH)
```

Rerun the project. You probably won't notice much difference since we only have one object moving. But, in more detailed animations, this image erasing approach is superior.

Collision Detection

Another requirement in animation is to determine if two images have collided. This is needed in games to see if a ball hits a paddle, if an alien rocket hits its target, or if a cute little character grabs some reward. Each image is described by a rectangular area, so the **collision detection** problem is to see if two rectangles collide, or overlap. This check is done using each image's position and dimensions.

Here are two images (**Image1** and **Image2**) in a panel control:

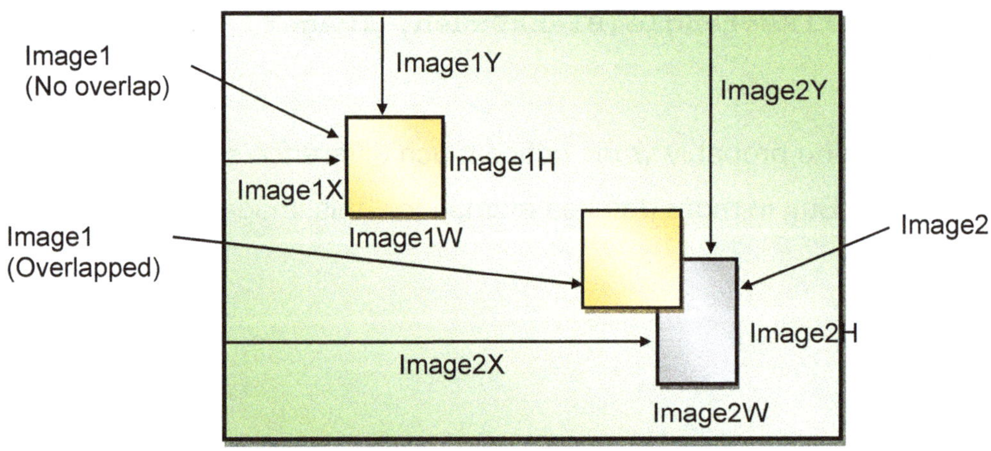

Image1 is positioned at (**Image1X**, **Image1Y**), is **Image1W** wide and **Image1H** high. Similarly, **Image2** is positioned at (**Image2X**, **Image2Y**), is **Image2W** wide and **Image2H** high.

Looking at this diagram, you should see there are four requirements for the two rectangles to overlap:

1. The right side of Image1 (**Image1X + Image1H**) must be "farther right" than the left side of Image2 (**Image2X**)
2. The left side of Image1 (**Image1X**) must be "farther left" than the right side of Image2 (**Image2X + Image2W**)
3. The bottom of Image1 (**Image1Y + Image1H**) must be "farther down" than the top of Image2 (**Image2Y**)
4. The top of Image1 (**Image1Y**) must be "farther up" than the bottom of Image2 (**Image2Y + Image2H**)

<u>All</u> four of these requirements must be met for a collision.

The BASIC code to check if these rectangles overlap is:

```
If (Image1X + Image1W) > Image2X Then
  If Image1X < (Image2X + Image2W) Then
    If (Image1Y + Image1H) > Image2Y Then
      If Image1Y < (Image2Y + Image2H) Then
          [BASIC code for overlap, or collision]
      End If
    End If
  End If
End If
```

This code checks the four conditions for overlap using four "nested" If/End If structures. The BASIC code for a collision is executed only if <u>all</u> four conditions are found to be True.

Let's try some collision detection with the bouncing soccer ball example. Add a button (default name **Button2**) control near the bottom of the panel – narrow the width a bit. Make sure the button is "attached" to the panel. Yes, we know a button is not an image, but it is a rectangle and the same overlap rules apply. We want to see if the image will collide with the button control and bounce up. Your form should look something like this:

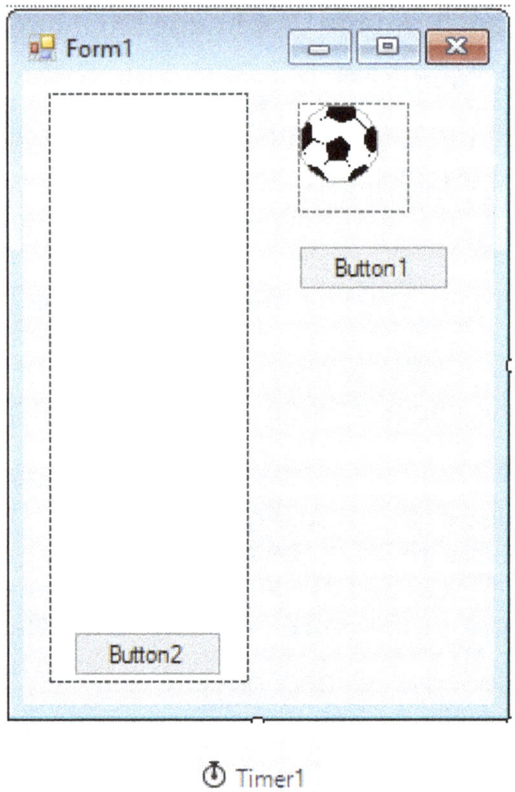

Change the **Timer1 Tick** event code to (added code is shaded):

```
  Private Sub Timer1_Tick(ByVal sender As System.Object,
ByVal e As System.EventArgs) Handles Timer1.Tick
    Dim ImageX As Integer
    Dim ImageW As Integer
    Dim ImageH As Integer
    Dim Collision As Boolean
    ImageX = 10
    ImageW = 30
    ImageH = 25
```

```
    MyGraphics.FillRectangle(BlankBrush, ImageX, ImageY,
ImageW, ImageH)
    ImageY = ImageY + ImageDir * Panel1.Height / 40
    MyGraphics.DrawImage(PictureBox1.Image, ImageX, ImageY,
ImageW, ImageH)
    Collision = False
    If (ImageX + ImageW) > Button2.Left Then
      If ImageX < (Button2.Left + Button2.Width) Then
        If (ImageY + ImageH) > Button2.Top Then
          If ImageY < (Button2.Top + Button2.Height) Then
            Collision = True
          End If
        End If
      End If
    End If
    If Collision = True Then
      ImageY = Button2.Top - ImageH
      ImageDir = -1
      Beep()
    ElseIf ImageY < 0 Then
      ImageY = 0
      ImageDir = 1
      Beep()
    End If
  End Sub
```

We declare a procedure level Boolean variable Collision to indicate an overlap (True for overlap, False for no overlap). The overlap code [using the button control properties for location (Left, Top) and size (Width, Height)] follows the DrawImage method. If a collision is detected, the image is repositioned so it just touches the top of Button2, its direction is reversed and a beep is played. The code for bouncing off the top of the panel is unchanged. Run the project. Notice the image now bounces off the button. Stop the project. Move Button2 out of the panel control so the image won't collide with it. The image should just drop off the screen. See how close the image can pass by Button2 without colliding to make sure the overlap routine works properly. Stop and save the project.

Now that you know how to detect collisions, you're well on your way to knowing how to build a simple video game. Next, we'll learn how to detect keyboard events from the user. One possible use for these events, among many, is to allow a user to move a little paddle to "hit" a dropping ball. The collision technique we just learned will come in handy for such a task.

Keyboard Events

In Class 8, we looked at ways for a user to interact with a Visual Basic project using the mouse for input. We studied three mouse events: MouseDown, MouseMove, and MouseUp. Another input device available for use is the computer keyboard. Here we look at **keyboard events** which give our projects the ability to detect user input from the keyboard. Two keyboard events are studied: the **KeyDown** event and the **KeyPress** event.

Several Visual Basic controls can recognize keyboard events, notably the form and the text box. Yet, only the control that has **focus** can receive a keyboard event. (Recall the control with focus is the active control.) When trying to detect a keyboard event for a certain control, we need to make sure that control has focus. We can give a control focus by clicking on it with the mouse. But, another way to assign focus to a control is with the **Focus** method. The format for such a statement is:

```
ControlName.Focus()
```

This command in BASIC will give **ControlName** focus and make it the active control. It has the same effect as clicking on the control. The control can then recognize any associated keyboard events. We use the Focus method with keyboard events to insure proper execution of each event.

To detect keyboard events on the form, you need to set the form **KeyPreview** property to **True**. This bypasses any keystrokes used by the controls to generate events.

KeyDown Event

The **KeyDown** event has the ability to detect the pressing of <u>any</u> key on the computer keyboard. It can detect:

- Special combinations of the Shift, Ctrl, and Alt keys
- Insert, Del, Home, End, PgUp, PgDn keys
- Cursor control keys
- Numeric keypad keys (it can distinguish these numbers from those on the top row of the keyboard)
- Function keys
- Letter, number and character keys

The KeyDown event for a control **ControlName** is executed whenever that control has focus and a key is pressed. The form of this event procedure is:

```
  Private Sub ControlName_KeyDown(ByVal sender As Object,
ByVal e As System.Windows.Forms.KeyEventArgs) Handles
ControlName.KeyDown

       [BASIC code for KeyDown Event]
  End Sub
```

The KeyDown event has two arguments: **sender** and **e**. We won't be concerned with the sender argument in this class. And, we won't be concerned with the status of any of the control keys (such as Shift, Ctrl, Alt). We only want to know what key was pressed down to invoke this procedure.

The property **e.KeyCode** can be used to determine which key was pressed down. There is a **KeyCode** value for each key on the keyboard. By evaluating the **e.KeyCode** argument, we can determine which key was pressed. There are nearly 100 KeyCode values, some of which are:

e.KeyCode	**Description**
Keys.Back	The BACKSPACE key.
Keys.Cancel	The CANCEL key.
Keys.Delete	The DEL key.
Keys.Down	The DOWN ARROW key.
Keys.Enter	The ENTER key.
Keys.Escape	The ESC key.
Keys.F1	The F1 key.
Keys.Home	The HOME key.
Keys.Left	The LEFT ARROW key.
Keys.NumPad0	The 0 key on the numeric keypad.
Keys.PageDown	The PAGE DOWN key.
Keys.PageUp	The PAGE UP key.
Keys.Right	The RIGHT ARROW key.
Keys.Space	The SPACEBAR key.
Keys.Tab	The TAB key.
Keys.Up	The UP ARROW key.

Using the KeyDown event is not easy. There is a lot of work involved in interpreting the information provided in the KeyDown event. For example, the KeyDown event cannot distinguish between an upper and lower case letter. You need to make that distinction in your BASIC code. You usually use a Select Case structure (based on e.KeyCode) to determine which key was pressed. Let's see how to use KeyDown to recognize some keys.

Start Visual Basic and start a new project. Put a text box control (**TextBox1**) on the form. Use this **TextBox1 KeyDown** event (make sure you pick the correct event):

```
  Private Sub TextBox1_KeyDown(ByVal sender As Object, ByVal
e As System.Windows.Forms.KeyEventArgs) Handles
TextBox1.KeyDown
    TextBox1.Text = e.KeyCode
  End Sub
```

Run the project. Type a letter. The letter and its corresponding e.KeyCode (a numeric value) are shown (there is no space between the two values). Press the same letter while holding down the <Shift> key. The same code will appear – there is no distinction between upper and lower case. Press each of the four arrow keys to see their different values. Notice for such 'non-printable' keys, only a number displays in the text box. Type numbers using the top row of the keyboard and the numeric keypad (make sure your **NumLock** key is selected). Notice the keypad numbers don't display and have different KeyCode values than the "keyboard numbers." This lets us distinguish the keypad from the keyboard. Try various keys on the keyboard to see which keys have a KeyCode (all of them). Notice it works with function keys, cursor control keys, letters, number, everything! Stop the project.

Add a second text box (**TextBox2**) to the form. Run the project. Click on this new text box and type some text. Notice the **TextBox1 KeyDown** event does not detect any key press. Why not? TextBox2 has focus - TextBox1 does not. The **TextBox2 KeyDown** event is being executed instead (but, there's no code there). Click on TextBox1 with the mouse - this gives it focus. Now, press a key. The key detection works again. Remember, for a keyboard event to be detected, the corresponding control must have focus.

KeyPress Event

The **KeyPress** event is similar to the KeyDown event, with one distinction. Many characters in the world of computers have what are called ASCII (pronounced as-key) codes. ASCII codes are simply numbers (ranging from 0 to 255) that represent all letters (upper and lower case), all numbers, all punctuation, and many special keys like Esc, Space, and Enter. The KeyPress event can detect the pressing of any key that has a corresponding ASCII code. A nice thing about the KeyPress event is that you immediately know what the user input is - no interpretation of any other key(s) is required (like with the KeyDown event). For example, there are different ASCII codes for upper and lower case letters. The KeyPress event procedure for a control named **ControlName** has the form:

```
  Private Sub ControlName_KeyPress(ByVal sender As Object,
ByVal e As System.Windows.Forms.KeyPressEventArgs) Handles
ControlName.KeyPress

        [BASIC code for KeyPress Event]

  End Sub
```

Again, there are two arguments, **sender** and **e**. We are interested in what key was pressed. That information is in the value of **e.KeyChar**. e.KeyChar is a **Char** type variable, returning a single string character, corresponding to the pressed key. The pressed key can be a readable character (letter, number, punctuation) or a non-readable character (Esc, Enter). It's easy to look at a readable character and know what it is. How can we distinguish one non-readable character from another?

To help recognize key presses of non-readable characters, known as control keys, Visual Basic has predefined values in the **ControlChars** structure. Some values for these keys we will use:

Value	**Definition**
ControlChars.Back	Backspace
ControlChars.Cr	Carriage return (<Enter> key)
ControlChars.Tab	Tab

Look at on-line help for more ControlChars values.

Recall each possible key recognized by the KeyPress event has an ASCII code. On-line help should have a table of ASCII values, if you're interested. If you want to know an ASCII value, you can use the Visual Basic **Asc** function. The format for using this function is:

```
KeyAscii = Asc(Character)
```

Here, **Character** is a string of length 1. The value (**KeyAscii**) returned by the Asc function is the integer ASCII code. To find the ASCII code of an upper case A, we would write:

```
KeyAscii = Asc("A")
```

The returned value of KeyAscii would be a 65. To find the ASCII code (8, by the way) for the backspace key, use:

```
KeyAscii = Asc(ControlChars.Back)
```

To determine the character represented by a specific ASCII code, you can use the Visual Basic **Chr** function. The format for Chr is:

```
Character = Chr(KeyAscii)
```

Here, **KeyAscii** is an integer ASCII code. The value (**Character**) returned by the Chr function is a single character string. To find the character represented by an ASCII code of 65 (recall, it is an upper case A), we would write:

```
Character = Chr(65)
```

Let's try an example with the KeyPress event.

Start a new project. Add a label control (**Label1**) and a text box (**TextBox1**) control. Add this code to the **TextBox1 KeyPress** event procedure:

```
  Private Sub TextBox1_KeyPress(ByVal sender As Object,
ByVal e As System.Windows.Forms.KeyPressEventArgs) Handles
TextBox1.KeyPress
    Label1.Text = e.KeyChar & Str(Asc(e.KeyChar))
  End Sub
```

Run the project. Press a key. The character typed (if it's printable) and its corresponding ASCII code will appear in the label control. Press as many keys as you like. Notice different values are displayed for upper and lower case letters. Notice not every key has an ASCII code. In particular, press a function key or one of the arrow keys. What happens? Nothing. You can't detect function key or arrow key presses with a KeyPress event. That's why we needed to talk about the KeyDown event. Stop and save the project.

Let's look at a very powerful use of the KeyPress event. Say we have an application where we only want the user to be able to type numbers in a text box. In that text box's KeyPress event, we would like to examine e.KeyChar and determine if it's a number. If it is a number, great! If not, we want to ignore that key! This process of detecting and ignoring unwanted key strokes is called **key trapping**. By comparing the input e.KeyChar with acceptable values, we can decide (in BASIC code) if we want to accept that value as input. Key trapping is a part of every sophisticated Visual Basic application.

The only question remaining is: if we decide a pressed key is <u>not</u> acceptable, how do we ignore it? We do that using the **e.Handled** property. If an unacceptable key is detected, we set **e.Handled** to **True**. This 'tricks' Visual Basic into thinking the KeyPress event has already been handled and the pressed key is ignored. If a pressed key is acceptable, we set the **e.Handled** property to **False**. This tells Visual Basic that this procedure has not been handled and the KeyPress should be allowed (by default, e.Handled is False, allowing all keystrokes).

Go back to the Visual Basic example we've been using. Change the code in the example **TextBox1 KeyPress** event to this:

```
  Private Sub TextBox1_KeyPress(ByVal sender As Object,
ByVal e As System.Windows.Forms.KeyPressEventArgs) Handles
TextBox1.KeyPress
    If e.KeyChar < "0" Or e.KeyChar > "9" Then
      e.Handled = True
      Label1.Text = "Not a number"
    Else
      e.Handled = False
      Label1.Text = e.KeyChar & Str(Asc(e.KeyChar))
    End If
  End Sub
```

Look at what's happening here. If e.KeyChar is outside the range of values from "0" to "9", **e.Handled** is set to **True**, ignoring this key press. This procedure will only accept a typed value from 0 to 9. We are restricting our user to just those keys. This comes in handy in applications where only numerical input is allowed. Run the project. Try typing numbers. Try typing non-numerical values - nothing will appear in the text control, indicating the key press was ignored.

Project – Beach Balls

In our final class project, we will build a little video game. Colorful beach balls are dropping from the sky. You maneuver your popping device under them to make them pop and get a point. You try to pop as many balls as you can in one minute. This project is saved as **BeachBalls** in the projects folder (**\CBGVB\BVB Projects**).

Project Design

All of the game action will go on in a panel control. There will be five possible balls, the image used is contained in a picture box. An picture box control will also hold the "popping arrow" image. This image will be moved using keys on the keyboard. A button will control starting and stopping the game. Another button will stop the program. The current score (number of balls popped) will be displayed in a titled text box.

Place Controls on Form

Start a new project in Visual Basic. Place a panel control on the form - make it fairly wide and tall. This is where the game will be played. Place two picture box controls on the form. Add a label control. Add a text box under the label for keeping score. Add larger text box to tell us when the game is over. Add two buttons. And, add two timer controls to use for animation and for timing the overall game.

Try to make your form look something like this when done:

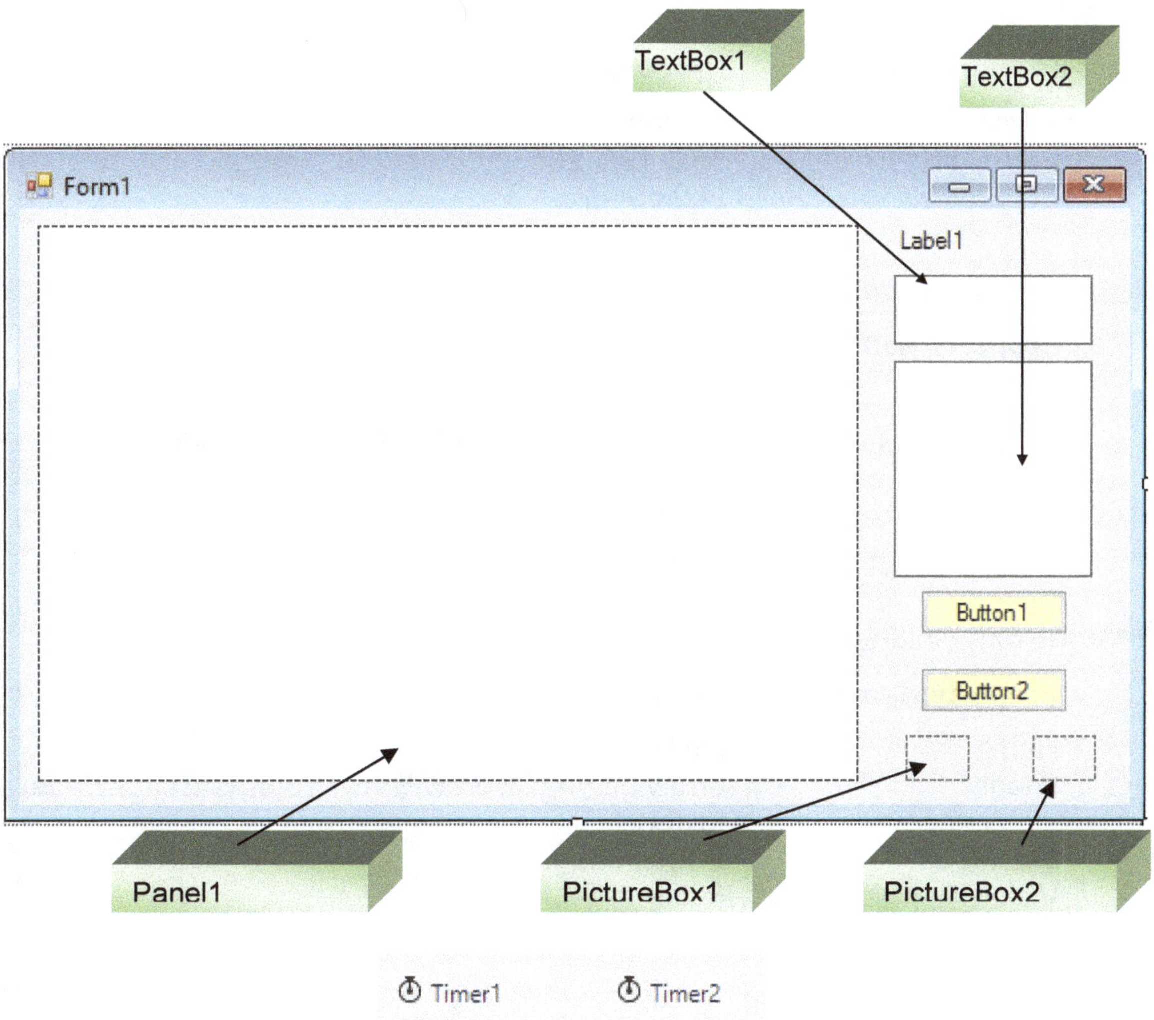

Set Control Properties

Set the control properties using the properties window:

Form1 Form:

Property Name	**Property Value**
BackColor	255, 192, 192
Text	Beach Balls
FormBorderStyle	FixedSingle
StartPosition	CenterScreen
KeyPreview	True (this allows us to detect key presses)

Panel1 Panel:

Property Name	**Property Value**
Name	pnlBeachBalls
BackColor	192, 192, 255
BorderStyle	FixedSingle

PictureBox1 Picture Box:

Property Name	**Property Value**
Name	picBall
Image	ball.gif (in **\CBGVB\BVB Projects\BeachBalls** folder)
SizeMode	StretchImage
Visible	False

PictureBox2 Picture Box:

Property Name	**Property Value**
Name	picArrow
Image	arrow.gif (in **\CBGVB\BVB Projects\BeachBalls** folder)
SizeMode	StretchImage
Visible	False

Label1 Label:

Property Name	Property Value
Name	lblHead
Text	Balls Popped
Font Size	10
Font Style	Bold
TextAlign	TopCenter

TextBox1 Text Box:

Property Name	Property Value
Name	txtScore
Text	0
Font Size	18
ReadOnly	True
TextAlign	Center
BackColor	White
ForeColor	Blue

TextBox2 Text Box:

Property Name	Property Value
Name	txtOver
Text	Game Over
Font Size	18
ReadOnly	True
TextAlign	Center
BackColor	White
ForeColor	Red

Button1 Button:

Property Name	Property Value
Name	btnStart
BackColor	Light Yellow
Text	Start

Button2 Button:

Property Name	**Property Value**
Name	btnExit
BackColor	Light Yellow
Text	Exit

Timer1 Timer:

Property Name	**Property Value**
Name	timBalls
Interval	100

Timer2 Timer:

Property Name	**Property Value**
Name	timGame
Interval	60000

When done setting properties, my form looks like this:

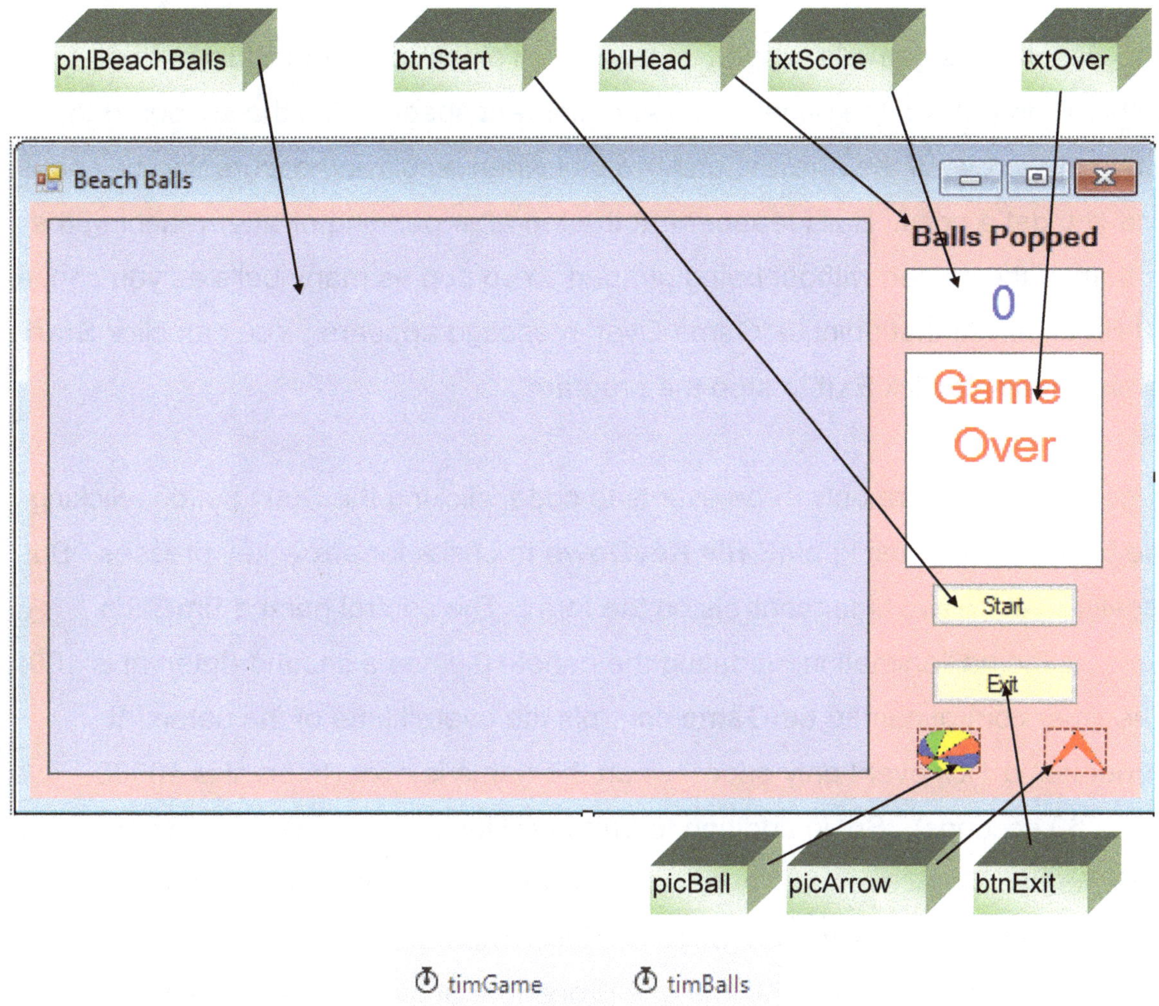

We have used **gif** files for our graphics (the ball and the arrow). With such graphics types, you can select one color to be transparent, allowing the background color to come through. How this is done is beyond the scope of this course. Do a little study on your own using paintbrush programs – PaintShop Pro by JASC (look on the Internet) is a great program for graphics.

Write Event Procedures

The Beach Balls game is simple, in concept. To play, click the **Start** button. Five balls will drop down the panel, each at a different speed. Use the keyboard to move the arrow. If the arrow is under a ball when a collision occurs, the ball pops and you get a point. Balls reappear at the top after popping or after reaching the bottom of the screen without being popped. You pop as many balls as you can in 60 seconds. At that point, a 'Game Over' message appears. You can click **Start** to play again or click **Exit** to stop the program.

It looks like there are only three events to code, clicking the **Start** button, clicking the **Exit** button, or using **picBalls KeyDown** to check for arrow key presses. But, recall there are two timer controls on the form. The control named **timBalls** controls the ball animation, updating the panel 10 times a second (Interval is 100). The timer control named **timGame** controls the overall time of the game. It generates a Tick event only once - when the game is over (Interval is 60000 - that's 60 seconds). So, in addition to button clicks and key down events, we need code for two Timer events. There is a substantial amount of BASIC code to write here, even though you will see there is a lot of repetition. We suggest writing the event procedures in stages. Write one procedure or a part of a procedure. Run the project. Make sure the code you wrote works. Add more code. Run the project again. Make sure the added code works. Continue adding code until complete. Building a project this way minimizes the potential for error and makes the debugging process much easier. Let's go.

Each ball will occupy a square region. We will compute the size (BallSize) of the ball to fit nicely on the panel. We need array variables to keep track of each ball's location (BallX, BallY) and dropping speed (BallSpeed). We need to know the arrow's size (ArrowSize) and position (ArrowX). We also need a graphics object to draw the balls (MyGraphics) and a blank brush object (BlankBrush, for erasing balls). Lastly, we need a random number object (MyRandom). Add this code to the **general declarations** area:

```
Dim BallSize As Integer
Dim BallX(5) As Integer
Dim BallY(5) As Integer
Dim BallSpeed(5) As Integer
Dim ArrowSize As Integer
Dim ArrowX As Integer
Dim MyGraphics As Graphics
Dim BlankBrush As Brush
Dim MyRandom As New Random
```

The array **BallSpeed** holds the five speeds, representing the number of pixels a ball will drop with each update of the viewing panel. We want each ball to drop at a different rate. In code, each speed will be computed using:

```
MyRandom.Next(4) + 3
```

Or, it will be a random value between 3 and 6. A new speed will be computed each time a ball starts its trip down the panel. How do we know this will be a good speed, providing reasonable dropping rates? We didn't before the project began. This expression was arrived at by 'trial and error.' We built the game and tried different speeds until we found values that worked. You do this a lot in developing games. You may not know values for some numbers before you start. So, you go ahead and build the game and try all kinds of values until you find ones that work. Then, you build these numbers into your code.

Use this **Form1 Load** procedure:

```
  Private Sub Form1_Load(ByVal sender As Object, ByVal e As
System.EventArgs) Handles MyBase.Load
    Dim X As Integer
    Dim I As Integer
    'Have the balls spread across the panel with 20 pixels
borders
    BallSize = Int((pnlBeachBalls.Width - 6 * 20) / 5)
    X = 10
    For I = 1 To 5
      BallX(I) = X
      X = X + BallSize + 20
    Next
    'Make arrow one-half the ball size
    ArrowSize = Int(BallSize / 2)
    MyGraphics = pnlBeachBalls.CreateGraphics
    BlankBrush = New SolidBrush(pnlBeachBalls.BackColor)
    'Give form focus
    Me.Focus()
  End Sub
```

In this code, initial horizontal positions for each of the balls are computed (BallX array). The balls are spread evenly across the panel (see if you can understand the code). The arrow is made to be one-half the ball size (ArrowSize). Lastly, the graphics object and brush object are created and the form is given focus so KeyDown events can occur.

Add this code to the **Form1 FormClosing** event to dispose of our objects:

```
  Private Sub Form1_FormClosing(ByVal sender As Object,
ByVal e As System.ComponentModel.CancelEventArgs) Handles
MyBase.FormClosing
    MyGraphics.Dispose()
    BlankBrush.Dispose()
  End Sub
```

To move the arrow (using DrawImage), we need a **Form1 KeyDown** event procedure (the panel control does not have a KeyDown event). Make sure you set the form's **KeyPreview** property to **True**, so the KeyDown event will be "seen." Pick a key that will move the arrow to the left and a key that will move it to the right. I chose **F** for **left** movement and **J** for **right** movement. Why? The keys are in the middle of the keyboard, with F to the left of J, and are easy to reach with a natural typing position. You could pick others. The arrow keys are one possibility. I hardly ever use these because they are always at some odd location on a keyboard and just not "naturally" reached. Also, the arrow keys are often used to move among controls on the form and this can get confusing. The code I use is (change the key code values if you pick different keys for arrow motion):

```
  Private Sub Form1_KeyDown(ByVal sender As Object, ByVal e
As System.Windows.Forms.KeyEventArgs) Handles MyBase.KeyDown
    'Erase arrow at old location
    MyGraphics.FillRectangle(BlankBrush, ArrowX,
pnlBeachBalls.Height - ArrowSize, ArrowSize, ArrowSize)
    'Check for F key (left) and J key (right) and compute
arrow position
    If e.KeyCode = Keys.F Then
      ArrowX = ArrowX - 5
    ElseIf e.KeyCode = Keys.J Then
      ArrowX = ArrowX + 5
    End If
    'Position arrow
    MyGraphics.DrawImage(picArrow.Image, ArrowX,
pnlBeachBalls.Height - ArrowSize, ArrowSize, ArrowSize)
  End Sub
```

Notice if the F key is pressed, the arrow (**imgArrow**) is moved to the left by 5 pixels. The arrow is moved right by 5 pixels if the J key is pressed. Again, the 5 pixels value was found by 'trial and error' - it seems to provide smooth motion. After typing in this procedure, save the project, then run it. Make sure the arrow moves as expected. Press the J key to see it. It should start at the left side of the form (ArrowX = 0) since we have not given it an initial position. This is what we meant when we suggested building the project in stages. Notice there is no code that keeps the arrow from moving out of the panel - you could add it if you like.

You would need to detect a left or right border crossing. Stop the project. Now, let's do the button events.

The **btnExit Click** procedure is simple, so let's get it out of the way first. It's the usual one line (well, two with the comment) that stops the project:

```
  Private Sub BtnExit_Click(ByVal sender As System.Object,
ByVal e As System.EventArgs) Handles btnExit.Click
     'Stop the program
     Me.Close()
  End Sub
```

Let's outline the steps involved in the **btnStart Click** event. We use this button for two purposes. It either starts the game (**Text** is **Start**) or stops the game (but, not the program - **Text** is **Stop**). So, the Click event has two segments. If Text is Start, the steps are:

- Hide 'Game Over' message
- Set btnStart Text to "Stop"
- Disable btnExit button
- Clear balls off screen
- Set score to 0
- Initialize each ball's position and speed
- Initialize arrow position
- Give form focus (so KeyDown can be recognized)
- Start the timers

If the Text is Stop when the button is clicked, the program steps are:

- Display 'Game Over' message
- Set btnStart Text to "Start"
- Enable btnExit button
- Stop the timers

Look at the **btnStart Click** event procedure and see if you can identify all of the outlined steps. Notice the balls are positioned just above the panel and the speeds are set using the formula given earlier:

```
  Private Sub BtnStart_Click(ByVal sender As System.Object,
ByVal e As System.EventArgs) Handles btnStart.Click
    Dim I As Integer
    If btnStart.Text = "Start" Then
      'New Game
      MyGraphics.Clear(pnlBeachBalls.BackColor)
      txtOver.Visible = False
      btnStart.Text = "Stop"
      btnExit.Enabled = False
      txtScore.Text = "0"
      'set each ball off top of panel and give new speed
      For I = 1 To 5
        BallY(I) = -BallSize
        BallSpeed(I) = MyRandom.Next(4) + 3
      Next I
      'Set arrow near center
      ArrowX = Int(pnlBeachBalls.Width / 2)
      MyGraphics.DrawImage(picArrow.Image, ArrowX,
pnlBeachBalls.Height - ArrowSize, ArrowSize, ArrowSize)
      'Give form focus so it can accept KeyDown events
      Me.Focus()
    Else
      'Game stopped
      txtOver.Visible = True
      btnStart.Text = "Start"
      btnExit.Enabled = True
    End If
    'Toggle timers
    timBalls.Enabled = Not (timBalls.Enabled)
```

```
    timGame.Enabled = Not (timGame.Enabled)
  End Sub
```

Save and run the project. There should be no balls displayed. Make sure you get no run-time errors. Make sure the arrow motion keys (F and J) still work OK. Stop the project.

The **btnStart Click** event procedure toggles the two timer controls. What goes on in the two Tick events? We'll do the easy one first. Each game lasts 60 seconds. This timing is handled by the timGame timer. It has an Interval of 60000, which means it's Tick event is executed every 60 seconds. We'll only execute that event once - when it is executed, we stop the game. The code to do this is identical to the code executed if the btnStart button is clicked when its Text is **Stop**. The **timGame Tick** event procedure should be:

```
  Private Sub TimGame_Tick(ByVal sender As System.Object,
ByVal e As System.EventArgs) Handles timGame.Tick
    '60 seconds have elapsed - stop game
    timBalls.Enabled = False
    timGame.Enabled = False
    txtOver.Visible = True
    btnStart.Text = "Start"
    btnExit.Enabled = True
  End Sub
```

Save the project. Run it. Click **Start**. Play with the arrow motion keys or just sit there. After 60 seconds, you should see the 'Game Over' notice pop up and see the buttons change appearance. If this happens, the timGame timer control is working properly. If it doesn't happen, you need to fix something. Stop the project.

Now, to the heart of the Beach Balls game - the **timBalls Tick** event. We haven't seen any dropping balls yet. Here's where we do that, and more. The timBalls timer control handles the animation sequence. It drops the balls down the screen, checks for popping, and checks for balls reaching the bottom of the panel. It gets new balls started. There's a lot going on. The procedure steps are identical for each ball. They are:

- Move the ball.
- Check to see if ball has popped. If so, sound a beep, make the ball disappear, increment score and make ball reappear at the top with a new speed.
- Check to see if ball has reached the bottom without being popped. If so, start a new ball with a new speed.

The steps are easy to write, just a little harder to code. Moving a ball simply involves erasing it at its old location and redrawing it at its new location (determined by the BallY value). To check if the ball has reached the bottom, we use the border crossing logic discussed earlier. The trickiest step is checking if a ball has popped. One way to check for a ball pop is to check to see if the ball image rectangle overlaps the arrow rectangle using the collision detection logic developed earlier. This would work, but a ball would pop if the arrow barely touched the ball. In our code, we modify the collision logic such that we will not consider a ball to be popped unless the <u>entire</u> width of the arrow is within the width of the ball.

Here's the complete **timBall Tick** event implementing these steps. The balls are handled individually within the structure of a For/Next loop:

```
  Private Sub TimBalls_Tick(ByVal sender As System.Object,
ByVal e As System.EventArgs) Handles timBalls.Tick
    Dim I As Integer
    For I = 1 To 5
      'erase ball
      MyGraphics.FillRectangle(BlankBrush, BallX(I),
BallY(I), BallSize, BallSize)
      'move ball
      BallY(I) = BallY(I) + BallSpeed(I)
      'check if ball has popped
      If (BallY(I) + BallSize) > (pnlBeachBalls.Height -
ArrowSize) Then
        If BallX(I) < ArrowX Then
          If (BallX(I) + BallSize) > (ArrowX + ArrowSize)
Then
            'Ball has popped
            'Increase score - move back to top
            Beep()
            txtScore.Text = Str(Val(txtScore.Text) + 1)
            BallY(I) = -BallSize
            BallSpeed(I) = MyRandom.Next(4) + 3
          End If
        End If
      End If
      'check for moving off bottom
      If (BallY(I) + BallSize) > pnlBeachBalls.Height Then
        'Ball reaches bottom without popping
        'Move back to top with new speed
        BallY(I) = -BallSize
        BallSpeed(I) = MyRandom.Next(4) + 3
      End If
      'redraw ball at new location, redraw arrow too
      MyGraphics.DrawImage(picBall.Image, BallX(I),
BallY(I), BallSize, BallSize)
    Next I
  End Sub
```

Do you see how all the steps are implemented? We added a Beep statement for some audio feedback when a ball pops.

Run the Project

Run the project. Make sure it works. Make sure each ball falls. Make sure when a ball reaches the bottom, a new one is initialized. Make sure you can pop each ball. And, following a pop, make sure a new ball appears. Make sure the score changes by one with each pop. Here's what my screen looks like in the middle of a game:

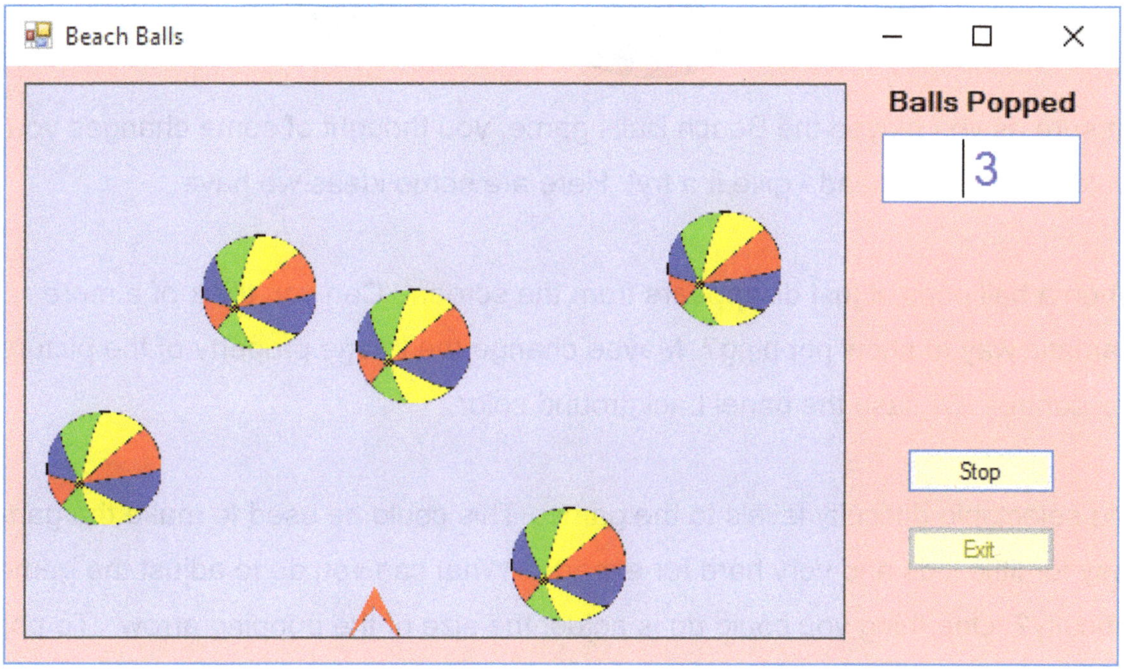

By building and testing the program in stages, you should now have a thoroughly tested, running version of Beach Balls. So relax and have fun playing it. Show your friends and family your great creation. If you do find any bugs and need to make any changes, make sure you resave your project.

Other Things to Try

I'm sure as you played the Beach Balls game, you thought of some changes you could make. Go ahead - give it a try! Here are some ideas we have.

When a ball pops, it just disappears from the screen. Can you think of a more dramatic way to show popping? Maybe change the Image property of the picture box control. Or flash the panel background color.

Add selectable difficulty levels to the game. This could be used to make the game easy for little kids and very hard for experts. What can you do to adjust the game difficulty? One thing you could do is adjust the size of the popping arrow. To pop a ball, the entire arrow width must fit within the width of a ball. Hence, a smaller (narrower) arrow would make it easier to pop balls before they reach the bottom of the picture box. A larger (wider) arrow makes popping harder. The ball dropping speed also affects game difficulty. Slowly dropping balls are easy to pop - fast ones are not. Play with the game to see what speeds would work for different difficulty levels.

Make it possible to play longer games and, as the game goes on, make the game more difficult using some of the ideas above (smaller arrow, faster balls). You've seen this in other games you may have played - games usually get harder as time goes on.

Players like to know how much time they have left in a game. Add this capability to your game. Use a text box control to display the number of seconds remaining. You'll need another timer control with an Interval of 1000 (one second). Whenever this timer's Tick event is executed, another second has gone by. In this event, subtract 1 from the value displayed in the label. You should be comfortable making such a change to your project.

Another thing players like to know is the highest score on a game. Add this capability. Declare a new variable to keep track of the highest score. After each game is played, compare the current score with the highest score to see if a new high has been reached. Add a text box control to display the highest score. One problem, though. When you stop the program, the highest score value will be lost. A new high needs to be established each time you run the project. As you become a more advanced Visual Basic programmer, you'll learn ways to save the highest score.

Summary

In this final class, we found that the timer control is a key element in computer animation. By periodically changing the display in a panel control, the sensation of motion was obtained. We studied "animation math" - how to detect if an image disappeared from a panel, how to detect if an image crosses the border of a panel, and how to detect if two images (rectangles) collide. We learned how to detect keyboard events. And, you built your first video game.

You've come a long way. Remember back in the first class when you first learned about events? You're an event expert by now. But, that doesn't mean you know everything there is to know about programming. Computer programming is a never-ending educational process. There are always new things to learn - ways to improve your skills. Believe it or not, you've just begun learning about Visual Basic.

Now let's look at how to build several two dimensional (2D) Computer Bible Games.

11

Noah's Ark Project

Preview

In Genesis, Noah was commanded by God to take two of every kind of animal into the ark. In this chapter, we build a game where turtles race to get on Noah's Ark. You pick two turtles (out of ten maximum) and see if your turtles are the winners. The purpose of this Bible story is to remember that God has promised never to flood the earth again. God displays a beautiful rainbow in the sky to remind us of His promises to us.

Noah's Ark Program Preview

In this chapter, we will build the **Noah's Ark** game. It's a simple game. Up to 10 turtles line up to race to the ark. You select two turtles you want to win the race. Clicking a '**Start'** button gets the race going. The turtles then move across the screen toward the finish line.

The finished project is saved as **NoahVB** in the **\BVB Projects\NoahVB** folder. Start Visual Basic and open the finished project. Open the form (double-click **Noah.vb** in Solution Explorer) and you will see:

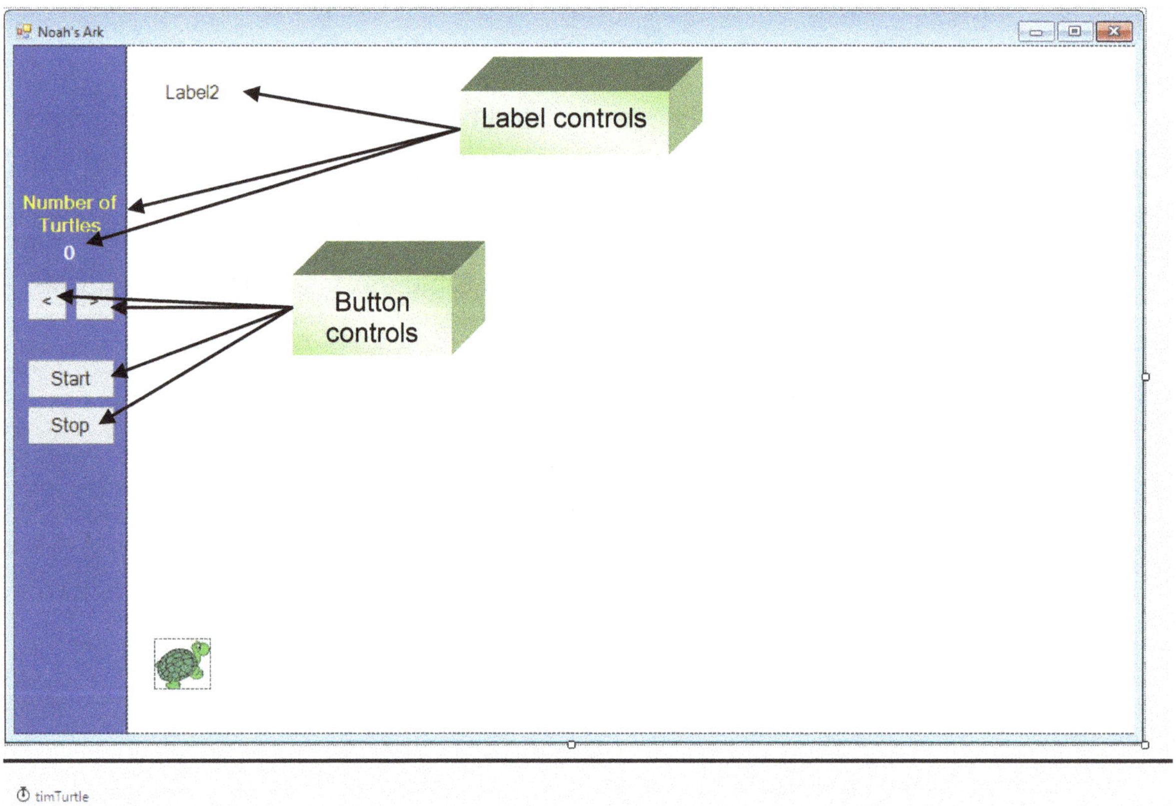

Labels are used for instructions and to display the number of turtles in the race. Four button controls are included: two to change the number of turtles, one to start the game and one to stop. A picture box control holds the turtle image. A timer control is used to update turtle motion during the race.

Run the program (press <**F5**>). The game will appear in its ‘initial’ state. A game description and program instructions are given. At this point, you can click the **Start** button to start the game, click arrow buttons to change the number of turtles racing or click **Stop** to stop the program.

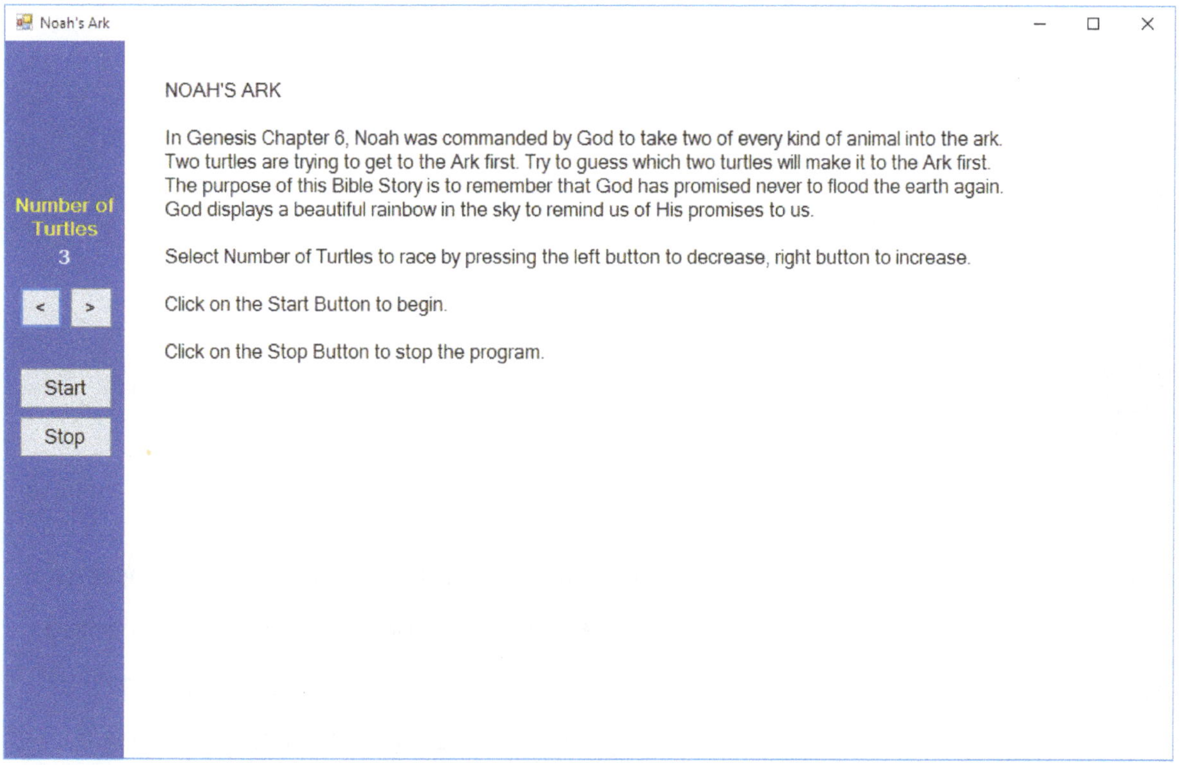

Change the number of turtles if you want (I picked five) by clicking the little arrows under **Number of Turtles**. Click the **Start** button to start playing. The program instructions disappear. Five turtles are poised, ready to race. This is the game's 'stopped' state:

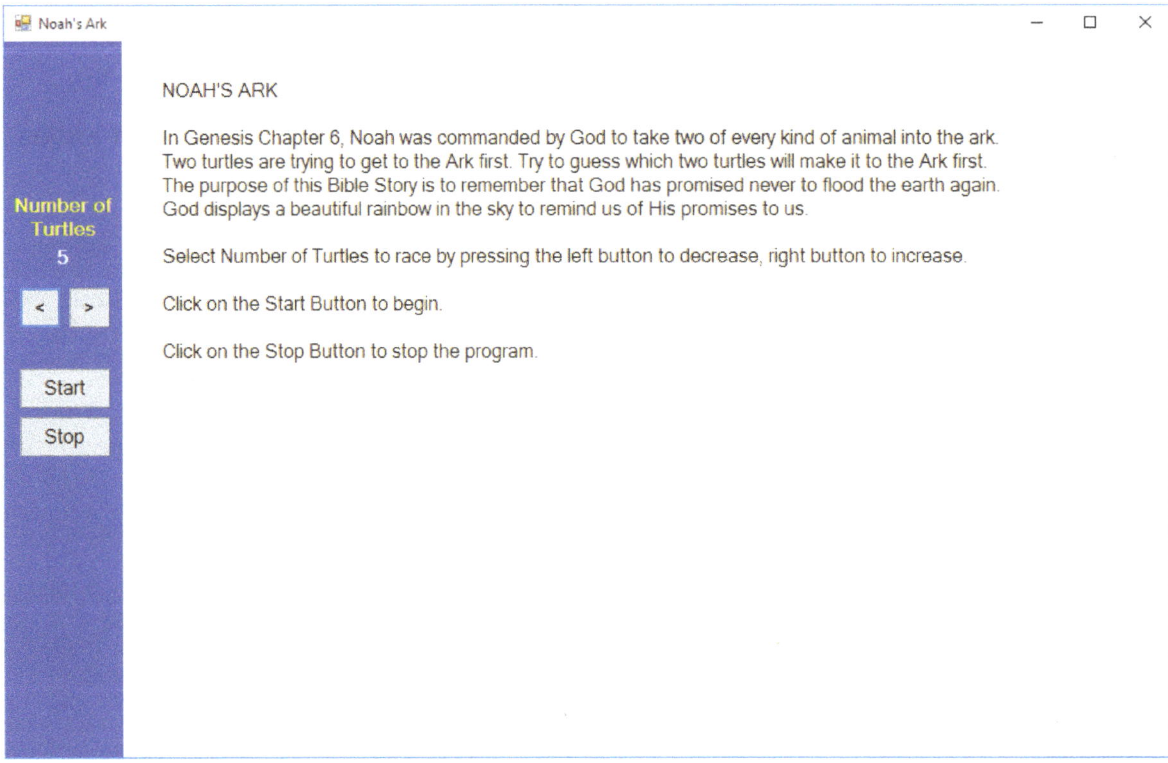

In this state, you pick two turtles you want to win the race. To do this, simple click on your selected turtle with the mouse – a red X will appear next to the selected turtle. Once two turtles are selected, you can start the race by clicking **Start**. If you select two turtles and want to change your mind, click on a selected turtle and the red X will disappear allowing you to pick another.

Choose two turtles. I picked the top one and the bottom one:

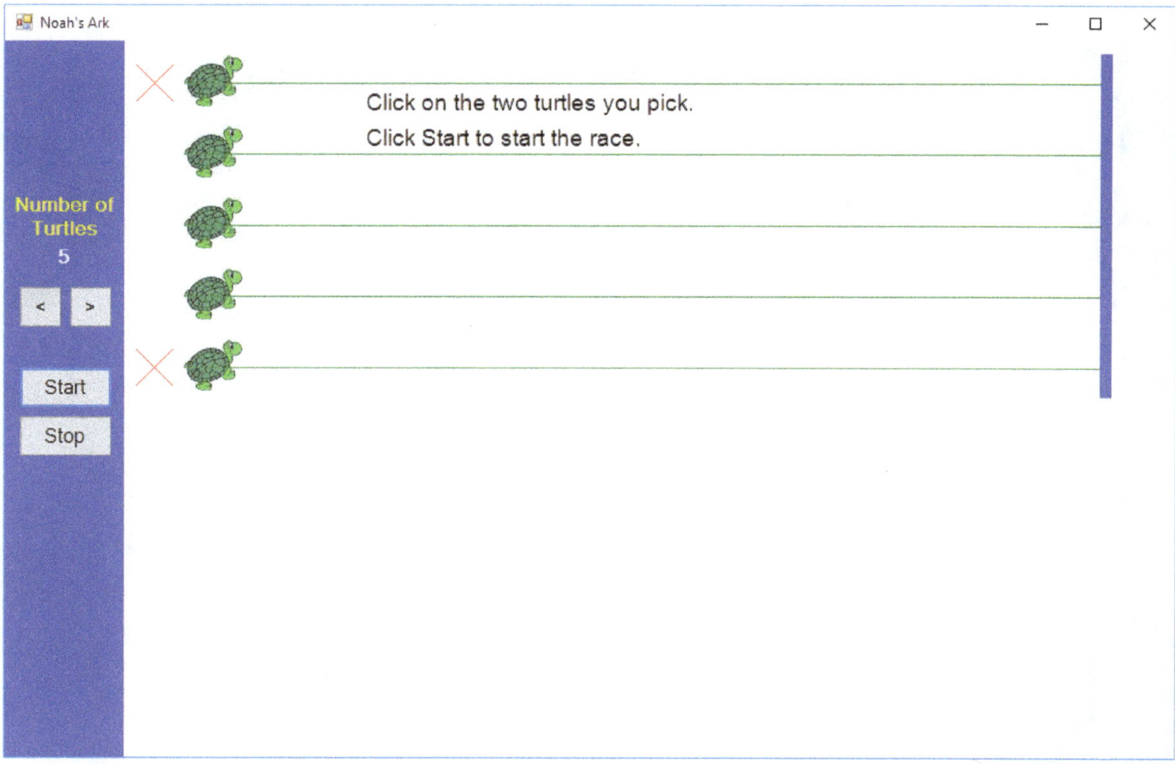

I then click **Start**. The race is on. The program is in 'moving' state. The turtles move across the screen until two cross the finish line.

Here's the results:

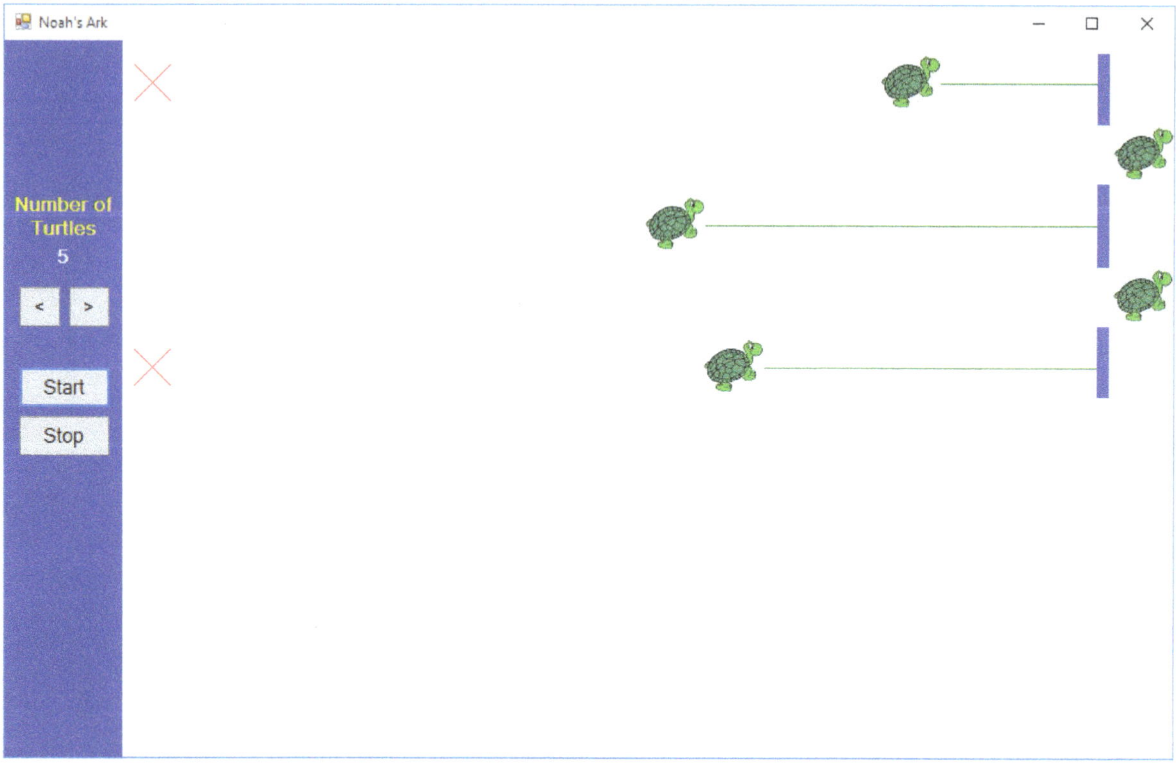

Bad news for my turtles! At this point, if you want, you can change the number of turtles. You can also click **Start** to race again or click **Stop** to stop the program. Continue playing the game to understand its operation.

You will now build this program in stages. As you build Visual Basic programs, we always recommend taking a slow, step-by-step process. It minimizes programming errors and helps build your confidence as things come together in a complete program. We address **form design**. And, we address **code design**. We discuss how to use the 'buttons', how to display the racing turtles, and how to move the turtles.

Noah's Ark Form Design

We begin building the **Noah's Ark** game project. Let's build the form. Start a new project in Visual Basic. Once started, we suggest you immediately save the project with a name you choose. This sets up the folder and file structure needed for your project.

Put two panel controls on the form (one 100 pixels wide on the left, one 900 pixels wide on the right). Put two labels and four buttons in the left panel. Put a label control and picture box control on the right panel. Add a timer control. The form should look like this:

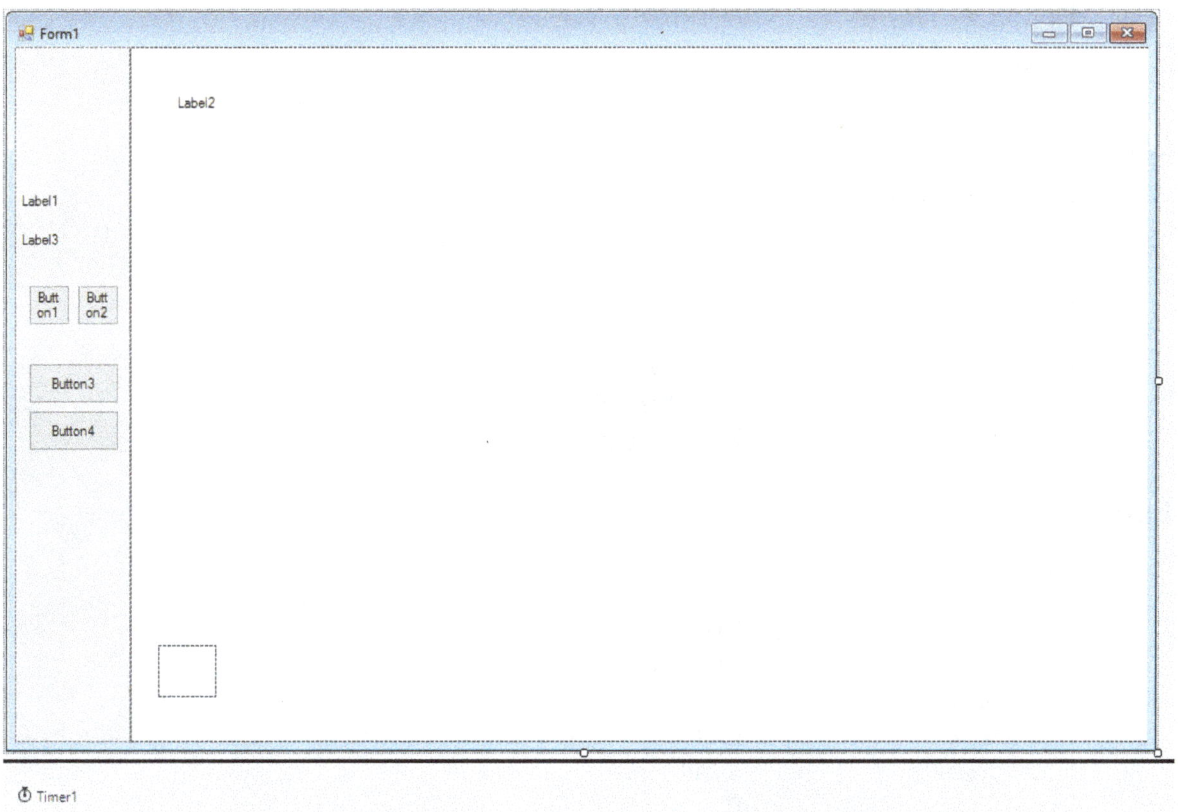

The labels are used for displaying information. Two buttons are used to change the number of turtles, two to start and stop the game. The timer control establishes the turtle motion.

Set the control properties using the properties window:

Form1 Form:

Property Name	**Property Value**
Name	frmNoah
Text	Noah's Ark
FormBorderStyle	Fixed Single
StartPosition	CenterScreen

Panel1 Panel:

Property Name	**Property Value**
BackColor	Blue

Label1 Label:

Property Name	**Property Value**
AutoSize	False
FontSize	12
FontStyle	Bold
ForeColor	Yellow
Text	Number of Turtles
TextAlign	Middle Center

Label3 Label:

Property Name	**Property Value**
AutoSize	False
Name	lblTurtles
FontSize	12
FontStyle	Bold
ForeColor	White
Text	0
TextAlign	Middle Center

Button1 Button:

Property Name	**Property Value**
Name	btnDecrease
FontSize	12
Text	<

Button2 Button:

Property Name	**Property Value**
Name	btnIncrease
FontSize	12
Text	>

Button3 Button:

Property Name	**Property Value**
Name	btnStart
FontSize	12
Text	Start

Button4 Button:

Property Name	**Property Value**
Name	btnStop
FontSize	12
Text	Stop

Panel2 Panel:

Property Name	**Property Value**
Name	pnlGame
BackColor	White

Label2 Label:

Property Name	**Property Value**
Name	lblInstructions
FontSize	12

PictureBox1 Picture Box:

Property Name	Property Value
Name	picTurtle
Image	Turtle.jpg (in **\BVB Projects\NoahVB** folder)
SizeMode	AutoSize
Visible	False

Timer1 Timer:

Property Name	Property Value
Name	timTurtle
Interval	100

When done, the form should look like this:

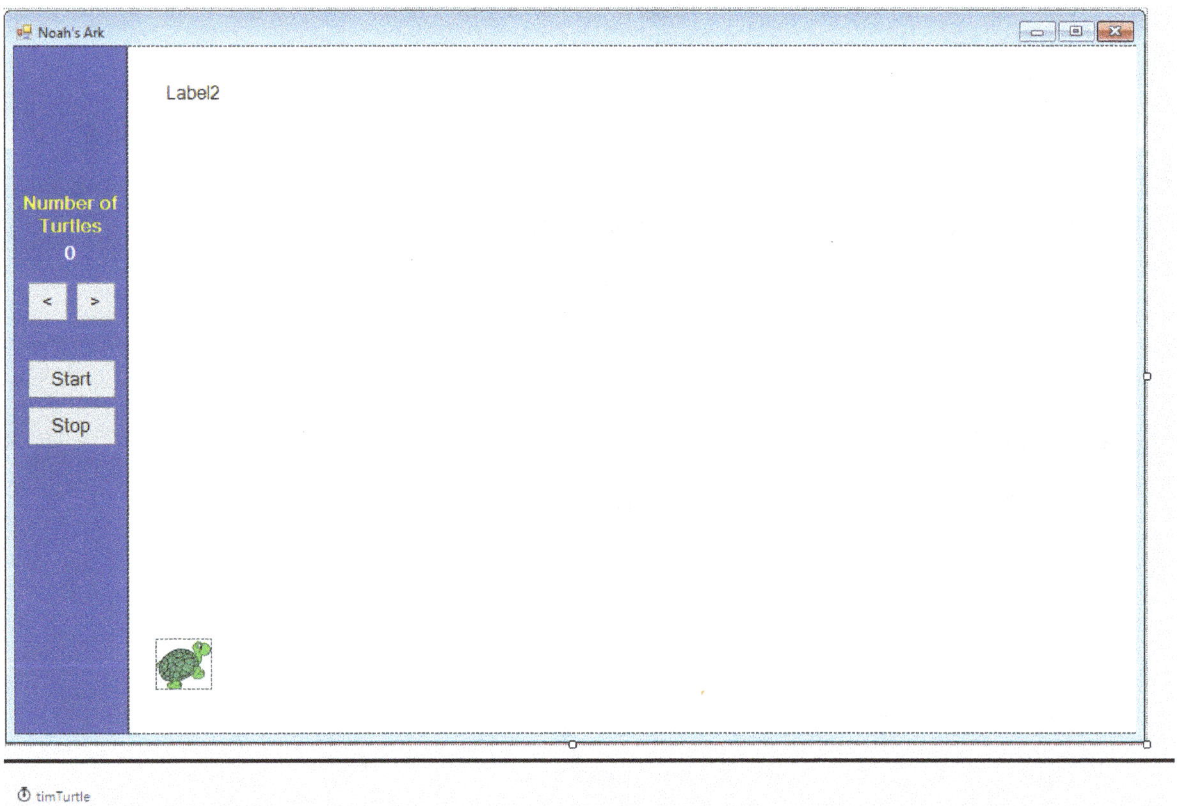

We now begin writing code for the **Noah's Ark** game. We will write the code in several steps. As a first step, we will write the code that starts the game and establishes its 'initial' state. Then, we look at how to go to 'stopped' state following clicking of the **Start** button from initial state. Lastly, we write code to race the turtles once **Start** is clicked again. During the code development process, recognize you may modify a particular procedure several times before arriving at the finished product.

Code Design – Initial State (Instructions)

Any time we start a program, there are certain initializations that must take place. Let's look at the initializations needed in the **Noah's Ark** game. When the program first begins, we want to display the game instructions. We also initialize the number of turtles (**NumberOfTurtles**) and the game status (**GameStatus**). These initializations are in the form's **Load** procedure.

We declare three variables (**NumberOfTurtles**, **GameStatus** and **GamePanel,** the game graphics object). Do this in the general declarations area:

```
Dim NumberOfTurtles As Integer
Dim GameStatus As String
Dim GamePanel As Graphics
```

Add this code to the **frmNoah Load** event procedure:

```
  Private Sub FrmNoah_Load(ByVal sender As System.Object, ByVal e
As System.EventArgs) Handles MyBase.Load
      ' Noah's Ark
      ' Visual Basic Version
      ' Intro screen
      NumberOfTurtles = 3
      GameStatus = "Initial"
      GamePanel = pnlGame.CreateGraphics()
      lblInstructions.Text = "NOAH'S ARK" + ControlChars.CrLf
      lblInstructions.Text += ControlChars.CrLf + "In Genesis
Chapter 6, Noah was commanded by God to take two of every kind of
animal into the ark."
      lblInstructions.Text += ControlChars.CrLf + "Two turtles are
trying to get to the Ark first. Try to guess which two turtles
will make it to the Ark first."
      lblInstructions.Text += ControlChars.CrLf + "The purpose of
this Bible Story is to remember that God has promised never to
flood the earth again."
```

```
    lblInstructions.Text += ControlChars.CrLf + "God displays a
beautiful rainbow in the sky to remind us of His promises to us."
    lblInstructions.Text += ControlChars.CrLf + ControlChars.CrLf
+ "Select Number of Turtles to race by pressing the left button to
decrease, right button to increase."
    lblInstructions.Text += ControlChars.CrLf + ControlChars.CrLf
+ "Click on the Start Button to begin."
    lblInstructions.Text += ControlChars.CrLf + ControlChars.CrLf
+ "Click on the Stop Button to stop the program."
    lblTurtles.Text = NumberOfTurtles
  End Sub
```

As mentioned, we set **NumberOfTurtles** to **3** and the **GameStatus** to "**Initial**". Next, after setting up the graphics object (**GamePanel**), using a series of statements, we write out the game instructions in **lblInstructions**.

Save and **Run** the program to see:

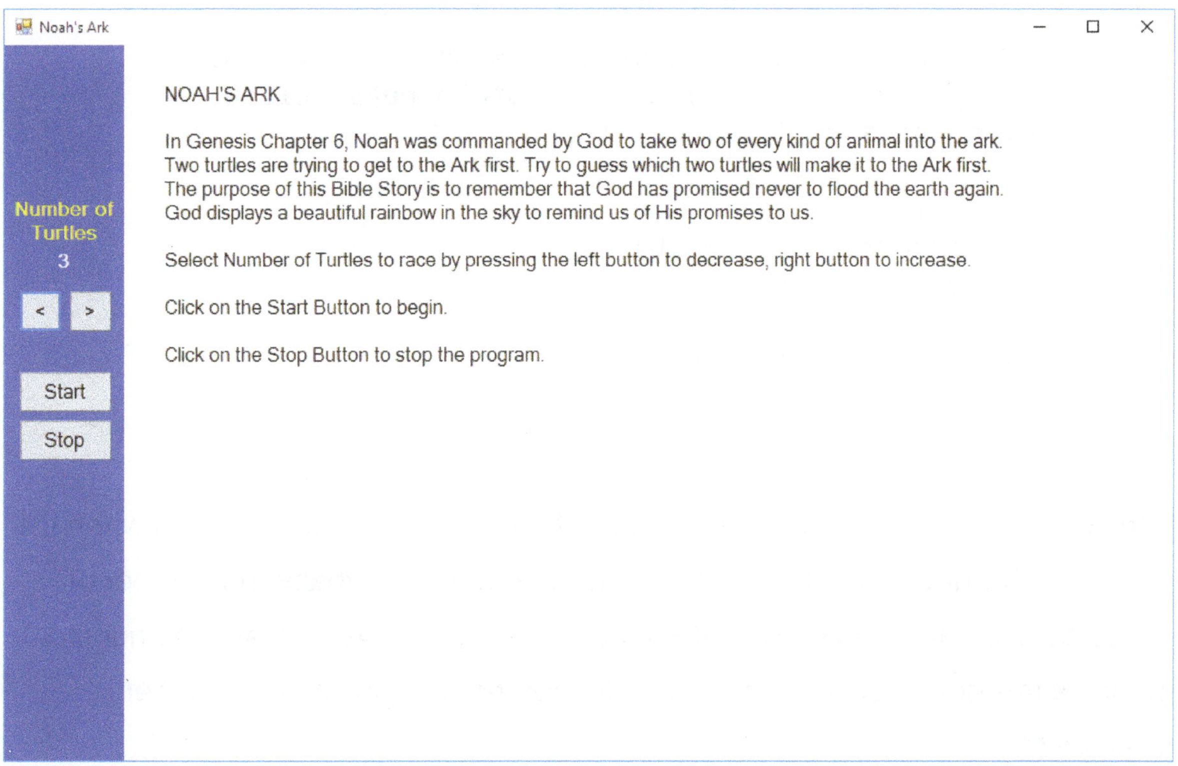

Code Design – Select Number of Turtles

To change the number of turtles, a user clicks on either of the two arrow buttons. The code to do this goes in the **btnDecrease** and **btnIncrease Click** event procedures:

```
  Private Sub BtnDecrease_Click(ByVal sender As System.Object,
ByVal e As System.EventArgs) Handles btnDecrease.Click
    If (GameStatus = "Initial") Then
      ' decrease number of turtles
      NumberOfTurtles -= 1
      If (NumberOfTurtles < 3) Then
        NumberOfTurtles = 3
      End If
      lblTurtles.Text = NumberOfTurtles
    End If
  End Sub

  Private Sub BtnIncrease_Click(ByVal sender As System.Object,
ByVal e As System.EventArgs) Handles btnIncrease.Click
    If (GameStatus = "Initial") Then
      ' increase number of turtles
      NumberOfTurtles += 1
      If (NumberOfTurtles > 10) Then
        NumberOfTurtles = 10
      End If
      lblTurtles.Text = NumberOfTurtles
    End If
  End Sub
```

The code is straightforward. The number of turtles can only be changed when the game is in "**Initial**" state. If the **<** button is clicked, we decrease the number of turtles by one (minimum of 3). If the **>** button is clicked, we increase the number of turtles (maximum of 10). The new value for the number of turtles is then displayed.

Save and **Run** the program. Make sure the arrow buttons work – make sure the number of turtles is always between 3 and 10. Here's my run where I changed the number of turtles to five:

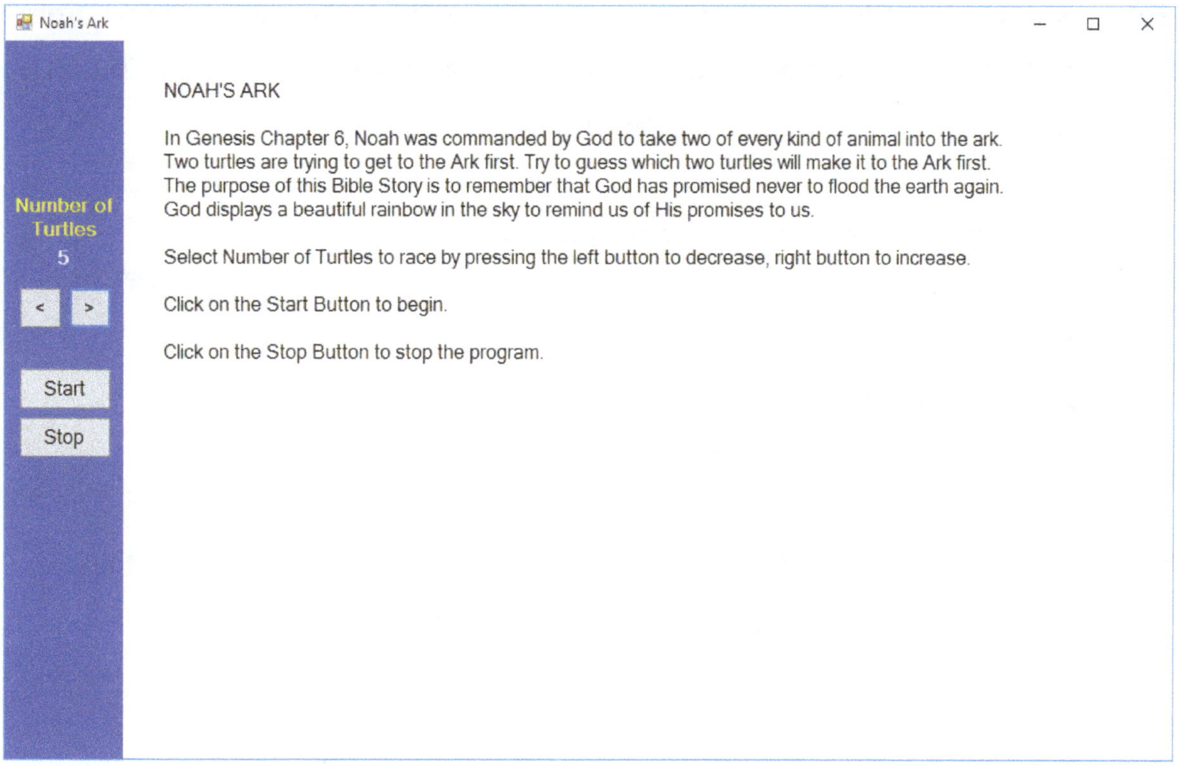

Code Design – Initial to Stopped State

Once the number of turtles is finalized, the next step is to click the **Start** button to allow selection of the turtles you want to win. Hence, we need code to move from the "**Initial**" state to "**Stopped**" state. When the **Start** button is clicked in "**Initial**" state, we need to take the following steps:

- Change **GameStatus** to "**Stopped**"
- Clear game screen
- Draw the turtles and "lane lines" for each
- Draw the finish line
- Display instructions for the user

To draw the turtles, we divide the race region into 10 equal size areas (set up for the maximum number of turtles). We then just move down the screen adding each turtle.

The image stored in **picTurtle** is used to represent the turtle:

The turtle is 50 pixels wide and 45 pixels high.

Now, add this code to **btnStart Click** event procedure::

```
  Private Sub BtnStart_Click(ByVal sender As System.Object, ByVal
e As System.EventArgs) Handles btnStart.Click
    If (GameStatus = "Initial") Then
      'clicked start
      GameStatus = "Stopped"
      lblInstructions.Visible = False
      GamePanel.Clear(Color.White)
      'draw turtles
      For i = 1 To NumberOfTurtles
        GamePanel.DrawImage(picTurtle.Image, 50, (i - 1) * 60 +
10)
        GamePanel.DrawLine(Pens.Green, 50, (i - 1) * 60 + 35, 820,
(i - 1) * 60 + 35)
      Next
      ' draw finish line
      GamePanel.FillRectangle(Brushes.Blue, 820, 10, 10,
NumberOfTurtles * 60 - 10)
      Dim MyFont As Font = New Font("Arial", 14)
      GamePanel.DrawString("Click on the two turtles you pick.",
MyFont, Brushes.Black, 200, 40)
      GamePanel.DrawString("Click Start to start the race.",
MyFont, Brushes.Black, 200, 70)
      TurtlesSelected = 0
      For i = 1 To NumberOfTurtles
        TurtlePicked(i) = 0
      Next
    End If
  End Sub
```

You should be able to identify each step in this new code. Notice in particular how we draw each turtle. Two new variables are introduced. **TurtlesSelected** (the number of turtles picked by the user) is initialized at zero. The array **TurtlePicked** is used to keep track of which turtles are selected by the user. Add these lines in the general declarations area:

```
  Dim TurtlePicked(10) As Integer
  Dim TurtlesSelected As Integer
```

Save and **Run** the program. Choose a number of turtles (I picked 5). Click **Start** and you should see:

The next step is to select two turtles you want in the race. We do that selection code soon. But first, let's take care of one last thing you can do while in "**Initial**" state – stop the program.

Code Design – Stop the Program

One last thing you can do while the game is in "**Initial**" state is to click on the **Stop** button. This will stop the game. The code here is simple. Add the few lines in the **btnStop Click** event procedure:

```
  Private Sub BtnStop_Click(ByVal sender As System.Object, ByVal e
As System.EventArgs) Handles btnStop.Click
    If (GameStatus = "Initial") Then
      'clicked stop
      End
    End If
  End Sub
```

As desired, if the **Stop** button is clicked, the program ends.

Save and **Run** the program. Make sure the **Stop** button works.

Code Design – Selecting Turtles

Once the game is in "**Stopped**" state, the user picks the two turtles they want in the **Noah's Ark** race. To detect clicks on a turtle, we need to know their location and size. From the code placing the turtles on **pnlGame**, you should see that for turtle i (where i goes from 1 to **NumberOfTurtles**):

located at (50, (i - 1) * 60 +10), width 50, height 45

The array **TurtlePicked** is used to tell us which turtles have been selected. A red **X** will appear next to a selected turtle. Once two turtles are selected (**TurtlesSelected = 2**), you can start the race by clicking **Start**. If you select two turtles and want to change your mind, click on a selected turtle and the red **X** will disappear allowing you to pick another.

When a turtle i is clicked, the following steps are taken:

- If turtle has been selected selected previously, decrement **TurtlesSelected**, set **TurtlePicked(i)** to **0**. Remove red **X** next to turtle.
- If turtle has not been selected and **TurtlesSelected** is less than 2, increment **TurtlesSelected**, set **TurtlePicked(i)** to **1**. Draw red **X** next to turtle.

We do the steps in this order to make sure we don't click on a turtle that has already been selected.

The code for turtle selection is placed in the **pnlGame MouseDown** event procedure:

```
  Private Sub PnlGame_MouseDown(ByVal sender As System.Object,
ByVal e As System.Windows.Forms.MouseEventArgs) Handles
pnlGame.MouseDown
    Dim TurtleClicked As Integer
    If (GameStatus = "Stopped") Then
      ' want to pick two and only two turtles
      'which turtle clicked
      TurtleClicked = Math.Floor((e.Y - 10) / 60) + 1
      'if clicked before, remove from list
      If (TurtlePicked(TurtleClicked) = 1) Then
        TurtlesSelected = TurtlesSelected - 1
        TurtlePicked(TurtleClicked) = 0
        GamePanel.FillRectangle(Brushes.White, 10, (TurtleClicked
- 1) * 60 + 20, 30, 30)
      ElseIf (TurtlesSelected < 2) Then
        'add to list if two have not been selected yet
        TurtlesSelected = TurtlesSelected + 1
        TurtlePicked(TurtleClicked) = 1
        GamePanel.DrawLine(Pens.Red, 10, (TurtleClicked - 1) * 60
+ 20, 40, (TurtleClicked - 1) * 60 + 50)
        GamePanel.DrawLine(Pens.Red, 10, (TurtleClicked - 1) * 60
+ 50, 40, (TurtleClicked - 1) * 60 + 20)
      End If
    End If
  End Sub
```

You should see how the clicks on the turtles are handled.

Save and **Run** the program. Choose a number of turtles (I picked 5). Click **Start**. Then, select two turtles for your race. I picked the first and last turtle:

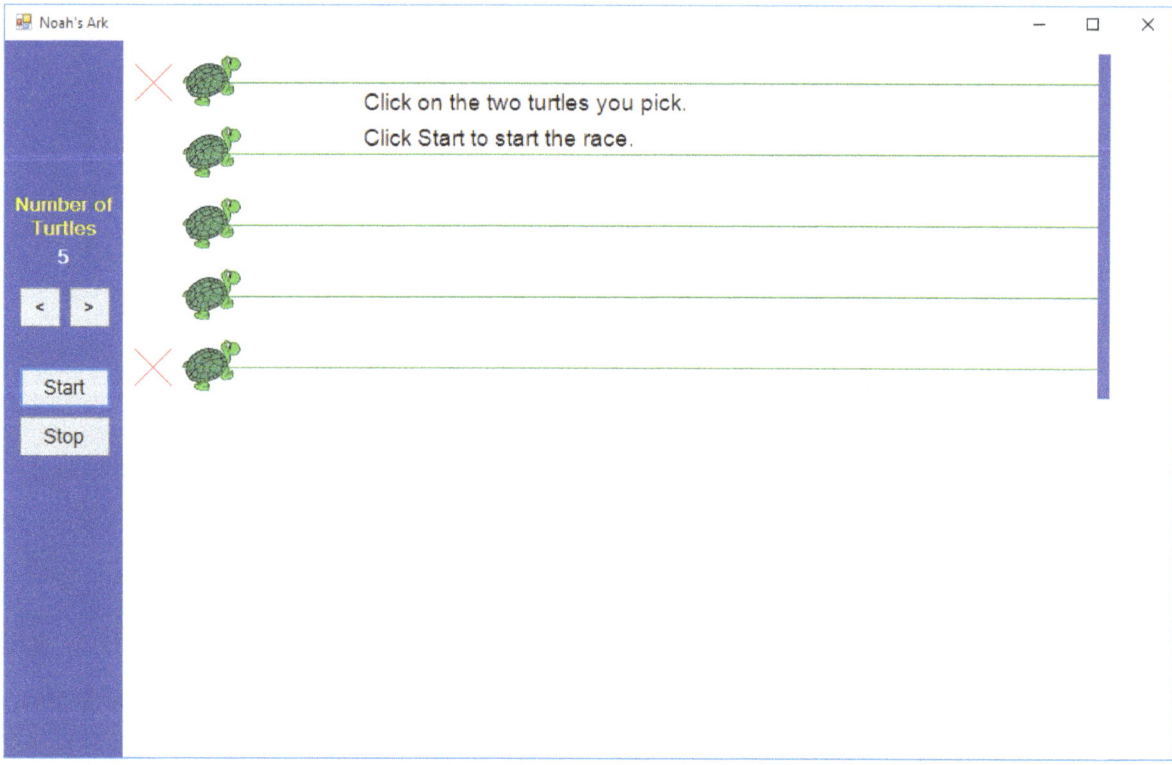

Make sure you can 'unselect' a turtle. Now, let's race!

Code Design – Stopped to Moving State

Once turtles are selected, we click the **Start** button to get the race started, moving to "**Moving**" state. So, when the **Start** button is clicked in "**Stopped**" state, we take these steps:

- Change **GameStatus** to "**Moving**".
- Clear instructions.
- For each turtle, pick a random final position <u>before</u> the finish line.
- Pick two winners at random. Assign these winners final positions <u>after</u> the finish line.
- Move the turtles to their final positions.
- Change **GameStatus** to "**Initial**" to allow another race.

What we do is pick two of the displayed turtles to be winners. These turtles finish across the line – all others finish before the line.

To move the turtles, we use the timer control (**timTurtle**). With each **Tick** event, we move each turtle some fraction of the difference between its initial and final postion. This method provides a smooth animation from start to finish. With the turtles, we want to move each from its starting position to final position in 5000 milliseconds (5 seconds). Since **Interval** is 100 milliseconds, we move each turtle 1/50th of its moved distance with each **Tick** event. You can change these values if you want.

The code that starts the turtles moving is shaded in the **btnStart Click** event procedure:

```
  Private Sub BtnStart_Click(ByVal sender As System.Object, ByVal
e As System.EventArgs) Handles btnStart.Click
    If (GameStatus = "Initial") Then
      'clicked start
      GameStatus = "Stopped"
      lblInstructions.Visible = False
      GamePanel.Clear(Color.White)
      'draw turtles
      For i = 1 To NumberOfTurtles
        GamePanel.DrawImage(picTurtle.Image, 50, (i - 1) * 60 +
10)
        GamePanel.DrawLine(Pens.Green, 50, (i - 1) * 60 + 35, 820,
(i - 1) * 60 + 35)
      Next
      ' draw finish line
      GamePanel.FillRectangle(Brushes.Blue, 820, 10, 10,
NumberOfTurtles * 60 - 10)
      Dim MyFont As Font = New Font("Arial", 14)
      GamePanel.DrawString("Click on the two turtles you pick.",
MyFont, Brushes.Black, 200, 40)
      GamePanel.DrawString("Click Start to start the race.",
MyFont, Brushes.Black, 200, 70)
      TurtlesSelected = 0
      For i = 1 To NumberOfTurtles
        TurtlePicked(i) = 0
      Next
    ElseIf (GameStatus = "Stopped" And TurtlesSelected = 2) Then
      'clicked start after picking two turtles
      GameStatus = "Moving"
      GamePanel.FillRectangle(Brushes.White, 150, 40, 350, 50)
      'set start position/get final positions
      NumberMoves = 0
      For i = 1 To NumberOfTurtles
        TurtlePosition(i) = 50
        FinalPosition(i) = 400 + MyRandom.Next(360)
      Next
      ' pick two winners
      Winner(1) = MyRandom.Next(NumberOfTurtles) + 1
NextWinner:
      Winner(2) = MyRandom.Next(NumberOfTurtles) + 1
      If (Winner(1) = Winner(2)) Then
```

```
        GoTo NextWinner
      End If
      FinalPosition(Winner(1)) = 850
      FinalPosition(Winner(2)) = 850
      timTurtle.Start()
    End If
  End Sub
```

Notice how the final positions and winners are determined. Several new variables are introduced and are declared in the general declarations area:

```
Dim NumberMoves As Integer
Dim TurtlePosition(10) As Integer
Dim FinalPosition(10) As Integer
Dim Winner(2) As Integer
Dim MyRandom As Random = New Random
```

NumberMoves is how many times the timer **Tick** event has been called. **TurtlePosition** is an array of current turtle locations, while **FinalPosition** is the array of final positions. The **Winner** array holds the two winners. **MyRandom** is used to generate random locations.

Motion begins by starting timTurtle. The code that moves the turtles is placed in the **timTurtle Tick** event procedure:

```
  Private Sub TimTurtle_Tick(ByVal sender As System.Object, ByVal
e As System.EventArgs) Handles timTurtle.Tick
    'increment number of moves and positions
    NumberMoves += 1
    For i = 1 To NumberOfTurtles
      GamePanel.FillRectangle(Brushes.White, TurtlePosition(i), (i
- 1) * 60 + 10, 50, 50)
      TurtlePosition(i) += (FinalPosition(i) - 50) / 50
      GamePanel.DrawImage(picTurtle.Image, TurtlePosition(i), (i -
1) * 60 + 10)
    Next
    If (NumberMoves = 49) Then
      timTurtle.Stop()
      GameStatus = "Initial"
    End If
  End Sub
```

Once the turtles are moved, you can play again by choosing a new number of turtles (if you want) and click **Start**. Or, you can click **Stop** to end the program.

One last time, **Save** and **Run** the program. Choose a number of turtles (again, I picked 5). Click **Start**, choose two turtles (I chose the top and bottom ones). Click **Start** –and the turtles start the race. Here's the middle of my race:

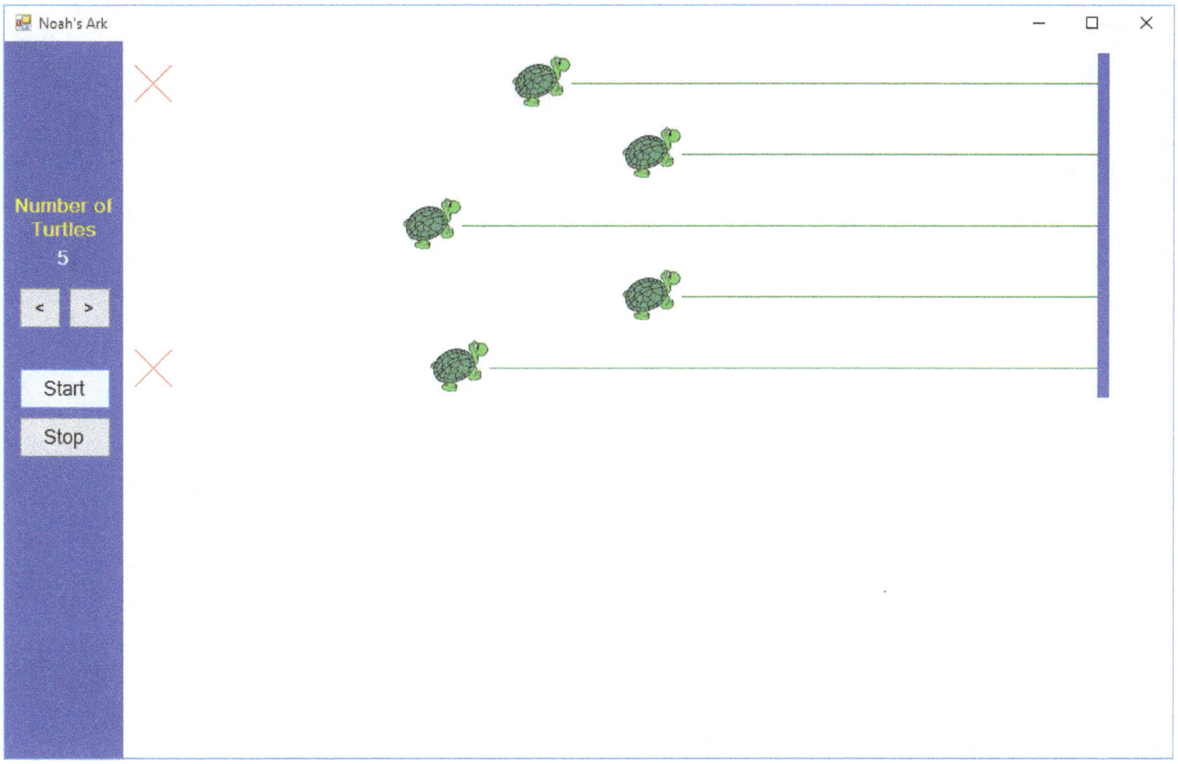

And the finish:

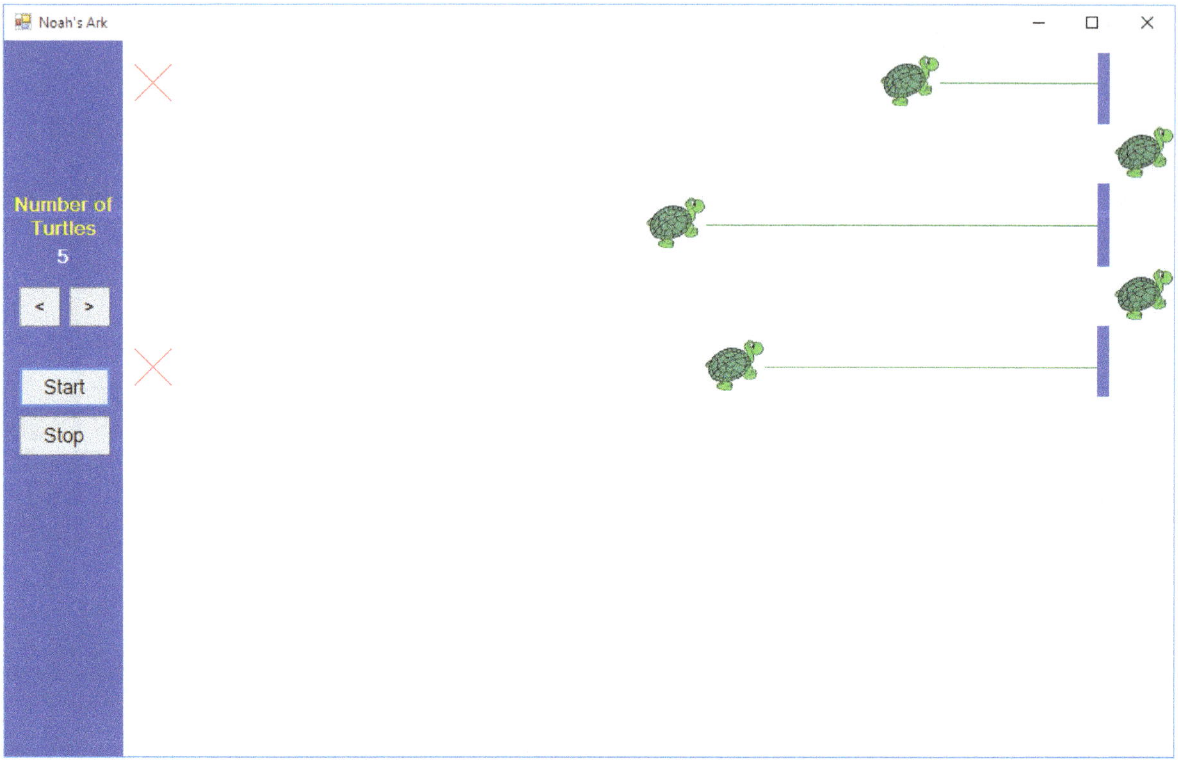

Our turtles lost … our work is done. Enjoy the game!

Noah's Ark Program Review

The **Noah's Ark** program is now complete. **Save** and **Run** the program and make sure it works as promised. Check that all options work correctly.

If there are errors in your implementation, go back over the steps of form and code design. Go over the developed code – make sure you understand how different parts of the program were coded. As mentioned in the beginning of this chapter, the completed program is saved as **NoahVB** in the **\BVB Projects\NoahVB** folder.

12

Elijah and the Ravens Project

Preview

In I Kings 17, God sends ravens to drop bread for Elijah while he hides from King Ahab. In this game, you try to catch as many falling loaves of bread as possible to feed Elijah. God always provides for our needs.

Elijah and the Ravens Program Preview

In this chapter, we will build the **Elijah and the Ravens** game. Flying ravens drop loaves of bread from the sky. You position Elijah under the falling loaves to catch them for food.

The finished project is saved as **ElijahVB** in the **\BVB Projects \ElijahVB** folder. Start Visual Basic and open the finished project. Open the form (double-click **Elijah.vb** in Solution Explorer) and you will see:

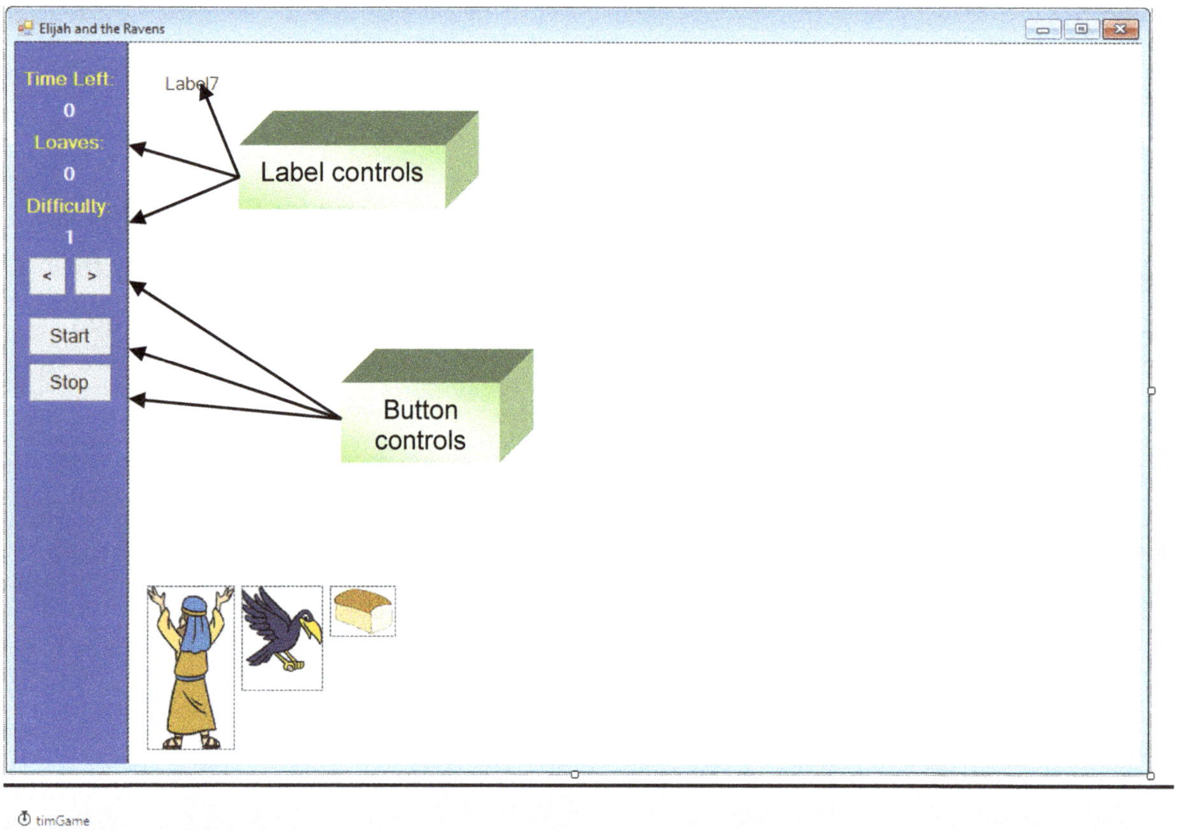

Labels are used for instructions and to display game information (time remaining, loaves caught, difficulty). Two buttons are used to change the difficulty, one to start the game and one to stop. Picture box controls hold images for Elijah, the raven and the bread.

Run the program (press <**F5**>). The game will appear in its 'initial' state. A game description and program instructions are given. At this point, you can click the **Start** button to start the game, click arrow buttons to change the game difficulty or click **Stop** to stop the program.

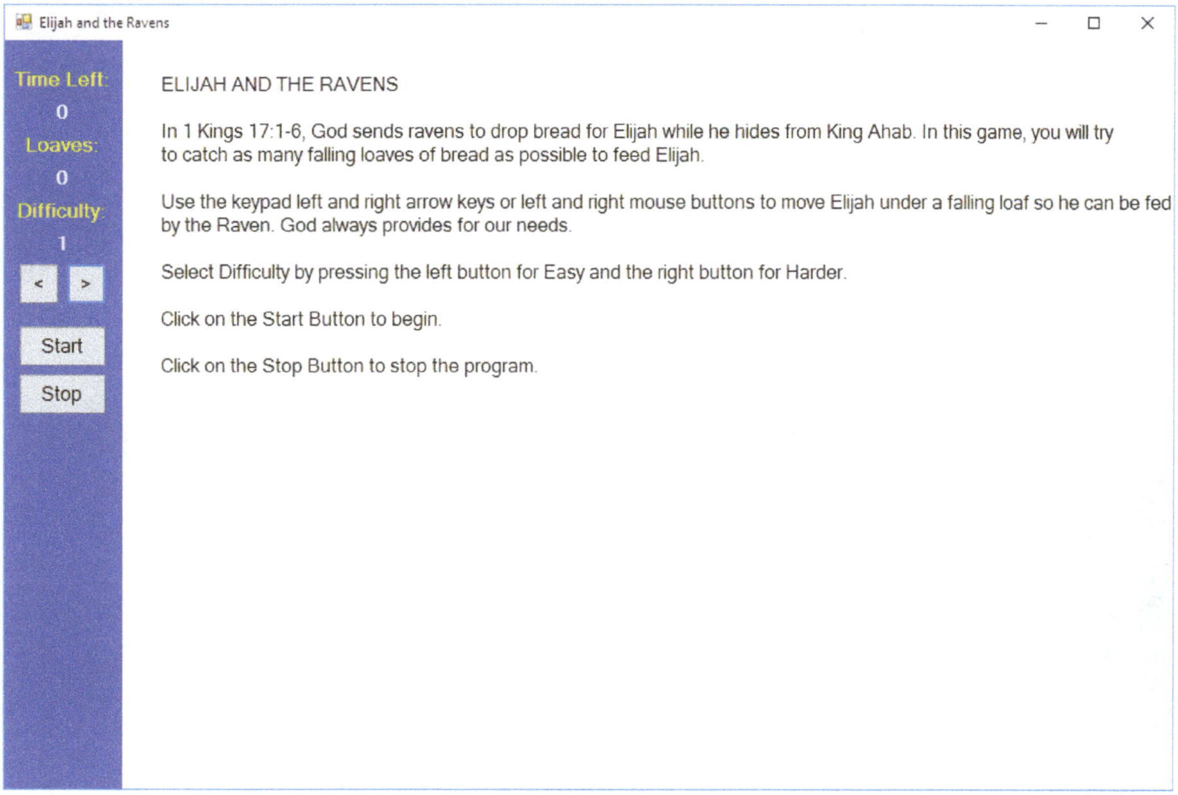

Change the difficulty if you want (I picked 3) by clicking the little arrows under **Difficulty**. Click the **Start** button to start playing. The program instructions disappear. A raven appears at the top of the screen holding a loaf of bread. Elijah is at the bottom of the screen. The loaf of bread will start falling. This is the game's 'playing' state:

You move Elijah under the falling loaf to catch it. You can move Elijah using the keypad arrow keys (**NumLock** must be on) or by holding down the left or right mouse button. When the loaf reaches Elijah, you score a point (under **Loaves**). If the loaf passes without catching it, you score nothing. Either way, another raven appears dropping another loaf.

Here's a screen where Elijah is about to catch a loaf of bread:

The game continues for 60 seconds. The remaining time is shown under **Time Left**. You are given your final score at this point. Here's mine:

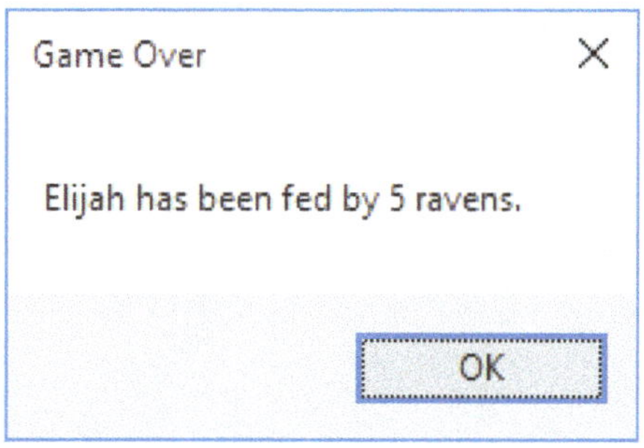

Next, if you want, you can change the difficulty – higher difficulties give you faster dropping bread. You can also click **Start** to race again or click **Stop** to stop the program. Continue playing the game to understand its operation.

You will now build this program in stages. As you build Visual Basic programs, we always recommend taking a slow, step-by-step process. It minimizes programming errors and helps build your confidence as things come together in a complete program. We address **form design**. And, we address **code design**. We discuss how to use the buttons, how to display the raven, the bread and Elijah, and how to move the different graphic images and detect whether a loaf of bread has been caught.

Elijah and the Ravens Form Design

We begin building the **Elijah and the Ravens** game project. Let's build the form. Start a new project in Visual Basic. Once started, we suggest you immediately save the project with a name you choose. This sets up the folder and file structure needed for your project.

Put two panel controls on the form (one 100 pixels wide on the left, one 900 pixels wide on the right). Make both panels around 600 pixels high. Put six labels and four buttons on the left panel. Put a label control and three picture box controls on the right panel. Add a timer control. The form should look like this:

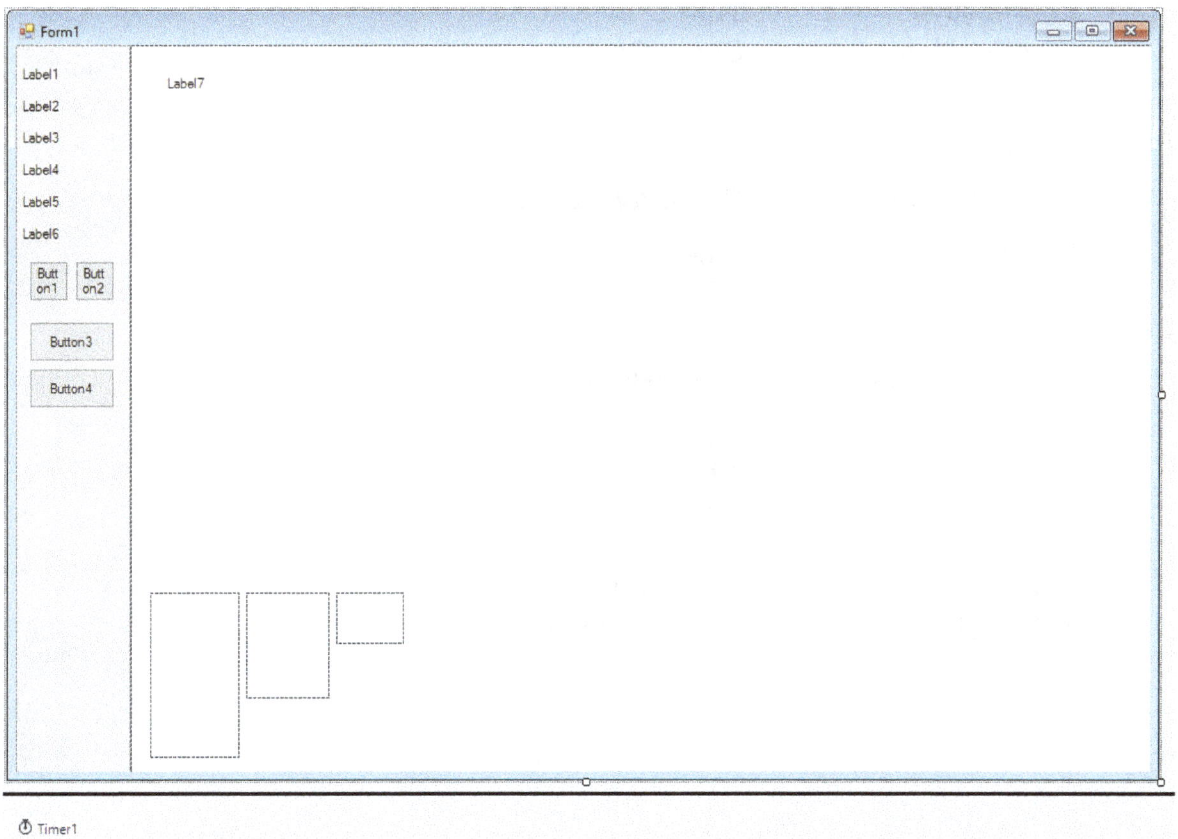

The labels on the left are used to display game information. Two buttons are used to change the difficulty, one to start the game, and one to stop the program. The label control in the second panel is used to display game instructions. The picture boxes hold the images of Elijah, a raven and the bread. The timer controls game play.

Set the control properties using the properties window:

Form1 Form:

Property Name	**Property Value**
Name	frmElijah
Text	Elijah and the Ravens
FormBorderStyle	Fixed Single
KeyPreview	True
StartPosition	CenterScreen

Panel1 Panel:

Property Name	**Property Value**
BackColor	Blue

Label1 Label:

Property Name	**Property Value**
AutoSize	False
FontSize	12
FontStyle	Bold
ForeColor	Yellow
Text	Time Left:
TextAlign	Middle Center

Label2 Label:

Property Name	Property Value
Name	lblTime
AutoSize	False
FontSize	12
FontStyle	Bold
ForeColor	White
Text	0
TextAlign	Middle Center

Label3 Label:

Property Name	Property Value
AutoSize	False
FontSize	12
FontStyle	Bold
ForeColor	Yellow
Text	Loaves:
TextAlign	Middle Center

Label4 Label:

Property Name	Property Value
Name	lblScore
AutoSize	False
FontSize	12
FontStyle	Bold
ForeColor	White
Text	0
TextAlign	Middle Center

Label5 Label:

Property Name	Property Value
AutoSize	False
FontSize	12
FontStyle	Bold
ForeColor	Yellow
Text	Difficulty:
TextAlign	Middle Center

Label6 Label:

Property Name	Property Value
Name	lblDifficulty
AutoSize	False
FontSize	12
FontStyle	Bold
ForeColor	White
Text	1
TextAlign	Middle Center

Button1 Button:

Property Name	Property Value
Name	btnDecrease
FontSize	12
Text	<

Button2 Button:

Property Name	Property Value
Name	btnIncrease
FontSize	12
Text	>

Button3 Button:

Property Name	Property Value
Name	btnStart
FontSize	12
Text	Start

Button4 Button:

Property Name	Property Value
Name	btnStop
FontSize	12
Text	Stop

Label7 Label:

Property Name	Property Value
Name	lblInstructions
FontSize	12

PictureBox1 Picture Box:

Property Name	Property Value
Name	picElijah
Image	Elijah.gif (in **\BVB Projects \ElijahVB** folder)
SizeMode	AutoSize
Visible	False

PictureBox2 Picture Box:

Property Name	Property Value
Name	picRaven
Image	Raven.gif (in **\BVB Projects \ElijahVB** folder)
Visible	False

PictureBox3 Picture Box:

Property Name	Property Value
Name	picBread
Image	Bread.gif (in **\BVB Projects \ElijahVB** folder)
Visible	False

When done, the form should look like this:

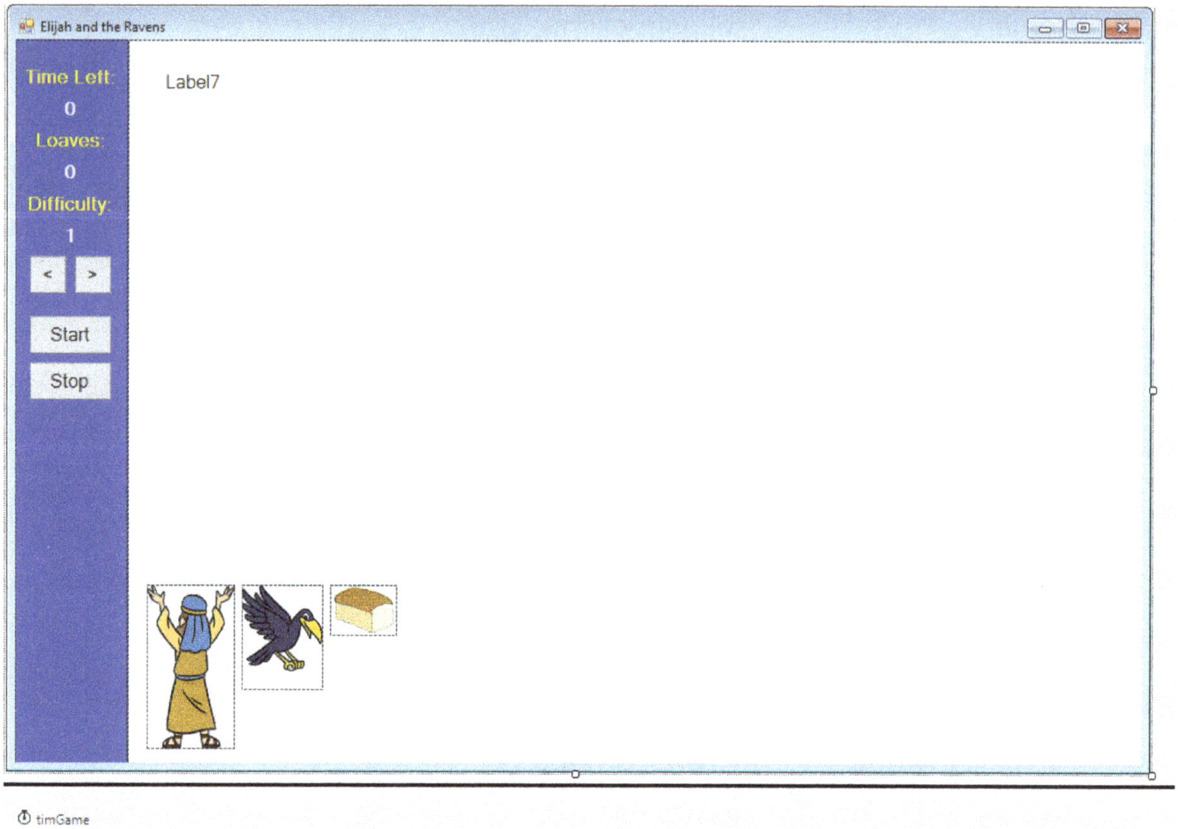

We now begin writing code for the **Elijah and the Ravens** game. We will write the code in several steps. As a first step, we will write the code that starts the program and establishes its 'initial' state. Then, we look at how to go to 'playing' state (positioning all the graphics elements) following clicking of the **Start** button. We then write code to move the bread down the screen, move Elijah (using mouse clicks or keyboard presses), and check for caught loaves of bread. During the code development process, recognize you may modify a particular procedure several times before arriving at the finished product.

Code Design – Initial State (Instructions)

Any time we start a program, there are certain initializations that must take place. Let's look at the initializations needed in the **Elijah and the Ravens** game. When the program first begins, we want to display the game instructions. We also initialize the difficulty (**Difficulty**) and the game status (**GameStatus**). We set up the game screen and display the instructions first. These initializations are in the form **Load** procedure.

We declare two variables (**Difficulty** and **GameStatus**). Do this in the general declarations area:

```
Dim Difficulty As Integer
Dim GameStatus As String
```

Add this code to the **frmElijah Load** event procedure:

```
Private Sub FrmElijah_Load(ByVal sender As System.Object, ByVal
e As System.EventArgs) Handles MyBase.Load
    ' Elijah and the Ravens
    ' Visual Basic Version
    ' Intro screen
    Difficulty = 1
    GameStatus = "Initial"
    lblInstructions.Text = "ELIJAH AND THE RAVENS"
    lblInstructions.Text += ControlChars.CrLf + ControlChars.CrLf
+ "In 1 Kings 17:1-6, God sends ravens to drop bread for Elijah
while he hides from King Ahab. In this game, you will try"
    lblInstructions.Text += ControlChars.CrLf + "to catch as many
falling loaves of bread as possible to feed Elijah."
    lblInstructions.Text += ControlChars.CrLf + ControlChars.CrLf
+ "Use the keypad left and right arrow keys or left and right
mouse buttons to move Elijah under a falling loaf so he can be
fed"
    lblInstructions.Text += ControlChars.CrLf + "by the Raven. God
always provides for our needs."
```

```
    lblInstructions.Text += ControlChars.CrLf + ControlChars.CrLf
+ "Select Difficulty by pressing the left button for Easy and the
right button for Harder."
    lblInstructions.Text += ControlChars.CrLf + ControlChars.CrLf
+ "Click on the Start Button to begin."
    lblInstructions.Text += ControlChars.CrLf + ControlChars.CrLf
+ "Click on the Stop Button to stop the program."
  End Sub
```

As mentioned, we set **Difficulty** to **1** and the **GameStatus** to "**Initial**". Next, using a series of statements, we write out the game instructions in **lblInstructions**.

Save and **Run** the program to see:

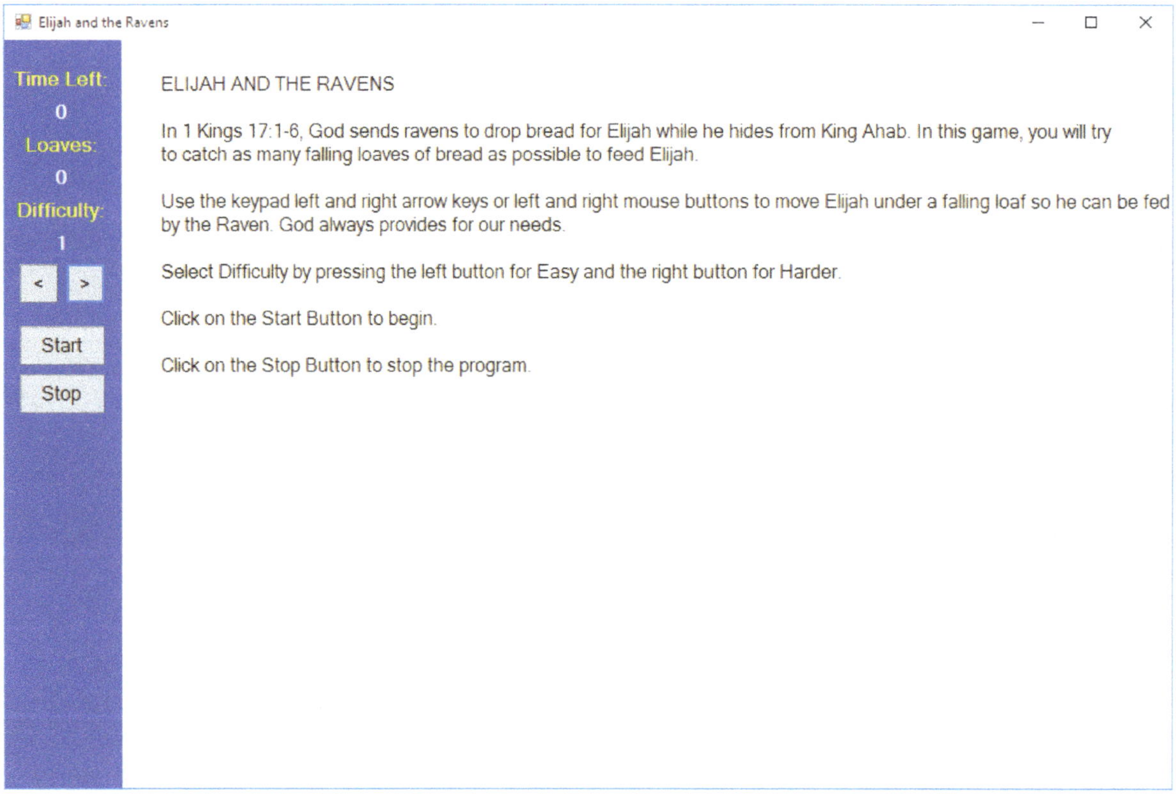

Code Design – Select Difficulty

The **Difficulty** variable is used to determine how fast the bread falls (the higher the difficulty, the faster it falls). To change the difficulty, a user clicks on either of the two arrow buttons. The code to do this goes in the **btnDecrease** and **btnIncrease Click** event procedures:

```
  Private Sub BtnDecrease_Click(ByVal sender As System.Object,
ByVal e As System.EventArgs) Handles btnDecrease.Click
    If (GameStatus = "Initial") Then
      ' decrease difficulty
      Difficulty = Difficulty - 1
      If (Difficulty < 1) Then
        Difficulty = 1
      End If
      lblDifficulty.Text = Difficulty
    End If
  End Sub

  Private Sub BtnIncrease_Click(ByVal sender As System.Object,
ByVal e As System.EventArgs) Handles btnIncrease.Click
    If (GameStatus = "Initial") Then
      'increase difficulty
      Difficulty = Difficulty + 1
      If (Difficulty > 10) Then
        Difficulty = 10
      End If
      lblDifficulty.Text = Difficulty
    End If
  End Sub
```

The code is straightforward. The difficulty can only be changed when the game is in "**Initial**" state. If the **<** button is clicked, we decrease the difficulty by one (minimum of 1). If the **>** button is clicked, we increase the difficulty (maximum of 10). The new value for the difficulty is then displayed in **lblDifficulty**.

Save and **Run** the program. Make sure the arrow buttons work – make sure the difficulty is always between 1 and 10. Here's my run where I changed the difficulty to three:

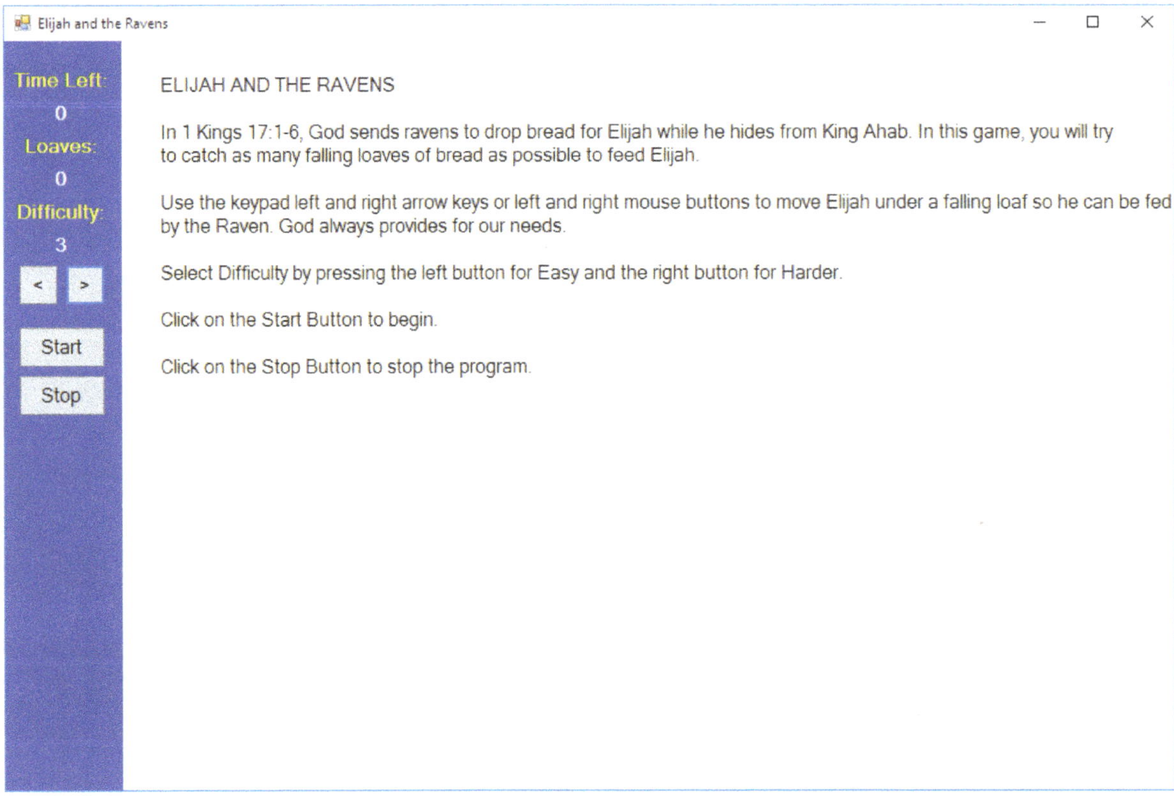

Code Design – Position Elijah

Once the difficulty is set, the next step is to click the **Start** button to allow the game to begin. Hence, we need code to move from the "**Initial**" state to what we'll call "**Playing**" state. When the **Start** button is clicked in "**Initial**" state, we need to take the following steps:

- Change **GameStatus** to "**Playing**"
- Clear the screen.
- Initialize score and time left.
- Place Elijah at bottom of screen
- Randomly place Raven and bread at top of screen
- Start dropping bread

There is a lot to do here, so we will take it in steps. First, we'll initialize variables and position Elijah at the bottom of the screen.

Two variables are used in game control. **TimeLeft** is an integer value telling us how much time is left in the game (in milliseconds). We choose to let a game last 60 seconds. **Score** tells us how many loaves of bread have been caught by Elijah. **GamePanel** is the graphics region we play the game in. Add these general variable declarations:

```
Dim TimeLeft As Integer
Dim Score As Integer
Dim GamePanel As Graphics
```

The image stored in **picElijah** is used for Elijah:

picElijah

In the code, we determine both the width (**ElijahW**) and height of this graphic (**ElijahH**). Elijah is positioned at the bottom of the screen, near the middle. The variables **ElijahX** and **ElijahY** tell us where Elijah is. **ElijahDeltaX** is used to tell us how much to move Elijah with each button click or mouse press. All of these variables will be helpful when checking to see if Elijah catches or misses falling bread. Add these new variable declarations:

```
  Dim ElijahW As Integer, ElijahH As Integer, ElijahX As Integer,
ElijahY As Integer
  Dim ElijahDeltaX As Integer
```

Add this code to the **btnStart Click** event procedure:

```
  Private Sub BtnStart_Click(ByVal sender As System.Object, ByVal
e As System.EventArgs) Handles btnStart.Click
    'clicked start
    GameStatus = "Playing"
    lblInstructions.Visible = False
    GamePanel = pnlGame.CreateGraphics()
    GamePanel.Clear(Color.White)
    'time/score
    TimeLeft = 60 * 1000 ' milliseconds remaining
    Score = 0
    DisplayTimeScore()
    'Elijah
    ElijahW = picElijah.Width
    ElijahH = picElijah.Height
```

```
    ElijahDeltaX = 5
    ElijahX = 375
    ElijahY = pnlGame.Height - ElijahH
    GamePanel.DrawImage(picElijah.Image, ElijahX, ElijahY)
  End Sub
```

You should be able to identify each step in this new code. We clear the area and set variables. We establish the variables for Elijah and position him at the bottom.

Notice this line of code:

```
DisplayTimeScore()
```

This line calls a subroutine that updates the displayed value for **TimeLeft** and **Score**. Add this subroutine at the end of your program:

```
  Private Sub DisplayTimeScore()
    lblTime.Text = CInt(TimeLeft / 1000).ToString()
    lblScore.Text = Score.ToString()
  End Sub
```

Here, we set the appropriate values in **lblTime** and **lblScore**. Note how we convert milliseconds to seconds.

Save and **Run** the program. Choose a difficulty (I picked 3). Click **Start** and you should see:

Notice the displayed values for **Time Left** and **Loaves**. Notice Elijah down there waiting for bread to fall. Let's get a raven and loaf of bread on the screen.

Code Design – Position Raven and Bread

The last initialization step is to randomly place the raven and bread at the top of the screen. The images stored in **picDaniel** and **picLion** are are used:

picRaven

picBread

We determine the width and height of the raven (**RavenW** and **RavenH**) and the width and height for the bread (**BreadW** and **BreadH**). These help in determining if Elijah catches a loaf of bread. Add these general declarations:

```
  Dim RavenW As Integer, RavenH As Integer, RavenX As Integer
  Dim BreadW As Integer, BreadH As Integer, BreadX As Integer,
BreadY As Integer
  Dim MyRandom As Random = New Random()
```

RavenX is the x position of the raven (the y position is zero – the top of the screen). The bread is a (**BreadX**, **BreadY**). **MyRandom** is needed for random number generation.

Add the shaded code to the **btnStart Click** event procedure:

```
  Private Sub BtnStart_Click(ByVal sender As System.Object, ByVal
e As System.EventArgs) Handles btnStart.Click
    'clicked start
    GameStatus = "Playing"
    lblInstructions.Visible = False
    GamePanel = pnlGame.CreateGraphics()
    GamePanel.Clear(Color.White)
    'time/score
    TimeLeft = 60 * 1000 ' milliseconds remaining
    Score = 0
    DisplayTimeScore()
    'Elijah
    ElijahW = picElijah.Width
    ElijahH = picElijah.Height
    ElijahDeltaX = 5
    ElijahX = 375
    ElijahY = pnlGame.Height - ElijahH
    GamePanel.DrawImage(picElijah.Image, ElijahX, ElijahY)
    'Raven
    RavenW = picRaven.Width
    RavenH = picRaven.Height
    'Bread
    BreadW = picBread.Width
    BreadH = picBread.Height
    PositionRavenAndBread()
  End Sub
```

The above code uses a separate subroutine (**PositionRavenAndBread**) to randomly place the raven and bread on the screen. Add this subroutine to your program:

```
Private Sub PositionRavenAndBread()
  RavenX = MyRandom.Next(pnlGame.Width - RavenW)
  GamePanel.DrawImage(picRaven.Image, RavenX, 0)
  BreadX = RavenX + 0.5 * (RavenW - BreadW)
  BreadY = RavenH - 20
  GamePanel.DrawImage(picBread.Image, BreadX, BreadY)
End Sub
```

Notice how the random horizontal position is selected. The coordinates **BreadX** and **BreadY** let us know where a falling loaf of bread is at all times.

Save and **Run** the program. Set the **Difficulty** (I used 3). Click **Start**. The complete initialized game is now seen:

We still need to code to get the bread to drop and to move Elijah along the bottom of the screen. We write code to do these steps soon. But first, let's take care of one last thing you can do while in "**Initial**" state – stop the program.

Code Design – Stop the Program

One last thing you can do while the game is in "**Initial**" state is to click on the **Stop** button. This will stop the program. The code here is simple. Add these lines to the **btnStop Click** event procedure:

```
  Private Sub BtnStop_Click(ByVal sender As System.Object, ByVal e
As System.EventArgs) Handles btnStop.Click
    If (GameStatus = "Initial") Then
      'clicked stop
      Me.Close()
    End If
  End Sub
```

As desired, if the **Stop** button is clicked, the program ends.

Save and **Run** the program. Make sure the **Stop** button works. This completes the code for moving from "**Initial**" game status to "**Playing**" status. Now, let's look at code to move Elijah along the bottom of the screen.

Code Design – Dropping Bread

Once the game begins, the loaf of bread will drop. You move Elijah along the bottom of the screen to try and catch the dropping bread. Here we do the code that drops the bread. A variable **BreadSpeed** will determine how fast the bread drops down the screen. Add this general declaration:

```
Dim BreadSpeed As Integer
```

We assign **BreadSpeed** based on the value of **Difficulty**:

```
BreadSpeed = 0.5 * Difficulty + 3
```

Note, the higher the difficulty, the faster the speed. You can change this if you like.

The timer control (**timGame**) is used to control bread motion. Add the shaded lines to the **btnStart Click** event procedure to turn on the timer and set the value for **BreadSpeed**:

```
  Private Sub BtnStart_Click(ByVal sender As System.Object, ByVal
e As System.EventArgs) Handles btnStart.Click
    'clicked start
    GameStatus = "Playing"
    lblInstructions.Visible = False
    GamePanel = pnlGame.CreateGraphics()
    GamePanel.Clear(Color.White)
    'time/score
    TimeLeft = 60 * 1000 ' milliseconds remaining
    Score = 0
    DisplayTimeScore()
    'Elijah
    ElijahW = picElijah.Width
    ElijahH = picElijah.Height
    ElijahDeltaX = 5
    ElijahX = 375
    ElijahY = pnlGame.Height - ElijahH
```

```
    GamePanel.DrawImage(picElijah.Image, ElijahX, ElijahY)
    'Raven
    RavenW = picRaven.Width
    RavenH = picRaven.Height
    'Bread
    BreadW = picBread.Width
    BreadH = picBread.Height
    PositionRavenAndBread()
    'start timer
    BreadSpeed = 0.5 * Difficulty + 3 ' base on difficulty
    timGame.Start()
  End Sub
```

The bread position is updated in the **timGame Tick** event procedure. Use this code:

```
  Private Sub TimGame_Tick(ByVal sender As System.Object, ByVal e
As System.EventArgs) Handles timGame.Tick
    ' move bread
    RemoveBread()
    BreadY = BreadY + BreadSpeed
    GamePanel.DrawImage(picBread.Image, BreadX, BreadY)
  End Sub
```

With each **Tick** event, the bread vertical position changes. This uses a new subroutine **RemoveBread** that erases the bread from its current location prior to moving it to its new one. Add this new subroutine:

```
  Private Sub RemoveBread()
    GamePanel.FillRectangle(Brushes.White, BreadX, BreadY, BreadW,
BreadH)
  End Sub
```

Save and **Run** the program. Click **Start**. The bread is falling:

But it just keeps on falling! We need to add two more pieces of code – one to move Elijah under the bread and one to determine whether Elijah has caught the bread.

Code Design – Moving Elijah

The object of the game is to move Elijah under falling bread so he can catch the loaves for food. Elijah can be moved using two different methods. First, he can be moved by using the left and right arrow buttons on the numeric keypad (this will not work with the cursor control keys). With each key press, we change **ElijahX** by **ElijahDeltaX** in the appropriate direction. We use a new variable **KeyPressed** to keep track of which key is being held. Add the general declaration (initializing **KeyPressed** to **None**):

```
Dim KeyPressed As String = "None"
```

We detect key presses in the form's **KeyDown** event procedure. The code is:

```
  Private Sub FrmElijah_KeyDown(ByVal sender As System.Object,
ByVal e As System.Windows.Forms.KeyEventArgs) Handles
MyBase.KeyDown
    ' check for left or right numpad arrow key to move Elijah
    If (e.KeyCode = Keys.NumPad4) Then
      KeyPressed = "Left"
    ElseIf (e.KeyCode = Keys.NumPad6) Then
      KeyPressed = "Right"
    End If
  End Sub
```

This tells us which key is being pressed (**KeyPressed**). It is used in the **timGame Tick** event procedure to update the position of Elijah.

We also need code to tell us when a pressed key is released. This goes in the form's **KeyUp** procedure:

```
  Private Sub FrmElijah_KeyUp(ByVal sender As System.Object, ByVal
e As System.Windows.Forms.KeyEventArgs) Handles MyBase.KeyUp
    KeyPressed = "None"
  End Sub
```

When a key is released, **KeyPressed** is set back to "**None**".

Add the shaded code to the **timGame Tick** procedure:

```
  Private Sub TimGame_Tick(ByVal sender As System.Object, ByVal e
As System.EventArgs) Handles timGame.Tick
    ' move bread
    RemoveBread()
    BreadY = BreadY + BreadSpeed
    GamePanel.DrawImage(picBread.Image, BreadX, BreadY)
    ' move elijah
    RemoveElijah()
    If (KeyPressed = "Left") Then
      ElijahX = ElijahX - ElijahDeltaX
      If ElijahX < 0 Then
        ElijahX = 0
      End If
    ElseIf (KeyPressed = "Right") Then
      ElijahX = ElijahX + ElijahDeltaX
      If ElijahX > pnlGame.Width - ElijahW Then
        ElijahX = pnlGame.Width - ElijahW
      End If
    End If
    GamePanel.DrawImage(picElijah.Image, ElijahX, ElijahY)
  End Sub
```

If the left key is pressed, Elijah's position is decremented by **ElijahDeltaX** – if the right key is pressed, the position is incremented by **ElijahDeltaX**.

Like the bread moving code, this code uses another subroutine **RemoveElijah** to erase Elijah from his current location. Add this subroutine:

```
  Private Sub RemoveElijah()
    GamePanel.FillRectangle(Brushes.White, ElijahX, ElijahY,
ElijahW, ElijahH)
  End Sub
```

Save and **Run** the program. Click **Start**. Try moving Elijah using the left and right arrow keys on the numeric keypad (make sure **NumLock** is on):

Here I've moved him far to the left.

When we started this section, we said there were two ways to move Elijah. Let's write code for the second method – using the left and mouse button keys. It's a fairly easy change. Define a variable to keep track of the pressed button (**ButtonPressed**):

```
  Dim ButtonPressed As String = "None"
```

Now, add this code to the **pnlGame MouseDown** event procedure:

```
  Private Sub PnlGame_MouseDown(ByVal sender As System.Object,
ByVal e As System.Windows.Forms.MouseEventArgs) Handles
pnlGame.MouseDown
    ' check for left or right mouse button.y to move Elijah
    If (e.Button = MouseButtons.Left) Then
      ButtonPressed = "Left"
    ElseIf (e.Button = MouseButtons.Right) Then
      ButtonPressed = "Right"
    End If
  End Sub
```

With this, when the mouse is over the game panel, the left and right mouse buttons replicate the action of clicking on the left and right arrow keys on the keypad. Add this code to the **pnlGame MouseUp** event procedure:

```
  Private Sub PnlGame_MouseUp(ByVal sender As System.Object, ByVal
e As System.Windows.Forms.MouseEventArgs) Handles pnlGame.MouseUp
    ButtonPressed = "None"
  End Sub
```

This tells us when a mouse button is released.

Finally, add the shaded changes to the **timGame Tick** event procedure:

```
  Private Sub TimGame_Tick(ByVal sender As System.Object, ByVal e
As System.EventArgs) Handles timGame.Tick
    ' move bread
    RemoveBread()
    BreadY = BreadY + BreadSpeed
    GamePanel.DrawImage(picBread.Image, BreadX, BreadY)
    ' move elijah
    RemoveElijah()
    If (KeyPressed = "Left" Or ButtonPressed = "Left") Then
      ElijahX = ElijahX - ElijahDeltaX
      If ElijahX < 0 Then
        ElijahX = 0
      End If
    ElseIf (KeyPressed = "Right" Or ButtonPressed = "Right") Then
      ElijahX = ElijahX + ElijahDeltaX
      If ElijahX > pnlGame.Width - ElijahW Then
        ElijahX = pnlGame.Width - ElijahW
      End If
    End If
    GamePanel.DrawImage(picElijah.Image, ElijahX, ElijahY)
  End Sub
```

In this code, if the left mouse button is being held down, Elijah moves to the left. Similarly, if the right mouse button is being held down, Elijah moves to the right. In the changes, we just use the code we used for the arrow keys.

Save and **Run** the program. Make sure you can move Elijah with both the keypad arrow keys and by using the mouse buttons. Recall the mouse must be over the panel for the mouse buttons to work properly.

Code Design – Catching Bread

When the bread approaches the bottom of the screen, we need to see if Elijah catches it. The code to do this check is in the **timGame Tick** event procedure. We need to do two things:

- Check to see if the bread has been caught. If so, make the bread disappear, increment score and make raven and bread reappear at a random location at the top of the screen.
- Check to see if bread has reached the same vertical position of Elijah without being caught. If so, start a new raven and bread.

How do we know if Elijah catches the bread? We want to see if the Elijah graphic collides with the bread graphic. The check cannot be made until the bread passes the top of Elijah. This happens when:

```
BreadY + BreadH > ElijahY
```

We will use a boolean variable (**Passed**) to see if this is true. Once this condition is met, we can see that Elijah collides with bread (or catches it) when:

```
ElijahX + ElijahW > BreadX And ElijahX < BreadX + BreadW
```

This says that the right side of Elijah must be "farther right" than the left side of the bread and the left side of Elijah must be "farther left" than the right side of the bread. Another boolean variable (**Collision**) is used to check this condition.

Declare the two new variables:

```
Dim Passed As Boolean
Dim Collision As Boolean
```

Add the shaded code to the **timGame Tick** event procedure:

```
Private Sub TimGame_Tick(ByVal sender As System.Object, ByVal e
As System.EventArgs) Handles timGame.Tick
    ' move bread
    RemoveBread()
    BreadY = BreadY + BreadSpeed
    GamePanel.DrawImage(picBread.Image, BreadX, BreadY)
    ' move elijah
    RemoveElijah()
    If (KeyPressed = "Left" Or ButtonPressed = "Left") Then
      ElijahX = ElijahX - ElijahDeltaX
      If ElijahX < 0 Then
        ElijahX = 0
      End If
    ElseIf (KeyPressed = "Right" Or ButtonPressed = "Right") Then
      ElijahX = ElijahX + ElijahDeltaX
      If ElijahX > pnlGame.Width - ElijahW Then
        ElijahX = pnlGame.Width - ElijahW
      End If
    End If
    GamePanel.DrawImage(picElijah.Image, ElijahX, ElijahY)
    ' check for bread collision or passed elijah
    Passed = False
    Collision = False
    If (BreadY + BreadH > ElijahY) Then
      Passed = True
      If (ElijahX + ElijahW > BreadX And ElijahX < BreadX +
BreadW) Then
        Collision = True
      End If
    End If
    If (Passed) Then
      If (Collision) Then
        Score = Score + 1
      End If
      RemoveRaven()
      RemoveBread()
```

```
      PositionRavenAndBread()
    End If
    DisplayTimeScore()
  End Sub
```

You should see how the listed steps are implemented. In particular, note how a new raven is positioned once **Passed** is **true** (and how the score is incremented if **Collision** is also **true**. This new code requires **RemoveRaven** – a subroutine to erase the raven from its current location:

```
  Private Sub RemoveRaven()
    GamePanel.FillRectangle(Brushes.White, RavenX, 0, RavenW, 
RavenH)
  End Sub
```

Save and **Run** the program. Change **Difficulty** if you want (I used 3). Click **Start**. Now when you move Elijah under a falling loaf, the score will increment and another raven will appear. If Elijah misses a loaf, the score will not increment and another raven will appear. Here's my screen after catching three loaves and waiting on another:

Code Design – Stop the Game

We're almost done. With the current code, you can play the game as long as you like – notice the displayed **Time Left** is always 60. We need to implement the logic that ends the game after 60 seconds (and updates the time display). To do this, add the shaded code to the **timGame Tick** event procedure:

```
  Private Sub TimGame_Tick(ByVal sender As System.Object, ByVal e
As System.EventArgs) Handles timGame.Tick
    ' move bread
    RemoveBread()
    BreadY = BreadY + BreadSpeed
    GamePanel.DrawImage(picBread.Image, BreadX, BreadY)
    ' move elijah
    RemoveElijah()
    If (KeyPressed = "Left" Or ButtonPressed = "Left") Then
      ElijahX = ElijahX - ElijahDeltaX
      If ElijahX < 0 Then
        ElijahX = 0
      End If
    ElseIf (KeyPressed = "Right" Or ButtonPressed = "Right") Then
      ElijahX = ElijahX + ElijahDeltaX
      If ElijahX > pnlGame.Width - ElijahW Then
        ElijahX = pnlGame.Width - ElijahW
      End If
    End If
    GamePanel.DrawImage(picElijah.Image, ElijahX, ElijahY)
    ' check for bread collision or passed elijah
    Passed = False
    Collision = False
    If (BreadY + BreadH > ElijahY) Then
      Passed = True
      If (ElijahX + ElijahW > BreadX And ElijahX < BreadX +
BreadW) Then
        Collision = True
      End If
    End If
    If (Passed) Then
      If (Collision) Then
        Score = Score + 1
      End If
      RemoveRaven()
```

```
      RemoveBread()
      PositionRavenAndBread()
    End If
    'update time
    TimeLeft = TimeLeft - timGame.Interval
    DisplayTimeScore()
    If (TimeLeft = 0) Then
      RemoveRaven()
      RemoveBread()
      RemoveElijah()
      timGame.Stop()
      MessageBox.Show("Elijah has been fed by " + Score.ToString()
+ " ravens.", "Game Over")
      GameStatus = "Initial"
    End If
  End Sub
```

In this new code, with each **Tick** event, the **TimeLeft** is decremented by **Interval**. Once **TimeLeft** is zero, the graphic elements (raven, bread, Elijah) are removed from the screen, the timer is turned off and the results displayed.

Save and **Run** the program. Click **Start**. The time will count down. Here's my game in the middle:

And here's my final result:

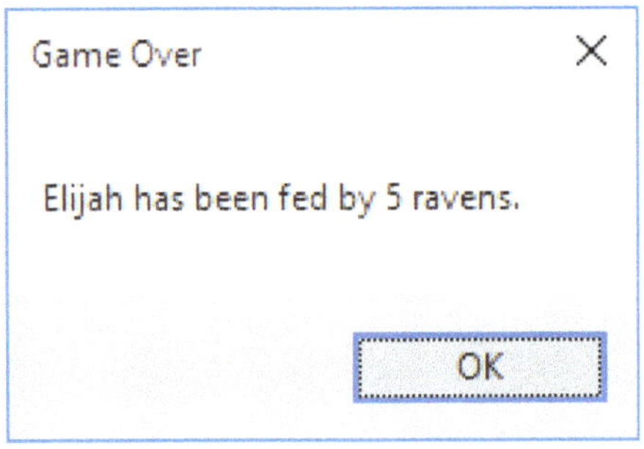

I did okay.

Just one last change. You may want to stop a game before 60 seconds goes by. To do this, you can click the **Stop** button while the game is in "**Playing**" status. The code here is simple. Add the few shaded lines at the end of the **btnStop Click** event procedure:

```
  Private Sub BtnStop_Click(ByVal sender As System.Object, ByVal e
As System.EventArgs) Handles btnStop.Click
    If (GameStatus = "Initial") Then
      'clicked stop
      Me.Close()
    Else
      'clicked stop while playing
      timGame.Stop()
      GameStatus = "Initial"
      MessageBox.Show("You stopped the game.", "Game Over")
      RemoveElijah()
      RemoveRaven()
      RemoveBread()
    End If
  End Sub
```

Here, when stopped is pressed the game screen is cleared and a message displayed.

Save and **Run** the program. Click **Start**, then click **Stop**. You should see this message:

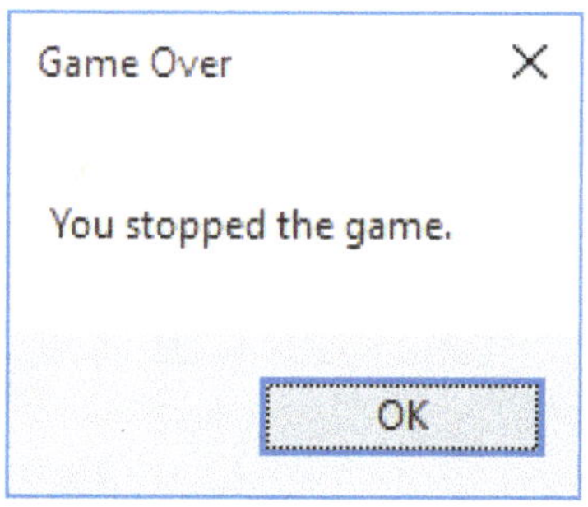

The game is now complete.

Elijah and the Ravens Program Review

The **Elijah and the Ravens** program is now complete. **Save** and **Run** the program and make sure it works as promised. Check that all options work correctly.

If there are errors in your implementation, go back over the steps of window and code design. Go over the developed code – make sure you understand how different parts of the program were coded. As mentioned in the beginning of this chapter, the completed program is saved as **Elijah** in the **\BVB Projects \Elijah** folder.

13

Daniel and the Lions Project

Preview

In Daniel 6, King Darius is tricked into putting Daniel into the lion's den. Daniel prays for God's protection and god sends His Angel to shut the lion's mouth. In this chapter, you build a computer game based on this story. Daniel is surrounded by lion's in a grid. As he moves, they move closer to him. He shoots prayers at the lions to dispatch them.

Daniel and the Lions Program Preview

In this chapter, we will build the **Daniel and the Lions** game. Daniel is placed in a grid with a number of lions (and four rocks). The idea is for Daniel to dispatch (eliminate) each lion by shooting a prayer at it. The game is over when Daniel has dispatched all the lions or the moving lions reach Daniel first.

The finished project is saved as **DanielVB** in the **\BVB Projects** folder. Start Visual Basic and open the finished project. Open the form (double-click **Daniel.vb** in Solution Explorer) and you will see:

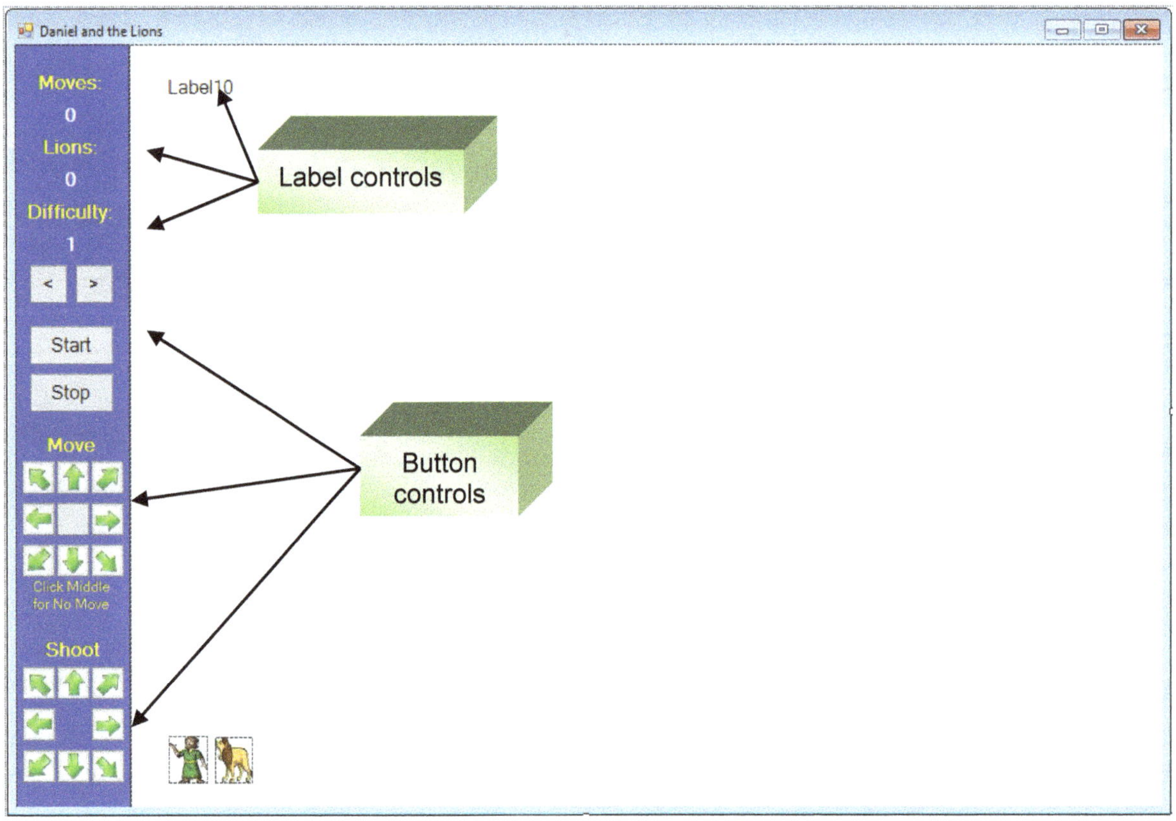

Labels are used for instructions and to display game information (number of moves, number of lions, difficulty). There are many button controls. Two are used to change the difficulty, one to start the game and one to stop. Nine button controls (with arrows) are used to move Daniel, while eight buttons (with arrows) are used to shoot prayers at lions. Picture box controls hold images for Daniel and lions.

Run the program (press <**F5**>). The game will appear in its 'initial' state. A game description and program instructions are given. At this point, you can click the **Start** button to start the game, click arrow buttons to change the game **Difficulty** or click **Stop** to stop the program.

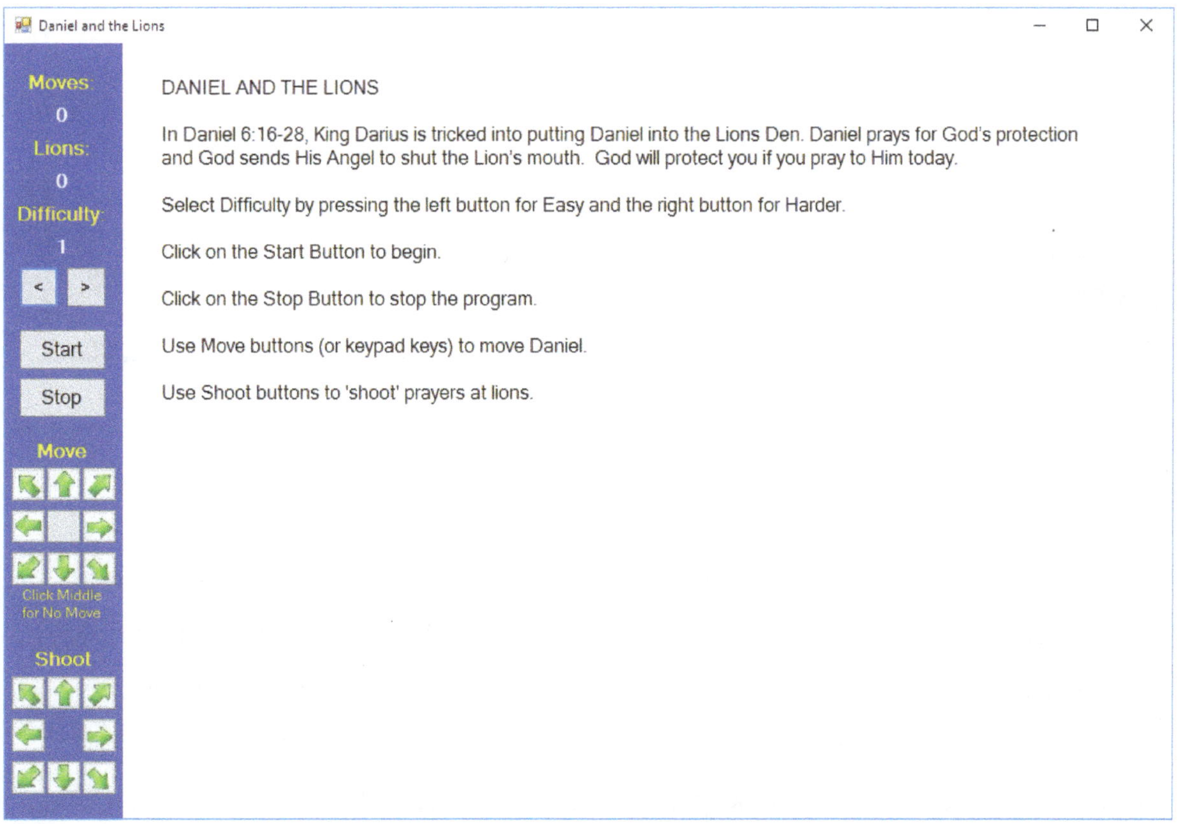

Change the **Difficulty** if you want. The higher the difficulty, the more lions that Daniel must dispatch. I set the value to **3** by clicking the little arrows under **Difficulty**. Click the **Start** button to start playing. The program instructions disappear. Daniel and the lions appear in the game grid This is the game's '**DanielMove'** state:

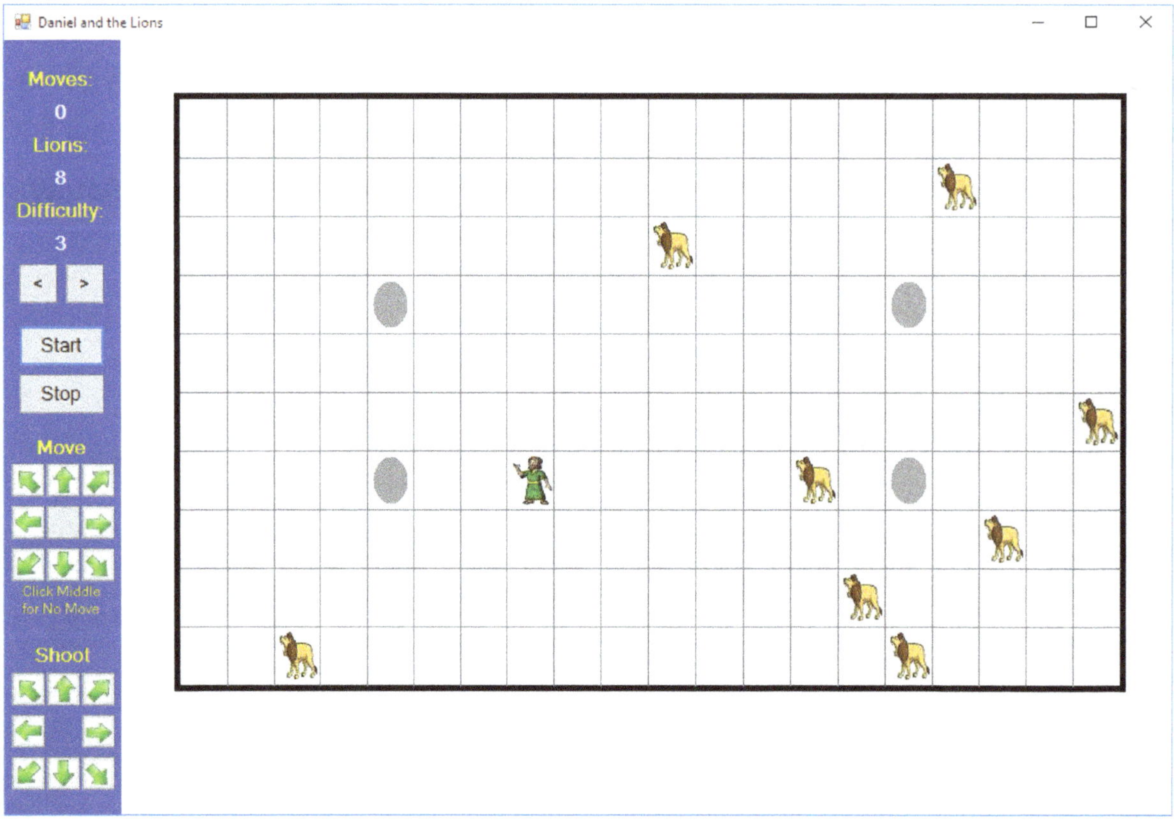

You can see Daniel in the middle of the grid. A number of lions are in the grid along with four rocks (gray ovals). In the upper left corner you are shown how many **Moves** you have taken and how many **Lions** remain. You have two choices. You can move Daniel by clicking one of the arrows under **Move** (or alternately use corresponding key on the numeric keypad). Or, you can shoot a prayer at a lion by clicking one of the green arrows under **Shoot**.

If you move Daniel, he will move one square in the chosen direction (or click the middle to have him remain where he is). Following his move, all the lions will move closer to Daniel, so be careful. Note lions cannot move through the rocks. If you shoot a prayer, it will travel in the selected direction. If it intercepts a lion, that lion is dispatched (taken out of the grid). A prayer will not move through a rock. The goal of the game is to dispatch all the lions before one reaches Daniel.

In our example, notice a lion to the right of Daniel. Click the right **Shoot** arrow and that lion is gone:

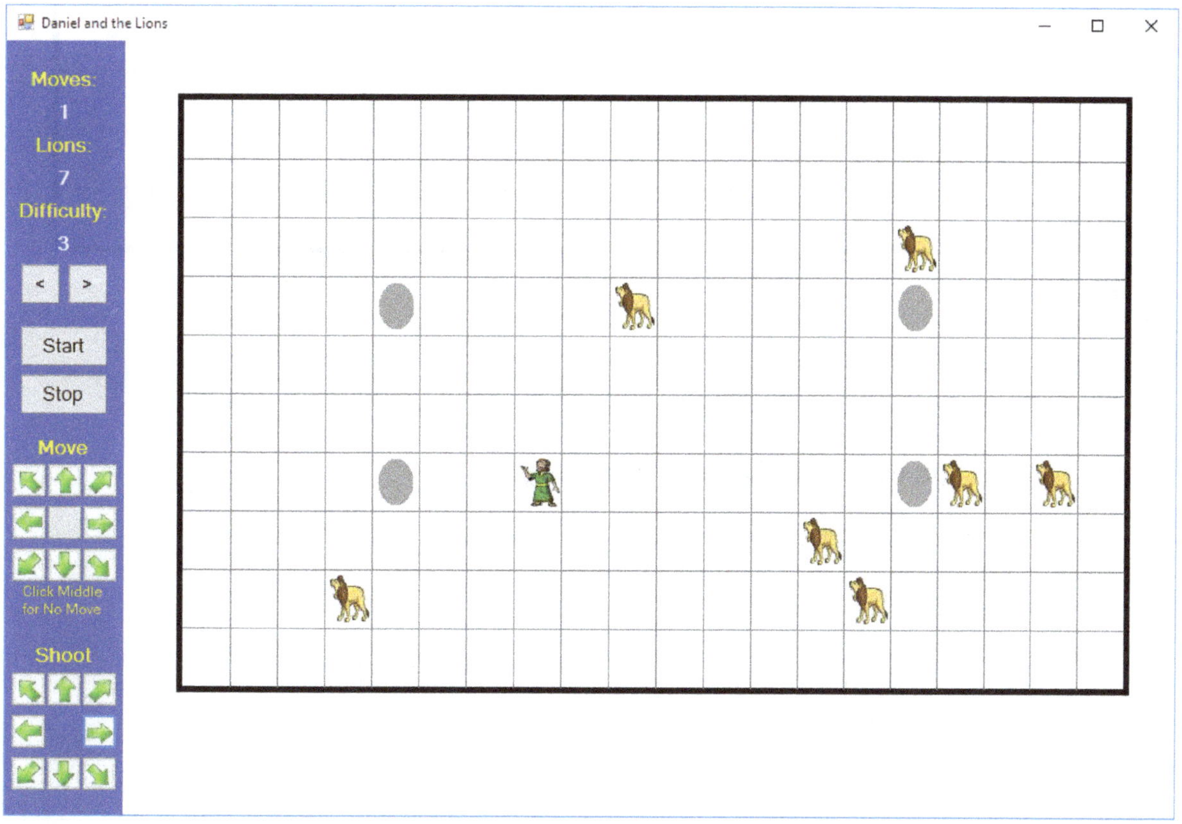

Also notice the remaining lions have moved toward Daniel. At this point, no lions are in the direct path of a 'prayer shot' so we can only move Daniel.

I moved him up and the lions moved too:

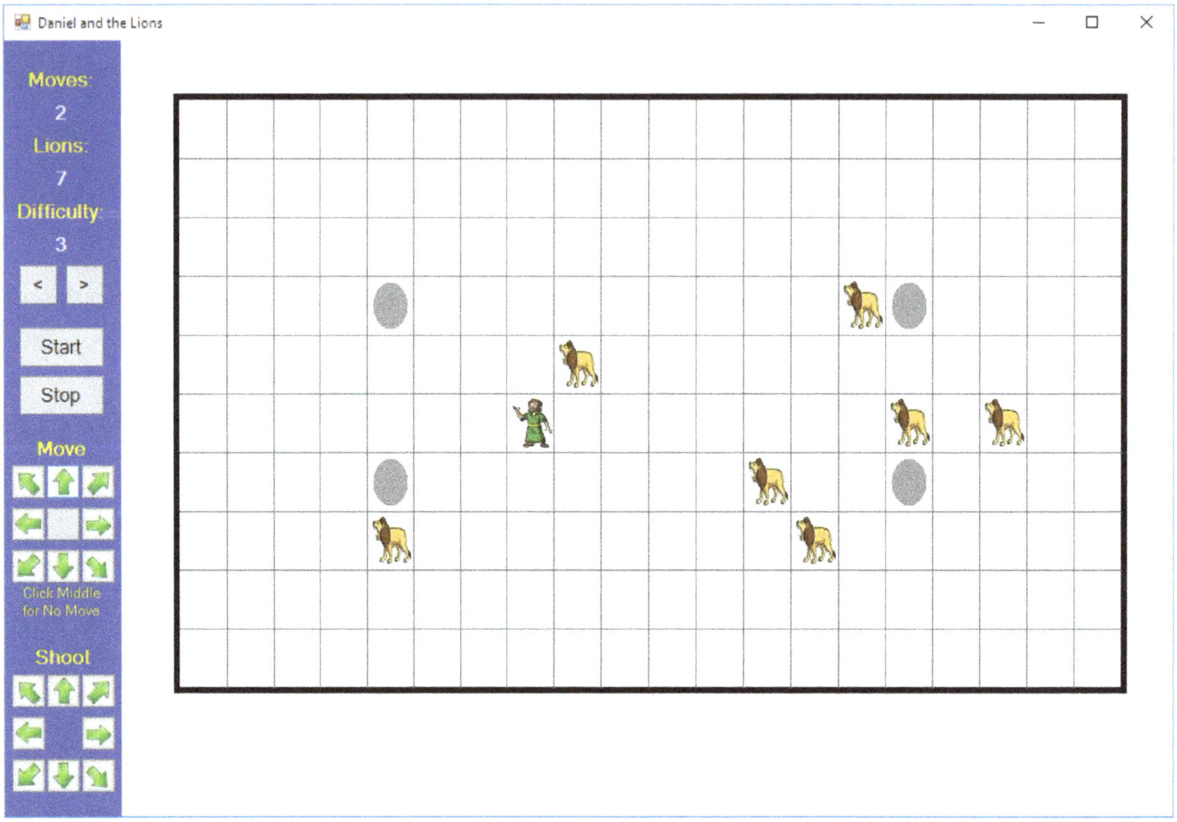

I have another lion to shoot. Up and to the right.

Another lion is dispatched, but they continue to close in on Daniel:

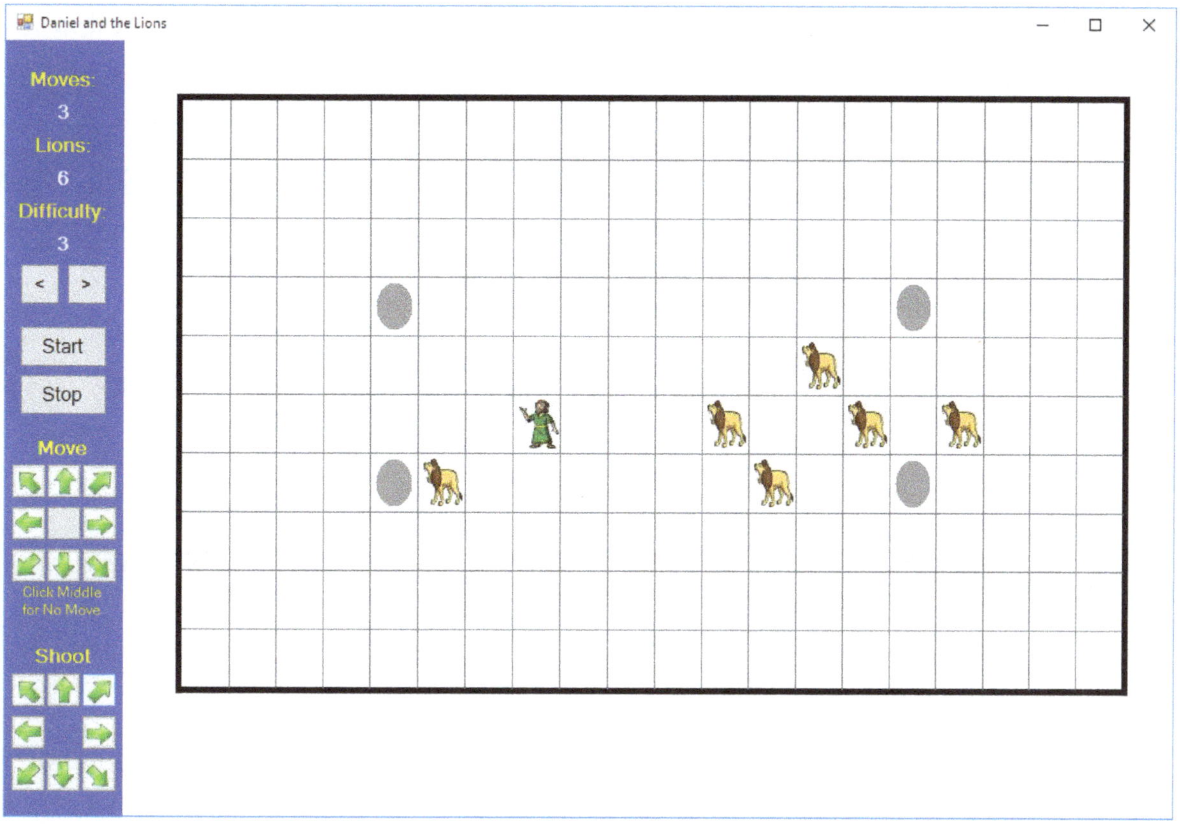

If I keep shooting, I should be able to eliminate all the lions.

You should see how the game is played. When a lion is in shot range, take a shot. If a lion gets stuck behind a rock, you need to move Daniel until the lion moves in range. I continued this game and dispatched all 8 lions in just 9 moves. At this point, I got this message:

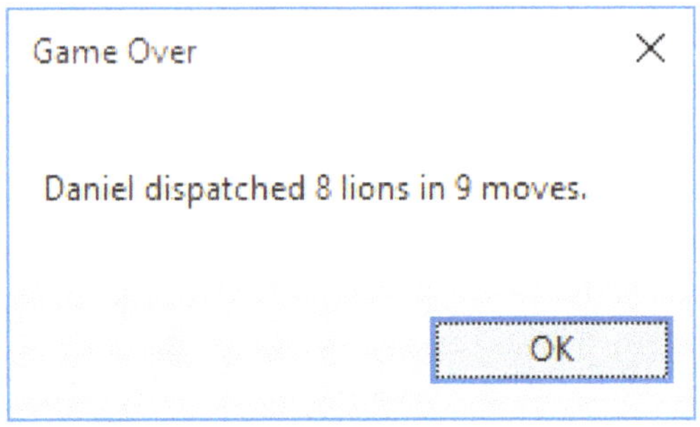

If you aren't successful in dispatching all the lions, you will see this message:

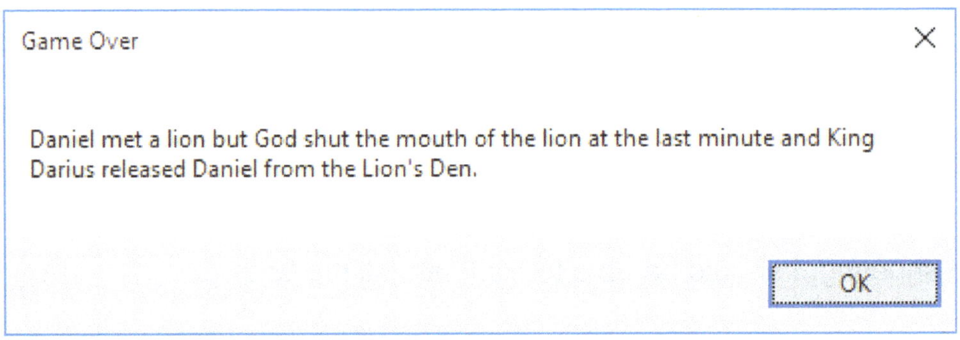

When a game is over, you can change the **Difficulty**. You can also click **Start** to play again or click **Stop** to stop the program. Continue playing the game to understand its operation.

You will now build this project in stages. As you build Visual Basic programs, we always recommend taking a slow, step-by-step process. It minimizes programming errors and helps build your confidence as things come together in a complete program. We address **form design**. And, we address **code design**. We discuss how to use the buttons, how to draw the grid, how to display Daniel, the lions and the rocks, and how to move Daniel and the lions.

Daniel and the Lions Form Design

We begin building the **Daniel and the Lions** game project. Let's build the form. Start a new project in Visual Basic. Once started, we suggest you immediately save the project with a name you choose. This sets up the folder and file structure needed for your project.

Put two panel controls on the form (one 100 pixels wide on the left, one 900 pixels wide on the right). Put six labels and four buttons at the top of the left panel. Under these put another label, then a 3 x 3 grid of nine small buttons, followed by two labels. Lastly, place another grid of eight small button controls. Put a label control and two picture box controls on the right panel. The form should look like this:

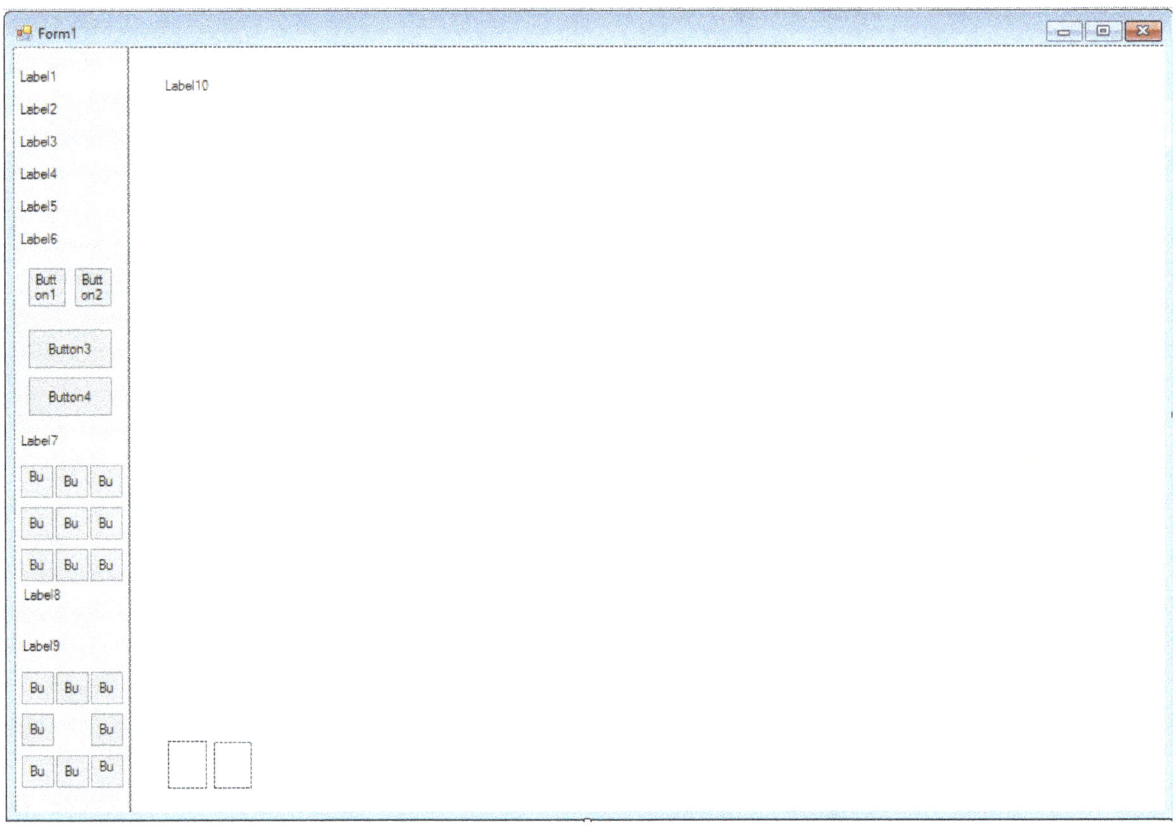

The labels on the left are used to display game information. Two buttons are used to change the difficulty, one to start the game, and one to stop the program. Under the game control buttons are two sets of directional buttons. The first set of nine buttons are used to move Daniel. The last set of eight buttons are used to fire prayers at the lions. The label control in the second panel is used to display game instructions. The picture boxes hold the images of Daniel and a lion.

Set the control properties using the properties window:

Form1 Form:

Property Name	**Property Value**
Name	frmDaniel
Text	Daniel and the Lions
FormBorderStyle	Fixed Single
KeyPreview	True
StartPosition	CenterScreen

Panel1 Panel:

Property Name	**Property Value**
BackColor	Blue

Label1 Label:

Property Name	**Property Value**
AutoSize	False
FontSize	12
FontStyle	Bold
ForeColor	Yellow
Text	Moves:
TextAlign	Middle Center

Label2 Label:

Property Name	Property Value
Name	lblMoves
AutoSize	False
FontSize	12
FontStyle	Bold
ForeColor	White
Text	0
TextAlign	Middle Center

Label3 Label:

Property Name	Property Value
AutoSize	False
FontSize	12
FontStyle	Bold
ForeColor	Yellow
Text	Lions:
TextAlign	Middle Center

Label4 Label:

Property Name	Property Value
Name	lblLions
AutoSize	False
FontSize	12
FontStyle	Bold
ForeColor	White
Text	0
TextAlign	Middle Center

Label5 Label:

Property Name	Property Value
AutoSize	False
FontSize	12
FontStyle	Bold
ForeColor	Yellow
Text	Difficulty:
TextAlign	Middle Center

Label6 Label:

Property Name	Property Value
Name	lblDifficulty
AutoSize	False
FontSize	12
FontStyle	Bold
ForeColor	White
Text	1
TextAlign	Middle Center

Button1 Button:

Property Name	Property Value
Name	btnDecrease
FontSize	12
Text	<

Button2 Button:

Property Name	Property Value
Name	btnIncrease
FontSize	12
Text	>

Button3 Button:

Property Name	Property Value
Name	btnStart
FontSize	12
Text	Start

Button4 Button:

Property Name	Property Value
Name	btnStop
FontSize	12
Text	Stop

Label7 Label:

Property Name	Property Value
AutoSize	False
FontSize	12
FontStyle	Bold
ForeColor	Yellow
Text	Move
TextAlign	Middle Center

Button5 Button:

Property Name	Property Value
Name	btnMoveUpLeft
Image	UpLeft.jpg (in **\BVB Projects\DanielVB** folder)
Text	[blank]

Button6 Button:

Property Name	Property Value
Name	btnMoveUp
Image	Up.jpg (in **\BVB Projects\DanielVB**
Text	[blank]

Button7 Button:

Property Name	Property Value
Name	btnMoveUpRight
Image	UpRight.jpg (in **\BVB Projects\DanielVB** folder)
Text	[blank]

Button8 Button:

Property Name	Property Value
Name	btnMoveLeft
Image	Left.jpg (in **\BVB Projects\DanielVB** folder)
Text	[blank]

Button9 Button:

Property Name	**Property Value**
Name	btnNoMove
Text	[blank]

Button10 Button:

Property Name	**Property Value**
Name	btnMoveRight
Image	Right.jpg (in **\BVB Projects\DanielVB** folder)
Text	[blank]

Button11 Button:

Property Name	**Property Value**
Name	btnMoveDownLeft
Image	DownLeft.jpg (in **\BVB Projects\DanielVB** folder)
Text	[blank]

Button12 Button:

Property Name	**Property Value**
Name	btnMoveDown
Image	Down.jpg (in **\BVB Projects\DanielVB** folder)
Text	[blank]

Button13 Button:

Property Name	**Property Value**
Name	btnMoveDownRight
Image	DownRight.jpg (in **\BVB Projects\DanielVB** folder)
Text	[blank]

Label8 Label:

Property Name	**Property Value**
AutoSize	False
FontSize	9
ForeColor	Yellow
Text	Click Middle for No Move
TextAlign	Middle Center

Label9 Label:

Property Name	**Property Value**
AutoSize	False
FontSize	12
FontStyle	Bold
ForeColor	Yellow
Text	Shoot
TextAlign	Middle Center

Button14 Button:

Property Name	**Property Value**
Name	btnShootUpLeft
Image	UpLeft.jpg (in **BeginVB\BVB Code\DanielVB** folder)
Text	[blank]

Button15 Button:

Property Name	**Property Value**
Name	btnShootUp
Image	Up.jpg (in **BeginVB\BVB Code\DanielVB** folder)
Text	[blank]

Button16 Button:

Property Name	**Property Value**
Name	btnShootUpRight
Image	UpRight.jpg (in **BeginVB\BVB Code\DanielVB** folder)
Text	[blank]

Button17 Button:

Property Name	Property Value
Name	btnShootLeft
Image	Left.jpg (in **\BVB Projects\DanielVB** folder)
Text	[blank]

Button18 Button:

Property Name	Property Value
Name	btnShootRight
Image	Right.jpg (in **\BVB Projects\DanielVB** folder)
Text	[blank]

Button19 Button:

Property Name	Property Value
Name	btnShootDownLeft
Image	DownLeft.jpg (in **\BVB Projects\DanielVB** folder)
Text	[blank]

Button20 Button:

Property Name	Property Value
Name	btnShootDown
Image	Down.jpg (in **BeginVB\BVB Projects\DanielVB** folder)
Text	[blank]

Button21 Button:

Property Name	Property Value
Name	btnShootDownRight
Image	DownRight.jpg (in **\BVB Projects\DanielVB** folder)
Text	[blank]

Panel2 Panel:

Property Name	Property Value
Name	pnlGame
BackColor	White

Label10 Label:

Property Name	Property Value
Name	lblInstructions
FontSize	12

PictureBox1 Picture Box:

Property Name	Property Value
Name	picDaniel
Image	Daniel.jpg (in **\BVB Projects\DanielVB** folder)
SizeMode	AutoSize
Visible	False

PictureBox2 Picture Box:

Property Name	Property Value
Name	picLion
Image	Lion.jpg (in **\BVB Projects\DanielVB** folder)
Visible	False

When done, the form should look like this:

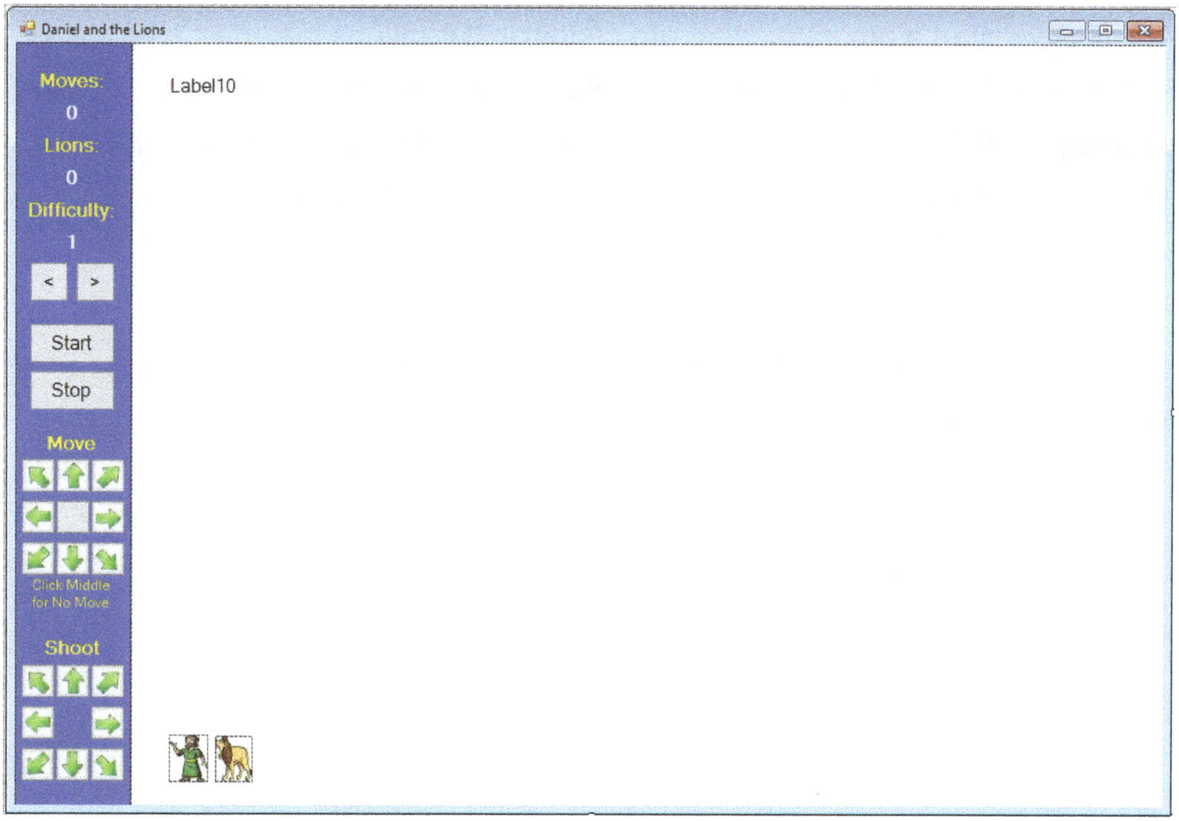

We now begin writing code for the **Daniel and the Lions** game. We will write the code in several steps. As a first step, we will write the code that starts the program and establishes its 'initial' state. Then, we look at how to go to the state allowing Daniel to move following clicking of the **Start** button. We then write code to move Daniel (using mouse clicks or keyboard presses), move the lions toward Daniel and shoot prayers at the lions. During the code development process, recognize you may modify a particular procedure several times before arriving at the finished product.

Code Design – Initial State (Instructions)

Any time we start a program, there are certain initializations that must take place. Let's look at the initializations needed in the **Daniel and the Lions** game. When the program first begins, we want to display the game instructions. We also initialize the difficulty (**Difficulty**) and the game status (**GameStatus**). These initializations are in the forms **Load** procedure.

We declare two variables (**Difficulty** and, **GameStatus**). Do this in the general declarations area:

```
Dim Difficulty As Integer
Dim GameStatus As String
```

Add this code to the **frmNoah Load** event procedure:

```
  Private Sub FrmDaniel_Load(ByVal sender As System.Object, ByVal
e As System.EventArgs) Handles MyBase.Load
    ' Daniel and the Lions
    ' Visual Basic Version
    ' Intro screen
    Difficulty = 1
    GameStatus = "Initial"
    lblInstructions.Text = "DANIEL AND THE LIONS"
    lblInstructions.Text += ControlChars.CrLf + ControlChars.CrLf
+ "In Daniel 6:16-28, King Darius is tricked into putting Daniel
into the Lions Den. Daniel prays for God's protection"
    lblInstructions.Text += ControlChars.CrLf + "and God sends His
Angel to shut the Lion's mouth.  God will protect you if you pray
to Him today."
    lblInstructions.Text += ControlChars.CrLf + ControlChars.CrLf
+ "Select Difficulty by pressing the left button for Easy and the
right button for Harder."
    lblInstructions.Text += ControlChars.CrLf + ControlChars.CrLf
+ "Click on the Start Button to begin."
    lblInstructions.Text += ControlChars.CrLf + ControlChars.CrLf
+ "Click on the Stop Button to stop the program."
```

```
    lblInstructions.Text += ControlChars.CrLf + ControlChars.CrLf
+ "Use Move buttons (or keypad keys) to move Daniel."
    lblInstructions.Text += ControlChars.CrLf + ControlChars.CrLf
+ "Use Shoot buttons to 'shoot' prayers at lions."
  End Sub
```

As mentioned, we set **Difficulty** to **1** and the **GameStatus** to “**Initial**”. Next, using a series of statements, we write out the game instructions in **lblInstructions**.

Save and **Run** the program to see:

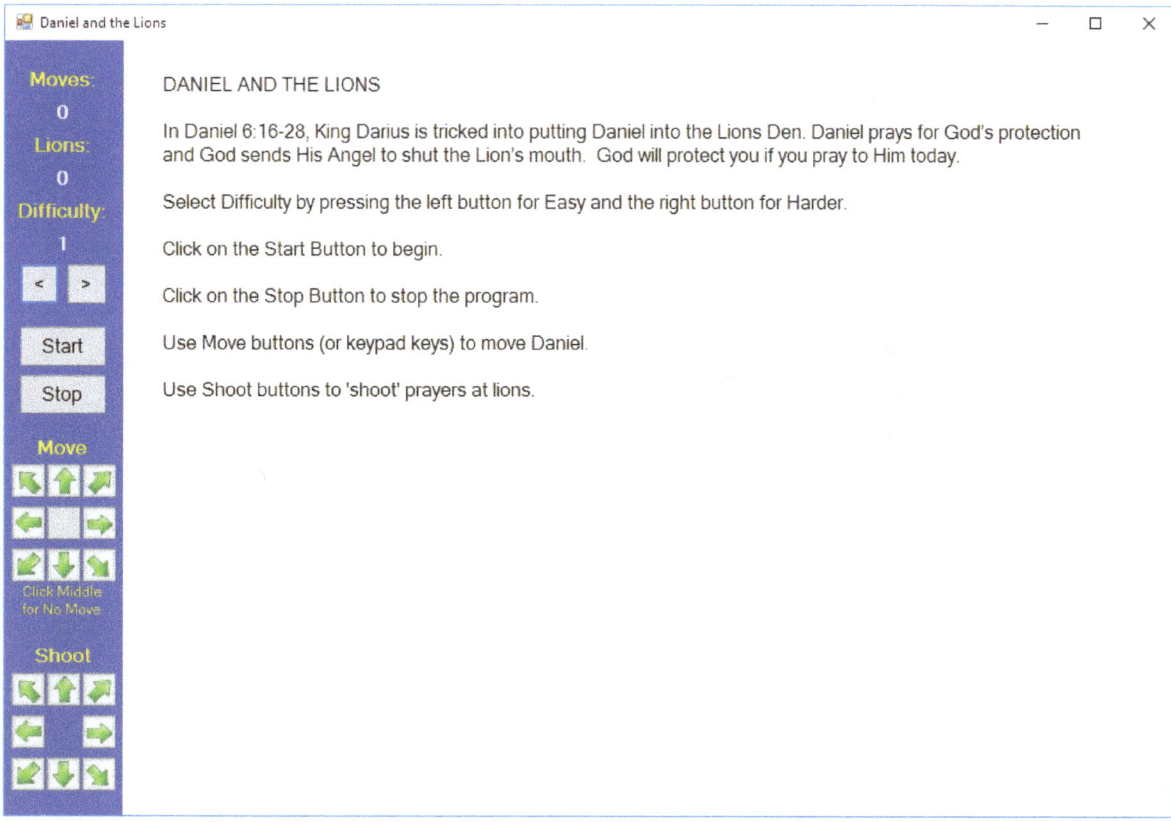

Code Design – Select Difficulty

The **Difficulty** variable is used to determine how many lions are put on the game grid (the higher the difficulty, the more lions). To change the difficulty, a user clicks on either of the two arrow buttons. The code to do this goes in the **btnDecrease** and **btnIncrease Click** event procedures:

```
  Private Sub BtnDecrease_Click(ByVal sender As System.Object,
ByVal e As System.EventArgs) Handles btnDecrease.Click
    If (GameStatus = "Initial") Then
      ' decrease difficulty
      Difficulty = Difficulty - 1
      If (Difficulty < 1) Then
        Difficulty = 1
      End If
      lblDifficulty.Text = Difficulty
    End If
  End Sub

  Private Sub BtnIncrease_Click(ByVal sender As System.Object,
ByVal e As System.EventArgs) Handles btnIncrease.Click
    If (GameStatus = "Initial") Then
      'increase difficulty
      Difficulty = Difficulty + 1
      If (Difficulty > 10) Then
        Difficulty = 10
      End If
      lblDifficulty.Text = Difficulty
    End If
  End Sub
```

The code is straightforward. The difficulty can only be changed when the game is in "**Initial**" state. If the **<** button is clicked, we decrease the difficulty by one (minimum of 1). If the **>** button is clicked, we increase the difficulty (maximum of 10). The new value for the difficulty is then displayed in **lblDifficulty**.

Save and **Run** the program. Make sure the arrow buttons work – make sure the difficulty is always between 1 and 10. Here's my run where I changed the difficulty to three:

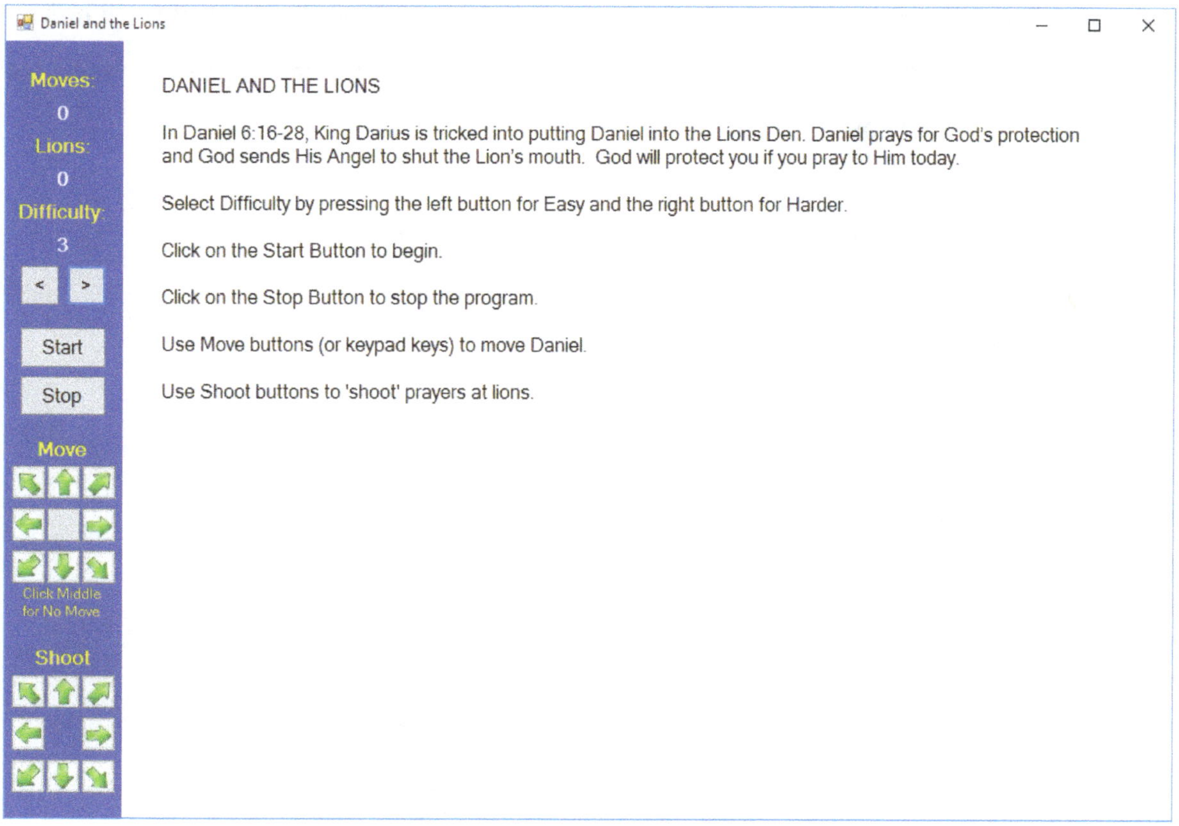

Code Design – Draw Grid

Once the difficulty is set, the next step is to click the **Start** button to allow the game to begin. Hence, we need code to move from the "**Initial**" state to what we'll call "**DanielMove**" state. When the **Start** button is clicked in "**Initial**" state, we need to take the following steps:

- Change **GameStatus** to "**DanielMove**"
- Initialize variables
- Clear game screen
- Draw game grid with rocks
- Randomly place Daniel on the grid
- Randomly place lions on the grid

There is a lot to do here, so we will take it in steps. First, we'll initialize variables and draw the grid.

Several variables are used in game control. **GameOver** is a Boolean variable that tells us if the game has ended – it is initialized at **False**. **Moves** (initialized at zero) tells us how many times Daniel has moved. **NumberLions** tells us how many lions are placed in the grid (initialized to **Difficulty + 5**) and **LionsLeft** tells us how many lions remain in the grid. The game grid has 10 rows and 20 columns (each grid space 40 pixels wide by 50 pixels high). **GamePanel** is the graphics region we play the game in. Add these general declarations:

```
Dim GameOver As Boolean
Dim Moves As Integer
Dim NumberLions As Integer
Dim LionsLeft As Integer
Dim GamePanel As Graphics
```

Add this code to the **btnStart Click** event procedure:

```
  Private Sub BtnStart_Click(ByVal sender As System.Object, ByVal
e As System.EventArgs) Handles btnStart.Click
    'clicked start
    GameStatus = "DanielMove"
    GameOver = False
    Label10.Visible = False
    Moves = 0
    NumberLions = Difficulty + 5
    LionsLeft = NumberLions
    lblMoves.Text = Moves
    lblLions.Text = LionsLeft
    '  draw grid structure
    GamePanel = pnlGame.CreateGraphics()
    GamePanel.FillRectangle(Brushes.Black, 45, 45, 810, 510)
    GamePanel.FillRectangle(Brushes.White, 50, 50, 800, 500)
    For i = 1 To 9
      GamePanel.DrawLine(Pens.Gray, 50, (i + 1) * 50, 850, (i + 1)
* 50)
    Next
    For i = 1 To 19
      GamePanel.DrawLine(Pens.Gray, 50 + i * 40, 50, 50 + i * 40,
550)
    Next
  End Sub
```

You should be able to identify each step in this new code. We clear the area and set variables. The grid structure is established as a white rectangle with a black border. Horizontal lines are drawn every 50 pixels and vertical lines are drawn every 40 pixels.

Save and **Run** the program. Choose a difficulty (I picked 3). Click **Start** and you should see:

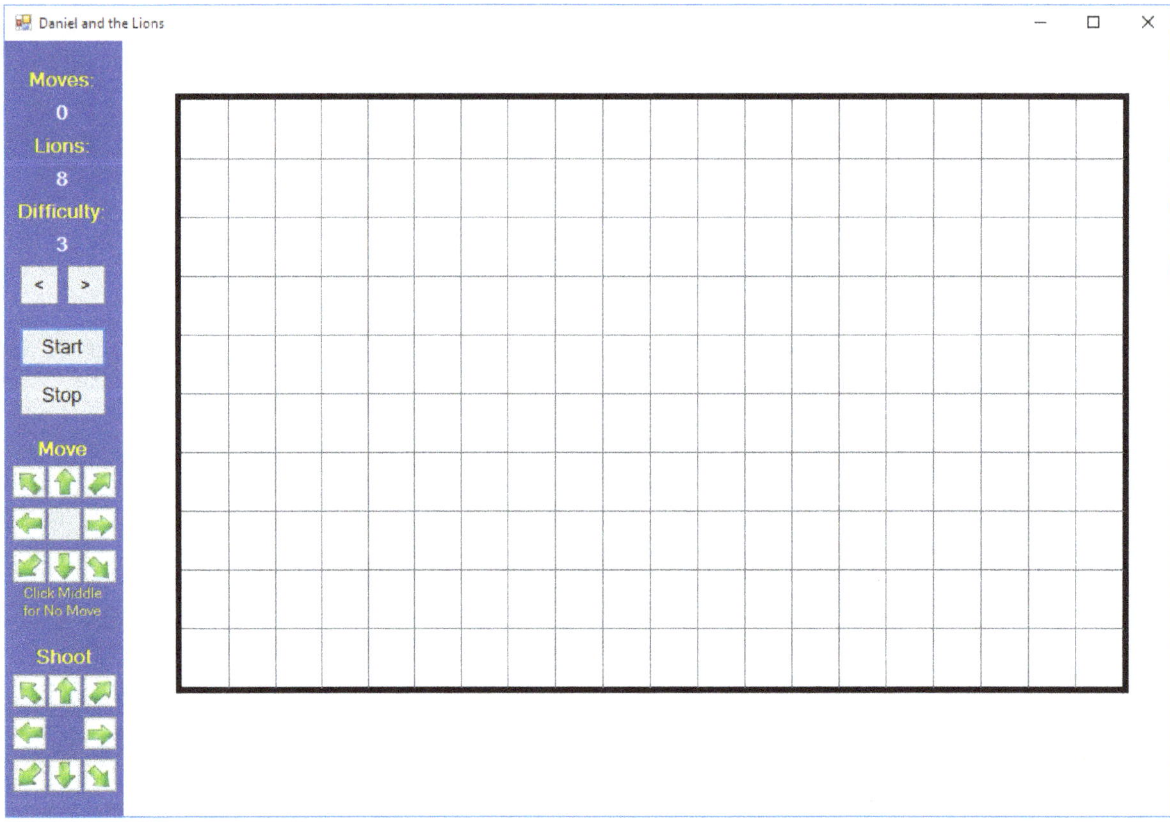

Notice the displayed values for **Moves** and **Lions**. Notice the nice grid structure.

Code Design – Position Rocks

Four rocks are placed in the grid. Daniel can hide behind these rocks if needed for protection from the lions. Elliptical shapes are used for each of the rocks.

Recall the grid has 10 rows and 20 columns. We use a two-dimensional array **A** to keep track of what is in each location within the grid. The first index in the array is the **Row**, the second is the **Column**, so the value at:

```
A(Row, Column)
```

tells us what is in that location. We use this system:

`A(Row, Column) = 0`	Nothing is there
`A(Row, Column) = 1`	Rock is there
`A(Row, Column) = 2`	Lion is there
`A(Row, Column) = 3`	Daniel is there

The rocks are in fixed locations: Row 4, Column 5 and Column 16 and Row 7, Column 5 and Column 16.

Add this line to the general declarations area to define the **A** array:

```
Dim A(10, 20) As Integer
```

Add the shaded code to the **btnStart Click** event procedure to initialize the **A** array to all zeroes, then position the four rocks on the grid:

```
  Private Sub BtnStart_Click(ByVal sender As System.Object, ByVal
e As System.EventArgs) Handles btnStart.Click
    'clicked start
    GameStatus = "DanielMove"
    GameOver = False
    Label10.Visible = False
    Moves = 0
    NumberLions = Difficulty + 5
    LionsLeft = NumberLions
    lblMoves.Text = Moves
    lblLions.Text = LionsLeft
    '  draw grid structure
    GamePanel = pnlGame.CreateGraphics()
    GamePanel.FillRectangle(Brushes.Black, 45, 45, 810, 510)
    GamePanel.FillRectangle(Brushes.White, 50, 50, 800, 500)
    For i = 1 To 9
      GamePanel.DrawLine(Pens.Gray, 50, (i + 1) * 50, 850, (i + 1)
* 50)
    Next
    For i = 1 To 19
      GamePanel.DrawLine(Pens.Gray, 50 + i * 40, 50, 50 + i * 40,
550)
    Next
    For i = 1 To 10
      For j = 1 To 20
        A(i, j) = 0
      Next
    Next
    '  Place rocks
    ' A array (0- nothing, 1-rock, 2-lion, 3-Daniel)
    A(4, 5) = 1
    A(4, 16) = 1
    A(7, 5) = 1
    A(7, 16) = 1
    GamePanel.FillEllipse(Brushes.DarkGray, 215, 205, 30, 40)
    GamePanel.FillEllipse(Brushes.DarkGray, 655, 205, 30, 40)
    GamePanel.FillEllipse(Brushes.DarkGray, 215, 355, 30, 40)
    GamePanel.FillEllipse(Brushes.DarkGray, 655, 355, 30, 40)
  End Sub
```

The (x, y) coordinates used in the **FillEllipse** methods were found by knowing where the grid lines are located (by looking at the code that draws these lines). For example, the first rock is at row 4, column 5. The top left corner at that position is (**210**, **200**).

Save and **Run** the program. Click **Start**. The rocks will appear:

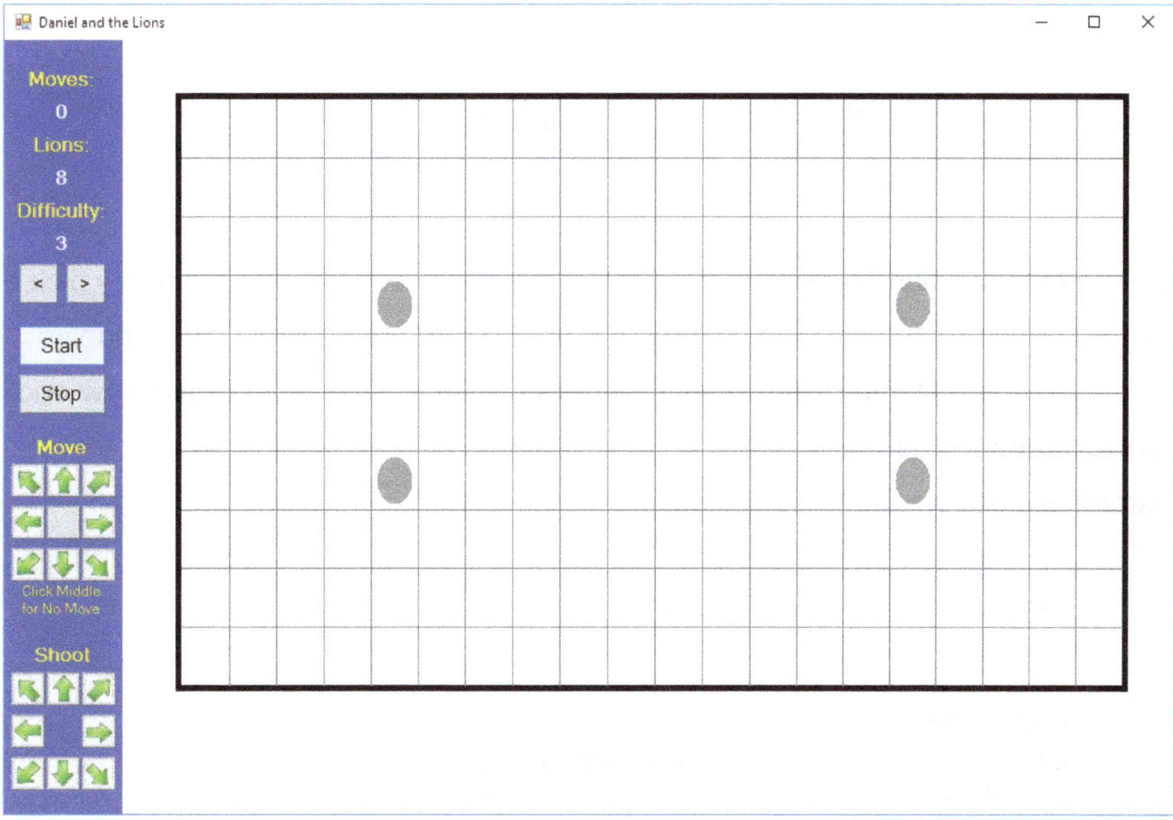

Code Design – Position Daniel and Lions

The last initialization step is to randomly place Daniel and the lions (**NumberLions**) onto the grid. The images stored in **picDaniel** and **picLion** are are used:

picDaniel

picLion

The code to position Daniel and the lions in the grid is similar. We randomly pick a row and column. If nothing is already at that position, put it there. The variables **DanielRow** and **DanielColumn** tell us where Daniel is. The arrays **LionRow** and **LionColumn** tell us where each lion is. Positioning coordinates (x, y) are determined like we did for rock placement.

Add these new variable declarations:

```
Dim MyRandom As Random = New Random()
Dim DanielRow As Integer, DanielColumn As Integer
Dim LionRow(15) As Integer, LionColumn(15) As Integer
```

MyRandom is needed for random number generation.

Add the shaded code to the **btnStart Click** event procedure:

```
  Private Sub BtnStart_Click(ByVal sender As System.Object, ByVal
e As System.EventArgs) Handles btnStart.Click
    'clicked start
    GameStatus = "DanielMove"
    GameOver = False
    Label10.Visible = False
    Moves = 0
    NumberLions = Difficulty + 5
    LionsLeft = NumberLions
    lblMoves.Text = Moves
    lblLions.Text = LionsLeft
    '  draw grid structure
    GamePanel = pnlGame.CreateGraphics()
    GamePanel.FillRectangle(Brushes.Black, 45, 45, 810, 510)
    GamePanel.FillRectangle(Brushes.White, 50, 50, 800, 500)
    For i = 1 To 9
      GamePanel.DrawLine(Pens.Gray, 50, (i + 1) * 50, 850, (i + 1)
* 50)
    Next
    For i = 1 To 19
      GamePanel.DrawLine(Pens.Gray, 50 + i * 40, 50, 50 + i * 40,
550)
    Next
    For i = 1 To 10
      For j = 1 To 20
        A(i, j) = 0
      Next
    Next
    '  Place rocks
    ' A array (0- nothing, 1-rock, 2-lion, 3-Daniel)
    A(4, 5) = 1
    A(4, 16) = 1
    A(7, 5) = 1
    A(7, 16) = 1
    GamePanel.FillEllipse(Brushes.DarkGray, 215, 205, 30, 40)
    GamePanel.FillEllipse(Brushes.DarkGray, 655, 205, 30, 40)
    GamePanel.FillEllipse(Brushes.DarkGray, 215, 355, 30, 40)
    GamePanel.FillEllipse(Brushes.DarkGray, 655, 355, 30, 40)
    'Place Daniel
    Dim Row As Integer
    Dim Column As Integer
PlaceDaniel:
    Row = MyRandom.Next(10) + 1
```

```
    Column = MyRandom.Next(20) + 1
    If (A(Row, Column) = 0) Then
      A(Row, Column) = 3
      DanielRow = Row
      DanielColumn = Column
      GamePanel.DrawImage(picDaniel.Image, DanielColumn * 40 + 15,
DanielRow * 50 + 5)
    Else
      GoTo PlaceDaniel
    End If
    'Place lions
    For i = 1 To NumberLions
PlaceLion:
      Row = MyRandom.Next(10) + 1
      Column = MyRandom.Next(20) + 1
      If (A(Row, Column) = 0) Then
        A(Row, Column) = 2
        LionRow(i) = Row
        LionColumn(i) = Column
        GamePanel.DrawImage(picLion.Image, LionColumn(i) * 40 +
15, LionRow(i) * 50 + 5)
      Else
        GoTo PlaceLion
      End If
    Next
  End Sub
```

Save and **Run** the program. Set the **Difficulty** (I used 3). Click **Start**. The complete initialized game grid is now seen:

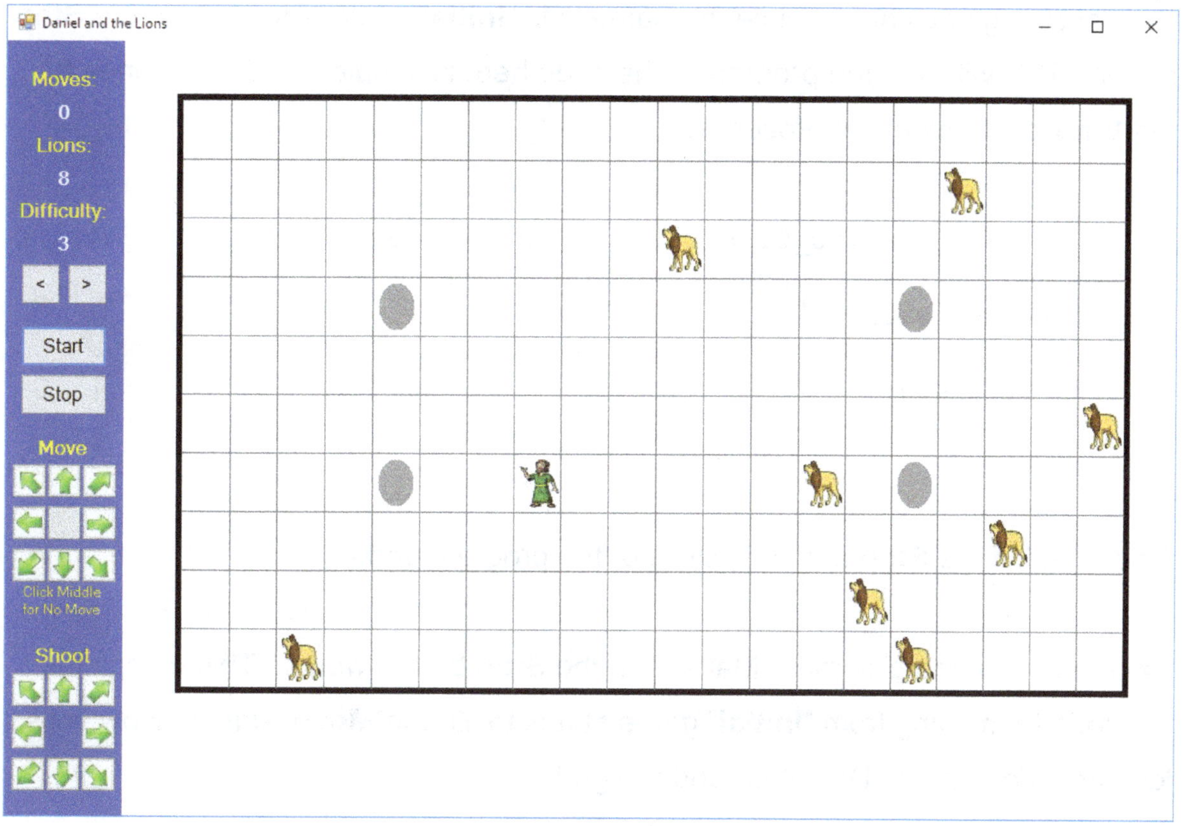

Since **Difficulty** is 3, there are 8 lions. The next step is to either move Daniel or shoot a prayer at a lion. We write code to do these steps soon. But first, let's take care of one last thing you can do while in "**Initial**" state – stop the program.

Code Design – Stop the Program

One last thing you can do while the game is in "**Initial**" state is to click on the **Stop** button. This will stop the program. The code here is simple. Add these lines to the **btnStop Click** event procedure:

```
  Private Sub BtnStop_Click(ByVal sender As System.Object, ByVal e
As System.EventArgs) Handles btnStop.Click
    If (GameStatus = "Initial") Then
      'clicked stop
      Me.Close()
    End If
  End Sub
```

As desired, if the **Stop** button is clicked, the program ends.

Save and **Run** the program. Make sure the **Stop** button works. This completes the code for moving from "**Initial**" game status to '**DanielMove**' status. Now, let's look at code to move Daniel around the grid.

Code Design – Moving Daniel

Once the game begins, you move Daniel around the grid so he can begin 'shooting' prayers at the lions. Daniel can be moved using two different methods. First, he can be moved by using the 'buttons' under the **Move** heading on the game screen:

Clicking on any of the arrow buttons will move Daniel one grid square in the corresponding direction. Clicking the middle button will leave Daniel at his current position.

The code to detect clicking on any of these buttons is placed in the corresponding button's **Click** event procedure. Once a move is made, we need to check to see if it is a valid move. Invalid moves include moving off the top, bottom, left or right side of the grid, moving onto a rock or moving into a lion. If an invalid move is attempted, it is not allowed, and, if a move is into a lion, the game ends! Let's do the code.

We use a subroutine **CheckMove** (will be presented in a bit) to see if a move is valid. **CheckMove** requires two pieces of information: **DeltaRow** and **DeltaColumn**. **DeltaRow** tells us how many rows to move Daniel – it will be either +1 (down one row), 0 (no row change), or -1 (up one row). Similarly, **DeltaColumn** tells us how many columns to move Daniel - it will be either +1 (right one column), 0 (no column change), or -1 (left one column). You should be able to see that clicking any arrow button in the top row yields **DeltaRow** = - 1, any button in the middle row yields **DeltaRow** = 0 and any button in the bottom row yields

DeltaRow = +1. Likewise, clicking any button in the left column gives **DeltaColumn** = - 1, any button in the middle column gives **DeltaColumn** = 0 and any button in the right column gives **DeltaColumn** = +1. Using this, we write the nine button **Click** event procedures:

```
  Private Sub BtnMoveUpLeft_Click(ByVal sender As System.Object,
ByVal e As System.EventArgs) Handles btnMoveUpLeft.Click
    CheckMove(-1, -1)
  End Sub

  Private Sub BtnMoveUp_Click(ByVal sender As System.Object, ByVal
e As System.EventArgs) Handles btnMoveUp.Click
    CheckMove(-1, -0)
  End Sub

  Private Sub BtnMoveUpRight_Click(ByVal sender As System.Object,
ByVal e As System.EventArgs) Handles btnMoveUpRight.Click
    CheckMove(-1, 1)
  End Sub

  Private Sub BtnMoveLeft_Click(ByVal sender As System.Object,
ByVal e As System.EventArgs) Handles btnMoveLeft.Click
    CheckMove(0, -1)
  End Sub

  Private Sub BtnNoMove_Click(ByVal sender As System.Object, ByVal
e As System.EventArgs) Handles btnNoMove.Click
    CheckMove(0, 0)
  End Sub

  Private Sub BtnMoveRight_Click(ByVal sender As System.Object,
ByVal e As System.EventArgs) Handles btnMoveRight.Click
    CheckMove(0, 1)
  End Sub

  Private Sub BtnMoveDownLeft_Click(ByVal sender As System.Object,
ByVal e As System.EventArgs) Handles btnMoveDownLeft.Click
    CheckMove(1, -1)
  End Sub
```

```
  Private Sub BtnMoveDown_Click(ByVal sender As System.Object,
ByVal e As System.EventArgs) Handles btnMoveDown.Click
    CheckMove(1, 0)
  End Sub

  Private Sub BtnMoveDownRight_Click(ByVal sender As
System.Object, ByVal e As System.EventArgs) Handles
btnMoveDownRight.Click
    CheckMove(1, 1)
  End Sub
```

In each procedure, **CheckMove** is called with the appropriate values for **DeltaRow** (the first number) and **DeltaColumn** (the second number). Now, let's add **CheckMove**.

Add this subroutine to your program:

```
  Private Sub CheckMove(ByVal DeltaRow As Integer, ByVal
DeltaColumn As Integer)
    Dim NewRow As Integer, NewColumn As Integer
    Dim MoveOkay As Boolean
    Moves += 1
    'check if move is okay
    NewRow = DanielRow + DeltaRow
    NewColumn = DanielColumn + DeltaColumn
    MoveOkay = True
    If (NewRow < 1 Or NewRow > 10 Or NewColumn < 1 Or NewColumn >
20) Then
      ' off grid
      MoveOkay = False
    ElseIf (A(NewRow, NewColumn) = 1) Then
      'moving to rock
      MoveOkay = False
    ElseIf (A(NewRow, NewColumn) = 2) Then
      'moving to lion
      MoveOkay = False
      GameOver = True
      'remove Daniel
      RemoveDaniel()
    End If
    If (MoveOkay = True) Then
      ' move to new location
```

```
      RemoveDaniel()
      GamePanel.DrawImage(picDaniel.Image, NewColumn * 40 + 15,
NewRow * 50 + 5)
      A(DanielRow, DanielColumn) = 0
      DanielRow = NewRow
      DanielColumn = NewColumn
      A(DanielRow, DanielColumn) = 3
    End If
    UpdateGame()
  End Sub
```

We increment **Moves** and set new values for Daniel's row and column (**NewRow** and **NewColumn**). We then check the validity of the move. If Daniel moves off the grid, onto a rock, or into a lion, we set **MoveOkay** to **False**. If Daniel moves into a lion, we set **GameOver** to **True** and remove Daniel from the grid. If we have a valid move, Daniel is moved to his new location from his old location.

We use this little subroutine (**RemoveDaniel**) to clear Daniel from his current location:

```
  Private Sub RemoveDaniel()
    GamePanel.FillRectangle(Brushes.White, DanielColumn * 40 + 15,
DanielRow * 50 + 5, 35, 45)
  End Sub
```

And, notice the last line in **CheckMove** is a call to another subroutine **UpdateGame**. This subroutine is used to change the game status after Daniel moves or after Daniel shoots a prayer (that code is added later). For now, **CheckMove** just updates the number of moves and number of lions. Add this subroutine to your code:

```
  Private Sub UpdateGame()
    lblMoves.Text = Moves
    lblLions.Text = LionsLeft
  End Sub
```

Save and **Run** the program. Choose a difficulty (I picked 3). Click **Start**. Here's what I see:

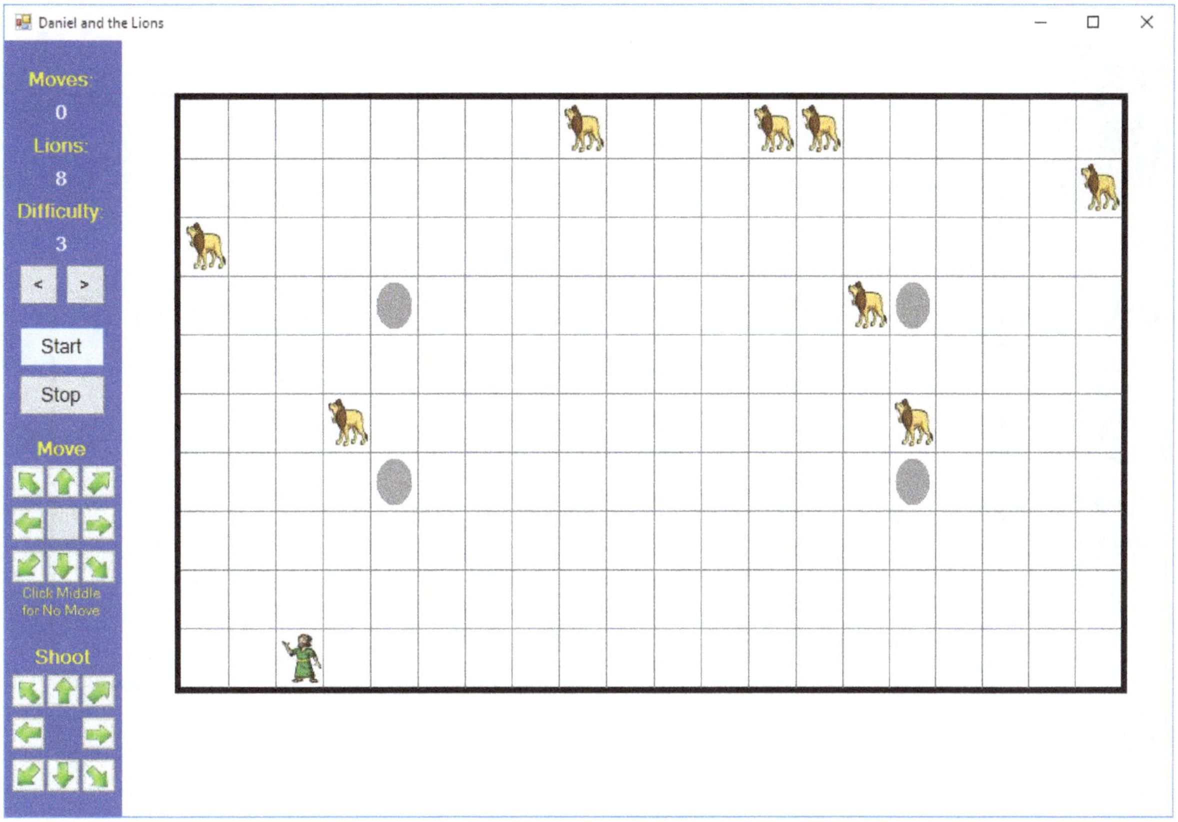

Daniel's in the lower left area (your Daniel will be at a different random location).

If I click the right move arrow, he moves one column to the right (**DeltaRow** = 0, **DeltaColumn** = 1):

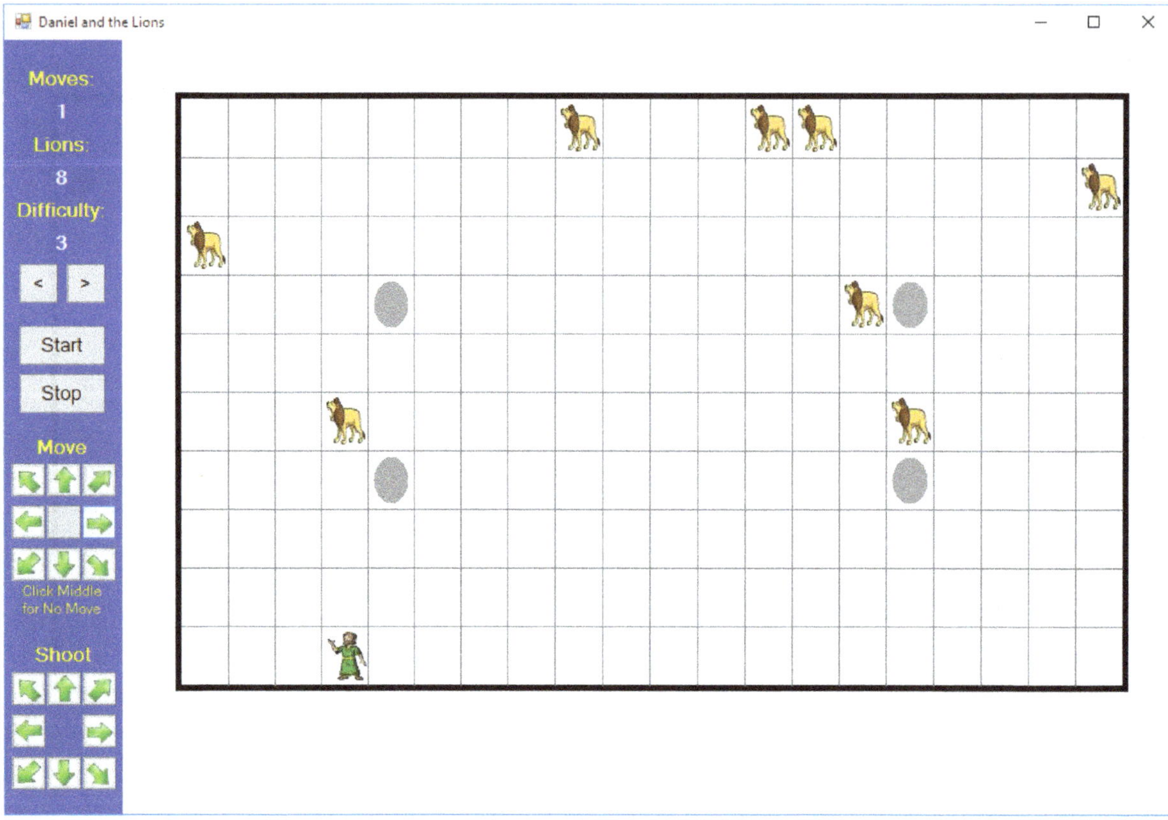

Try all the **Move** buttons to make sure they work properly. Try moving off the grid. Try moving onto a rock. Stay away from lions for now – we don't have logic to end a game yet.

When we started this section, we said there were two ways to move Daniel. Let's write code for the second method – using the numeric keypad on your keyboard. Here's a numeric keypad:

Notice the 9 number keys line up just like the **Move** buttons on the game screen. Many times, users prefer using the keyboard to the mouse. We'll add code so the 7, 8, and 9 keys work like the top row of the move buttons, the 4, 5, and 6 keys work like the middle row and the 1, 2, and 3 keys work like the bottom row.

We detect key presses in the form's **KeyDown** event procedure. The code there just replicates what we use for clicking on the corresponding arrow key. Add this code to the **frmDaniel KeyDown** event procedure:

```
  Private Sub FrmDaniel_KeyDown(ByVal sender As System.Object,
ByVal e As System.Windows.Forms.KeyEventArgs) Handles
MyBase.KeyDown
    Select Case e.KeyCode
      Case Keys.NumPad7
        CheckMove(-1, -1)
      Case Keys.NumPad8
        CheckMove(-1, -0)
      Case Keys.NumPad9
        CheckMove(-1, 1)
      Case Keys.NumPad4
        CheckMove(0, -1)
      Case Keys.NumPad5
        CheckMove(0, 0)
      Case Keys.NumPad6
        CheckMove(0, 1)
      Case Keys.NumPad1
        CheckMove(1, -1)
      Case Keys.NumPad2
        CheckMove(1, 0)
      Case Keys.NumPad3
        CheckMove(1, 1)
    End Select
  End Sub
```

Here, based on whatever key is pressed, the correct values for **DeltaRow** and **DeltaColumn** are set and **CheckMove** is called.

Save and **Run** the program again. Click **Start**. Make sure you can move Daniel both by clicking the move buttons and using the numeric keypad (**NumLock** must be selected to use this option). Again, be careful not to move into a lion – there is no game ending logic. We'll fix that now.

Code Design – Moving Lions

Once Daniel makes a move, all the lions also make a move – closer to Daniel! If Daniel and a lion meet, the game ends. We put this basic logic in **UpdateGame** subroutine. Add the shaded framework:

```
Private Sub UpdateGame()
  lblMoves.Text = Moves
  lblLions.Text = LionsLeft
  If (GameOver = False) Then
    'move lions
  End If
  If (GameOver = True) Then
    'game is over
  End If
End Sub
```

If **GameOver** is **False**, we move the lions. If **GameOver** is **True**, we end the game. Let's add the code for both options..

For now, we'll program the game over logic. When the game ends, we change **GameStatus** to "**Initial**". If there are lions remaining (**LionsLeft > 0**), Daniel has met a lion. If no lions remain, Daniel has dispatched all the lions with prayers. This logic is reflected in the shaded code in UpdateGame:

```
Private Sub UpdateGame()
  lblMoves.Text = Moves
  lblLions.Text = LionsLeft
  If (GameOver = False) Then
    'move lions
  End If
  If (GameOver = True) Then
    'game is over
    GameStatus = "Initial"
    If (LionsLeft > 0) Then
      MessageBox.Show("Daniel met a lion but God shut the mouth
of the lion at the last minute and King Darius released Daniel
from the Lion's Den.", "Game Over")
      For i = 1 To NumberLions
        ' clear all the lions
        RemoveLion(i)
      Next
    Else
      MessageBox.Show("Daniel dispatched " +
NumberLions.ToString() + " lions in " + Moves.ToString() + "
moves.", "Game Over")
      RemoveDaniel()
    End If
  End If
End Sub
```

This new code needs a subroutine (**RemoveLion**) that removes lion i from its current location:

```
Private Sub RemoveLion(ByVal i As Integer)
  GamePanel.FillRectangle(Brushes.White, LionColumn(i) * 40 +
15, LionRow(i) * 50 + 5, 35, 45)
End Sub
```

Save and **Run** the program. Click **Start**. Move Daniel around until he meets a lion. You should see this message:

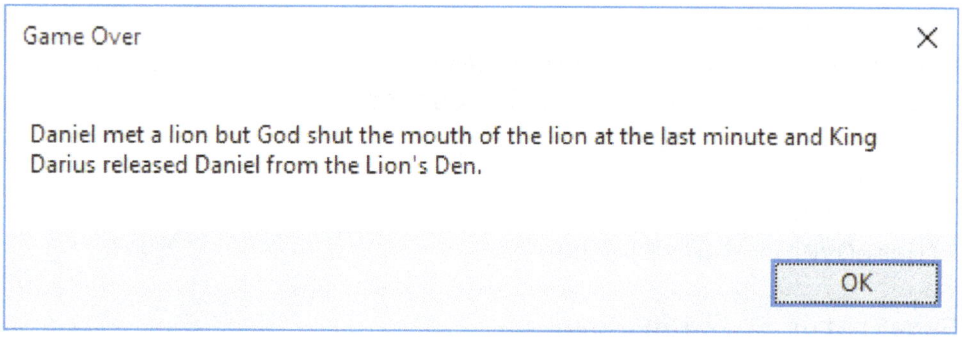

You will see a different message if Daniel dispatches all the lions. Before this can happen, though, we need code to move the lions, then code to shoot the prayers.

When the lions move, the game is switched to "**LionsMove**" status. The goal is move each lion one grid square closer to Daniel. So, for each lion remaining, the steps taken are:

- If Daniel is above lion, move lion up one grid square. If Daniel is below lion, move lion down one grid square. If Daniel and lion are in same row, do not move lion vertically.
- If Daniel is to left of lion, move lion left one grid square. If Daniel is to right of lion, move lion righ one grid square. If Daniel and lion are in same column, do not move lion horizontally.
- Lion cannot move off of grid.
- Lion cannot move into rock or another lion.
- If lion moves into Daniel, the game ends.
- Once move is complete, change **GameStatus** to "**DanielMove**"

The code that implements these steps is placed in the top part of the **UpdateGame** subroutine. The code is shaded:

```
Private Sub UpdateGame()
  Dim NewRow As Integer, NewColumn As Integer
  Dim DeltaRow As Integer, DeltaColumn As Integer
  Dim MoveOkay As Boolean
  lblMoves.Text = Moves
  lblLions.Text = LionsLeft
  If (GameOver = False) Then
    'move lions
    GameStatus = "LionsMove"
    For i = 1 To NumberLions
      If (A(LionRow(i), LionColumn(i)) = 2) Then
        If (LionRow(i) > DanielRow) Then
          DeltaRow = -1
        ElseIf (LionRow(i) < DanielRow) Then
          DeltaRow = 1
        Else
          DeltaRow = 0
        End If
        If (LionColumn(i) > DanielColumn) Then
          DeltaColumn = -1
        ElseIf (LionColumn(i) < DanielColumn) Then
          DeltaColumn = 1
        Else
          DeltaColumn = 0
        End If
        NewRow = LionRow(i) + DeltaRow
        NewColumn = LionColumn(i) + DeltaColumn
        MoveOkay = True
        If (NewRow < 1 Or NewRow > 10 Or NewColumn < 1 Or
NewColumn > 20) Then
          ' off grid
          MoveOkay = False
        ElseIf (A(NewRow, NewColumn) = 1) Then
          'moving to rock
          MoveOkay = False
        ElseIf (A(NewRow, NewColumn) = 2) Then
          'moving to another lion
          MoveOkay = False
        End If
        If (MoveOkay = True) Then
          If (A(NewRow, NewColumn) = 3) Then
```

```
                'moving to Daniel
                GameOver = True
                RemoveDaniel()
              End If
              RemoveLion(i)
              GamePanel.DrawImage(picLion.Image, NewColumn * 40 +
15, NewRow * 50 + 5)
              A(LionRow(i), LionColumn(i)) = 0
              LionRow(i) = NewRow
              LionColumn(i) = NewColumn
              A(LionRow(i), LionColumn(i)) = 2
            End If
          End If
        Next
        GameStatus = "DanielMove"
      End If
      If (GameOver = True) Then
        'game is over
        GameStatus = "Initial"
        If (LionsLeft > 0) Then
          MessageBox.Show("Daniel met a lion but God shut the mouth
of the lion at the last minute and King Darius released Daniel
from the Lion's Den.", "Game Over")
          For i = 1 To NumberLions
            ' clear all the lions
            RemoveLion(i)
          Next
        Else
          MessageBox.Show("Daniel dispatched " +
NumberLions.ToString() + " lions in " + Moves.ToString() + "
moves.", "Game Over")
          RemoveDaniel()
        End If
      End If
    End Sub
```

We declare some new variables at the top. We cycle through all the lions (**NumberLions**) in a **For/Next** loop. If a lion is still on the grid, we determine values for **DeltaRow** and **DeltaColumn** (how much a lion moves) and the proposed new position (**NewRow** and **NewColumn**). If it is an acceptable move, the lion is moved by first removing it from its current location, then redrawn at its new location. Notice if the lion moves into Daniel, **GameOver** is set to **True** and Daniel is removed from the grid. This will end the game.

Save and **Run** the program. Choose a **Difficulty** (I used 3). Click **Start**. My game looks like this:

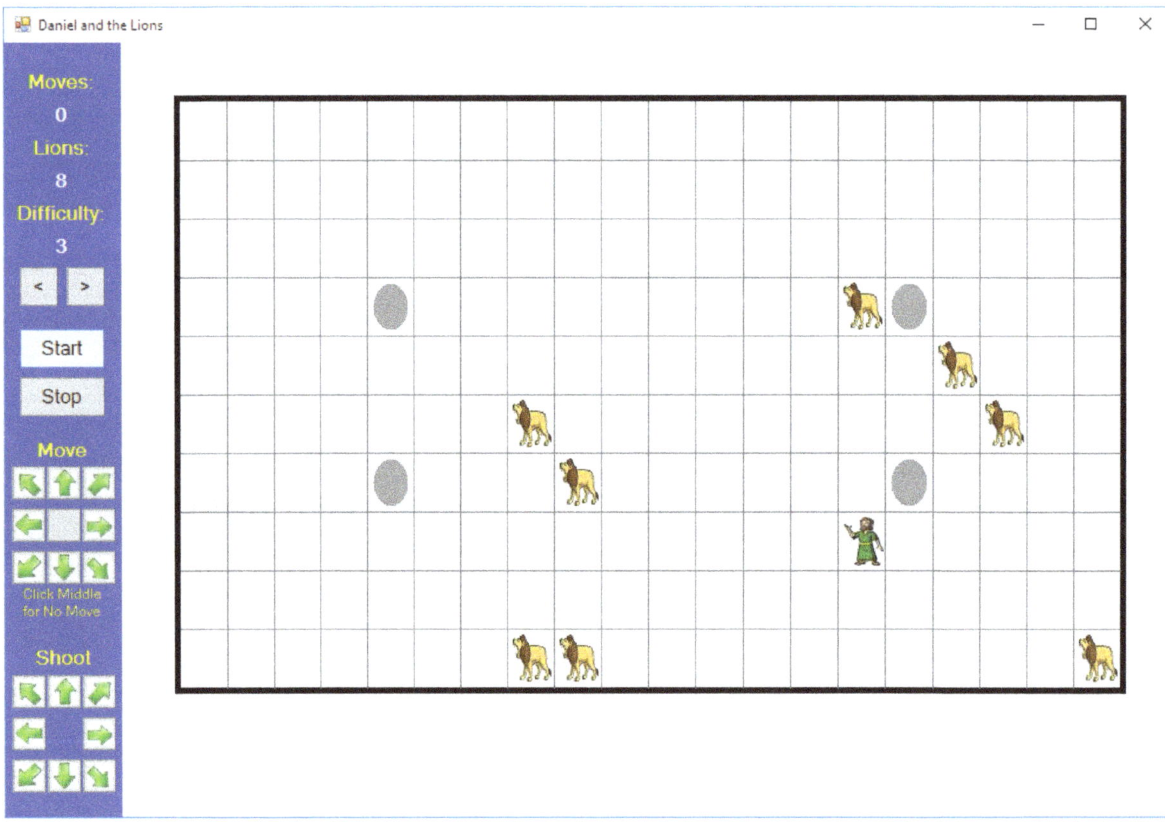

I move Daniel one square to the left.

Following my move, all the lions are closer:

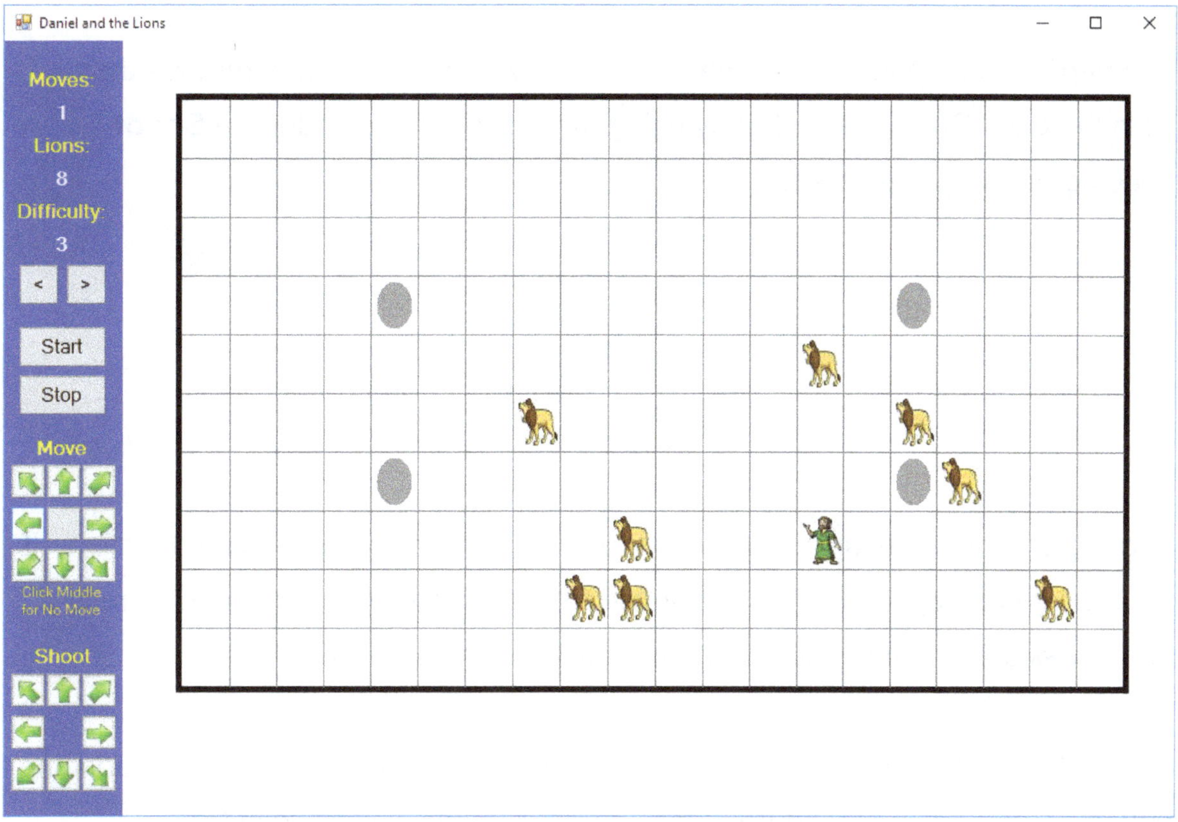

After two more moves left, the ultimate happens:

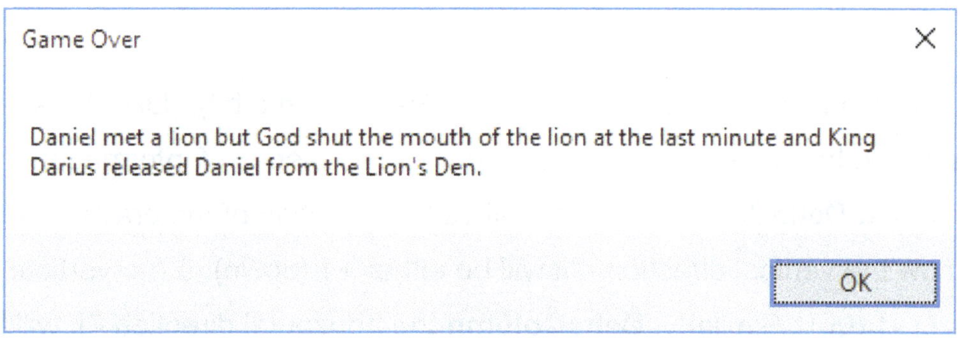

If Daniel could have shot some prayers, the lions wouldn't have gotten to him. Let's add that logic now.

Code Design – Shooting Prayers

To keep the lions away, Daniel can 'shoot' prayers at the lions to remove them from the grid. Prayers are shot by using the eight buttons under the **Shoot** heading on the game screen:

Clicking on any of the arrows will shoot a prayer in the corresponding direction. If the prayer intercepts a lion, it is removed from the grid. The logic used here is nearly identical to that used for the buttons used to move Daniel.

The code to detect clicking on any of these buttons is placed in the corresponding button's **Click** event procedure. Once a shot is taken, we move in the corresponding direction until we hit a rock, move off the grid or hit a lion. If a lion is hit, that lion is removed. Once all lions are removed, the game ends! Let's do the code.

We use a subroutine **ShootPrayer** (will be presented in a bit). Like the similar **CheckMove** subroutine, **ShootPrayer** requires two pieces of information: **DeltaRow** and **DeltaColumn**. These tell us the direction of the prayer. **DeltaRow** tells us how the vertical direction – it will be either +1 (down), 0 (no vertical motion), or -1 (up). Similarly, **DeltaColumn** the horizontal direction - it will be either +1 (right), 0 (no horizontal motion), or -1 (left). You should be able to see that clicking any arrow button in the top row yields **DeltaRow** = - 1, either button in the middle row yields **DeltaRow** = 0 and any button in the bottom row yields **DeltaRow** = +1. Likewise, clicking any button in the left column gives **DeltaColumn** = - 1, either button in the middle column gives **DeltaColumn** = 0 and any button in the right column gives **DeltaColumn** = +1. Using this, we write the eight button **Click** event procedures:

```
  Private Sub BtnShootUpLeft_Click(ByVal sender As System.Object,
ByVal e As System.EventArgs) Handles btnShootUpLeft.Click
    ShootPrayer(-1, -1)
  End Sub

  Private Sub BtnShootUp_Click(ByVal sender As System.Object,
ByVal e As System.EventArgs) Handles btnShootUp.Click
    ShootPrayer(-1, 0)
  End Sub

  Private Sub BtnShootUpRight_Click(ByVal sender As System.Object,
ByVal e As System.EventArgs) Handles btnShootUpRight.Click
    ShootPrayer(-1, 1)
  End Sub

  Private Sub BtnShootLeft_Click(ByVal sender As System.Object,
ByVal e As System.EventArgs) Handles btnShootLeft.Click
    ShootPrayer(0, -1)
  End Sub

  Private Sub BtnShootRight_Click(ByVal sender As System.Object,
ByVal e As System.EventArgs) Handles btnShootRight.Click
    ShootPrayer(0, 1)
  End Sub

  Private Sub BtnShootDownLeft_Click(ByVal sender As
System.Object, ByVal e As System.EventArgs) Handles
btnShootDownLeft.Click
    ShootPrayer(1, -1)
  End Sub

  Private Sub BtnShootDown_Click(ByVal sender As System.Object,
ByVal e As System.EventArgs) Handles btnShootDown.Click
    ShootPrayer(1, 0)
  End Sub
```

```
  Private Sub BtnShootDownRight_Click(ByVal sender As
System.Object, ByVal e As System.EventArgs) Handles
btnShootDownRight.Click
    ShootPrayer(1, 1)
  End Sub
```

In each procedure, **ShootPrayer** is called with the appropriate values for **DeltaRow** (the first number) and **DeltaColumn** (the second number). Now, let's add **ShootPrayer**.

Add this subroutine to your program:

```
  Private Sub ShootPrayer(ByVal DeltaRow As Integer, ByVal
DeltaColumn As Integer)
    Dim PrayerRow As Integer, PrayerColumn As Integer
    Dim MoveOkay As Boolean
    Dim i As Integer
    If (DeltaRow <> 0 Or DeltaColumn <> 0) Then
      Moves = Moves + 1
    End If
    PrayerRow = DanielRow
    PrayerColumn = DanielColumn
MoveAgain:
    'check if move is okay
    PrayerRow = PrayerRow + DeltaRow
    PrayerColumn = PrayerColumn + DeltaColumn
    MoveOkay = True
    If (PrayerRow < 1 Or PrayerRow > 10 Or PrayerColumn < 1 Or
PrayerColumn > 20 Or (DeltaRow = 0 And DeltaColumn = 0)) Then
      ' off grid or center button area clicked
      MoveOkay = False
    ElseIf (A(PrayerRow, PrayerColumn) = 1) Then
      'moving to rock
      MoveOkay = False
    End If
    If (MoveOkay) Then
      If (A(PrayerRow, PrayerColumn) = 2) Then
        ' dispatched a lion - find that lion
        For i = 1 To NumberLions
          If (PrayerRow = LionRow(i) And PrayerColumn =
LionColumn(i)) Then
            GoTo FoundHim
```

```
          End If
        Next
FoundHim:
        MoveOkay = False
        A(PrayerRow, PrayerColumn) = 0
        RemoveLion(i)
        LionRow(i) = 0
        LionColumn(i) = 0
        LionsLeft -= 1
        If (LionsLeft = 0) Then
          GameOver = True
        End If
      End If
    End If
    If (MoveOkay = True) Then
      GoTo MoveAgain
    End If
    UpdateGame()
  End Sub
```

Though long, the code is fairly easy to follow. We initialize **PrayerRow** and **PrayerColumn** to Daniel's position (where the prayer starts). From that point on, we change **PrayerRow** and **PrayerColumn** (by the known **DeltaRow** and **DeltaColumn** values) until the prayer moves off the grid, hits a rock or hits a lion. If a lion is hit, we determine which lion and remove it from the grid. As a last step, we call **UpdateGame**. Make sure you understand how all this works.

Save and **Run** the program again. The game is nearly complete. Choose a difficulty (I use 3) and click **Start**. Here's my screen:

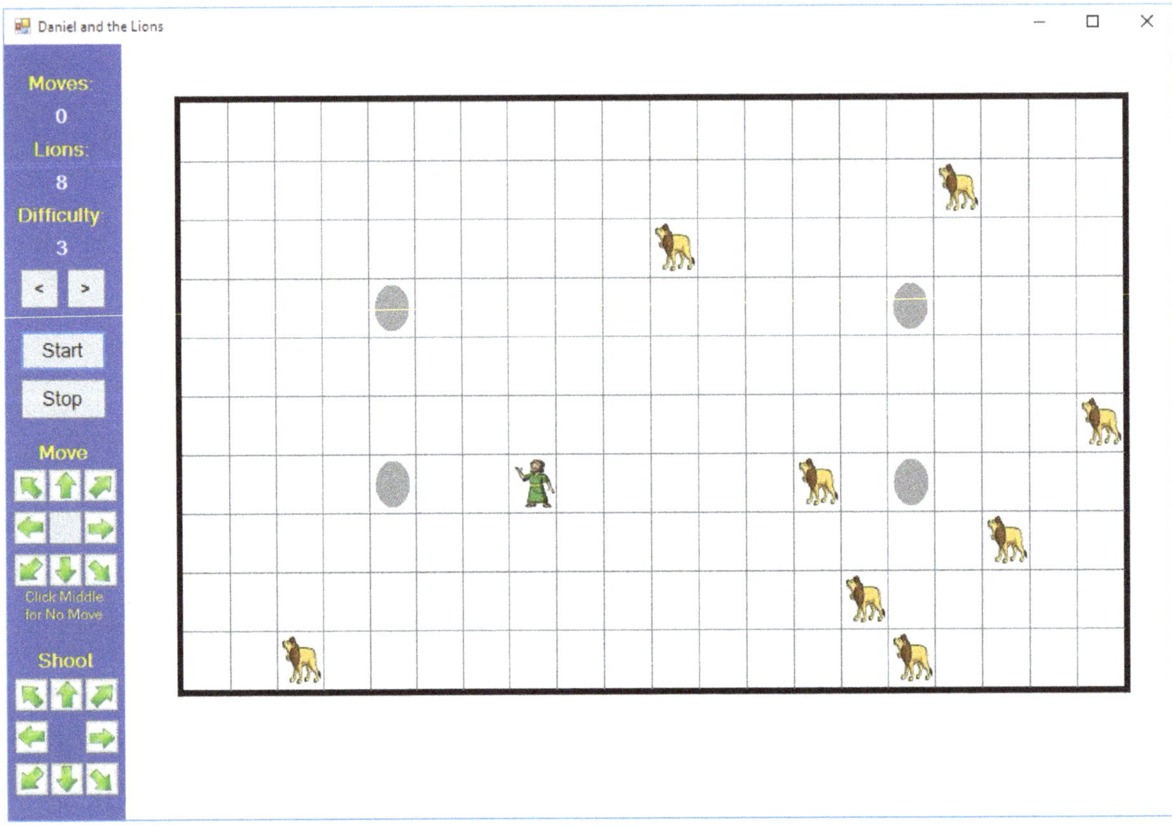

There are 8 lions to eliminate.

Notice a lion next to Daniel in the same row. Click the right **Shoot** arrow and that lion is gone:

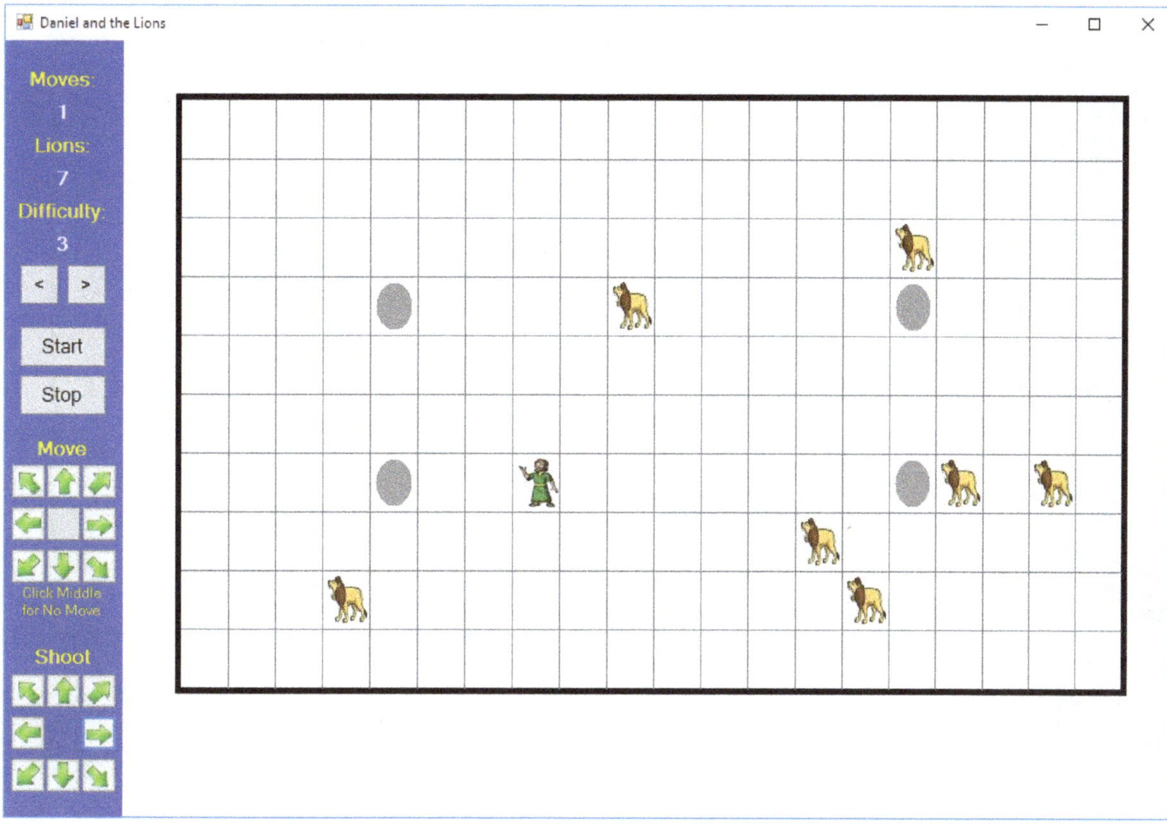

Also notice the remaining lions have moved toward Daniel. At this point, no lions are in the direct path of a 'prayer shot' so we can only move Daniel.

I moved him up (and the lions moved too):

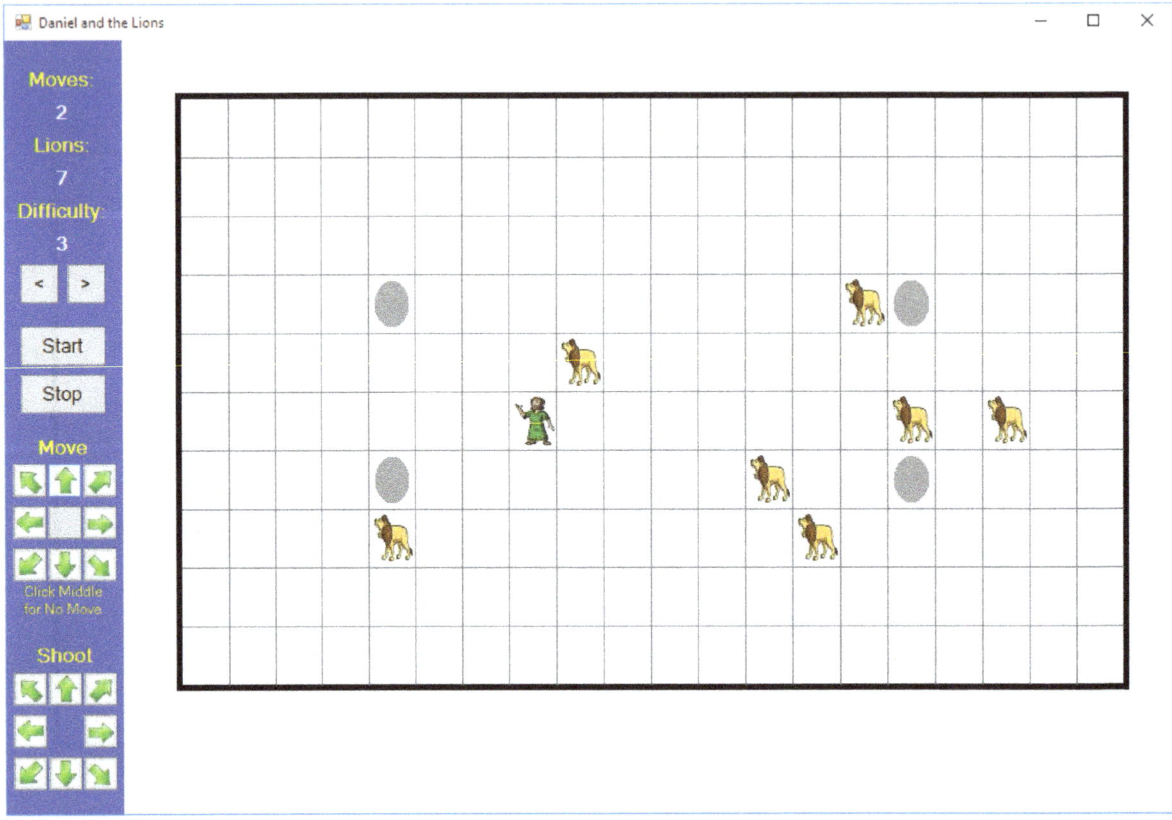

I have another lion to shoot. Up and to the right.

The next shot to the right led me to this state (six lions left):

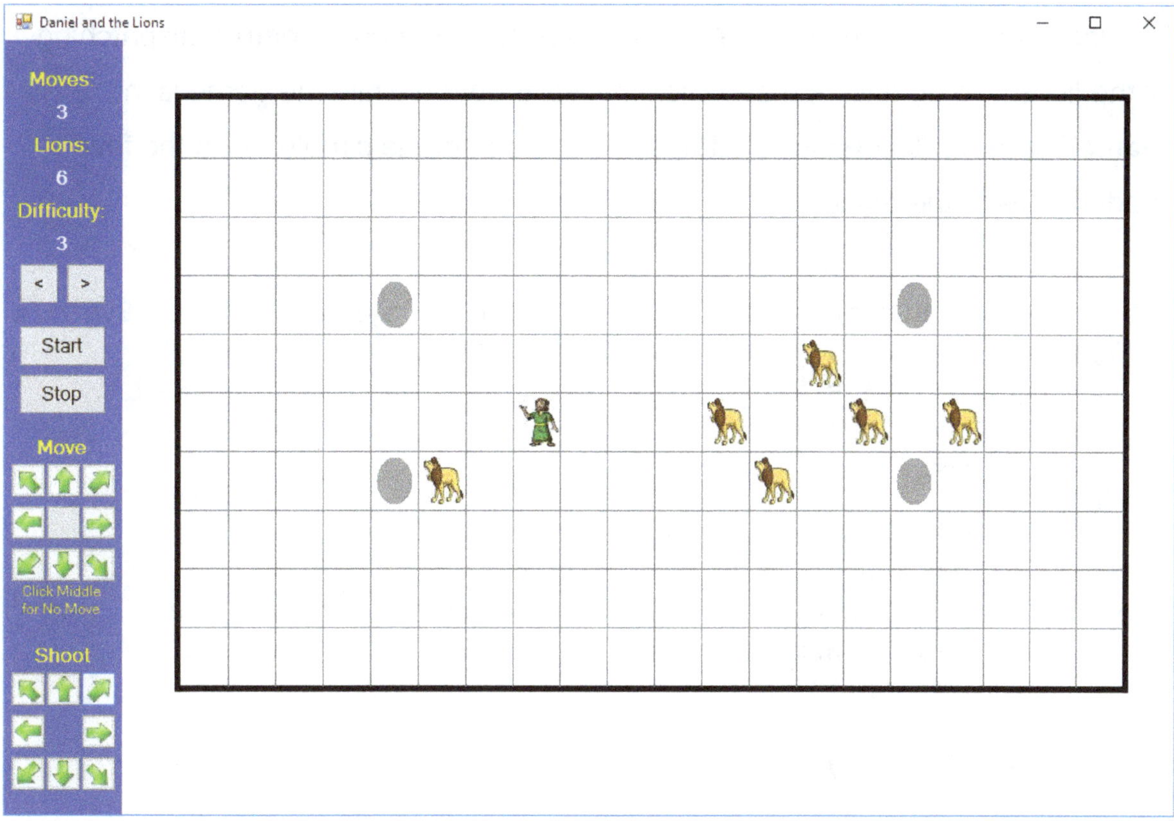

I continued this game and dispatched all 8 lions in just 9 moves. At this point, I got this message:

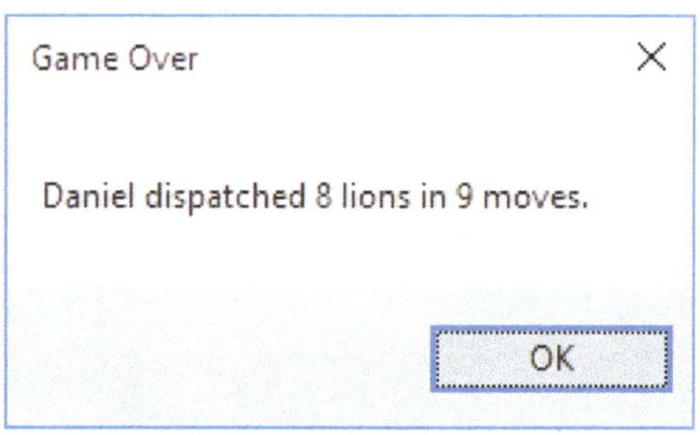

Code Design – Stop the Game

One last step and we're done. You may want to stop a game before dispatching all the lions. To do this, you can click the **Stop** button while the game is in "**DanielMove**" or "**LionsMove**" status. The code here is simple. Add the few shaded lines to the btnStop Click event procedure:

```
  Private Sub BtnStop_Click(ByVal sender As System.Object, ByVal e
As System.EventArgs) Handles btnStop.Click
    If (GameStatus = "Initial") Then
      'clicked stop
      Me.Close()
    Else
      'clicked stop while playing
      GameStatus = "Initial"
      MessageBox.Show("You stopped the game.", "Game Over")
      For i = 1 To NumberLions
        RemoveLion(i)
      Next
      RemoveDaniel()
    End If
  End Sub
```

Save and **Run** the program. Click **Start**, then click **Stop**. You should see this message:

All the lions and Daniel should be removed from the screen. The game is now complete.

Daniel and the Lions Program Review

The **Daniel and the Lions** program is now complete. **Save** and **Run** the program and make sure it works as promised. Check that all options work correctly.

If there are errors in your implementation, go back over the steps of window and code design. Go over the developed code – make sure you understand how different parts of the program were coded. As mentioned in the beginning of this chapter, the completed program is saved as **Daniel** in the **\BVB Projects\DanielVB** folder.

Bonus Projects

Preview

By now, you should feel pretty comfortable with the steps involved in building a Visual Basic project. In this bonus chapter, we give you more projects you can build and try. We'll present the steps involved in building each project - **Project Design**, **Place Controls on Form**, **Set Control Properties**, **Write Event Procedures**, **Run the Project**, and **Other Things to Try**. But, we won't give you detailed discussion of what's going on in the code (we will point out new ideas). You should be able to figure that out by now (with the help of the code comments). Actually, a very valuable programming skill to have is the ability to read and understand someone else's code.

The twelve new projects included are: Computer Stopwatch, Times Tables, Dice Rolling, State Capitals, Memory Game, Unit Conversions, Loan Calculator, Checkbook Balancer, Portfolio Manager, Decode and Frown. And, as another bonus, we'll throw in a Visual Basic version of the first video game ever – Pong!

Project 1 - Computer Stopwatch

Project Design

In this project, we will build a computer stopwatch that measures elapsed time in seconds. One button will start and stop the timing and one will reset the display (a label). Elapsed time is measured using the BASIC **Now** function that provides the current time and date in a **Date** type function. The project you are about to build is saved as **Stopwatch** in the project folder (**\CBGVB\BVB Projects**).

Place Controls on Form

Start a new project in Visual Basic. Place a text box control on the form. Then place two buttons on the form. Add a timer control. When done, your form should look something like this:

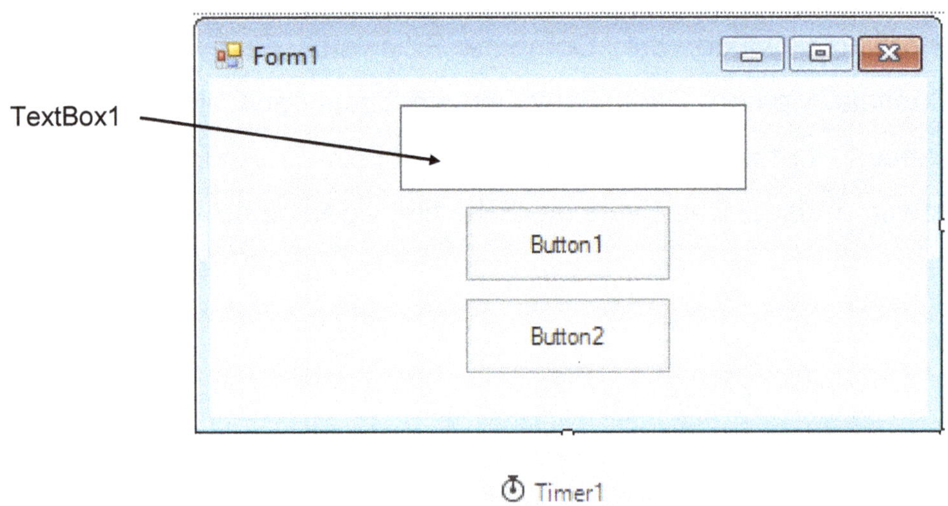

Set Control Properties

Set the control properties using the properties window:

Form1 Form:

Property Name	Property Value
Text	Stopwatch
FormBorderStyle	Fixed Single
StartPosition	CenterScreen

TextBox1 Text Box:

Property Name	Property Value
Name	txtTime
Text	00:00:00
BackColor	White
Font	Arial
Font Size	24
Font Style	Bold
ReadOnly	True
TextAlign	Center
TabStop	False

Button1 Button:

Property Name	Property Value
Name	btnStartStop
Text	Start
Font	Arial
Font Size	12

Button2 Command Button:

Property Name	Property Value
Name	btnReset
Text	Reset
Enabled	False
Font	Arial
Font Size	12

Timer1 Timer:

Property Name	Property Value
Name	timDisplay
Interval	1000

When done setting properties, my form looks like this:

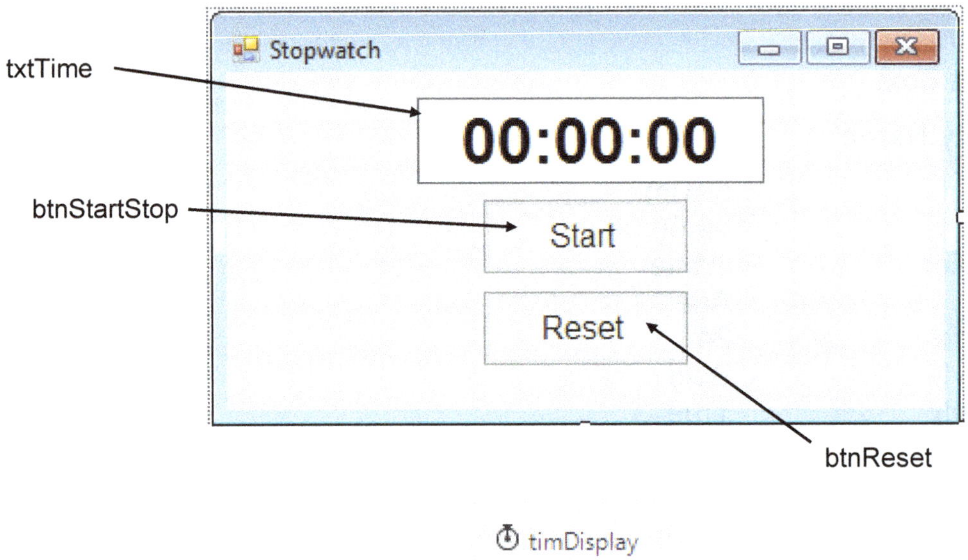

Write Event Procedures

To start the stopwatch, click **Start**. To stop, click **Stop**. Click **Reset** to reset the display to zero. Each of these buttons has a **Click** event. The timer control **Tick** event controls the display of the time.

Add this code to the **general declarations** area:

```
Dim StartTime As Date ' Time when Start clicked
```

The **btnStartStop Click** event procedure:

```
  Private Sub BtnStartStop_Click(ByVal sender As
System.Object, ByVal e As System.EventArgs) Handles
btnStartStop.Click
    'Starting timer?
    If btnStartStop.Text = "Start" Then
      'Reset Text on Start/Stop button
      btnStartStop.Text = "Stop"
      'Start timer and get starting time
      timDisplay.Enabled = True
      StartTime = Now
    Else
      'Stop timer
      timDisplay.Enabled = False
      'Disable Start/Stop button, enable Reset button
      btnStartStop.Enabled = False
      btnReset.Enabled = True
    End If
  End Sub
```

The **btnReset Click** event procedure:

```
  Private Sub BtnReset_Click(ByVal sender As System.Object,
ByVal e As System.EventArgs) Handles btnReset.Click
    'Reset display to zero
    txtTime.Text = "00:00:00"
    'Reset button Text and enable Start, disable Reset
    btnStartStop.Text = "Start"
    btnStartStop.Enabled = True
    btnReset.Enabled = False
  End Sub
```

The **timDisplay Tick** event procedure:

```
  Private Sub TimDisplay_Tick(ByVal sender As System.Object,
ByVal e As System.EventArgs) Handles timDisplay.Tick
    Dim Hours As Integer, Minutes As Integer, Seconds As
Integer
    Dim ElapsedTime As Integer
    'Determine elapsed time since Start was clicked
    ElapsedTime = DateDiff(DateInterval.Second, StartTime,
Now)
    'Break elapsed time down into hours, minutes, and
seconds
    Hours = Int(ElapsedTime / 3600)
    Minutes = Int((ElapsedTime - Hours * 3600) / 60)
    Seconds = Int(ElapsedTime - Hours * 3600 - Minutes * 60)
    'Display time in label box
    txtTime.Text = Format(Hours, "00") & ":" &
Format(Minutes, "00") & ":" & Format(Seconds, "00")
  End Sub
```

Run the Project

Save your work. Run the project. Click **Start** to start the timer. Make sure the display updates every second. Here's a run I made:

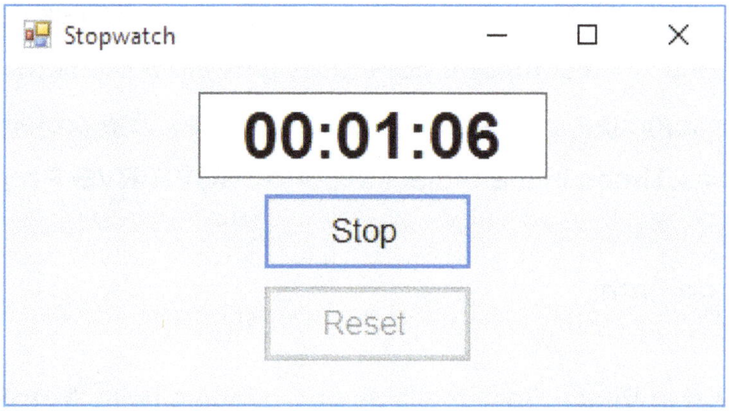

Study the Tick event if you're unsure of how this is done – especially look at how to subtract two date types (using the BASIC **DateDiff** function) to get the elapsed time. Click **Stop** to stop the timer. Make sure the **Reset** button works properly.

Other Things to Try

Many stopwatches allow you to continue timing after you've stopped one or more times. That is, you can measure total elapsed time in different segments. Modify this project to allow such measurement. You'll need a separate Stop button and a variable to keep track of total elapsed time. You'll also need to determine which buttons you want to have enabled at different times in the project. Add a "lap timing" feature by displaying the time measured in each segment (a segment being defined as the time between each Start and Stop click).

Project 2 – Times Tables

Project Design

In this project, you can give a child practice with the times tables using the numbers from 0 to 9. The computer generates a random problem. The child answers and the computer evaluates the performance. The project you are about to build is saved as **Times** in the project folder (**\CBGVB\BVB Projects**).

Place Controls on Form

Start a new project in Visual Basic. Place seven labels (with **AutoSize** set to **False**, to allow resizing), a text box and a button on the form. When done, your form should look something like this (I've temporarily set the border style of each label control to **FixedSingle** to show placement; you might also like to do this, but remember to change border style back to None):

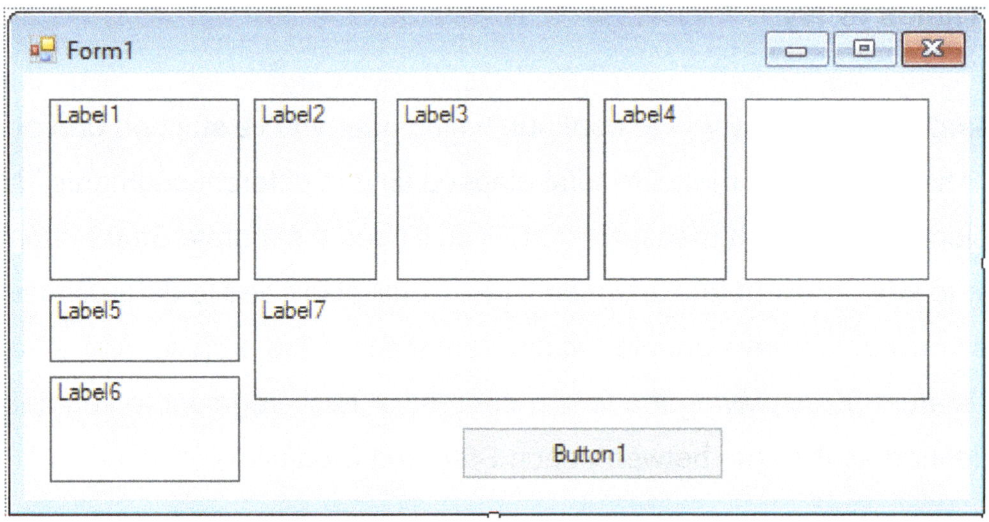

Set Control Properties

Set the control properties using the properties window:

Form1 Form:

Property Name	Property Value
Text	Times Tables
FormBorderStyle	FixedSingle
StartPosition	CenterScreen

Label1 Label:

Property Name	Property Value
Name	lblNum1
Text	[Blank]
TextAlign	MiddleCenter
Font	Arial
Font Size	48

Label2 Label:

Property Name	Property Value
Text	x
TextAlign	MiddleCenter
Font	Arial
Font Size	48

Label3 Label:

Property Name	Property Value
Name	lblNum2
Text	[Blank]
TextAlign	MiddleCenter
Font	Arial
Font Size	48

Label4 Label:

Property Name	Property Value
Text	=
TextAlign	MiddleCenter
Font	Arial
Font Size	48

Label5 Label:

Property Name	Property Value
Text	Score:
TextAlign	MiddleCenter
Font Size	18

Label6 Label:

Property Name	Property Value
Name	lblScore
Text	0%
TextAlign	MiddleCenter
BackColor	Light Yellow
BorderStyle	Fixed3D
Font Size	20

Label7 Label:

Property Name	Property Value
Name	lblMessage
Text	[Blank]
TextAlign	MiddleCenter
BackColor	Light Yellow
BorderStyle	Fixed3D
Font Size	24

TextBox1 Text Box:

Property Name	**Property Value**
Name	txtAnswer
Text	[Blank]
TextAlign	Center
Font	Arial
Font Size	48
MaxLength	2

Button1 Button:

Property Name	**Property Value**
Name	btnNext
Text	Next Problem

When done setting properties, my form looks like this:

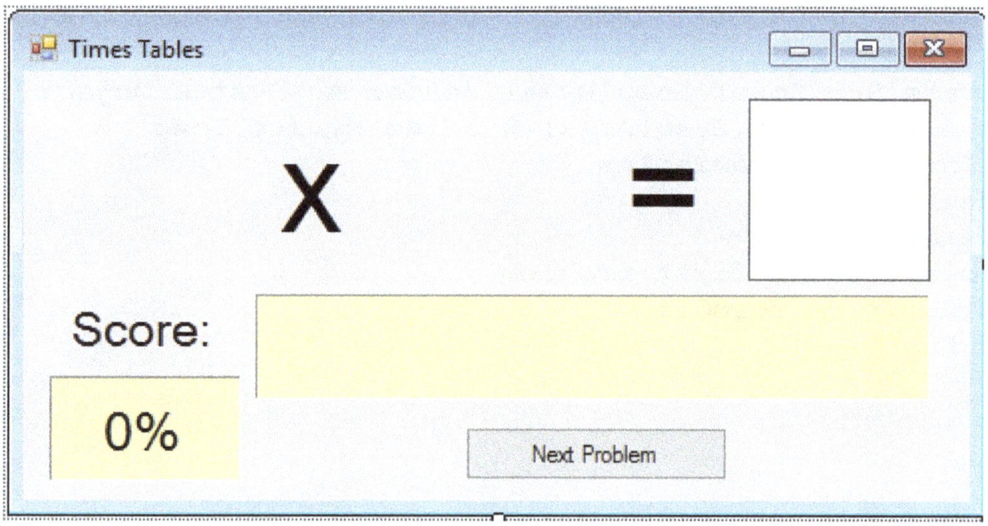

Write Event Procedures

When the user clicks **Next Problem**, the computer generates and displays a multiplication problem. The user types an answer and presses **<Enter>.** If correct, you are told so. If incorrect, the correct answer is given. In either case, the score is updated. Continue answering as long as you would like.

Add this code to the **general declarations** area:

```
Dim Product As Integer
Dim NumProb As Integer
Dim NumRight As Integer
Dim MyRandom As New Random
```

The **Form1 Load** event procedure:

```
Private Sub Form1_Load(ByVal sender As System.Object,
ByVal e As System.EventArgs) Handles MyBase.Load
    'Initialize variables
    NumProb = 0
    NumRight = 0
    'display the first problem
    btnNext.PerformClick()
End Sub
```

The **btnNext Click** event procedure:

```
  Private Sub BtnNext_Click(ByVal sender As System.Object,
ByVal e As System.EventArgs) Handles btnNext.Click
    'Generate next multiplication problem
    Dim Number1 As Integer
    Dim Number2 As Integer
    txtAnswer.Text = ""
    lblMessage.Text = ""
    NumProb = NumProb + 1
    'Generate random numbers for factors
    Number1 = MyRandom.Next(10)
    Number2 = MyRandom.Next(10)
    lblNum1.Text = Format(Number1, "0")
    lblNum2.Text = Format(Number2, "0")
    'Find product
    Product = Number1 * Number2
    btnNext.Enabled = False
    txtAnswer.Focus()
  End Sub
```

The **txtAnswer KeyPress** event procedure:

```
  Private Sub TxtAnswer_KeyPress(ByVal sender As Object,
ByVal e As System.Windows.Forms.KeyPressEventArgs) Handles
txtAnswer.KeyPress
    Dim Ans As Integer
    'Check for number only input and for return key
    If (e.KeyChar >= "0" And e.KeyChar <= "9") Or e.KeyChar
= ControlChars.Back Then
      e.Handled = False
    ElseIf e.KeyChar = ControlChars.Cr Then
      'Check answer and update score
      Ans = Val(txtAnswer.Text)
      If Ans = Product Then
        NumRight = NumRight + 1
        lblMessage.Text = "That's correct!"
      Else
        lblMessage.Text = "Answer is " + Format(Product,
"0")
      End If
      lblScore.Text = Format(100 * (NumRight / NumProb),
"0") + "%"
      btnNext.Enabled = True
      btnNext.Focus()
    Else
      e.Handled = True
    End If
  End Sub
```

Run the Project

Save your work. Run the project. A multiplication problem will be displayed. Type an answer and press <Enter>. If correct, that's great. If not, you will be shown the correct answer. Click **Next Problem** for another problem. Try for a high score. Here's a run I made:

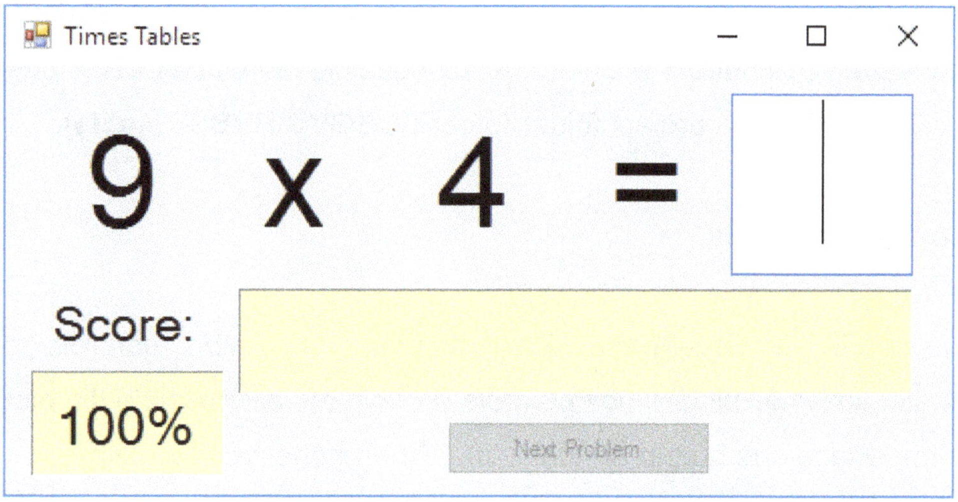

Other Things to Try

Some suggested changes to make this a more useful program are: (1) make the range of factors an option (small numbers for little kids, large numbers for older kids), (2) allow practice with a specific factor only, (3) give the user more chances at the correct answer with a decreasing score for each try, (4) set up a timer so the faster the user answers, the higher the score and (5) expand the program to include other operations such as addition, subtraction and division.

Project 3 – Dice Rolling

Project Design

It happens all the time. You get your favorite game out and the dice are missing! This program comes to the rescue – it uses the BASIC random number generator to roll two dice for you. Simply click a button to see the two dice displayed. A group of picture box controls will hold the six possible die values. This project is saved as **DiceRoll** in the project folder folder **(\CBGVB\BVB Projects).**

Place Controls on Form

Start a new project in Visual Basic. Place two large picture box controls (to display the dice) and six small picture box controls (to hold the six possible die pictures) on the form. Place one button on the form. When done, you form should resemble this:

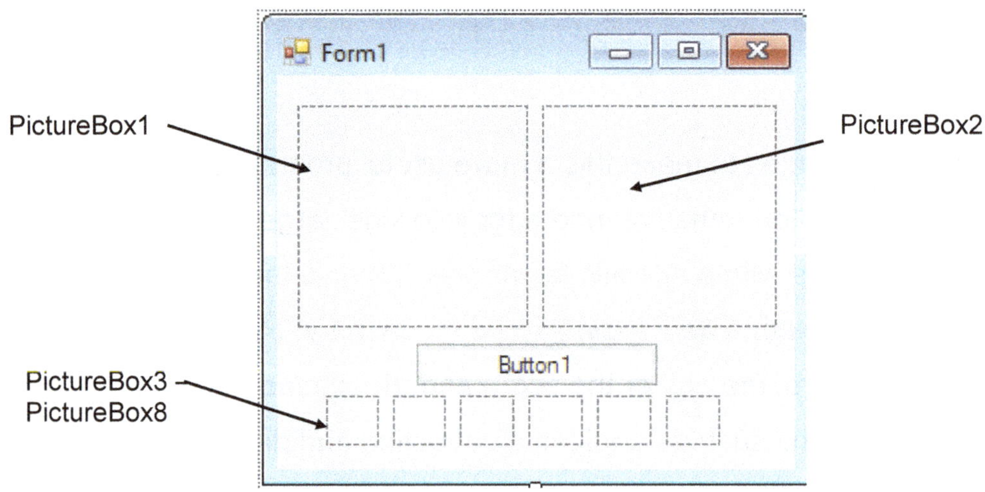

Set Control Properties

Set the control properties using the properties window:

Form1 Form:

Property Name	**Property Value**
Text	Dice Rolling
BackColor	Red
FormBorderStyle	FixedSingle
StartPosition	CenterScreen

PictureBox1 Picture Box:

Property Name	**Property Value**
Name	picDice1
SizeMode	StretchImage

PictureBox2 Picture Box:

Property Name	**Property Value**
Name	picDice2
SizeMode	StretchImage

PictureBox3 Picture Box:

Property Name	**Property Value**
Name	picDots1
Image	Dice1.gif (in **\CBGVB\BVB Projects\DiceRoll** folder)
SizeMode	StretchImage
Visible	False

PictureBox4 Picture Box:

Property Name	Property Value
Name	picDots2
Image	Dice2.gif (in **\CBGVB\BVB Projects\DiceRoll** folder)
SizeMode	StretchImage
Visible	False

PictureBox5 Picture Box:

Property Name	Property Value
Name	picDots3
Image	Dice3.gif (in **\CBGVB\BVB Projects\DiceRoll** folder)
SizeMode	StretchImage
Visible	False

PictureBox6 Picture Box:

Property Name	Property Value
Name	picDots4
Image	Dice4.gif (in **\CBGVB\BVB Projects\DiceRoll** folder)
SizeMode	StretchImage
Visible	False

PictureBox7 Picture Box:

Property Name	Property Value
Name	picDots5
Image	Dice5.gif (in **\CBGVB\BVB Projects\DiceRoll** folder)
SizeMode	StretchImage
Visible	False

PictureBox8 Picture Box:

Property Name	Property Value
Name	picDots6
Image	Dice6.gif (in **\CBGVB\BVB Projects\DiceRoll** folder)
SizeMode	StretchImage
Visible	False

Button1 Button:

Property Name	Property Value
Name	btnRoll
Text	Roll Dice

When, done my form looks like this:

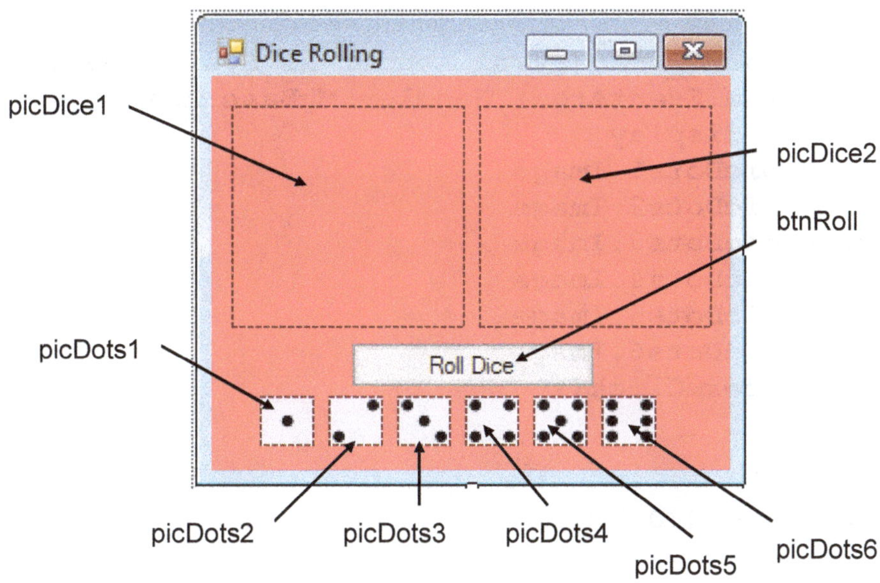

Notice we use two sets of picture boxes. The first, picDice1 and picDice2, is used to display the two dice. The second, picDots1 – picDots6, is used to store the six possible die pictures. This second group has a Visible property of False. Hence, you only see them displayed at design time.

Write Event Procedures

To roll the dice, simply click **Roll Dice**.

Declare an array of images in the **general declarations** area. This array will be used to choose which of the six possible images to display. You also need a random number object:

```
Dim Dots(6) As Image
Dim MyRandom As New Random
```

Add this code to the **Form1 Load** event. Here, we establish the image array and 'click' the **btnRoll** button to 'roll' the dice before the display is activated:

```
Private Sub Form1_Load(ByVal sender As System.Object,
ByVal e As System.EventArgs) Handles MyBase.Load
    'initialize display
    Dots(1) = picDots1.Image
    Dots(2) = picDots2.Image
    Dots(3) = picDots3.Image
    Dots(4) = picDots4.Image
    Dots(5) = picDots5.Image
    Dots(6) = picDots6.Image
    btnRoll.PerformClick()
End Sub
```

The **btnRoll Click** event procedure:

```
Private Sub BtnRoll_Click(ByVal sender As System.Object,
ByVal e As System.EventArgs) Handles btnRoll.Click
    'Roll Dice 1 and set display
    picDice1.Image = Dots(MyRandom.Next(6) + 1)
    'Roll Dice 2 and set display
    picDice2.Image = Dots(MyRandom.Next(6) + 1)
End Sub
```

Run the Project

Save your work. Run the project. Click **Roll Dice** to see the dice change with each click. Look at the code to see how the random number (1 through 6) is generated and how the image array (**Dots**) sets the display. Here's one of my rolls:

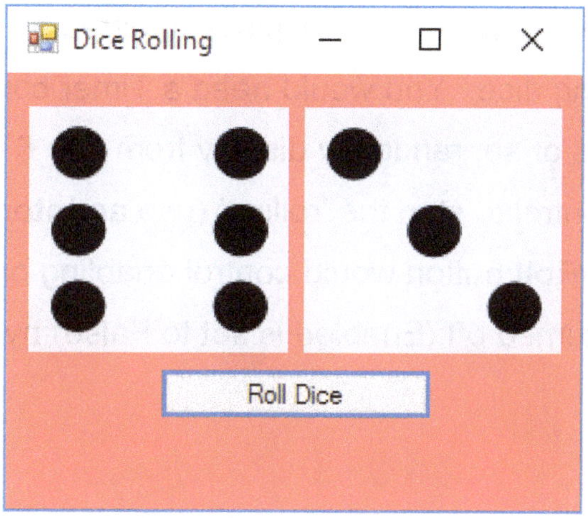

Other Things to Try

The game of Yahtzee requires 5 dice. Modify the project to roll and display five dice. Or, let the user decide how many dice to display (you could more 'display' picture boxes and use the **Visible** property to specify whether a particular die is displayed). Add a label control that displays the sum of the displayed dice.

A fun change would be to have the die displays updated by a **Timer** control to give the appearance of rolling dice. You would need a Timer control for each die (every 100 milliseconds or so, randomly display from 1 to 6 dots). And, then you would need a Timer control to stop the 'rolling' (use an **Interval** of about 2000 milliseconds). The **btnRoll** button would control enabling on the Timer controls. All Timer controls are turned off (Enabled is set to False) by the Timer event that stops the rolling.

Project 4 – State Capitals

Project Design

In this project, we build a fun game for home and school. You will be given the name of a state in the United States and four possible choices for its capital city. You click on the guess of your choice to see if you are right. (We apologize to our foreign readers – perhaps you can modify this project to build a similar multiple choice type game). Click on **Next State** for another question. This project is saved as **StateCapitals** in the project folder (**\CBGVB\BVB Projects**).

Place Controls on Form

Start a new project in Visual Basic. Place two label controls, five text boxes and two buttons on the form. When done, you form should resemble this:

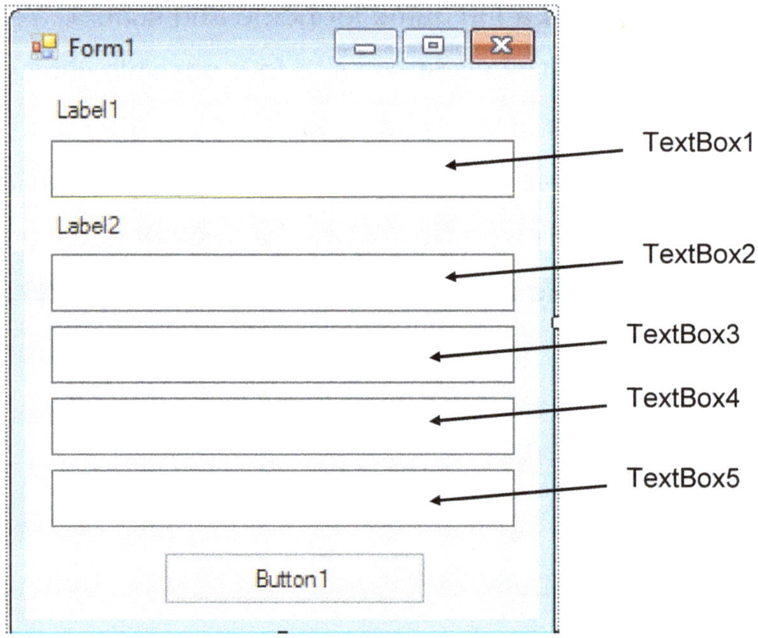

Set Control Properties

Set the control properties using the properties window:

Form1 Form:

Property Name	Property Value
Text	State Capitals
FormBorderStyle	FixedSingle
StartPosition	CenterScreen

Label1 Label:

Property Name	Property Value
Name	lblHeadState
Text	State:
Font Size	14
Font Style	Italic

TextBox1 Text Box:

Property Name	Property Value
Name	txtState
BackColor	White
Font Size	14
ReadOnly	True
TextAlign	Center
TabStop	False

Label2 Label:

Property Name	Property Value
Name	lblHeadCapital
Text	Capital:
Font Size	14
Font Style	Italic

TextBox2 Text Box:

Property Name	**Property Value**
Name	txtCapital1
BackColor	White
Font Size	14
ReadOnly	True
TextAlign	Center
TabStop	False

TextBox3 Text Box:

Property Name	**Property Value**
Name	txtCapital2
BackColor	White
Font Size	14
ReadOnly	True
TextAlign	Center
TabStop	False

TextBox4 Text Box:

Property Name	**Property Value**
Name	txtCapital3
BackColor	White
Font Size	14
ReadOnly	True
TextAlign	Center
TabStop	False

TextBox5 Text Box:

Property Name	**Property Value**
Name	txtCapital4
BackColor	White
Font Size	14
ReadOnly	True
TextAlign	Center
TabStop	False

Button1 Button:

Property Name	Property Value
Name	btnNext
Text	Next State

Button2 Button:

Property Name	Property Value
Name	btnCheck

Resize the form so **btnCheck** does not appear (we'll use this as a general procedure button). When done, the form looks like this :

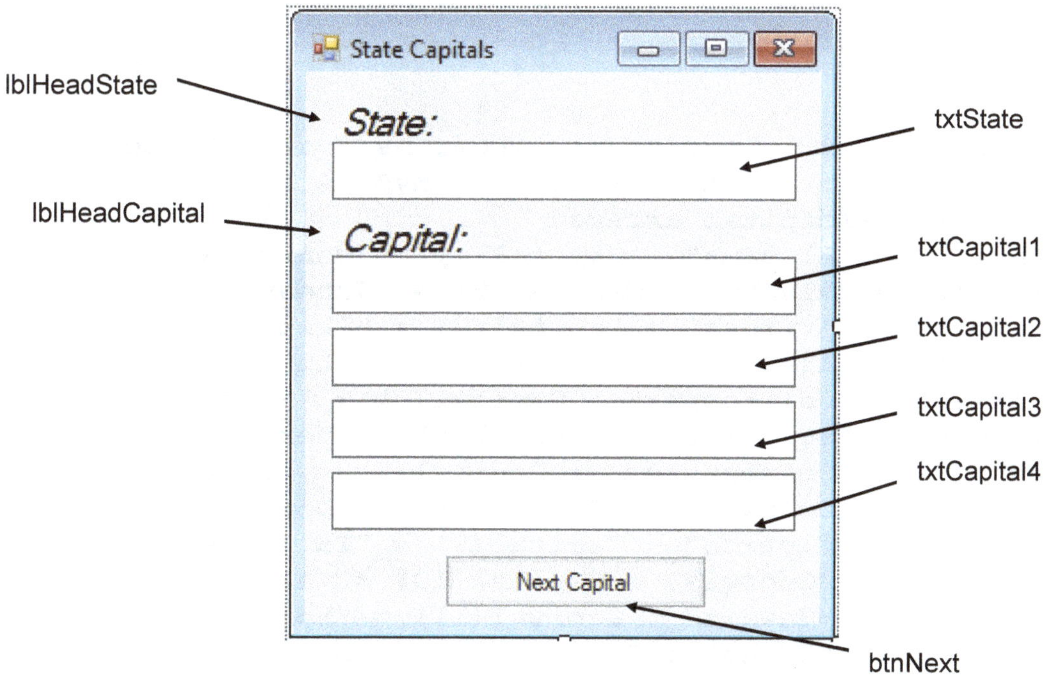

Write Event Procedures

To display a state and possible capitals, click **Next State**. Click on your choice for answer.

Put this code in the general declarations area:

```
Dim Answer As Integer
Dim State(50) As String, Capital(50) As String
Dim ListedCapital(4) As TextBox
Dim CapitalClicked As Integer
Dim MyRandom As New Random
```

Add this code to the **Form1 Load** event (yes, it's a lot of typing or just copy and paste from these notes):

```
  Private Sub Form1_Load(ByVal sender As System.Object,
ByVal e As System.EventArgs) Handles MyBase.Load
    'Load state/capital arrays
    State(1) = "Alabama" : Capital(1) = "Montgomery"
    State(2) = "Alaska" : Capital(2) = "Juneau"
    State(3) = "Arizona" : Capital(3) = "Phoenix"
    State(4) = "Arkansas" : Capital(4) = "Little Rock"
    State(5) = "California" : Capital(5) = "Sacramento"
    State(6) = "Colorado" : Capital(6) = "Denver"
    State(7) = "Connecticut" : Capital(7) = "Hartford"
    State(8) = "Delaware" : Capital(8) = "Dover"
    State(9) = "Florida" : Capital(9) = "Tallahassee"
    State(10) = "Georgia" : Capital(10) = "Atlanta"
    State(11) = "Hawaii" : Capital(11) = "Honolulu"
    State(12) = "Idaho" : Capital(12) = "Boise"
    State(13) = "Illinois" : Capital(13) = "Springfield"
    State(14) = "Indiana" : Capital(14) = "Indianapolis"
    State(15) = "Iowa" : Capital(15) = "Des Moines"
    State(16) = "Kansas" : Capital(16) = "Topeka"
    State(17) = "Kentucky" : Capital(17) = "Frankfort"
    State(18) = "Louisiana" : Capital(18) = "Baton Rouge"
    State(19) = "Maine" : Capital(19) = "Augusta"
    State(20) = "Maryland" : Capital(20) = "Annapolis"
    State(21) = "Massachusetts" : Capital(21) = "Boston"
    State(22) = "Michigan" : Capital(22) = "Lansing"
```

```
    State(23) = "Minnesota" : Capital(23) = "Saint Paul"
    State(24) = "Mississippi" : Capital(24) = "Jackson"
    State(25) = "Missouri" : Capital(25) = "Jefferson City"
    State(26) = "Montana" : Capital(26) = "Helena"
    State(27) = "Nebraska" : Capital(27) = "Lincoln"
    State(28) = "Nevada" : Capital(28) = "Carson City"
    State(29) = "New Hampshire" : Capital(29) = "Concord"
    State(30) = "New Jersey" : Capital(30) = "Trenton"
    State(31) = "New Mexico" : Capital(31) = "Santa Fe"
    State(32) = "New York" : Capital(32) = "Albany"
    State(33) = "North Carolina" : Capital(33) = "Raleigh"
    State(34) = "North Dakota" : Capital(34) = "Bismarck"
    State(35) = "Ohio" : Capital(35) = "Columbus"
    State(36) = "Oklahoma" : Capital(36) = "Oklahoma City"
    State(37) = "Oregon" : Capital(37) = "Salem"
    State(38) = "Pennsylvania" : Capital(38) = "Harrisburg"
    State(39) = "Rhode Island" : Capital(39) = "Providence"
    State(40) = "South Carolina" : Capital(40) = "Columbia"
    State(41) = "South Dakota" : Capital(41) = "Pierre"
    State(42) = "Tennessee" : Capital(42) = "Nashville"
    State(43) = "Texas" : Capital(43) = "Austin"
    State(44) = "Utah" : Capital(44) = "Salt Lake City"
    State(45) = "Vermont" : Capital(45) = "Montpelier"
    State(46) = "Virginia" : Capital(46) = "Richmond"
    State(47) = "Washington" : Capital(47) = "Olympia"
    State(48) = "West Virginia" : Capital(48) = "Charleston"
    State(49) = "Wisconsin" : Capital(49) = "Madison"
    State(50) = "Wyoming" : Capital(50) = "Cheyenne"
    'Set listed capital labels
    ListedCapital(1) = txtCapital1
    ListedCapital(2) = txtCapital2
    ListedCapital(3) = txtCapital3
    ListedCapital(4) = txtCapital4
    'set first question
    btnNext.PerformClick()
End Sub
```

The **btnNext Click** event procedure generates the next multiple choice question:

```
  Private Sub BtnNext_Click(ByVal sender As System.Object,
ByVal e As System.EventArgs) Handles btnNext.Click
    Dim VUsed(50) As Integer
    Dim Index(4) As Integer
    Dim I As Integer
    Dim J As Integer
    'Generate the next question at random
    btnNext.Enabled = False
    Answer = MyRandom.Next(50) + 1
    'Display selected state
    txtState.Text = State(Answer)
    'Vused array is used to see which state capitals have
    'been selected as possible answers
    For I = 1 To 50
      VUsed(I) = 0
    Next I
    'Pick four different state indices (J) at random
    'These are used to set up multiple choice answers
    'Stored in the Index array
    For I = 1 To 4
      'Find index not used yet and not the answer
      Do
        J = MyRandom.Next(50) + 1
      Loop Until VUsed(J) = 0 And J <> Answer
      VUsed(J) = 1
      Index(I) = J
    Next I
    'Now replace one index (at random) with correct answer
    Index(MyRandom.Next(4) + 1) = Answer
    'Display multiple choice answers in label boxes
    For I = 1 To 4
      ListedCapital(I).Text = Capital(Index(I))
    Next I
  End Sub
```

A new concept in this routine is the **Do** loop (shaded line) to pick the different possible answers. Let's explain how this particular loop works.

The form used in this code is:

```
Do

    [BASIC code]

Loop Until Condition
```

In this "loop," the BASIC code between the **Do** line and the **Loop** line is repeated until the specified **Condition** is True. See if you can see how this loop allows us to pick four distinct capital cities for the multiple choice answers (no repeated values).

The event procedures for clicking the capital city text box controls simply identify which text box was clicked and "clicks" the hidden **btnCheck** button:

```
  Private Sub TxtCapital1_Click(ByVal sender As
System.Object, ByVal e As System.EventArgs) Handles
txtCapital1.Click
    CapitalClicked = 1
    btnCheck.PerformClick()
  End Sub

  Private Sub TxtCapital2_Click(ByVal sender As
System.Object, ByVal e As System.EventArgs) Handles
txtCapital2.Click
    CapitalClicked = 2
    btnCheck.PerformClick()
  End Sub

  Private Sub TxtCapital3_Click(ByVal sender As
System.Object, ByVal e As System.EventArgs) Handles
txtCapital3.Click
    CapitalClicked = 3
    btnCheck.PerformClick()
  End Sub

  Private Sub TxtCapital4_Click(ByVal sender As
System.Object, ByVal e As System.EventArgs) Handles
txtCapital4.Click
    CapitalClicked = 4
    btnCheck.PerformClick()
  End Sub
```

We write a **btnCheck Click** "hidden" general procedure to check the answer (when it is selected by clicking a text box control):

```
  Private Sub BtnCheck_Click(ByVal sender As Object, ByVal e
As System.EventArgs) Handles btnCheck.Click
    Dim I As Integer
    'If already answered, ignore click
    If ListedCapital(CapitalClicked).Text <> "" And
btnNext.Enabled = False Then
      'Check clicked answer
      If ListedCapital(CapitalClicked).Text =
Capital(Answer) Then
        'Correct answer - clear out other answers and enable
Next button
        For I = 1 To 4
          If I <> CapitalClicked Then
            ListedCapital(I).Text = ""
          End If
        Next I
        btnNext.Enabled = True
        btnNext.Focus()
      Else
        'Incorrect answer - clear out selected answer
        ListedCapital(CapitalClicked).Text = ""
      End If
    End If
  End Sub
```

Run the Project

Save your work. Run the project. A state name and four possible capital cities will be displayed. (Study the code used to choose and sort the possible answers – this kind of code is very useful.) Choose an answer. If correct, the other answers will be cleared. Click **Next State** to continue. If incorrect, your choice will be cleared. Keeping answering until correct. Here's a run I made:

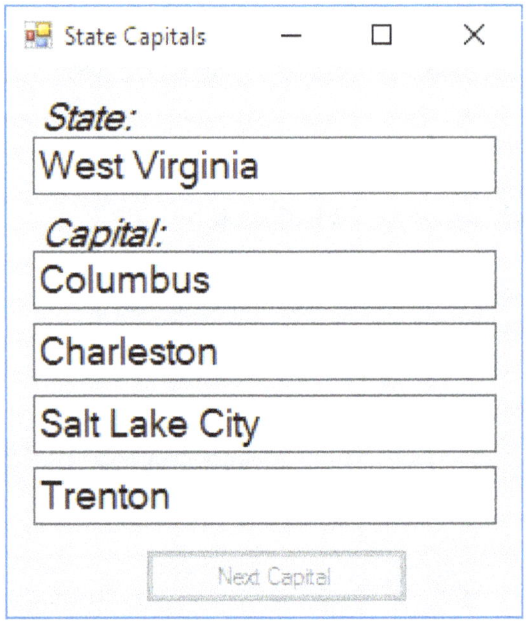

Other Things to Try

This would be a fun project to modify. How about changing it to display a capital city with four states as the multiple choices? Allow the user to type in the answer (use a text box) instead of picking from a list. Add some kind of scoring system.

This program could also be used to build general multiple choice tests from any two lists. You could do language translations (given a word in English, choose the corresponding word in Spanish), given a book, choose the author, or given an invention, name the inventor. Use your imagination.

Project 5 – Memory Game

Project Design

In this game for little kids, sixteen squares are used to hide eight different pairs of pictures. The player chooses two squares on the board and the pictures behind them are revealed. If the pictures match, those squares are removed from the board. If there is no match, the pictures are recovered and the player tries again. The play continues until all eight pairs are matched up. The game is saved as **MemoryGame** in the project folder (**\CBGVB\BVB Projects**).

Place Controls on Form

Start a new project in Visual Basic. Place sixteen large picture box controls and nine smaller picture box controls on the form. Place two buttons and a timer on the form. When done, you form should resemble this:

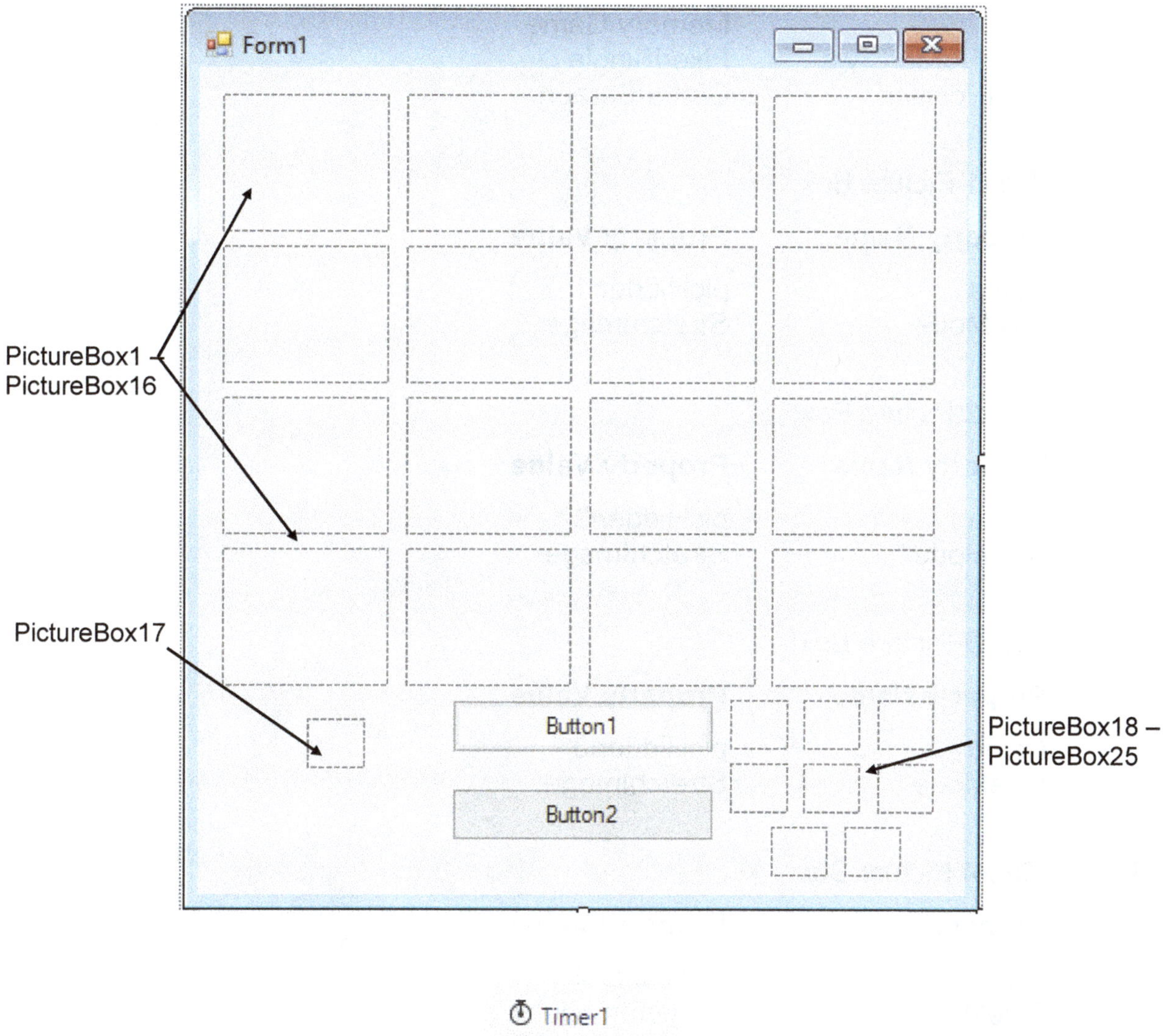

Set Control Properties

Set the control properties using the properties window:

Form1 Form:

Property Name	**Property Value**
Text	Memory Game
FormBorderStyle	FixedSingle
StartPosition	CenterScreen

PictureBox1 Picture Box:

Property Name	**Property Value**
Name	picHidden1
SizeMode	StretchImage

PictureBox2 Picture Box:

Property Name	**Property Value**
Name	picHidden2
SizeMode	StretchImage

PictureBox3 Picture Box:

Property Name	**Property Value**
Name	picHidden3
SizeMode	StretchImage

PictureBox4 Picture Box:

Property Name	**Property Value**
Name	picHidden4
SizeMode	StretchImage

PictureBox5 Picture Box:

Property Name	**Property Value**
Name	picHidden5
SizeMode	StretchImage

PictureBox6 Picture Box:

Property Name	**Property Value**
Name	picHidden6
SizeMode	StretchImage

PictureBox7 Picture Box:

Property Name	**Property Value**
Name	picHidden7
SizeMode	StretchImage

PictureBox8 Picture Box:

Property Name	**Property Value**
Name	picHidden8
SizeMode	StretchImage

PictureBox9 Picture Box:

Property Name	**Property Value**
Name	picHidden9
SizeMode	StretchImage

PictureBox10 Picture Box:

Property Name	**Property Value**
Name	picHidden10
SizeMode	StretchImage

PictureBox11 Picture Box:

Property Name	**Property Value**
Name	picHidden11
SizeMode	StretchImage

PictureBox12 Picture Box:

Property Name	**Property Value**
Name	picHidden12
SizeMode	StretchImage

PictureBox13 Picture Box:

Property Name	**Property Value**
Name	picHidden13
SizeMode	StretchImage

PictureBox14 Picture Box:

Property Name	**Property Value**
Name	picHidden14
SizeMode	StretchImage

PictureBox15 Picture Box:

Property Name	**Property Value**
Name	picHidden15
SizeMode	StretchImage

PictureBox16 Picture Box:

Property Name	**Property Value**
Name	picHidden16
SizeMode	StretchImage

PictureBox17 Picture Box:

Property Name	Property Value
Name	picBack
SizeMode	StretchImage
Image	Back.gif (in **\CBGVB\BVB Projects\MemoryGame** folder)
Visible	False

PictureBox18 PictureBox:

Property Name	Property Value
Name	picChoice1
SizeMode	StretchImage
Image	Ball.gif (in **\CBGVB\BVB Projects\MemoryGame** folder)
Visible	False

PictureBox19 PictureBox:

Property Name	Property Value
Name	picChoice2
SizeMode	StretchImage
Image	Gift.gif (in **\CBGVB\BVB Projects\MemoryGame** folder)
Visible	False

PictureBox20 PictureBox:

Property Name	Property Value
Name	picChoice3
SizeMode	StretchImage
Image	Bear.gif (in **\CBGVB\BVB Projects\MemoryGame** folder)
Visible	False

PictureBox21 PictureBox:

Property Name	Property Value
Name	picChoice4
SizeMode	StretchImage
Image	Block.gif (in **\CBGVB\BVB Projects\MemoryGame** folder)
Visible	False

PictureBox22 PictureBox:

Property Name	Property Value
Name	picChoice5
SizeMode	StretchImage
Image	Ducky.gif (in **\CBGVB\BVB Projects\MemoryGame** folder)
Visible	False

PictureBox23 PictureBox:

Property Name	Property Value
Name	picChoice6
SizeMode	StretchImage
Image	Burger.gif (in **\CBGVB\BVB Projects\MemoryGame** folder)
Visible	False

PictureBox24 PictureBox:

Property Name	Property Value
Name	picChoice7
SizeMode	StretchImage
Image	Hotdog.gif (in **\CBGVB\BVB Projects\MemoryGame** folder)
Visible	False

PictureBox25 PictureBox:

Property Name	Property Value
Name	picChoice8
SizeMode	StretchImage
Image	Cake.gif (in **\CBGVB\BVB Projects\MemoryGame** folder)
Visible	False

Button1 Button:

Property Name	Property Value
Name	btnNew
Text	New Game

Button2 Button:

Property Name	Property Value
Name	btnCheck

Timer1 Timer:

Property Name	Property Value
Name	timDelay
Interval	1000

The completed form appears like this:

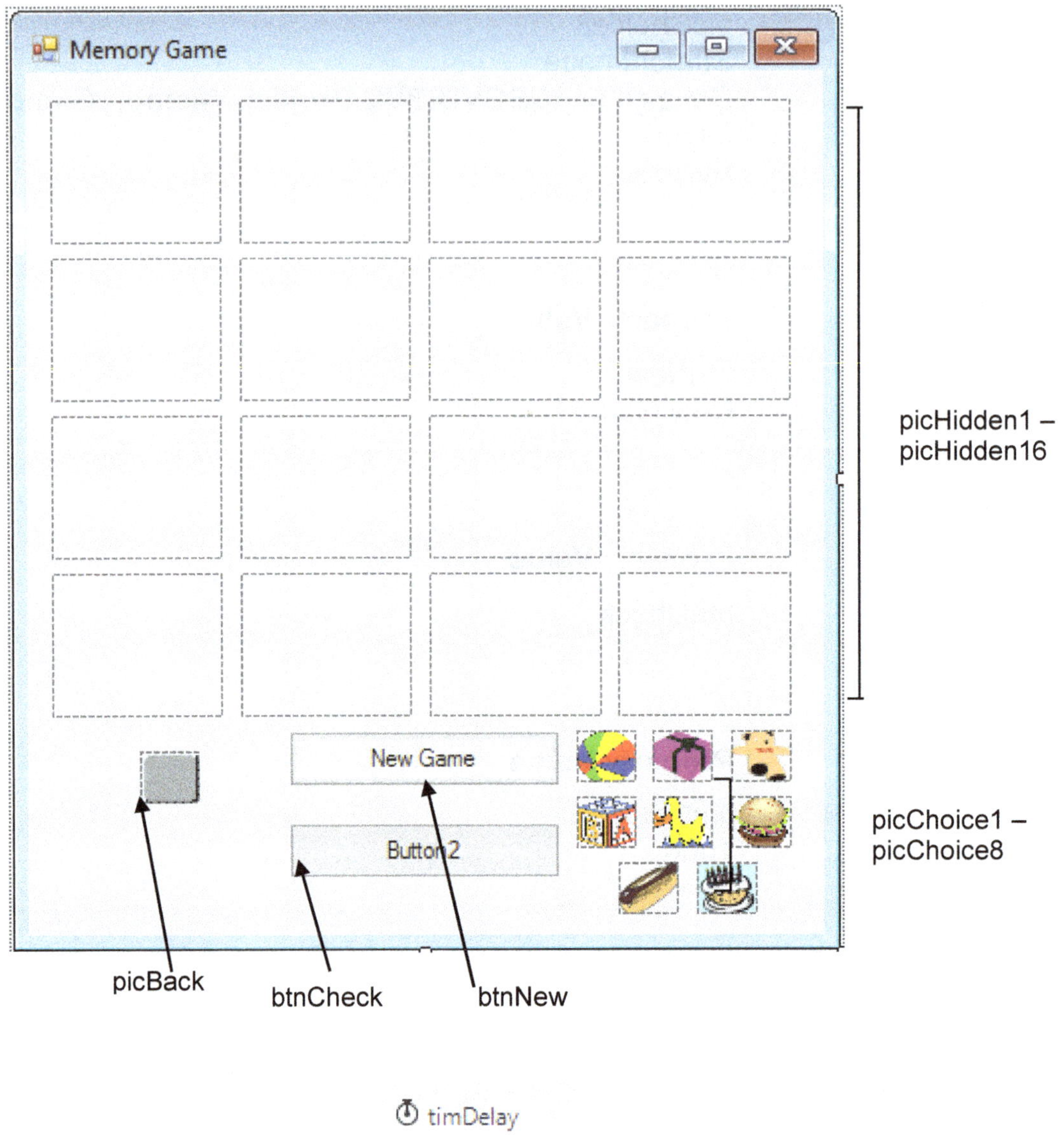

Before continuing, resize the form to hide **btnCheck**, a button we use for a general procedure. A few of the graphics will disappear, but that's okay since their Visible property is False anyway.

Write Event Procedures

When the game starts, pick one box, then another. The game stops when all matching picture pairs have been found. A delay is used to display the pictures for one second before deciding whether or not there is a match. At any time, click **New Game** to start again.

Add this code to the **general declarations** area:

```
Dim Choice As Integer
Dim Picked(2) As Integer
Dim Behind(16) As Integer
Dim Displayed(16) As PictureBox
Dim Choices(8) As PictureBox
Dim MyRandom As New Random
```

The **Form1 Load** event establishes images to pick from

```
  Private Sub Form1_Load(ByVal sender As System.Object,
ByVal e As System.EventArgs) Handles MyBase.Load
    'establish display and choices picture boxes
    Displayed(1) = picHidden1
    Displayed(2) = picHidden2
    Displayed(3) = picHidden3
    Displayed(4) = picHidden4
    Displayed(5) = picHidden5
    Displayed(6) = picHidden6
    Displayed(7) = picHidden7
    Displayed(8) = picHidden8
    Displayed(9) = picHidden9
    Displayed(10) = picHidden10
    Displayed(11) = picHidden11
    Displayed(12) = picHidden12
    Displayed(13) = picHidden13
    Displayed(14) = picHidden14
    Displayed(15) = picHidden15
    Displayed(16) = picHidden16
    Choices(1) = picChoice1
    Choices(2) = picChoice2
    Choices(3) = picChoice3
    Choices(4) = picChoice4
    Choices(5) = picChoice5
    Choices(6) = picChoice6
    Choices(7) = picChoice7
    Choices(8) = picChoice8
    'start new game
    btnNew.PerformClick()
  End Sub
```

The **btnNew Click** event procedure sets up the hidden pictures:

```
  Private Sub BtnNew_Click(ByVal sender As System.Object,
ByVal e As System.EventArgs) Handles btnNew.Click
    Dim I As Integer
    Dim TempValue As Integer
    Dim Remaining As Integer
    For I = 1 To 16
      'replace with card back
      Displayed(I).Image = picBack.Image
      Displayed(I).Visible = True
      Behind(I) = I
    Next I
    'Randomly sort 16 integers using Shuffle routine from
Class 9
    'Behind array contains indexes (1-8) for hidden pictures
    'Work through Remaining values
    'Start at 16 and swap one value
    'at each For/Next loop step
    'After each step, Remaining is decreased by 1
    For Remaining = 16 To 2 Step -1
      'Pick item at random
      I = MyRandom.Next(Remaining) + 1
      'Swap picked item with bottom item
      TempValue = Behind(Remaining)
      Behind(Remaining) = Behind(I)
      Behind(I) = TempValue
    Next Remaining
    For I = 1 To 16
      If Behind(I) > 8 Then
        Behind(I) = Behind(I) - 8
      End If
    Next I
    Choice = 1
  End Sub
```

The **Click** event procedures for the 16 picture boxes:

```
  Private Sub PicHidden1_Click(ByVal sender As
System.Object, ByVal e As System.EventArgs) Handles
picHidden1.Click
    Picked(Choice) = 1
    btnCheck.PerformClick()
   End Sub

  Private Sub PicHidden2_Click(ByVal sender As
System.Object, ByVal e As System.EventArgs) Handles
picHidden2.Click
    Picked(Choice) = 2
    btnCheck.PerformClick()
  End Sub

  Private Sub PicHidden3_Click(ByVal sender As
System.Object, ByVal e As System.EventArgs) Handles
picHidden3.Click
    Picked(Choice) = 3
    btnCheck.PerformClick()
  End Sub

  Private Sub PicHidden4_Click(ByVal sender As
System.Object, ByVal e As System.EventArgs) Handles
picHidden4.Click
    Picked(Choice) = 4
    btnCheck.PerformClick()
  End Sub

  Private Sub PicHidden5_Click(ByVal sender As
System.Object, ByVal e As System.EventArgs) Handles
picHidden5.Click
    Picked(Choice) = 5
    btnCheck.PerformClick()
  End Sub

  Private Sub PicHidden6_Click(ByVal sender As
System.Object, ByVal e As System.EventArgs) Handles
picHidden6.Click
    Picked(Choice) = 6
    btnCheck.PerformClick()
  End Sub
```

```
  Private Sub PicHidden7_Click(ByVal sender As
System.Object, ByVal e As System.EventArgs) Handles
picHidden7.Click
    Picked(Choice) = 7
    btnCheck.PerformClick()
  End Sub
```

```
  Private Sub PicHidden8_Click(ByVal sender As
System.Object, ByVal e As System.EventArgs) Handles
picHidden8.Click
    Picked(Choice) = 8
    btnCheck.PerformClick()
  End Sub

  Private Sub PicHidden9_Click(ByVal sender As
System.Object, ByVal e As System.EventArgs) Handles
picHidden9.Click
    Picked(Choice) = 9
    btnCheck.PerformClick()
  End Sub

  Private Sub PicHidden10_Click(ByVal sender As
System.Object, ByVal e As System.EventArgs) Handles
picHidden10.Click
    Picked(Choice) = 10
    btnCheck.PerformClick()
  End Sub

  Private Sub PicHidden11_Click(ByVal sender As
System.Object, ByVal e As System.EventArgs) Handles
picHidden11.Click
    Picked(Choice) = 11
    btnCheck.PerformClick()
  End Sub

  Private Sub PicHidden12_Click(ByVal sender As
System.Object, ByVal e As System.EventArgs) Handles
picHidden12.Click
    Picked(Choice) = 12
    btnCheck.PerformClick()
  End Sub

  Private Sub PicHidden13_Click(ByVal sender As
System.Object, ByVal e As System.EventArgs) Handles
picHidden13.Click
    Picked(Choice) = 13
    btnCheck.PerformClick()
  End Sub
```

```
  Private Sub PicHidden14_Click(ByVal sender As
System.Object, ByVal e As System.EventArgs) Handles
picHidden14.Click
    Picked(Choice) = 14
    btnCheck.PerformClick()
  End Sub

  Private Sub PicHidden15_Click(ByVal sender As
System.Object, ByVal e As System.EventArgs) Handles
picHidden15.Click
    Picked(Choice) = 15
    btnCheck.PerformClick()
  End Sub

  Private Sub PicHidden16_Click(ByVal sender As
System.Object, ByVal e As System.EventArgs) Handles
picHidden16.Click
    Picked(Choice) = 16
    btnCheck.PerformClick()
  End Sub
```

The **btnCheck Click** "hidden" general procedure that displays the choices for a match:

```
  Private Sub BtnCheck_Click(ByVal sender As Object, ByVal e
As System.EventArgs) Handles btnCheck.Click
    'Only execute if not trying to pick same box
    If Choice = 1 Or (Choice = 2 And Picked(1) <> Picked(2))
Then
      'Display selected picture
      Displayed(Picked(Choice)).Image =
Choices(Behind(Picked(Choice))).Image
      Displayed(Picked(Choice)).Refresh()
      If Choice = 1 Then
        'first choice - just display
        Choice = 2
      Else
        'Delay for one second before checking
        timDelay.Enabled = True
      End If
    End If
  End Sub
```

The **timDelay Tick** procedure that checks for matches after a delay:

```
  Private Sub TimDelay_Tick(ByVal sender As System.Object,
ByVal e As System.EventArgs) Handles timDelay.Tick
    timDelay.Enabled = False
    'After delay, check for match
    If Behind(Picked(1)) = Behind(Picked(2)) Then
      'If match, remove pictures
      Displayed(Picked(1)).Visible = False
      Displayed(Picked(2)).Visible = False
    Else
      'If no match, blank picture, restore backs
      Displayed(Picked(1)).Image = picBack.Image
      Displayed(Picked(2)).Image = picBack.Image
    End If
    Choice = 1
  End Sub
```

Run the Project

Save your work. Run the project. Sixteen boxes appear. Click on one and view the picture. Click on another. If there is a match, the two pictures are removed (after a delay). If there is no match, the boxes are restored (also after a delay). Once all matches are found, click **New Game** to play again. Here's the middle of a game I was playing (notice the form has been resized at design time to hide the lower of the two button controls:

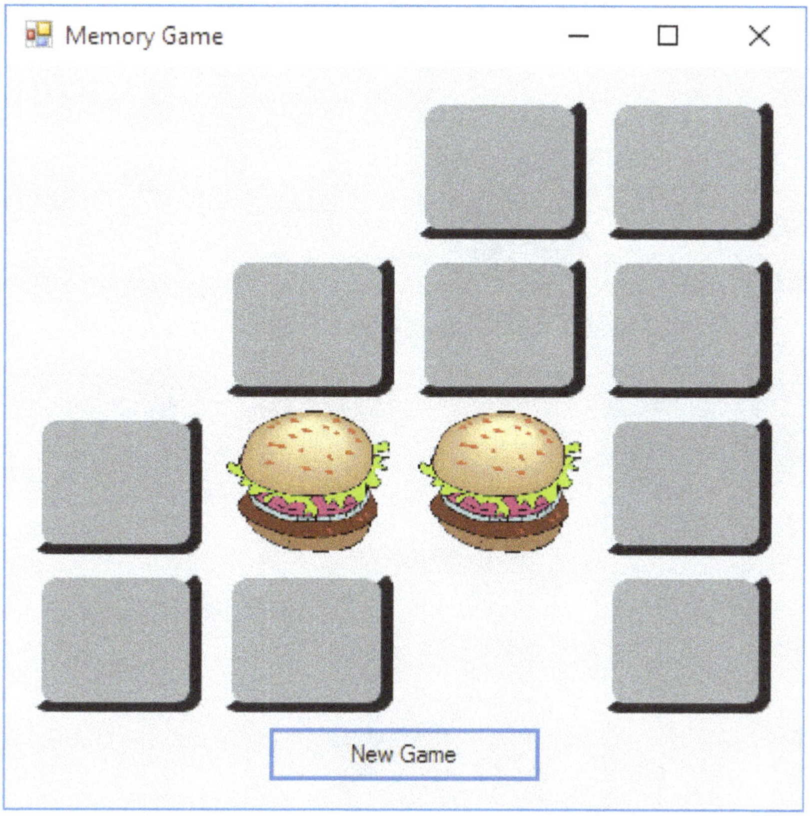

Other Things to Try

Some things to help improve or change this game: add a scoring system to keep track of how many tries you took to find all the matches, make it a two player game where you compete against another player or the computer, or set it up to match other items (shapes, colors, upper and lower case letters, numbers and objects, etc.).

Project 6 – Units Conversion

Project Design

In this project, we will build a program that converts length from one unit of measure (inch, foot, yard, mile, centimeter, meter, kilometer) to another. The program will allow you to choose (using radio buttons) how many decimal points you want to display in the result. The project you are about to build is saved as **Convert** in the project folder (**\CBGVB\BVB Projects**).

Place Controls on Form

Start a new project in Visual Basic. Place two text box controls and two domain updown controls on the form. The domain updown controls are like a numeric updown, with items listed instead of numbers. Also, place a group box with six radio buttons. When done, your form should look something like this:

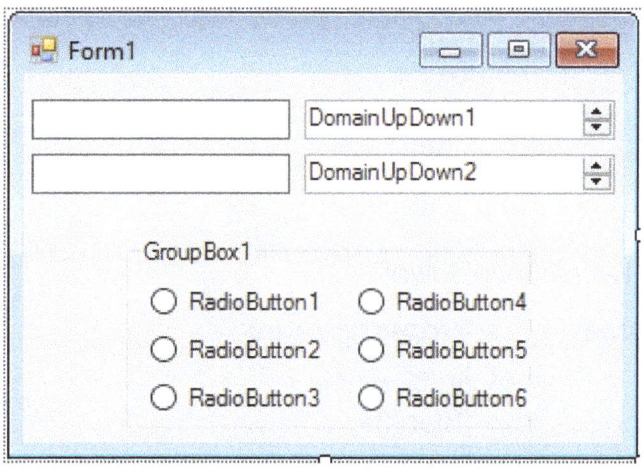

Set Control Properties

Set the control properties using the properties window:

Form1 Form:

Property Name	Property Value
Text	Units Conversion
BorderStyle	FixedSingle
StartPosition	CenterScreen

TextBox1 Text Box:

Property Name	Property Value
Name	txtFromValue
Text	0
TextAlign	Right
Font Size	12

TextBox2 Text Box:

Property Name	Property Value
Name	txtToValue
Text	0
TextAlign	Right
BackColor	White
Font Size	12
ReadOnly	True
TabStop	False

DomainUpDown1 Domain UpDown:

Property Name	Property Value
Name	dudFromUnit
Text	[Blank]
TextAlign	Right
BackColor	Light Yellow
Font Size	12

DomainUpDown2 Domain UpDown:

Property Name	Property Value
Name	dudToUnit
Text	[Blank]
TextAlign	Right
BackColor	Light Yellow
Font Size	12

GroupBox1 Group Box:

Property Name	Property Value
Name	grpConvert
Text	Number of Decimals
Font Size	10

RadioButton1 Radio Button:

Property Name	Property Value
Name	rdoDec0
Text	0
Checked	True

RadioButton2 Radio Button:

Property Name	Property Value
Name	rdoDec1
Text	1

RadioButton3 Radio Button:

Property Name	Property Value
Name	rdoDec2
Text	2

RadioButton4 Radio Button:

Property Name	Property Value
Name	rdoDec3
Text	3

RadioButton5 Radio Button:

Property Name	Property Value
Name	rdoDec4
Text	4

RadioButton6 Radio Button:

Property Name	Property Value
Name	rdoDec5
Text	5

My finished form looks like this:

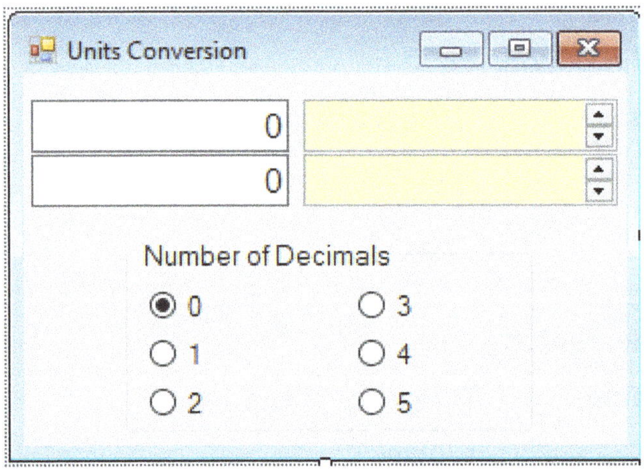

Write Event Procedures

The idea of the program is simple. Type a value in the text box and choose the units (both From and To). With each change in value, units or number of decimals, the conversion is updated. Most of the computation is involved with the **txtFromValue_Change** event. Note how the conversion factors are stored in a two-dimensional array (table).

Add this code to the **general declarations** area:

```
Dim Units(7) As String
Dim NumDecimals As Integer
Dim Conversions(7, 7) As Double
```

The **Form1 Load** event procedure:

```
  Private Sub Form1_Load(ByVal sender As System.Object,
ByVal e As System.EventArgs) Handles MyBase.Load
    Dim I As Integer
    'Establish conversion factors - stored in two
dimensional array
    'or table - the first number is the table row, the
second number
    'the table column
    Conversions(1, 1) = 1.0# 'in to in
    Conversions(1, 2) = 1 / 12 'in to ft
    Conversions(1, 3) = 1 / 36 'in to yd
    Conversions(1, 4) = (1 / 12) / 5280 'in to mi
    Conversions(1, 5) = 2.54 'in to cm
    Conversions(1, 6) = 2.54 / 100 'in to m
    Conversions(1, 7) = 2.54 / 100000 'in to km
    For I = 1 To 7
      Conversions(2, I) = 12 * Conversions(1, I)
      Conversions(3, I) = 36 * Conversions(1, I)
      Conversions(4, I) = 5280 * (12 * Conversions(1, I))
      Conversions(5, I) = Conversions(1, I) / 2.54
      Conversions(6, I) = 100 * Conversions(1, I) / 2.54
      Conversions(7, I) = 100000 * (Conversions(1, I) /
2.54)
    Next I
```

```
    'Initialize variables
    Units(1) = "inches (in)"
    Units(2) = "feet (ft)"
    Units(3) = "yards (yd)"
    Units(4) = "miles (mi)"
    Units(5) = "centimeters (cm)"
    Units(6) = "meters (m)"
    Units(7) = "kilometers (km)"
    For I = 0 To 6
      dudFromUnit.Items.Add(Units(I + 1))
      dudToUnit.Items.Add(Units(I + 1))
    Next I
    dudFromUnit.SelectedIndex = 0
    dudToUnit.SelectedIndex = 0
    NumDecimals = 0
    'Put cursor in text box
    txtFromValue.Focus()
  End Sub
```

The **txtFromValue KeyPress** event procedure:

```
  Private Sub TxtFromValue_KeyPress(ByVal sender As Object,
ByVal e As System.Windows.Forms.KeyPressEventArgs) Handles
txtFromValue.KeyPress
    'Numbers and decimal point only
    If (e.KeyChar >= "0" And e.KeyChar <= "9") Or e.KeyChar
= "." Or e.KeyChar = ControlChars.Back Then
      e.Handled = False
    Else
      e.Handled = True
    End If
  End Sub
```

The **txtFromValue TextChanged** event procedure:

```
  Private Sub TxtFromValue_TextChanged(ByVal sender As
Object, ByVal e As System.EventArgs) Handles
txtFromValue.TextChanged
    Call UpdateDisplay()
  End Sub
```

The **UpdateDisplay** general procedure (recall type the procedure, including header line, after any **End Sub** line):

```
  Private Sub UpdateDisplay()
    Dim V As Double
    'Do unit conversion
    V = Conversions(dudFromUnit.SelectedIndex + 1,
dudToUnit.SelectedIndex + 1) * Val(txtFromValue.Text)
    Select Case NumDecimals
      Case 0
        txtToValue.Text = Format(V, "0")
      Case 1
        txtToValue.Text = Format(V, "0.0")
      Case 2
        txtToValue.Text = Format(V, "0.00")
      Case 3
        txtToValue.Text = Format(V, "0.000")
      Case 4
        txtToValue.Text = Format(V, "0.0000")
      Case 5
        txtToValue.Text = Format(V, "0.00000")
    End Select
    txtFromValue.Focus()
  End Sub
```

The **dudFromUnit SelectedItemChanged** event procedure:

```
  Private Sub DudFromUnit_SelectedItemChanged(ByVal sender
As System.Object, ByVal e As System.EventArgs) Handles
dudFromUnit.SelectedItemChanged
    Call UpdateDisplay()
  End Sub
```

The **dudToUnit SelectedItemChanged** event procedure:

```
  Private Sub DudToUnit_SelectedItemChanged(ByVal sender As
System.Object, ByVal e As System.EventArgs) Handles
dudToUnit.SelectedItemChanged
    Call UpdateDisplay()
  End Sub
```

The **rdoDec0 CheckedChanged – rdoDec5 CheckedChanged** event procedures:

```
  Private Sub RdoDec0_CheckedChanged(ByVal sender As
System.Object, ByVal e As System.EventArgs) Handles
rdoDec0.CheckedChanged
    NumDecimals = 0
    Call UpdateDisplay()
  End Sub

  Private Sub RdoDec1_CheckedChanged(ByVal sender As
System.Object, ByVal e As System.EventArgs) Handles
rdoDec1.CheckedChanged
    NumDecimals = 1
    Call UpdateDisplay()
  End Sub

  Private Sub RdoDec2_CheckedChanged(ByVal sender As
System.Object, ByVal e As System.EventArgs) Handles
rdoDec2.CheckedChanged
    NumDecimals = 2
    Call UpdateDisplay()
  End Sub

  Private Sub RdoDec3_CheckedChanged(ByVal sender As
System.Object, ByVal e As System.EventArgs) Handles
rdoDec3.CheckedChanged
    NumDecimals = 3
    Call UpdateDisplay()
  End Sub

  Private Sub RdoDec4_CheckedChanged(ByVal sender As
System.Object, ByVal e As System.EventArgs) Handles
rdoDec4.CheckedChanged
    NumDecimals = 4
    Call UpdateDisplay()
  End Sub
```

```
  Private Sub RdoDec5_CheckedChanged(ByVal sender As
System.Object, ByVal e As System.EventArgs) Handles
rdoDec5.CheckedChanged
    NumDecimals = 5
    Call UpdateDisplay()
  End Sub
```

Run the Project

Save your work. Run the project. Type in a value. Watch the corresponding converted value change as you type. Change the From units and the To units using the updown controls. Change the number of decimals. Make sure all the options work as designed. Here's a run I tried:

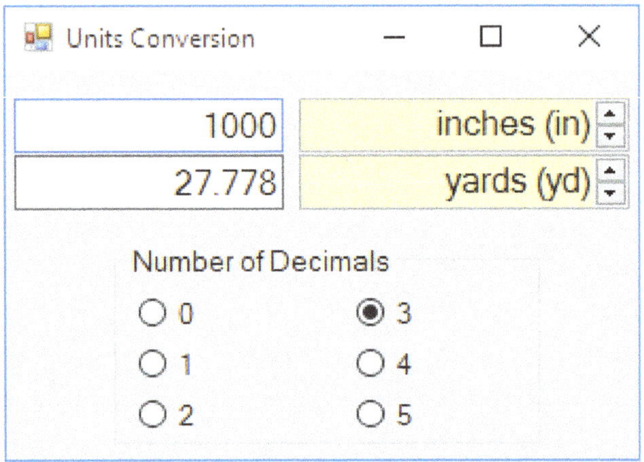

Other Things to Try

The most obvious change to this program is to include other units of measure. You could build a general purpose units conversion program that converts not only length, but weight, volume, density, area, temperature and many others. Such a program would be invaluable.

Project 7 - Decode

Project Design

This project is a classic computer game. The computer generates a four-digit code (with no repeating digits). You guess at the code. The computer then tells you how many digits in your guess are correct and how many digits are in the correct location. Based on these clues, you make a new guess. You continue guessing until you have cracked the code. The project you are about to build is saved as **Decode** in the project folder (**\CBGVB\BVB Projects**).

Place Controls on Form

Start a new project in Visual Basic. Place a label control (set **AutoSize** to **False** so it can be resized) and three group box controls on the form. In the first group box, place a text box control and a button. In the second group box, place two buttons. In the final group box, place a text box control. When done, your form should look something like this:

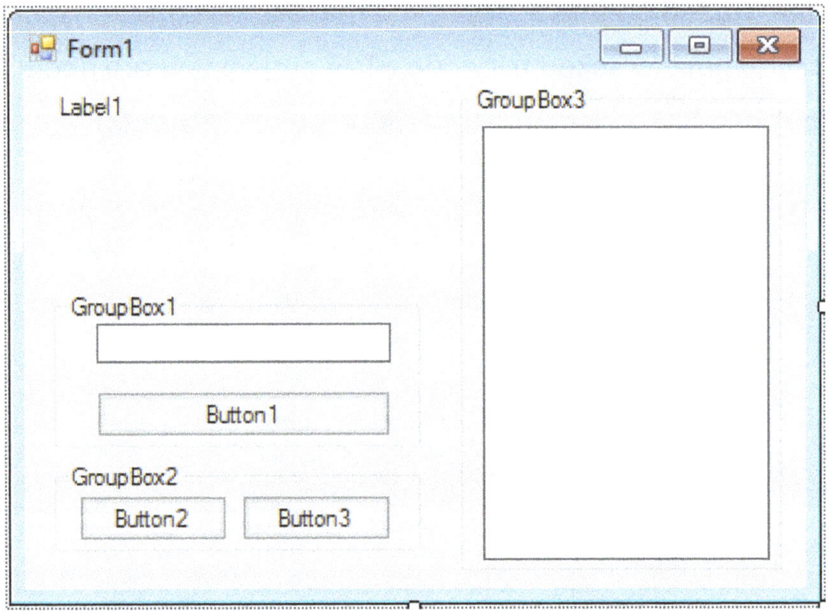

Set Control Properties

Set the control properties using the properties window:

Form1 Form:

Property Name	Property Value
Text	Decode
FormBorderStyle	FixedSingle
StartPosition	CenterScreen

Label1 Label:

Property Name	Property Value
Name	lblMessage
Text	[Blank]
TextAlign	MiddleCenter
BorderStyle	Fixed3D
BackColor	White
ForeColor	Blue
Font Size	12

GroupBox1 Group Box:

Property Name	Property Value
Name	grpGuess
BackColor	Red
Text	[Blank]
Visible	False

TextBox1 Text Box:

Property Name	Property Value
Name	txtGuess
TextAlign	Center
Font	Courier New
Font Size	16
MaxLength	4

Button1 Button:

Property Name	Property Value
Name	btnCheck
Text	Check Guess
Font	Arial
Font Size	12
BackColor	Light Yellow

GroupBox2 Group Box:

Property Name	Property Value
Name	grpChoice
Text	[Blank]
BackColor	Red

Button2 Button:

Property Name	Property Value
Name	btnNew
Text	New Game

Button3 Button:

Property Name	Property Value
Name	btnStop
Text	Stop
Enabled	False

GroupBox3 Group Box:

Property Name	Property Value
Name	grpGuesses
Text	Your Guesses
BackColor	Red
ForeColor	Yellow
Font Size	10
Font Style	Bold

TextBox2 Text Box:

Property Name	**Property Value**
Name	txtGuesses
Font	Courier New
Font Size	14
BackColor	White
MultiLine	True
ReadOnly	True
TabStop	False
ScrollBars	Vertical

When done setting properties, my form looks like this (I resized the text box under **Your Guesses** a bit):

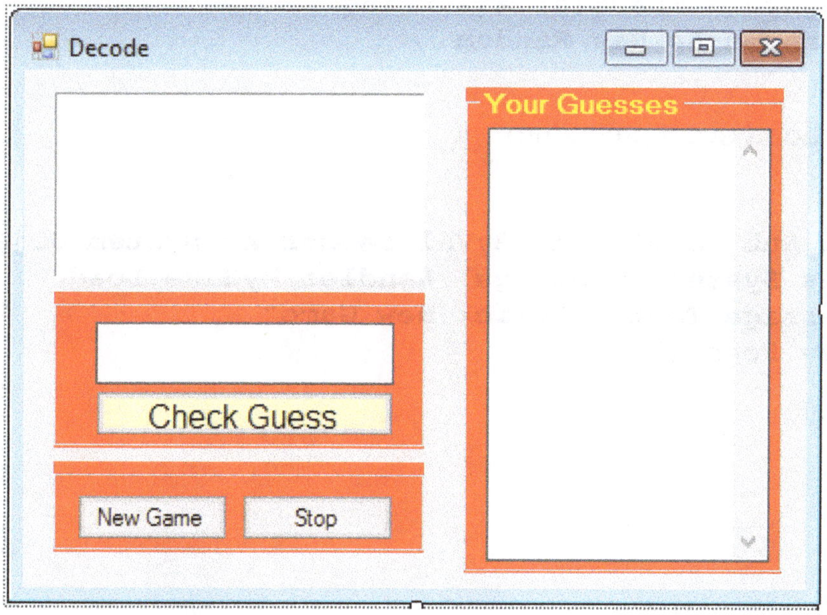

Write Event Procedures

Most of the code in this project is involved with generating a four-digit computer code (when you click **New Game**) and checking the guess you input (click **Check Guess**). The **Your Guesses** group box provides a history of each guess you made.

Add this code to the **general declarations** area:

```
Dim GameOver As Boolean
Dim MyGuess As String
Dim ComputerCode As String
Dim ComputerNumbers(4) As String
Dim MyRandom As New Random
```

The **Form1 Load** event procedure:

```
  Private Sub Form1_Load(ByVal sender As System.Object,
ByVal e As System.EventArgs) Handles MyBase.Load
    lblMessage.Text = "Click New Game"
    btnNew.Focus()
  End Sub
```

The **btnNew Click** event procedure:

```
  Private Sub BtnNew_Click(ByVal sender As System.Object,
ByVal e As System.EventArgs) Handles btnNew.Click
    Dim NArray(10) As String
    Dim T As Integer
    Dim I As Integer, J As Integer
    'Start new game
    btnStop.Enabled = True
    GameOver = False
    lblMessage.Text = ""
    txtGuesses.Text = ""
    txtGuess.Text = ""
    btnNew.Enabled = False
    'Choose code using modified version of card shuffling
routine
    'Order all digits initially
    ComputerCode = ""
    For I = 1 To 10 : NArray(I) = I - 1 : Next I
    'J is number of integers remaining
    For J = 10 To 7 Step -1
      I = MyRandom.Next(J) + 1
      ComputerNumbers(11 - J) = NArray(I)
      ComputerCode = ComputerCode & NArray(I)
      T = NArray(J)
      NArray(J) = NArray(I)
      NArray(I) = T
    Next J
    lblMessage.Text = "I have a 4 digit code." &
ControlChars.CrLf & "Try to guess it."
    grpGuess.Visible = True
    txtGuess.Focus()
  End Sub
```

The **btnStop Click** event procedure:

```
  Private Sub BtnStop_Click(ByVal sender As System.Object,
ByVal e As System.EventArgs) Handles btnStop.Click
    'Stop current game
    grpGuess.Visible = False
    btnNew.Enabled = True
    btnStop.Enabled = False
    If Not (GameOver) Then
      lblMessage.Text = "Game Stopped" & ControlChars.CrLf &
"My code was - " & ComputerCode
    End If
    btnNew.Focus()
  End Sub
```

The **txtGuess KeyPress** event procedure:

```
  Private Sub TxtGuess_KeyPress(ByVal sender As Object,
ByVal e As System.Windows.Forms.KeyPressEventArgs) Handles
txtGuess.KeyPress
    'Allow numbers only
    If e.KeyChar = ControlChars.Cr Then
      btnCheck.PerformClick()
    ElseIf (e.KeyChar >= "0" And e.KeyChar <= "9") Or
e.KeyChar = ControlChars.Back Then
      e.Handled = False
    Else
      e.Handled = True
    End If
  End Sub
```

The **btnCheck Click** event procedure:

```
  Private Sub BtnCheck_Click(ByVal sender As System.Object,
ByVal e As System.EventArgs) Handles btnCheck.Click
    Dim W As String
    Dim WNumbers(4) As String
    Dim I As Integer, J As Integer, K1 As Integer, K2 As
Integer
    Dim Distinct As Boolean
    'Check your guess
    W = txtGuess.Text
    'Check length validity
    If Len(W) <> 4 Then
      lblMessage.Text = "Guess must have 4 numbers ..." &
ControlChars.CrLf & "Try again!"
      txtGuess.Focus()
      Exit Sub
    Else
      'Get numbers and make sure they are distinct
      Distinct = True
      For I = 1 To 4
        WNumbers(I) = Mid(W, I, 1)
        If I <> 1 Then
          For J = I - 1 To 1 Step -1
            If WNumbers(I) = WNumbers(J) Then
              Distinct = False
            End If
          Next J
        End If
      Next I
      If Not (Distinct) Then
        lblMessage.Text = "Numbers must all be different
..." & ControlChars.CrLf & "Try again!"
        txtGuess.Focus()
        Exit Sub
      End If
      If W = ComputerCode Then
        lblMessage.Text = "Congratulations!" &
ControlChars.CrLf & "That's my code - " & ComputerCode
        GameOver = True
        btnStop.PerformClick()
        Exit Sub
      Else
        'Compute score
        K1 = 0
        K2 = 0
```

```
        For I = 1 To 4
          For J = 1 To 4
            If WNumbers(J) = ComputerNumbers(I) Then K1 = K1
+ 1
          Next J
          If WNumbers(I) = ComputerNumbers(I) Then K2 = K2 +
1
        Next I
        lblMessage.Text = "Your guess - " & W &
ControlChars.CrLf & Format(K1, "0") & " digit(s) correct" &
ControlChars.CrLf & Format(K2, "0") & " digit(s) in proper
place"
        txtGuesses.Text = W & "    " & Format(K1, "0") & "/"
& Format(K2, "0") & ControlChars.CrLf & txtGuesses.Text
        txtGuess.Text = ""
        txtGuess.Focus()
      End If
    End If
  End Sub
```

Run the Project

Save your work. Run the project. Click **New Game** to start. Type a guess for the four-digit code. Note the computer will not let you type an illegal guess (non-distinct, less than 4 digits). Click **Check Guess**. After each guess, the computer will tell you how many digits are correct and how many are in the correct location. For your reference, a history of your guesses is displayed under **Your Guesses**. The score is displayed as two numbers separated by a slash. The first number is the number of correct digits, the second the number in the correct location. Click **Stop** to stop guessing and see the computer's code. Here's a game I played:

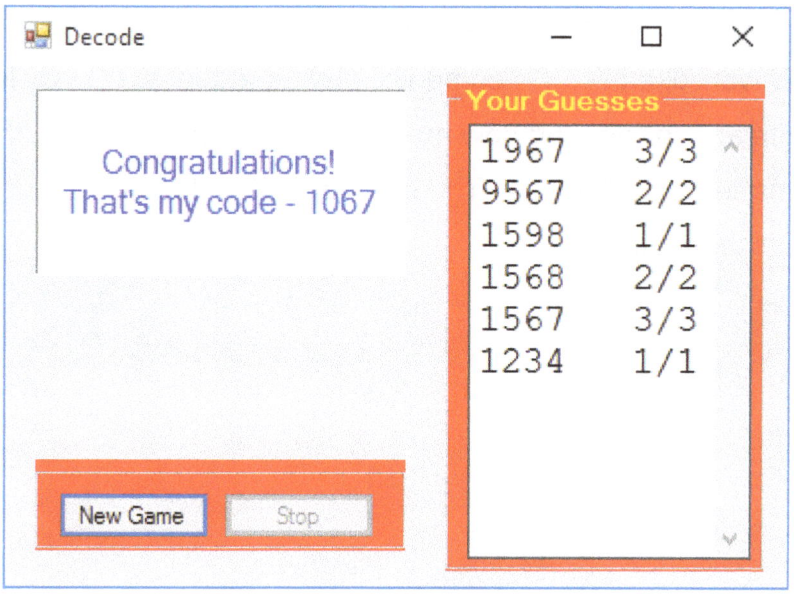

Other Things to Try

You can give this game a variable difficulty by allowing the user to choose how many digits are in the code, how many numbers are used to generate the code, and whether digits can repeat. See if you can code up and implement some of these options. The commercial version of this game (called MasterMind) uses colored pegs to set the code. This makes for a prettier game. See if you can code this variation.

Lastly, many mathematical papers have been written on developing a computer program that can decode the kinds of codes used here. Do you think you could write a computer program to determine a four digit code you make up? The program would work like this: (1) computer makes a guess, (2) you tell computer how many digits are correct and how many are in correct locations, then, (3) computer generates a new guess. The computer would continue guessing until it gave up or guessed your code.

Project 8 - Frown

Project Design

Frown is a fun two-player dice game you play against the computer. You play with a set of two dice that are normal except the side of the die where the "1" would be is replaced by a frowning face. The object of the game is to achieve a score of 100 points. Players alternate turns, which consist of a series of at least one roll of the dice, perhaps many, subject to the following rules.

As long as no frown appears on either die, the roller builds a running score for the current turn. After each roll with no frown, the player can choose to continue rolling or pass the dice to the other player. If the player passes the dice, the current score is added to any previous total. If a frown appears, the player loses the points gained on the current turn. If two frowns appear, the player loses the current points and all saved points! There is a considerable amount of luck involved. However, the skill of deciding when to pass the dice to your opponent also figures prominently. The project you are about to build is saved as **Frown** in the project folder (**\CBGVB\BVB Projects**).

Place Controls on Form

Start a new project in Visual Basic. There are lots of controls here. Place four group box controls on the form. Place four label controls in each of the first two group boxes. In the third group box, place a label, two picture box controls, and two buttons. Put two buttons in the last group box control. Finally, add a timer control and six small picture box controls to the form. Set **AutoSize** to **False** for each label to allow resizing. When done, your form should look something like this:

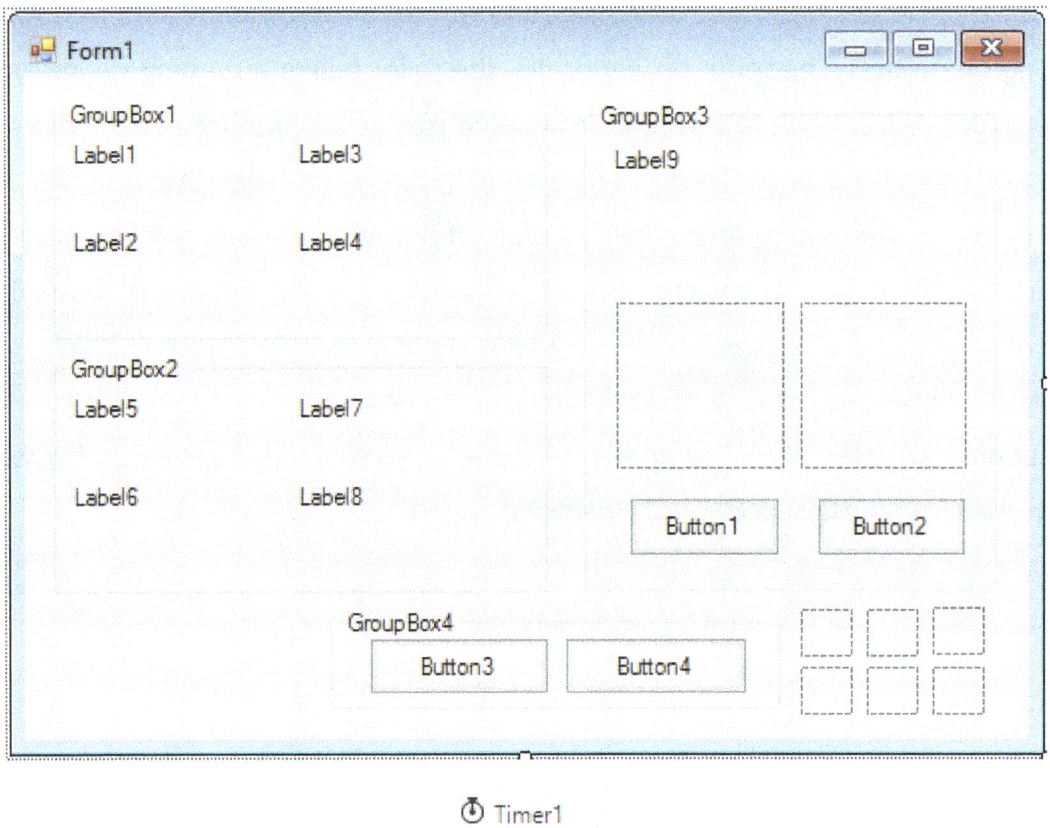

Set Control Properties

Set the control properties using the properties window:

Form1 Form:

Property Name	Property Value
Text	Frown
FormBorderStyle	FixedSingle
StartPosition	CenterScreen

GroupBox1 Group Box:

Property Name	Property Value
Name	grpYou
Text	You
BackColor	Blue
ForeColor	Yellow
Font Size	12
Font Style	Bold

Label1 Label:

Property Name	Property Value
Text	Score This Turn
TextAlign	MiddleLeft
ForeColor	White
Font Size	10

Label2 Label:

Property Name	Property Value
Text	Total Score
TextAlign	MiddleLeft
ForeColor	White
Font Size	10

Label3 Label:

Property Name	**Property Value**
Name	lblYouScore
Text	[Blank]
TextAlign	MiddleCenter
BorderStyle	Fixed3D
BackColor	White
ForeColor	Black
Font Size	12

Label4 Label:

Property Name	**Property Value**
Name	lblYouTotal
Text	0
TextAlign	MiddleCenter
BorderStyle	Fixed3D
BackColor	White
ForeColor	Black
Font Size	12

GroupBox2 Group Box:

Property Name	**Property Value**
Name	grpComputer
Text	Computer
BackColor	Blue
ForeColor	Yellow
Font Size	12
Font Style	Bold

Label5 Label:

Property Name	**Property Value**
Text	Score This Turn
TextAlign	MiddleLeft
ForeColor	White
Font Size	10

Label6 Label:

Property Name	**Property Value**
Text	Total Score
TextAlign	MiddleLeft
ForeColor	White
Font Size	10

Label7 Label:

Property Name	**Property Value**
Name	lblComputerScore
Text	[Blank]
TextAlign	MiddleCenter
BorderStyle	Fixed3D
BackColor	White
ForeColor	Black
Font Size	12

Label8 Label:

Property Name	**Property Value**
Name	lblComputerTotal
Text	0
TextAlign	MiddleCenter
BorderStyle	Fixed3D
BackColor	White
ForeColor	Black
Font Size	12

GroupBox3 Group Box:

Property Name	**Property Value**
Name	grpDice
Text	[Blank]
BackColor	Red

Label9 Label:

Property Name	Property Value
Name	lblMessage
Text	[Blank]
TextAlign	MiddleCenter
BorderStyle	Fixed3D
BackColor	Light Yellow
Font Size	10

PictureBox1 Picture Box:

Property Name	Property Value
Name	picDice1
BackColor	Green
SizeMode	StretchImage

PictureBox2 Picture Box:

Property Name	Property Value
Name	picDice2
BackColor	Green
SizeMode	StretchImage

Button1 Button:

Property Name	Property Value
Name	btnRoll
Text	Roll Dice
BackColor	Light Red
Enabled	False

Button2 Button:

Property Name	Property Value
Name	btnPass
Text	Pass Dice
BackColor	Light Red
Enabled	False

GroupBox4 Group Box:

Property Name	Property Value
Name	grpChoice
Text	[Blank]
BackColor	Yellow

Button3 Button:

Property Name	Property Value
Name	btnNew
Text	New Game

Button4 Button:

Property Name	Property Value
Name	btnStop
Text	Stop Game
Enabled	False

Timer1 Timer:

Property Name	Property Value
Name	timComputer
Interval	2000

PictureBox3 PictureBox:

Property Name	Property Value
Name	picDots1
Image	frown.gif (in the **\CBGVB\BVB Projects\Frown** folder)
SizeMode	StretchImage
Visible	False

PictureBox4 PictureBox:

Property Name	Property Value
Name	picDots2
Image	dice2.gif (in the **\CBGVB\BVB Projects\Frown** folder)
SizeMode	StretchImage
Visible	False

PictureBox5 PictureBox:

Property Name	Property Value
Name	picDots3
Image	dice3.gif (in the **\CBGVB\BVB Projects\Frown** folder)
SizeMode	StretchImage
Visible	False

PictureBox6 PictureBox:

Property Name	Property Value
Name	picDots4
Image	dice4.gif (in the **\CBGVB\BVB Projects\Frown** folder)
SizeMode	StretchImage
Visible	False

PictureBox7 PictureBox:

Property Name	Property Value
Name	picDots5
Image	dice5.gif (in the **\CBGVB\BVB Projects\Frown** folder)
SizeMode	StretchImage
Visible	False

PictureBox8 PictureBox:

Property Name	**Property Value**
Name	picDots6
Image	dice6.gif (in the **\CBGVB\BVB Projects\Frown** folder)
SizeMode	StretchImage
Visible	False

When done setting properties, my form looks like this:

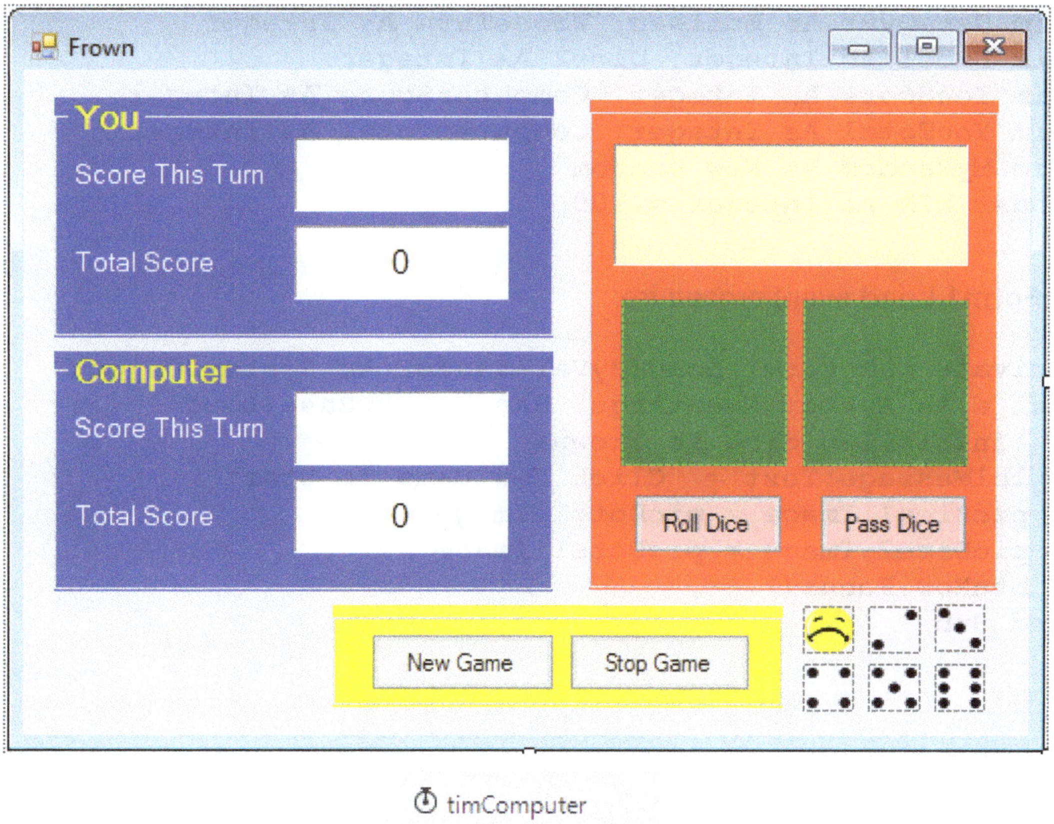

Write Event Procedures

Most of the code is involved with randomly rolling the two dice and passing control of the game from one player to the other. Study the logic carefully – it is used in many games where the human plays against the computer.

Add this code to the **general declarations** area:

```
Dim GameOver As Boolean, WhoseTurn As Integer
Dim Dice1 As Integer, Dice2 As Integer
Dim YouScore As Integer, ComputerScore As Integer
Dim YouTotal As Integer, ComputerTotal As Integer
Dim MyRandom As New Random
Const WIN As Integer = 100
```

The **Form1 Load** event procedure:

```
  Private Sub Form1_Load(ByVal sender As System.Object,
ByVal e As System.EventArgs) Handles MyBase.Load
    'Initialize dice to frowns
    lblMessage.Text = "Click New Game To Start"
    picDice1.Image = picDots1.Image
    picDice2.Image = picDots1.Image
    btnNew.Focus()
  End Sub
```

The **btnNew Click** event procedure:

```
  Private Sub BtnNew_Click(ByVal sender As System.Object,
ByVal e As System.EventArgs) Handles btnNew.Click
    'Start new game
    GameOver = False
    lblMessage.Text = ""
    btnNew.Enabled = False
    btnStop.Enabled = True
    YouScore = 0
    lblYouScore.Text = ""
    ComputerScore = 0
    lblComputerScore.Text = ""
    YouTotal = 0
    lblYouTotal.Text = "0"
    ComputerTotal = 0
    lblComputerTotal.Text = "0"
    If MyRandom.Next(100) < 50 Then
      'Computer goes first
      WhoseTurn = 0
      lblComputerScore.Text = "0"
      lblMessage.Text = "I'll roll first."
      'must call instead of performclick since button is not
      'enabeld
      Call BtnRoll_Click(Nothing, Nothing)
    Else
      'You go first
      WhoseTurn = 1
      lblYouScore.Text = "0"
      lblMessage.Text = "You roll first."
      btnRoll.Enabled = True
      btnRoll.Focus()
    End If
  End Sub
```

The **btnStop Click** event procedure:

```
  Private Sub BtnStop_Click(ByVal sender As System.Object,
ByVal e As System.EventArgs) Handles btnStop.Click
    'Stop current game
    timComputer.Enabled = False
    btnNew.Enabled = True
    btnStop.Enabled = False
    btnRoll.Enabled = False
    btnPass.Enabled = False
    If Not (GameOver) Then
      lblMessage.Text = "Game Stopped"
    End If
    btnNew.Focus()
  End Sub
```

The **btnRoll Click** event procedure:

```
  Private Sub BtnRoll_Click(ByVal sender As System.Object,
ByVal e As System.EventArgs) Handles btnRoll.Click
    'Dice rolling
    Dim Dice1 As Integer, Dice2 As Integer
    'Roll Dice 1 and set display
    Dice1 = MyRandom.Next(6) + 1
    Select Case Dice1
      Case 1
        picDice1.Image = picDots1.Image
      Case 2
        picDice1.Image = picDots2.Image
      Case 3
        picDice1.Image = picDots3.Image
      Case 4
        picDice1.Image = picDots4.Image
      Case 5
        picDice1.Image = picDots5.Image
      Case 6
        picDice1.Image = picDots6.Image
    End Select
    'Roll Dice 2 and set display
    Dice2 = MyRandom.Next(6) + 1
    Select Case Dice2
      Case 1
        picDice2.Image = picDots1.Image
      Case 2
        picDice2.Image = picDots2.Image
```

```
      Case 3
        picDice2.Image = picDots3.Image
      Case 4
        picDice2.Image = picDots4.Image
      Case 5
        picDice2.Image = picDots5.Image
      Case 6
        picDice2.Image = picDots6.Image
    End Select
    picDice1.Refresh()
    picDice2.Refresh()
    If WhoseTurn = 0 Then
      'Computer rolled
      If Dice1 > 1 And Dice2 > 1 Then
        'No frowns
        ComputerScore = ComputerScore + Dice1 + Dice2
        lblComputerScore.Text = Format(ComputerScore, "0")
        timComputer.Enabled = True
        lblMessage.Text = lblMessage.Text + " Let me think
..."
        Exit Sub
      ElseIf Dice1 = 1 And Dice2 = 1 Then
        'Two frowns - lose everything - must pass
        lblMessage.Text = lblMessage.Text +
ControlChars.CrLf + "I lost all my points!" +
ControlChars.CrLf + "Your turn."
        ComputerTotal = 0
        lblComputerTotal.Text = "0"
      Else
        'One frown - must pass
        lblMessage.Text = lblMessage.Text +
ControlChars.CrLf + "I lost my turn." + ControlChars.CrLf +
"Your turn."
      End If
      ComputerScore = 0
      lblComputerScore.Text = ""
      WhoseTurn = 1
      btnRoll.Enabled = True
      btnRoll.Focus()
    Else
      'You rolled
      lblMessage.Text = "Still your turn."
      btnPass.Enabled = True
      If Dice1 > 1 And Dice2 > 1 Then
        'No frowns
        YouScore = YouScore + Dice1 + Dice2
        lblYouScore.Text = Format(YouScore, "0")
```

```
      ElseIf Dice1 = 1 And Dice2 = 1 Then
        'Two frowns - lose everything - must pass
        YouScore = 0
        YouTotal = 0
        lblMessage.Text = "You lost everything." +
ControlChars.CrLf + "You must pass to me."
        btnRoll.Enabled = False
        btnPass.Focus()
      Else
        'One frown - must pass
        YouScore = 0
        lblMessage.Text = "You lost your turn." +
ControlChars.CrLf + "You must pass to me."
        btnRoll.Enabled = False
        btnPass.Focus()
      End If
    End If
  End Sub
```

The **btnPass Click** event procedure:

```
  Private Sub BtnPass_Click(ByVal sender As System.Object,
ByVal e As System.EventArgs) Handles btnPass.Click
    'You passed dice to computer
    btnRoll.Enabled = False
    btnPass.Enabled = False
    WhoseTurn = 0
    YouTotal = YouTotal + YouScore
    YouScore = 0
    lblYouScore.Text = ""
    lblYouTotal.Text = Format(YouTotal, "0")
    If YouTotal >= WIN Then
      GameOver = True
      lblMessage.Text = "You win!!"
      btnStop.PerformClick()
    Else
      lblMessage.Text = "I'll roll now."
      'call btnroll routine, we can't use performclick
method
      'since button is not enabled at this point
      Call BtnRoll_Click(Nothing, Nothing)
    End If
  End Sub
```

The **timComputer Timer** event procedure:

```
  Private Sub TimComputer_Tick(ByVal sender As
System.Object, ByVal e As System.EventArgs) Handles
timComputer.Tick
    Dim V As Integer
    Dim Odds As Single
    'Computer turn - decide wheter to roll again or pass
    timComputer.Enabled = False
    V = ComputerScore + ComputerTotal
    If V >= WIN Then
      'Computer wins!
      GameOver = True
      lblComputerTotal.Text = Format(V, "0")
      lblMessage.Text = "I win!!"
      btnStop.PerformClick()
      Exit Sub
    ElseIf WIN - YouTotal <= 10 Then
      'If you are close to win, computer rolls again
      lblMessage.Text = "I'll roll again."
      Call BtnRoll_Click(Nothing, Nothing)
    Else
      If ComputerTotal >= YouTotal Then
        'If computer already ahead, less likely to roll
again
        Odds = ComputerScore / 30
      ElseIf V < YouTotal Then
        'If computer behind, more likely
        Odds = ComputerScore / 50
      Else
        Odds = ComputerScore / 40
      End If
      If CSng(MyRandom.Next(100)/100) > Odds Then
        lblMessage.Text = "I'll roll again."
        Call BtnRoll_Click(Nothing, Nothing)
```

```
      Else
        'Stick with roll and pass
        lblMessage.Text = "I pass to you." +
ControlChars.CrLf + "Your turn."
        ComputerScore = 0
        ComputerTotal = V
        lblComputerTotal.Text = Format(ComputerTotal, "0")
        lblComputerScore.Text = ""
        WhoseTurn = 1
        btnRoll.Enabled = True
        btnRoll.Focus()
      End If
    End If
  End Sub
```

Run the Project

Save your work. Run the project. You should figure out the game fairly quickly. The computer will decide who goes first. When its your turn, click 'Roll Dice'. After each roll, decide whether to roll again or pass the dice to the computer (click 'Pass Dice'). If you get a frown on any roll, your score will be adjusted accordingly and the dice passed to the computer. When it's the computer's turn, you will watch the computer roll and make its decisions using the same rules. The game is over when either you or the computer has a Total Score of at least 100 points. Click **Stop** at any time to stop the game before its end. Here's the middle of a game I played:

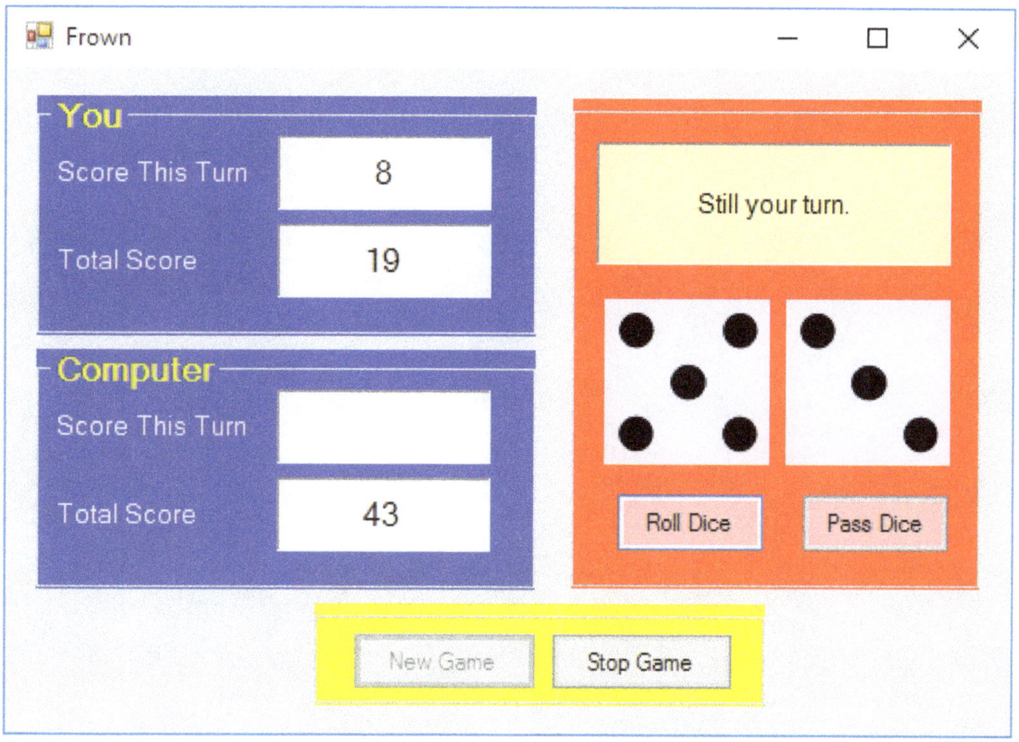

Other Things to Try

A first change to Frown would be to make it a two player game - eliminate the computer and play against a friend. You essentially need to have two group boxes and code like that for the human player. You might also like to have an adjustable winning score.

The computer logic used by the program is fairly simple – when it is far behind it tends to take more risks. This logic is in the **timComputer Tick** event procedure. Study the logic and see if you can improve upon it. Have your computer play someone else's computer.

Project 9 - Loan Calculator

Project Design

Do you want to know how much that new car will cost each month or how long it will take to pay off a credit card? This program will do the job. You enter a loan amount, a yearly interest, and a number of months, and the project computes your monthly payment. All entries will be in text boxes and a command button will initiate the payment calculation. The project you are about to build is saved as **Loan** in the project folder (**\CBGVB\BVB Projects**).

Place Controls on Form

Start a new project in Visual Basic. Place four label controls and four text boxes on the form. Then place a button on the form. When done, your form should look something like this:

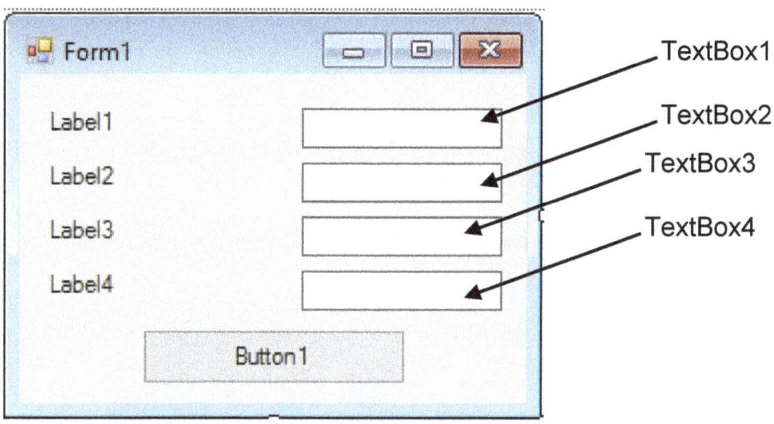

Set Control Properties

Set the control properties using the properties window:

Form1 Form:

Property Name	**Property Value**
Text	Loan Calculator
FormBorderStyle	FixedSingle
StartPosition	CenterScreen

Label1 Label:

Property Name	**Property Value**
Text	Loan Amount

Label2 Label:

Property Name	**Property Value**
Text	Yearly Interest

Label3 Label:

Property Name	**Property Value**
Text	Number of Months

Label4 Label:

Property Name	**Property Value**
Text	Monthly Payment

TextBox1 Text Box:

Property Name	Property Value
Name	txtLoan
Text	0
TextAlign	Right

TextBox2 Text Box:

Property Name	Property Value
Name	txtInterest
Text	0
TextAlign	Right

TextBox3 Text Box:

Property Name	Property Value
Name	txtMonths
Text	0
TextAlign	Right

TextBox4 Text Box:

Property Name	Property Value
Name	txtPayment
Text	0
TextAlign	Right
BackColor	White
ReadOnly	True
TabStop	False

Button1 Button:

Property Name	Property Value
Name	btnCompute
Text	Compute Payment

When done setting properties, my form looks like this:

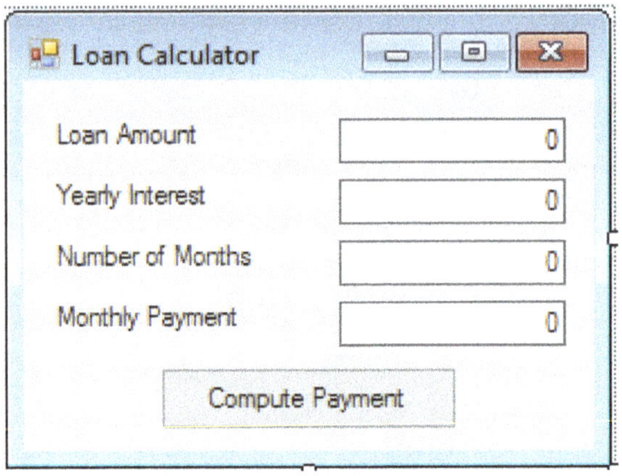

Write Event Procedures

Only one event is needed here - the **Click** event for **btnCompute**. Fill in values in the Loan Amount, Yearly Interest, and Number of Months text boxes, then click **Compute Payment**. The values are read and the payment is computed and displayed.

The **btnCompute Click** event procedure:

```
  Private Sub BtnCompute_Click(ByVal sender As
System.Object, ByVal e As System.EventArgs) Handles
btnCompute.Click
    Dim Loan As Single
    Dim Interest As Single
    Dim Months As Integer
    Dim Payment As Single
    Dim Multiplier As Single
    'Read text boxes
    Loan = Val(txtLoan.Text)
    Interest = Val(txtInterest.Text)
    Months = Val(txtMonths.Text)
    'Compute interest multiplier
    Multiplier = (1 + Interest / 1200) ^ Months
    'Compute payment
    Payment = Loan * Interest * Multiplier / (1200 *
(Multiplier - 1))
    txtPayment.Text = "$" & Format(Payment, "0.00")
  End Sub
```

Run the Project

Save your work. Run the project. Fill in a loan amount, an interest, and a number of months. Click **Compute Payment** to determine and display the monthly payment. Try a loan amount of $5,000 (don't type in the comma), an interest rate of 18%, and 24 months. Your payment should be $249.62:

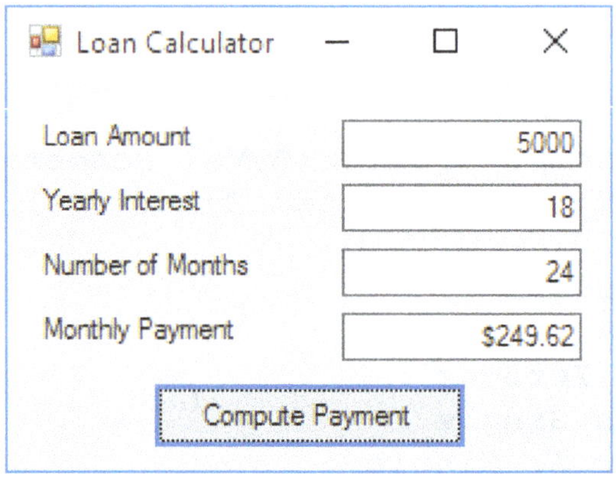

What can you do with this? Well, you can find monthly payments like we just did. Or, try this. Say you have a credit card balance of $2,000. The interest rate is 15% and you can make $100 payments each month. Put the 2000 in the loan amount box, the 15 in the interest. Then, try different numbers of months until the computed payment is close to $100. This will tell you how many months it will take you to pay off the credit card. I got 23 months with payments of $100.59 each month.

Other Things to Try

If you are going to let others use this program, it needs some improvements. Review the key trapping procedures discussed in Class 10 and make sure users can only type numbers, a decimal point, and a backspace key when using the text boxes for inputs. You need some logic to make sure the user has typed values in all three text boxes (Loan Amount, Yearly Interest, Number of Months). Also, what if the interest rate is zero (a very nice bank!)? The program won't work (try it). You'll need a way to compute payments with zero interest.

Project 10 - Checkbook Balancer

Project Design

This project will help you do that dreaded monthly task of balancing your checkbook. By entering requested information, you can find out just how much money you really have in your account. The project you are about to build is saved as **Checkbook** in the project folder (**\CBGVB\BVB Projects**).

Place Controls on Form

Start a new project in Visual Basic. Place three label controls (on one, set **AutoSize** to **False** and make it tall and skinny to use as a dividing line), eight text boxes, and eight buttons on the form. When done, your form should look something like this:

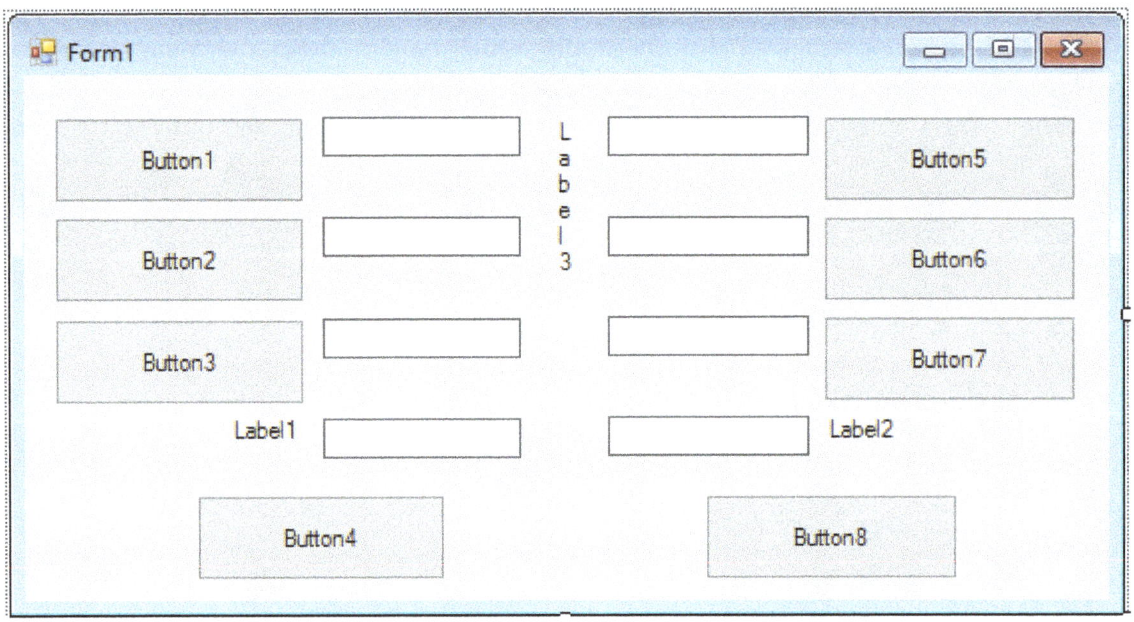

Set Control Properties

Set the control properties using the properties window:

Form1 Form:

Property Name	**Property Value**
Text	Checkbook Balancer
FormBorderStyle	FixedSingle
StartPosition	CenterScreen

Label1 Label:

Property Name	**Property Value**
AutoSize	False
Text	Adjusted Statement Balance
TextAlign	TopRight

Label2 Label:

Property Name	**Property Value**
AutoSize	False
Text	Adjusted Checkbook Balance

Label3 Label:

Property Name	**Property Value**
AutoSize	False
BackColor	Black
Text	[Blank it out]

TextBox1 Text Box:

Property Name	**Property Value**
Name	txtStmtBalance
Text	0
TextAlign	Right

TextBox2 Text Box:

Property Name	**Property Value**
Name	txtStmtDeposit
Text	0
TextAlign	Right
BackColor	White
ReadOnly	True
TabStop	False

TextBox3 Text Box:

Property Name	**Property Value**
Name	txtStmtCheck
Text	0
TextAlign	Right
BackColor	White
ReadOnly	True
TabStop	False

TextBox4 Text Box:

Property Name	**Property Value**
Name	txtAdjStmtBalance
Text	0
TextAlign	Right
BackColor	White
ReadOnly	True
TabStop	False

TextBox5 Text Box:

Property Name	**Property Value**
Name	txtChkBalance
Text	0
TextAlign	Right

TextBox6 Text Box:

Property Name	**Property Value**
Name	txtChkDeposit
Text	0
TextAlign	Right
BackColor	White
ReadOnly	True
TabStop	False

TextBox7 Text Box:

Property Name	**Property Value**
Name	txtChkCharge
Text	0
TextAlign	Right
BackColor	White
ReadOnly	True
TabStop	False

TextBox8 Text Box:

Property Name	**Property Value**
Name	txtAdjChkBalance
Text	0
TextAlign	Right
BackColor	White
ReadOnly	True
TabStop	False

Button1 Button:

Property Name	**Property Value**
Name	btnStmtBalance
Text	Enter Statement Balance

Button2 Button:

Property Name	**Property Value**
Name	btnStmtDeposit
Text	Add Uncredited Deposit
Enabled	False

Button3 Button:

Property Name	Property Value
Name	btnStmtCheck
Text	Subtract Outstanding Check
Enabled	False

Button4 Button:

Property Name	Property Value
Name	btnStmtReset
Text	Reset Statement Values

Button5 Button:

Property Name	Property Value
Name	btnChkBalance
Text	Enter Checkbook Balance

Button6 Button:

Property Name	Property Value
Name	btnChkDeposit
Text	Add Unrecorded Deposit
Enabled	False

Button7 Button:

Property Name	Property Value
Name	btnChkCharge
Text	Subtract Service Charge
Enabled	False

Button8 Button:

Property Name	Property Value
Name	btnChkReset
Text	Reset Checkbook Values

When done setting properties, my form looks like:

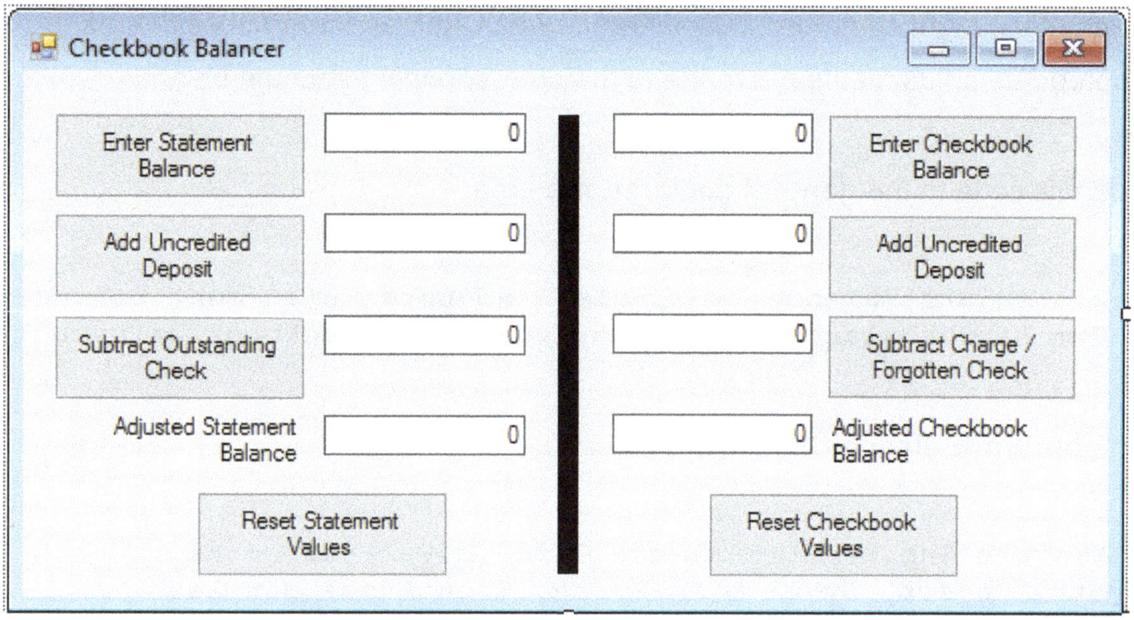

Write Event Procedures

Each of the eight command buttons requires a **Click** event. With each click, appropriate adjustments are made to the corresponding account balance.

Add this code to the **general declarations** area:

```
  Dim AdjStmtBalance As Single ' adjusted statement balance
  Dim AdjChkBalance As Single 'adjusted checkbook balance
```

The **btnStmtBalance Click** event procedure:

```
  Private Sub BtnStmtBalance_Click(ByVal sender As
System.Object, ByVal e As System.EventArgs) Handles
btnStmtBalance.Click
    'Read entered statement balance
    AdjStmtBalance = Val(txtStmtBalance.Text)
    'Disable balance, enable deposit and check
    btnStmtBalance.Enabled = False
    btnStmtDeposit.Enabled = True
    btnStmtCheck.Enabled = True
    txtStmtBalance.ReadOnly = True
    txtStmtDeposit.ReadOnly = False
    txtStmtCheck.ReadOnly = False
    btnStmtDeposit.Focus()
  End Sub
```

The **btnStmtDeposit_Click** event procedure:

```
  Private Sub BtnStmtDeposit_Click(ByVal sender As
System.Object, ByVal e As System.EventArgs) Handles
btnStmtDeposit.Click
    'Account for uncredited deposit
    AdjStmtBalance = AdjStmtBalance +
Val(txtStmtDeposit.Text)
    txtAdjStmtBalance.Text = "$" & Format(AdjStmtBalance,
"0.00")
  End Sub
```

The **btnStmtCheck Click** event procedure:

```
  Private Sub BtnStmtCheck_Click(ByVal sender As
System.Object, ByVal e As System.EventArgs) Handles
btnStmtCheck.Click
    'Account for outstanding check
    AdjStmtBalance = AdjStmtBalance - Val(txtStmtCheck.Text)
    txtAdjStmtBalance.Text = "$" & Format(AdjStmtBalance,
"0.00")
  End Sub
```

The **btnStmtReset Click** event procedure:

```
  Private Sub BtnStmtReset_Click(ByVal sender As
System.Object, ByVal e As System.EventArgs) Handles
btnStmtReset.Click
    'Reset statement values to defaults
    AdjStmtBalance = 0
    txtStmtBalance.Text = "0"
    txtStmtDeposit.Text = "0"
    txtStmtCheck.Text = "0"
    txtAdjStmtBalance.Text = "0"
    btnStmtBalance.Enabled = True
    btnStmtDeposit.Enabled = False
    btnStmtCheck.Enabled = False
    txtStmtBalance.ReadOnly = False
    txtStmtDeposit.ReadOnly = True
    txtStmtCheck.ReadOnly = True
    btnStmtBalance.Focus()
  End Sub
```

The **btnChkBalance Click** event procedure:

```
  Private Sub BtnChkBalance_Click(ByVal sender As
System.Object, ByVal e As System.EventArgs) Handles
btnChkBalance.Click
    'Read entered checkbook balance
    AdjChkBalance = Val(txtChkBalance.Text)
    'Disable balance, enabled deposit and charge
    btnChkBalance.Enabled = False
    btnChkDeposit.Enabled = True
    btnChkCharge.Enabled = True
    txtChkBalance.ReadOnly = True
    txtChkDeposit.ReadOnly = False
    txtChkCharge.readonly = False
    btnChkDeposit.Focus()
  End Sub
```

The **btnChkDeposit Click** event procedure:

```
  Private Sub BtnChkDeposit_Click(ByVal sender As
System.Object, ByVal e As System.EventArgs) Handles
btnChkDeposit.Click
    'Account for unrecorded deposit
    AdjChkBalance = AdjChkBalance + Val(txtChkDeposit.Text)
    txtAdjChkBalance.Text = "$" & Format(AdjChkBalance,
"0.00")
  End Sub
```

The **btnChkCharge Click** event procedure:

```
  Private Sub BtnChkCharge_Click(ByVal sender As
System.Object, ByVal e As System.EventArgs) Handles
btnChkCharge.Click
    'Account for service charge
    AdjChkBalance = AdjChkBalance - Val(txtChkCharge.Text)
    txtAdjChkBalance.Text = "$" & Format(AdjChkBalance,
"0.00")
  End Sub
```

The **btnChkReset Click** event procedure:

```
  Private Sub BtnChkReset_Click(ByVal sender As
System.Object, ByVal e As System.EventArgs) Handles
btnChkReset.Click
    'Reset all checkbook values to defaults
    AdjChkBalance = 0
    txtChkBalance.Text = "0"
    txtChkDeposit.Text = "0"
    txtChkCharge.Text = "0"
    txtAdjChkBalance.Text = "0"
    btnChkBalance.Enabled = True
    btnChkDeposit.Enabled = False
    btnChkCharge.Enabled = False
    txtChkBalance.ReadOnly = False
    txtChkDeposit.ReadOnly = True
    txtChkCharge.ReadOnly = True
    btnChkBalance.Focus()
  End Sub
```

Run the Project

Save your work. Run the project. Try balancing your latest bank statement with your checkbook - here's the procedure. Start on the left side of the form. Fill in your statement balance and click **Enter Statement Balance**. Next, enter each deposit you have made that is not recorded on the bank statement. After each entry, click **Add Uncredited Deposit**. Next, enter each check you have written that is not listed on the statement. After each check, click **Subtract Outstanding Check**. When done, your **Adjusted Statement Balance** is shown. Clicking **Reset Statement Values** will set everything on the left side back to default values.

Now to the right side of the form. Fill in your checkbook balance and click **Enter Checkbook Balance**. Next, enter each deposit shown on your bank statement that you forgot to enter in your checkbook. After each entry, click **Add Unrecorded Deposit**. Next, enter any service charge the bank may have charged or any check you that you haven't recorded in your checkbook. After each charge, click **Subtract Charge / Forgotten Check**. When done, your **Adjusted Checkbook Balance** is shown. Clicking **Reset Checkbook Values** will set everything on the left side back to default values.

At this point, the adjusted balances at the bottom of the form should be the same. If not, you need to dig deeper into your checks, deposits, and service charges to see what's missing or perhaps accounted for more than once. Here's a run on my account – what do you know? It balanced!!

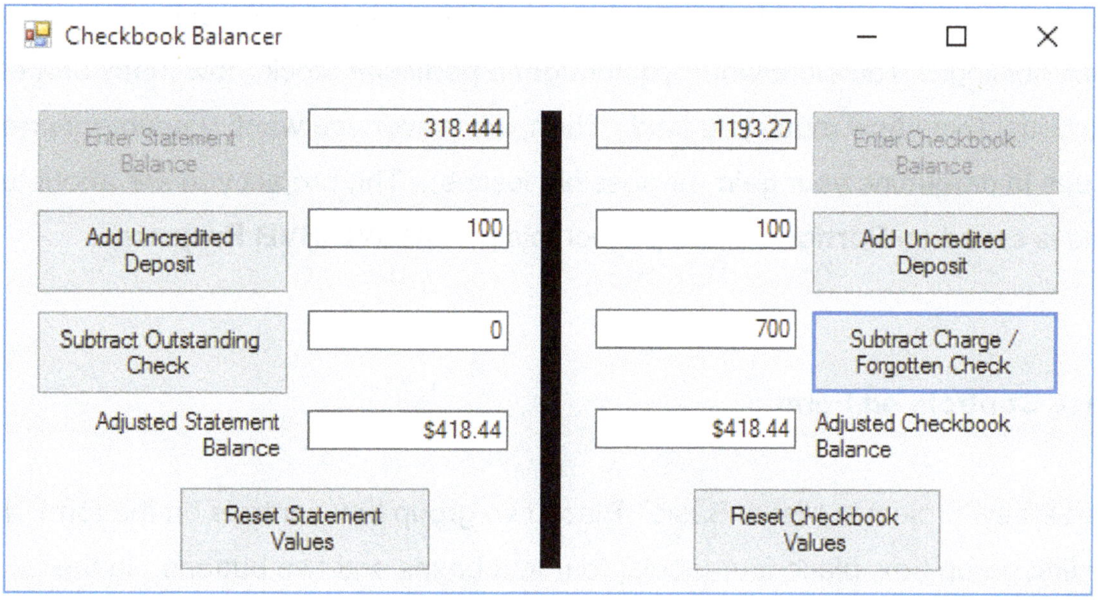

Other Things to Try

An interesting and useful modification to this project requires learning about a new control - the **Combo Box**. In this control, you can build up a list of entered information and edit it as you see fit. It would be useful to use combo boxes to store up the uncredited and unrecorded deposits, the outstanding checks, and any service charges. With complete lists, you could edit them as you see fit. This would make the checkbook balancing act an easier task. In time, you can even learn to add printing options to the project.

Project 11– Portfolio Manager

Project Design

In this project, we will build a tool that lets you determine the current value of your stock holdings. You store when you bought a particular stock, how many shares you bought and how much you paid. Then, whenever you want, you enter current values to determine your gain (or possible losses). The project you are about to build is saved as **Portfolio** in the project folder (**\CBGVB\BVB Projects**).

Place Controls on Form

Start a new project in Visual Basic. Place two group box controls on the form. In the first group box, place four labels, four text boxes and two buttons. In the second group box, place four labels, four text box controls and a button. When done, your form should look something like this:

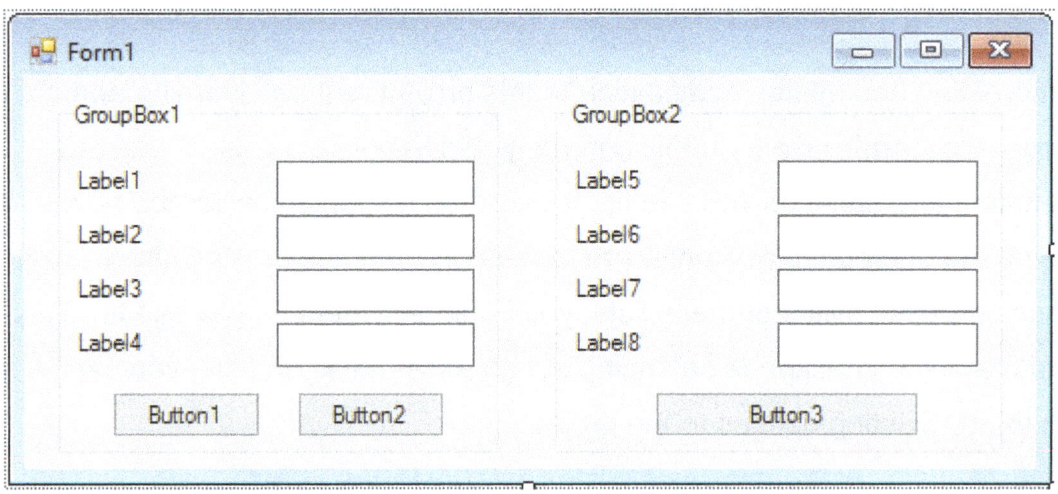

Set Control Properties

Set the control properties using the properties window:

Form1 Form:

Property Name	**Property Value**
Text	Portfolio Manager
FormBorderStyle	FixedSingle
StartPosition	CenterScreen

GroupBox1 Group Box:

Property Name	**Property Value**
Name	grpStock
Text	This Stock
Font Size	12
Font Style	Bold

Label1 Label:

Property Name	**Property Value**
Text	Date Purchased
Font Size	8
Font Style	Regular

Label2 Label:

Property Name	**Property Value**
Text	Price/Share
Font Size	8
Font Style	Regular

Label3 Label:

Property Name	Property Value
Text	Number of Shares
Font Size	8
Font Style	Regular

Label4 Label:

Property Name	Property Value
Text	Price Paid
Font Size	8
Font Style	Regular

TextBox1 Text Box:

Property Name	Property Value
Name	txtDate
TextAlign	Right
BackColor	White
Font Size	10
Font Style	Regular
ReadOnly	True
TabStop	False

TextBox2 Text Box:

Property Name	Property Value
Name	txtPrice
TextAlign	Right
BackColor	White
Font Size	10
Font Style	Regular
ReadOnly	True
TabStop	False

TextBox3 Text Box:

Property Name	Property Value
Name	txtShares
TextAlign	Right
BackColor	White
Font Size	10
Font Style	Regular
ReadOnly	True
TabStop	False

TextBox4 Text Box:

Property Name	Property Value
Name	txtPaid
TextAlign	Right
BackColor	White
Font Size	10
Font Style	Regular
ReadOnly	True
TabStop	False

Button1 Button:

Property Name	Property Value
Name	btnPrevious
Text	Previous
Font Size	8
Font Style	Regular

Button2 Button:

Property Name	Property Value
Name	btnNext
Text	Next
Font Size	8
Font Style	Regular

GroupBox2 Group Box:

Property Name	Property Value
Name	grpValue
Text	Current Value
Font Size	12
FontBold	True

Label5 Label:

Property Name	Property Value
Text	Today's Date
Font Size	8
Font Style	Regular

Label6 Label:

Property Name	Property Value
Text	Today's Price
Font Size	8
Font Style	Regular

Label7 Label:

Property Name	Property Value
Text	Yearly Return
Font Size	8
Font Style	Regular

Label8 Label:

Property Name	Property Value
Text	Today's Value
Font Size	8
Font Style	Regular

TextBox1 Text Box:

Property Name	Property Value
Name	txtTodayDate
TextAlign	Right
BackColor	White
Font Size	10
Font Style	Regular
ReadOnly	True
TabStop	False

TextBox2 Text Box:

Property Name	Property Value
Name	txtToday
TextAlign	Right
Font Size	10
Font Style	Regular

TextBox3 Text Box:

Property Name	Property Value
Name	txtReturn
TextAlign	Right
BackColor	White
Font Size	10
Font Style	Regular
ReadOnly	True
TabStop	False

TextBox4 Text Box:

Property Name	Property Value
Name	txtValue
TextAlign	Right
BackColor	White
Font Size	10
Font Style	Regular
ReadOnly	True
TabStop	False

Button3 Button:

Property Name	Property Value
Name	btnReturn
Text	Compute Return

When done setting properties, my form looks like this:

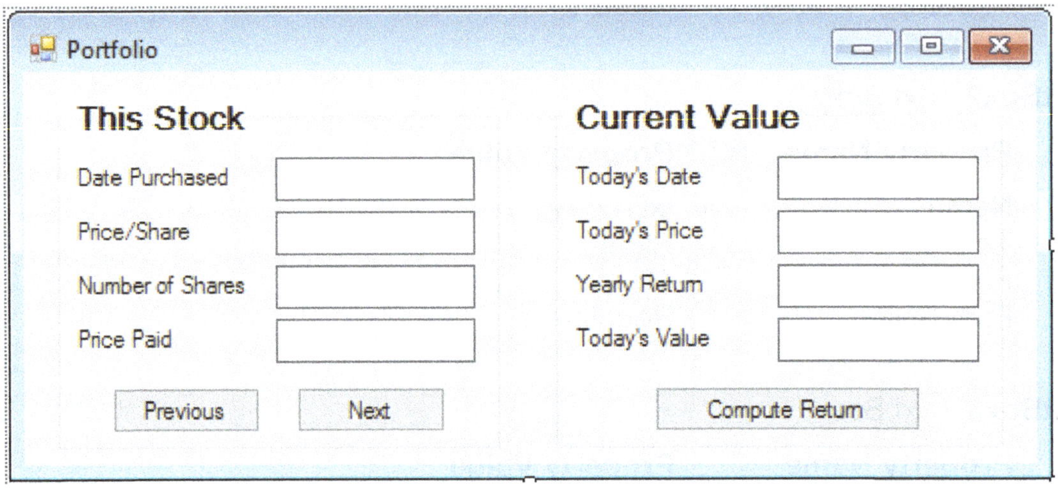

Write Event Procedures

In this program, you need to store information about your stocks (date purchased, purchase price and shares owned) in data arrays (the form **Load** procedure). Then, you use the **Previous** and **Next** buttons to view each stock. For the displayed stock, if you type in the current price (**Today's Price**) and click **Compute Return**, you will be shown the current value and yearly return for that stock.

In this project, we introduce an idea that's used all the time in computer programming. Whenever, there is a certain segment of code that needs to be repeated and used in various parts of a project, we put the corresponding code in something called a **general procedure**. This saves us from having to repeat code in different locations – a maintenance headache. A general procedure is identical in use to an event procedure, with the only difference being it is not invoked by some control event. We control invocation of a general procedure by **calling** it. In this project, we will use a general procedure to display the stock information after pressing the **Previous** or **Next** button. Look for the code (procedure is named **ShowStock**) and see how easy it is to use.

Add this code to the **general declarations** area:

```
Dim NumberStocks As Integer
Dim CurrentStock As Integer
Dim StockDate(25) As Date
Dim StockName(25) As String
Dim StockPrice(25) As Double
Dim StockShares(25) As Integer
```

The **Form1 Load** event procedure:

```
  Private Sub Form1_Load(ByVal sender As System.Object,
ByVal e As System.EventArgs) Handles MyBase.Load
    'Load Stock Information
    NumberStocks = 5
    StockDate(1) = "02/01/1999" : StockName(1) = "Big Deal"
    StockPrice(1) = 10 : StockShares(1) = 100
    StockDate(2) = "03/01/1999" : StockName(2) = "Web
Winner"
    StockPrice(2) = 20 : StockShares(2) = 300
    StockDate(3) = "04/01/1999" : StockName(3) = "Little
Blue"
    StockPrice(3) = 15 : StockShares(3) = 200
    StockDate(4) = "05/01/1999" : StockName(4) = "My
Company"
    StockPrice(4) = 40 : StockShares(4) = 400
    StockDate(5) = "05/01/2000" : StockName(5) = "Your
Company"
    StockPrice(5) = 30 : StockShares(5) = 200
    txtTodayDate.Text = Format(Today, "MM/dd/yyyy")
    CurrentStock = 1
    Me.Show()
    Call ShowStock()
  End Sub
```

The **btnPrevious Click** event procedure:

```
  Private Sub BtnPrevious_Click(ByVal sender As
System.Object, ByVal e As System.EventArgs) Handles
btnPrevious.Click
    'display previous stock
    If CurrentStock <> 1 Then
      CurrentStock = CurrentStock - 1
      Call ShowStock()
    End If
  End Sub
```

The **btnNext Click** event procedure:

```
  Private Sub BtnNext_Click(ByVal sender As System.Object,
ByVal e As System.EventArgs) Handles btnNext.Click
    'display next stock
    If CurrentStock <> NumberStocks Then
      CurrentStock = CurrentStock + 1
      Call ShowStock()
    End If
  End Sub
```

Next, we give the code for the **general procedure** called **ShowStock**. To type this in the code window, go to any line after an existing **End Sub** line. Type the first line of the procedure:

```
  Private Sub ShowStock
```

Then, press **<Enter>**. The following 'empty' procedure appears:

```
  Private Sub ShowStock()
                          ← Type code here
  End Sub
```

Type the code between the header you typed and this final line. The complete procedure is:

```
  Private Sub ShowStock()
    'Change displayed stock
    grpStock.Text = StockName(CurrentStock)
    txtDate.Text = StockDate(CurrentStock)
    txtPrice.Text = StockPrice(CurrentStock)
    txtShares.Text = StockShares(CurrentStock)
    txtPaid.Text = Format(StockPrice(CurrentStock) *
StockShares(CurrentStock), "0.00")
    'Allow computation of return
    txtToday.Text = ""
    txtValue.Text = "0.00"
    txtReturn.Text = "0.00%"
    txtToday.Focus()
  End Sub
```

The **txtToday KeyPress** event procedure:

```
  Private Sub TxtToday_KeyPress(ByVal sender As Object,
ByVal e As System.Windows.Forms.KeyPressEventArgs) Handles
txtToday.KeyPress
    'Only allow numbers,decimal backspace
    If e.KeyChar = ControlChars.Cr Then
    'If Return key pressed, then click the compute button
      btnReturn.PerformClick()
    ElseIf (e.KeyChar >= "0" And e.KeyChar <= "9") Or
e.KeyChar = "." Or e.KeyChar = ControlChars.Back Then
      e.Handled = False
    Else
      e.Handled = True
    End If
  End Sub
```

The **btnReturn Click** event procedure:

```
  Private Sub BtnReturn_Click(ByVal sender As System.Object,
ByVal e As System.EventArgs) Handles btnReturn.Click
    'compute todays value and percent return
    Dim P As Double, V As Double, R As Double
    P = Val(txtToday.Text)
    V = P * StockShares(CurrentStock)
    txtValue.Text = Format(V, "0.00")
    'Daily increase
    R = (V / Val(txtPaid.Text) - 1) /
DateDiff(DateInterval.Day, StockDate(CurrentStock), Today)
    'Yearly return
    R = 100 * (365 * R)
    txtReturn.Text = Format(R, "0.00") & "%"
  End Sub
```

Run the Project

Save your work. Run the project. Click the **Previous** and **Next** buttons to view the five stocks stored in the program (you can edit this information in the **Form1 Load** procedure to reflect your holdings). Make sure you understand the use of the general procedure (**ShowStock**). For a particular stock, type the current selling price in the displayed text box and click **Compute Return**. The yearly return percentage and current value of that particular stock to your portfolio is displayed. Here's a run I made:

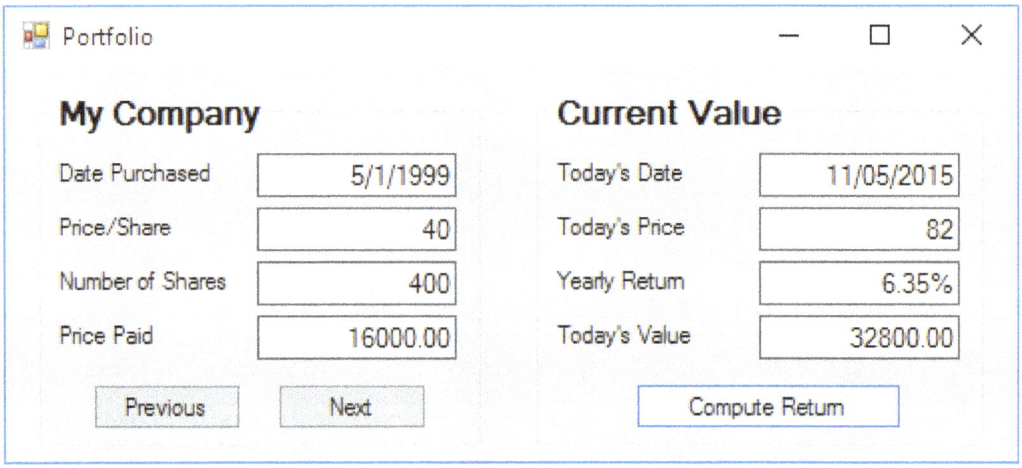

Other Things to Try

It's a hassle to have to store your holdings in the various arrays. You have to change the code every time you buy new stock or sell old stock. It would be nice to be able to save your holding information on a disk file. Then, it could be read in each time you run the program and any changes saved back to disk. With such saving capabilities, you could also modify the program to allow changing the number of shares you hold of a particular stock, allow addition of new stocks and deletion of old stocks. Accessing files on disk is an advanced topic you might like to study.

As written, the program gives returns on individual stocks. Try to write a summary function that computes the overall return on all the stocks in your current portfolio. I'm sure you can think of other changes to this program. Try them out.

Project 12 - Bonus Project - Pong!

In the early 1970's, while Bill Gates and Paul Allen were still in high school, a man named Nolan Bushnell began the video game revolution. He invented a very simple game - a computer version of Ping Pong. There were two paddles, one on each side of the screen. Players then bounced the ball back and forth. If you missed the ball, the other player got a point.

This first game was called Pong. And, Nolan Bushnell was the founder of Atari - the biggest video game maker for many years. (Nolan Bushnell also founded Chucky Cheese's Pizza Parlors, but that's another story!) In this bonus project, I give you my version of Pong written with Visual Basic. I don't expect you to build this project, but you can if you want. Just load the project (named **Pong**) and run it. Skim through the BASIC code - you should be able to understand a lot of it. The idea of giving you this project is to let you see what can be done with Visual Basic.

In this version of Pong, a ball moves from one end of a panel to the other, bouncing off side walls. Players try to deflect the ball at each end using a controllable paddle. In my simple game, the left paddle is controlled with the A and Z keys on the keyboard, while the right paddle is controlled with the K and M keys (detected using KeyPress events). My solution freely borrows code and techniques from several reference sources. The project relies heavily on lots of coding techniques you haven't seen. You will learn about these as you progress in your Visual Basic studies.

Start Visual Basic. Open the project named **Pong** in the project folder (**\CBGVB\BVB Projects**). Look at the form. Here's what my finished form looks like (with control names identified):

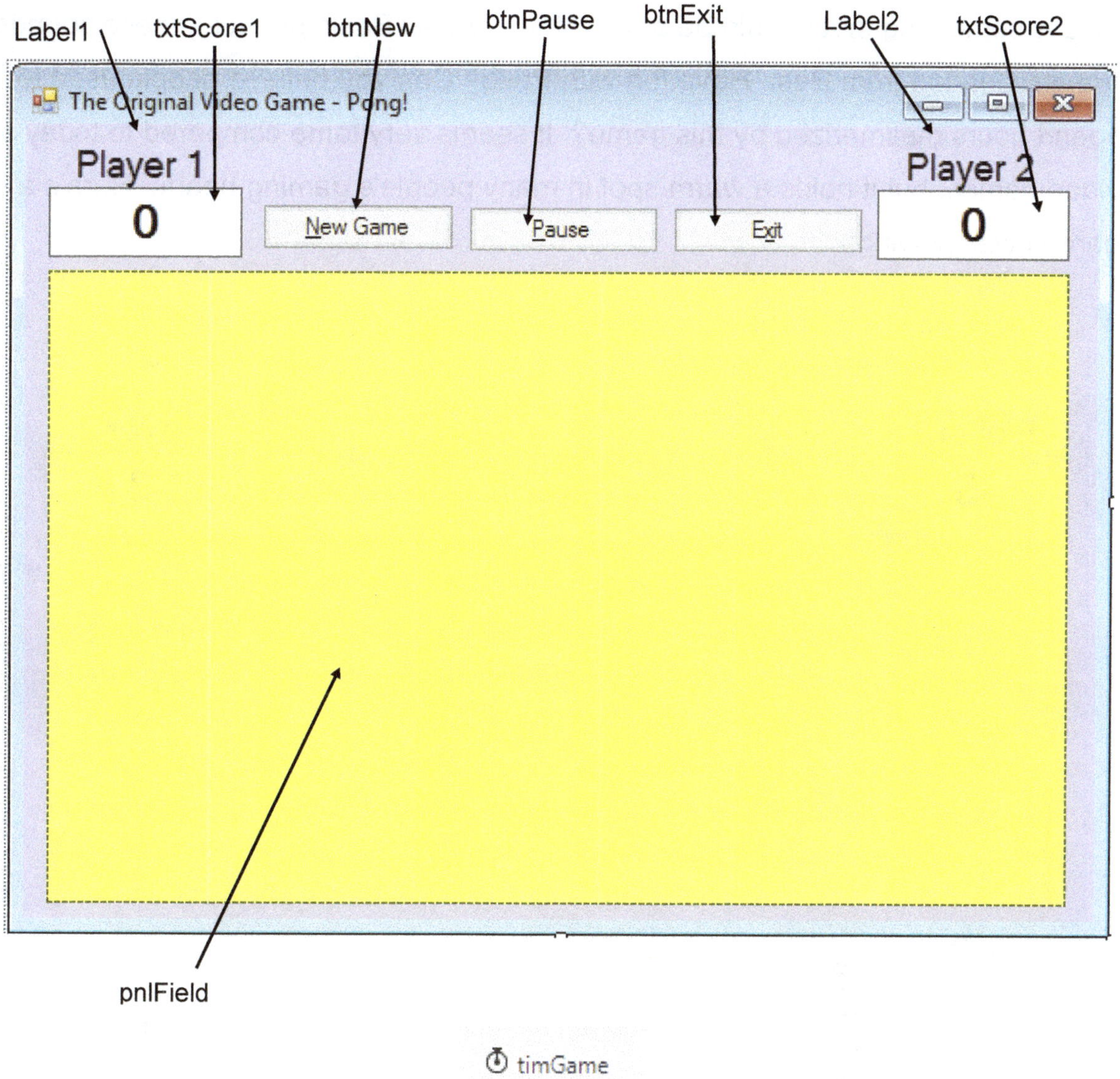

The graphics (paddles and ball) are loaded from files stored with the application. Try to identify controls you have seen before. Go to the properties window and look at the assigned properties. Run the project and play the game with someone. In particular, notice the cool sounds (if you have a sound card in your computer). This is something that should be a part of any Visual Basic project – these sounds are also loaded from files. Have fun with Pong! Can you believe people used to spend hours mesmerized by this game? It seems very tame compared to today's video games, but it holds a warm spot in many people's gaming hearts. Here's a game I was playing:

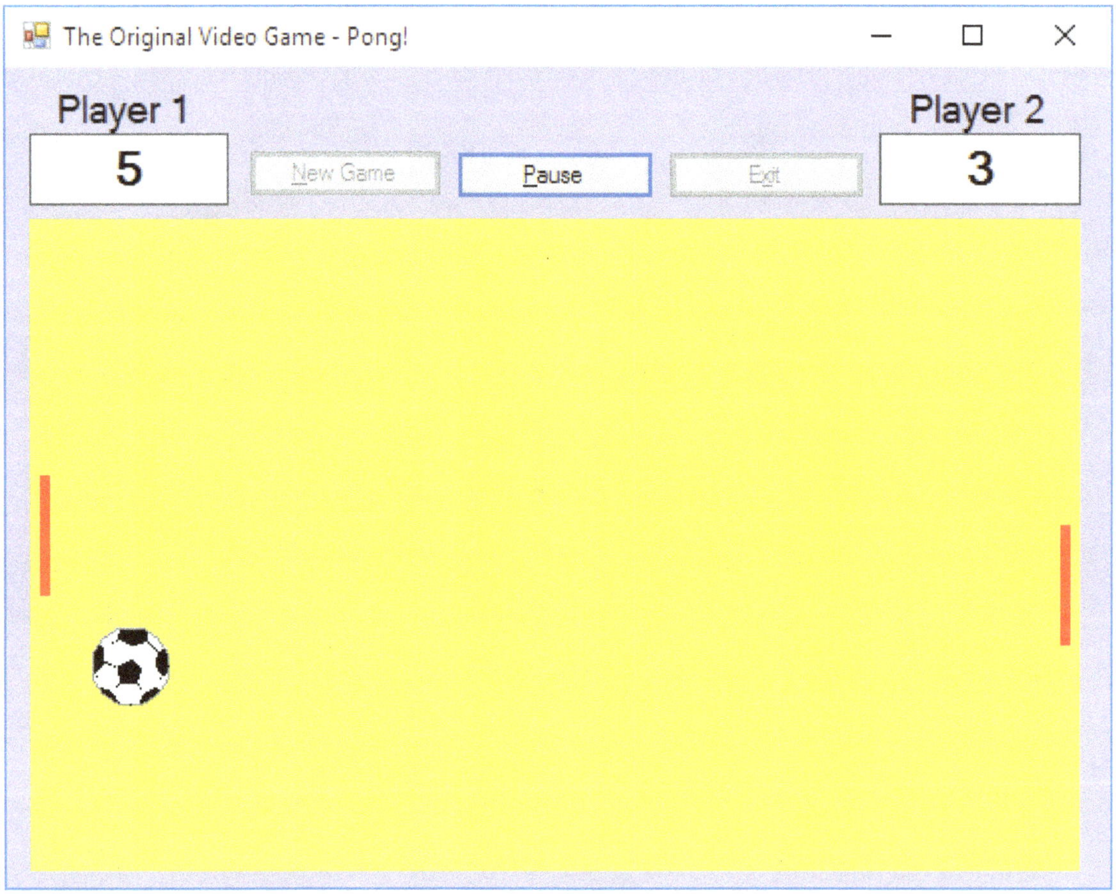

Classic Basic Computer Games

PREVIEW

Back in the early 1980's, there were many computers introduced to the market through such mass retailers as Sears, K Mart and JC Penneys. Names like Texas Instruments, Atari, Sinclair, Commodore, VIC and Coleco Adam appeared everywhere. Each of these computers was programmed in the BASIC language. Each computer also had monthly magazines being published containing BASIC programs you could type into your computer and play. Users eagerly awaited for each issue to have more programs for their computer. Many of these programs had roots back to the 1960's, when the BASIC language first appeared.

This chapter contains three BASIC computer games originally published using BASIC in the classic programming book called "101 Basic Computer Games" edited by David Ahl and published by DEC. The book was later re-published as "BASIC Computer Games" by David Ahl. The original games were simple 'text-only' programs. They had no fancy graphics and no sound. You had to use your imagination a lot back in those days. Much of the code is structured just like original BASIC programs. The original games were written long before the days of structured programs. However, the games are still fun and invoke a nostalgic feeling in many of us older programmers. Many of us stayed up very late at night typing in all these BASIC games on our computers just so we could learn how to program. BASIC Computer Games made learning the BASIC computer language fun and rewarding.

The games included are:

Even - Even Wins program files
Mugwump - Mugwump program files
Lunar - Lunar Lander program files

The program files are found in the **\CBGCB\BVB Projects** folder. To run one of these games, simply open the desired project file in the Visual Basic environment and click **Start**.

EVEN WINS (Original Author: Eric Peters of Digital Equipment Corporation)
BASIC COMPUTER GAMES, Edited by David H. Ahl, Published in 1978
The project is saved as **Even** in the project folder (**\CBGCB\BVB Projects**).

EVEN WINS is a game between you and the computer. To play, an odd number of markers are displayed on the screen. You take turns with the computer removing between one and four markers each turn. The game ends when there are no markers left and the winner is the one with an even number of markers removed.

When the game begins, the markers (asterisks) are displayed and the computer takes the first turn, removing from one to four markers. Then, on your turn, do the same. Remove from one to four markers by entering 1, 2, 3 or 4 key on your keyboard and pressing <Enter>. After each turn, you are shown how many markers you and the computer have. Continue alternating turns until all markers are gone. You win if you are left with an even number of markers. The computer wins if its score is an even number.

This is an interesting version of this game. The computer starts out only knowing the rules of the game and doesn't play very well. Using simple techniques of artificial intelligence, the computer gradually learns to play from its mistakes until it plays a very good game. After 20 games, the computer is a challenge to beat. Variation in your style of play seems to make the computer learn more quickly. I personally don't know how this code works - maybe you can figure it out. I just typed the code from a magazine - a technique used by many programmers (code 'borrowing').

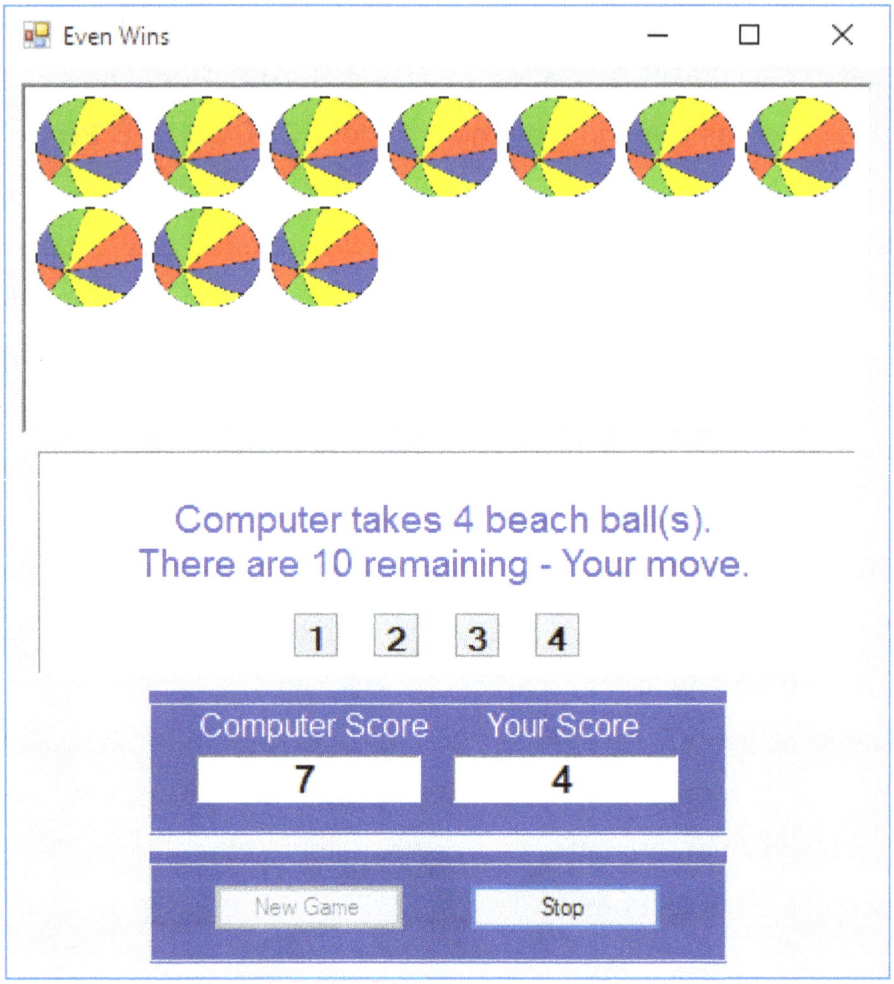
Even Wins
Computer takes 4 beach ball(s).
There are 10 remaining - Your move.
1
2
3
4
Computer Score
Your Score
7
4
New Game
Stop

MUGWUMP (Original Author: Bob Albrecht of Peoples Computer Company)
BASIC COMPUTER GAMES, Edited by David H. Ahl, Published in 1978
The project is saved as **Mugwump** in the project folder (**\CBGCB\BVB Projects**).

The objective in this game is to find the four Mugwumps hiding on various squares of a 10 x 10 grid. After guessing a location, the computer gives you distance clues on how far you are from each Mugwump.

At the beginning of each game, a blank grid is shown. Choose a square to guess the location of a Mugwump. To choose a square, you are asked to enter the row (0 to 9) and column (0 to 9) of the selected square. After your guess, you are told how far (the famous Pythagorean triangle formula is used) you are from each remaining Mugwump. Use this information for your next guess. The program tells you how many Mugwumps are remaining and how many guesses you have taken. The game ends when all the Mugwumps have been found.

Playing the game with aid of graph paper and a compass should allow you to find all the Mugwumps in six or seven moves using triangulation similar to old Loran radio navigation (do some research to find out what this is).

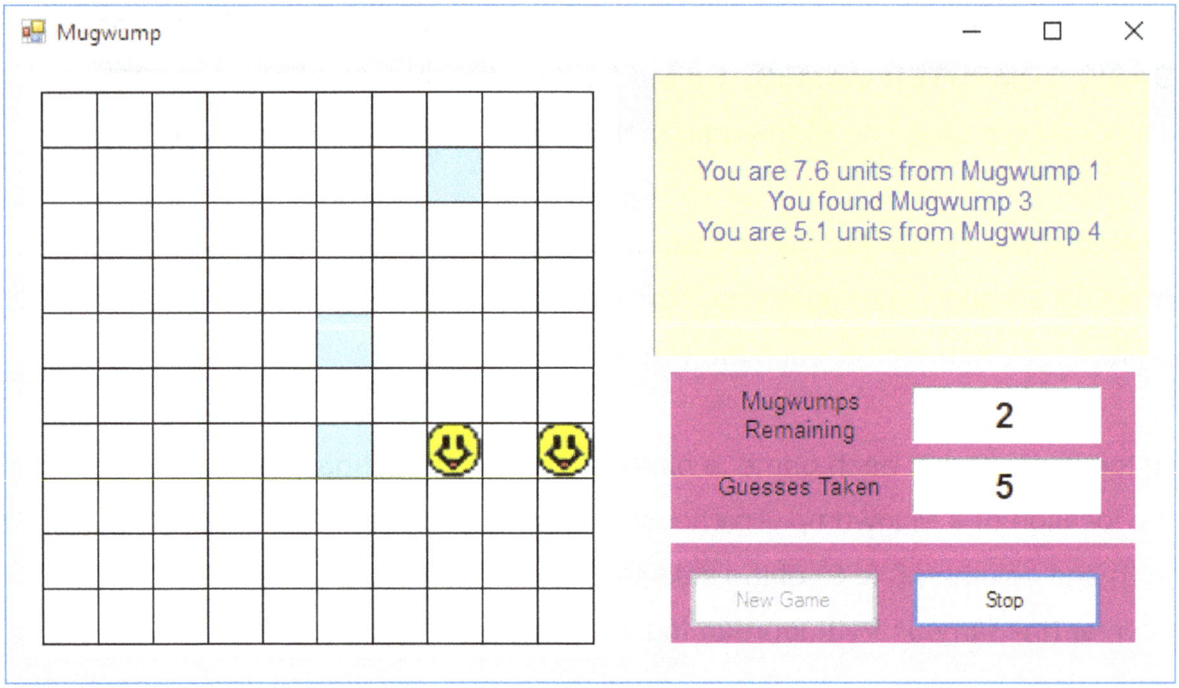
Mugwump
You are 7.6 units from Mugwump 1
You found Mugwump 3
You are 5.1 units from Mugwump 4
Mugwumps Remaining
2
Guesses Taken
5
New Game
Stop

LUNAR LANDER (Original Author: Eric Peters of DEC)

BASIC COMPUTER GAMES, Edited by David H. Ahl, Published in 1978

The project is saved as **Lunar** in the project folder (**\CBGCB\BVB Projects**).

This has been called the single most popular computer game ever. It was one of the first games written by little Billy Gates in his early programming days. You are hovering over the moon in your lunar module. You must land it safely by controlling the retrorocket burns.

When the game begins, you are 500 feet above the lunar surface and control the rocket burns in 1-second bursts. Displayed on the screen are Time, Altitude, Speed and Fuel Remaining. Each unit of fuel used slows your descent by 1 ft/sec. The maximum burn is 30 units of fuel in one second. To slow the module, enter the amount of fuel you want to burn over the next second (0 accelerates the module toward the lunar surface). Press the <Enter> key and the screen is updated with the latest data. A safe landing is achieved with final speeds less than 10 ft/sec.

The biggest mistake people make playing this game is yielding to the temptation of slowing the module much too soon. With this strategy, you run out of fuel for the lower part of the journey and the resulting free-fall is disastrous! Use small burns early on to slow slight or maintain speed (a burn of 5 units does this). Then, really crank it on near the surface. You'll find some burn rates that work well.

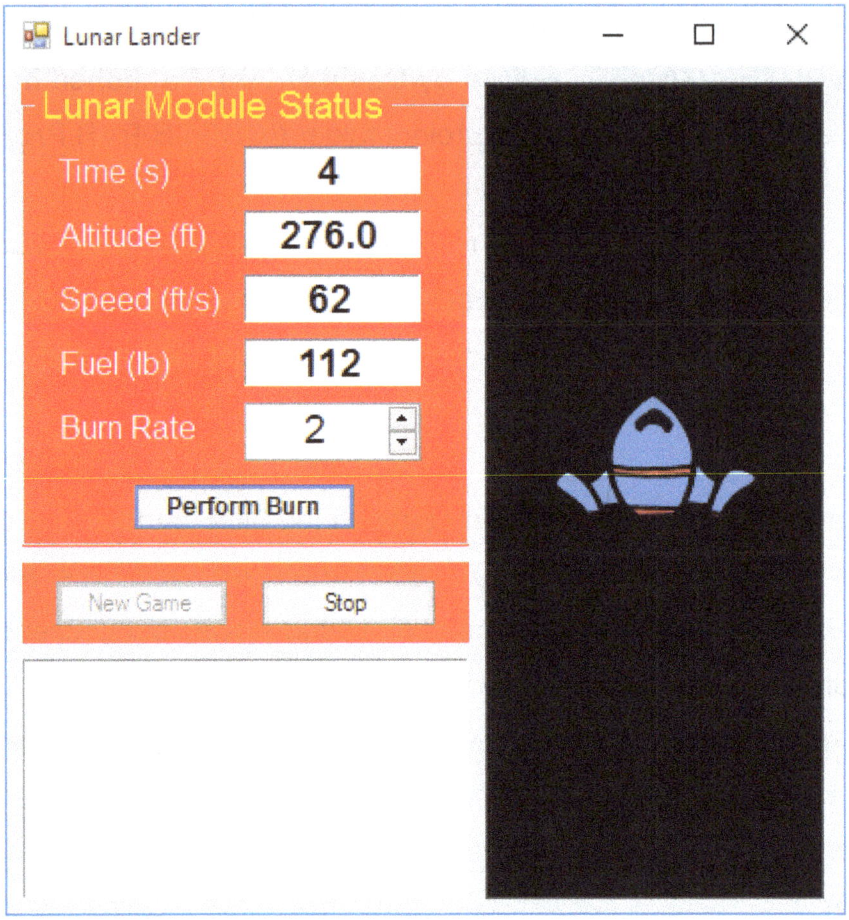
Lunar Lander
Lunar Module Status
Time (s)
4
Altitude (ft)
276.0
Speed (ft/s)
62
Fuel (lb)
112
Burn Rate
2
Perform Burn
New Game
Stop

Other Self-Study and/or Instructor-Led Programming Tutorials By BibleByte Books

Computer Bible Games for Microsoft Small Basic is a self-paced "beginner" programming tutorial for Middle-School students. This tutorial consists of 13 chapters explaining (in simple, easy-to-follow terms) how to build Computer Bible Games in Small Basic. It also includes the Small Basic source code for the several of the original Computer Bible Games. The Computer Bible Games built include Noah's Ark, Daniel and the Lions, Elijah and the Ravens, The Good Shepherd, The Prodigal Son, The Lost Coin, and Bible Scramble. Other learning projects include a card game, an allowance calculator, a drawing program, a state capitals game, and a video game.

Computer Bible Games with Visual Basic® is a self-paced semester long self-study "beginner" programming tutorial consisting of 13 chapters explaining (in simple, easy-to-follow terms) how to build a Visual Basic Express Windows application and Computer Bible Games. The Computer Bible Games built include Noah's Ark, Elijah & the Ravens, and Daniel & the Lions. Other learning projects include a card game, an allowance calculator, a drawing program, a state capitals game, and a video game. We also include several college prep bonus projects including a loan calculator, portfolio manager, and checkbook balancer.

Computer Bible Games with Visual C#® is a semester long self-paced "beginning "programming tutorial consisting of 13 chapters explaining (in simple, easy-to-follow terms) how to build a C# Express Windows applications and several Computer Bible Games. The Computer Bible Games built include Noah's Ark, Elijah & the Ravens, Daniel & the Lions and a Unity 3D Cartoon Moses Rod Adventure game. Other learning projects include a card game, an allowance calculator, a drawing program, a state capitals game, and the Pong video game. We also include several bonus projects including a loan calculator, portfolio manager, and checkbook balancer.

Introduction to Unity 3D with C# – The Exodus Adventure is a 2nd semester self-paced tutorial that teaches you how to build a high quality Third Person 3D Puzzle Adventure game based on the Book of Exodus. Students are provided with high quality 3D Character models and 3D Environment models to work with. We teach students how to build the following game mechanics: 3rd person Mecanim controller to Interact with actors and objects; Dialogue; Item Management; Full screen map and mini-map showing key locations; Quest Journal to manage quests; Cut-scenes; Cinematics for Game Opening and Ending, Game soundtrack, and building 3D Character Models using the Unity Multipurpose Avatar (UMA).

Computer Bible Games with Java™ is a semester long self-paced programming tutorial consisting of 7 chapters explaining (in simple, easy-to-follow terms) how to build a Java® Computer Bible Games. This Tutorial requires a complete understanding of the Java Swing Control Library before attempting so it is an Advanced Java Tutorial. We recommend that you compete the *Learn Java GUI Applications* tutorial by Kidware Software before attempting this advanced tutorial. The Computer Bible Games built include Noah's Ark, Elijah & the Ravens, and Daniel & the Lions, Bible Safecracker, Bible Match, and Bible Trivia Tic-Tac-Toe.

www.ingramcontent.com/pod-product-compliance
Lightning Source LLC
Chambersburg PA
CBHW081431090925
32270CB00146B/6031
* 9 7 8 1 9 5 1 0 7 7 1 4 3 *